The *Chronicle* of Eusebius and Greek Chronographic Tradition

Alden A. Mosshammer

Lewisburg
Bucknell University Press
London: Associated University Presses

© 1979 by Associated University Presses, Inc.

Associated University Presses, Inc.
Cranbury, New Jersey 08512

Associated University Presses
Magdalen House
136–148 Tooley Street
London SE1 2TT, England

Library of Congress Cataloging in Publication Data
Mosshammer, Alden A
The Chronicle of Eusebius and Greek
chronographic tradition.
Bibliography: p.
Includes index.
1. Eusebious Pamphili, Bp. of Caesarea.
Chronicon. 2. World history—Early works to
1800. I. Title.
D17.E73M67   930   76-1029
ISBN 0-8387-1939-2

PRINTED IN THE UNITED STATES OF AMERICA

The *Chronicle* of Eusebius
and
Greek Chronographic Tradition

In Memoriam Patris Carissimi
Qui Transit ad Gloriam MCMLXXV

Contents

Plates

(following page 21)

Acknowledgments

Several leaves of the Bodleian manuscript of St. Jerome's version of the *Chronicle* of Eusebius are reproduced among the plates, by permission of the Bodleian Library. The photographs were prepared directly from the manuscript by the staff of the Bodleian Library. Page 192 of Karst's edition of the Armenian version is reproduced by permission of the Kommission für Spätantike Religionsgeschichte, Berlin. The photograph was prepared by the Scripps Institution of Oceanography, San Diego, from a copy in the UCLA library. My typescript illustrating a hypothetical reconstruction of the original Greek was also photographed at Scripps.

Of the many persons who have assisted this project at various stages of its development, I owe especial thanks to Frances Newman of the Interlibrary Loan Department at the University of California, San Diego. Without her patience and persistence in obtaining material unavailable at so youthful a library as San Diego's, my research would not have been possible. I am grateful also to Dolores Swetland, who prepared the final typescript with painstaking care, undeterred by the presence of so many citations in Greek. Much of the cost of preparing the typescript was defrayed by the Research Committee of the San Diego division of the Academic Senate of the University of California.

The editorial staff at Associated University Presses, especially Mathilde E. Finch, have been most helpful in answering my many questions of technical detail.

Professor Charles W. Fornara of the Department of Classics at Brown University read the penultimate draft closely. His comments have rescued me from infelicities of expression, as well as substantive errors. Those which remain are, of course, my own responsibility.

Finally, I must express my sincerest appreciation to my family—my wife and my four stepsons—for their Herculean endurance of a scholar's preoccupations and an author's moods.

San Diego, May, 1976

Abbreviations

Abh.Berl.	Abhandlungen der Berliner Akademie
Abh.Gött.	Abhandlungen von der Gesellschaft der Wissenschaften zu Göttingen
AJP	*American Journal of Philology*
AntCl	*L'Antiquité classique*
BCH	*Bulletin de correspondance hellénique*
BICS	*Bulletin of the London Institute for Classical Studies*
CJ	*Classical Journal*
CQ	*Classical Quarterly*
DK	H. Diels and W. Kranz, *Die Fragmente der Vorsokratiker*
FGrHist	Felix Jacoby, *Die Fragmente der griechischen Historiker*
GGA	*Göttingische gelehrte Anzeigen*
GRBS	*Greek, Roman, and Byzantine Studies*
Helm	Rudolf Helm, *Die Chronik des Hieronymus*
JHS	*Journal of Hellenic Studies*
JThS	*Journal of Theological Studies*
Karst	Josef Karst, *Die Chronik des Eusebius aus dem armenischen übersetz*
MH	*Museum Helveticum*
MusB	*Musée belge*
RE	*Real-Encyclopädie der klassischen Altertumswissenschaft*
RFIC	*Rivista di Filologia e d'Istruzione Classica*
RhM	*Rheinisches Museum für Philologie*
SBBerl	*Sitzungsberichte der preussische Akademie*
TAPA	*Transactions of the American Philological Association*
Wehrli	Fritz Wehrli, *Die Schule des Aristoteles*
West.	Anton Westermann, *Biographi Graeci Minores*

Manuscripts

A	Codex Amandinus, Valenciennes 495
B	Codex Bongarsianus, Bern 219
F	Codex Freherianus, Leyden Scal. 14
L	Codex Luccensis, Lucca Bibl. Capit. 490
M	Codex Middlehillensis, Berlin Phillipps 1829
N	Codex Middlehillensis, Berlin Phillipps 1872
O	Codex Oxoniensis, Bodleian Auct. T. II. 26
P	Codex Petavianus, Leyden Voss. Lat. Qu. 110
S	Codicis Floriacensis Fragmenta
	Vatican Reg. Lat. 1709A
	Paris Lat. 6400B
	Leyden Voss. Lat. Qu. 110A
T	Codex Oxoniensis, Merton 315
X	Codex Londinensis, Mus. Brit. Add. 16974

Introduction

From the time of its composition in the early fourth century A.D. until the Reformation period, the *Chronicle* of Eusebius was the standard text for world chronology from the birth of Abraham (2016 B.C.) to the Vicennalia of Constantine (A.D. 325). Its scope was universal, including biblical history and the Near Eastern kingdoms as well as the Greco-Roman world. A prefatory volume contained excerpts from earlier authors summarizing the chronological systems of all the peoples of antiquity. In the main body of the work Eusebius transcribed the various systems in an innovative format with parallel columns of vertically numbered lists synchronized with each other and aligned with two universal standards—years since Abraham and the Alexandrian system of numbered Olympiads. Horizontally, in the middle of the page, Eusebius noted what persons and events were to be dated to the years specified in the lists. Reading from left to right across the page, the user obtained a universal synchronism at a glance.

So useful a work was early translated, adapted, epitomized, and extended. In fact, the original had been entirely supplanted by the seventh century, so that it does not have a continuous manuscript tradition of its own. In substance, however, the work was never superseded. Through secondary versions in Latin, Syriac, and Armenian, as well as Greek, the Eusebian chronology was considered definitive, not only in Europe, but also in the Near East.

We no longer rely primarily on Eusebius for the reconstruction of ancient historical chronology. Nevertheless, the *Chronicle* of Eusebius is more than an antique curiosus. It remains an important source of chronological evidence. As a historian of his own times Eusebius provides information both in the *Chronicle* and in his *Historia Ecclesiastica* about the crisis of the Roman Empire in the late third and early fourth centuries, as well as

15

about the early history of the Church. Eusebius' lists of the Hellenistic kings are fundamental for the reconstruction of the chronology of the successor kingdoms to the empire of Alexander the Great during the third century B.C. Most significant, the *Chronicle* of Eusebius is the one great repository of Greek scholarly opinion about the absolute chronology of the Greeks' own distant past. Neither official dating systems nor the idea of historical chronology existed before the middle of the fifth century B.C. The archaic period of Greece was prehistoriographic, and the modern historian obviously has no way of confronting the remembered traditions directly. Besides the *Histories* of Herodotus—a good, but secondary source—what remains of the epic and lyric poetry provides the only direct link. For the rest, the historian must rely on a literary tradition formulated often centuries after the fact and transmitted at second or third hand, usually in fragmentary form.

Greek historiography lies in ruins, and the work of the Greek chronologists suffered a more disastrous wreck than the rest. The *Chronicle* of Eusebius is the earliest work extant in anything like its original form that deals with early Greek chronology in a continuous and comprehensive manner. What use the historian can legitimately make of Eusebius' information is a fundamental problem. It is generally agreed that all chronological data before the middle of the eighth century (traditionally 776 B.C., the first Olympic festival) are almost pure fiction and historically worthless. For the period between the middle of the eighth and the middle of the fifth centuries, it remains an open and controversial question to what extent and in what manner the dates of the Greek chronologists, preserved chiefly by Eusebius, are the numerical representation on an absolute chronological scale of a solid tradition of relative chronology based partly on oral tradition, partly on literary or documentary evidence now lost to posterity. The *Chronicle* of Eusebius and the seven hundred years of a complex chronological tradition that it almost alone represents stand between us and the orally transmitted memories of the past as they existed in the middle of the fifth century B.C., when professional historians and official archivists began to make the art of memory obsolete.

To evaluate Eusebius' information as historical evidence for Greek chronology in the archaic period, one must first understand it in its own context. Three separate but interrelated problems are involved. The extant texts are difficult, witnessing to the original in different ways, so that analysis of Eusebian evidence must always begin with textual criticism. Second, the chrono-graphic tradition from which Eusebius' dates derive defies defini-tive analysis; one wonders how the Greeks could possbly have established a credible absolute chronology for events that took place before there was any such thing as a date. Finally, the quality of Eusebius' evidence depends on the type of sources he used and the accuracy with which they transmitted the earlier chronographic tradition. In Part 1, each of these problems is discussed generally to develop the critical techniques necessary for the management of Eusebian evidence. Part 2 consists of a series of case studies in early Greek chronology, using those techniques for the detailed analysis of specific entries in the *Chronological Canons*. This organizational procedure is required by the nature of the problem. Individual notices can be analyzed and evaluated, but no abstract solution can do justice to the complexities of the issues. This is as true of the *Chronicle* of Eusebius as it is for the traditional dates of early Greek history in general.

The *Chronicle* of Eusebius
and
Greek Chronographic Tradition

Part 1

The *Chronicle* of Eusebius
and
Greek Chronographic Tradition

CODEX OXONIENSIS BODLEIANUS AUCT. T. 2. 26, folio 65ᵛ

Facing pages of the Bodleian manuscript of St. Jerome's Chronicle, showing the twin-page format used for the earlier portion of the work.

CODEX OXONIENSIS BODLEIANUS AUCT. T. 2. 26, folio 66ʳ

latinorum	maced		lydorum	aegyptiorum
XX	X		III	LI
XXI	XI	ARETINUSMILESIUSUERSI picatokflorentissimus	LIII	LII
XXII	XII	habetur	LI	LIII

MACEDON III
TYRIMMAS XXXIIII

XXIII	I	reusetromulusgene RANTUR KMARTIETILIA	LII	LIIII
XXIIII	II		LIII	LIIII
XXU	III	atheniensesprimum	LIIII	X
XXUI	IIII	trierisnauigauitamino cleocupsusdirigente	LIIII	XI
XXUII	U		X	XII
XXUIII	LII	hesiodussecundumquos	XI	XIIII
XXUIIII	LII	damelakushabetur	XII	XIIII
XXX	LIIII		XIII	XU
XXXI	LIIII		XIIII	XUI
		cinaethonlacedaemonius poetaquirelegoniamscri		
XXXII	X	bsitagnoscitur	XU	XUII
XXXIII	XI		XUI	XUIIII
XXXIIII	XII		XUII	XUIIII
		theraeicyrenencondide runtoraculosiciubente conditurkurbisbattus		
XXXU	XIII	ciiuspropkiumnomen aristoteles	XUIIII	XX
XXXUI	XIIII		XUIIII	XXI
XXXUII	XU	aradusinsulacondita	XX	XXII
XXXUIIII	XUI		XXI	XXIII

THE ARMENIAN VERSION, page 192 Karst

192			Eusebius, Chronik aus dem Armenischen			

K		Olp.	Abr.	Mak. Alexandros	Pers. Xerxes	
			1537	24	6 ·	· Der Kampf bei Thermupolis[a] und die Seeschlacht bei Salamin.
			1538	25	7 ·	· Die Schlacht bei Plataes[b][7] und die bei Mikalen.
			1539	26	8	
		76	1540	27	9	
	· Éschilos der Gesangdichter war gekannt[3].		1541	28	10	
			1542	29	11	
280	· Jeron[4] ward Gewaltherrscher der Syrakusaner nach Gelon.		1543	30	12	
	· Sophokles der Gesangdichter erschien zuerst.	77	1544	31	13 ·	· Pindaros war gerade um diese Zeiten.
			1545	·32	14 ·	· Themestokles floh zu den Persern.
71. Jobeläum			1546[5]	33	15 ·	· Zu Rom ward Sunia die Jungfrau[6], bei der Schändung befunden, lebendig begraben.
			1547	34	16	
		78	1548	35	17 ·	· Sophekles und Euripides waren gekannt.
			1549	36	18 ·	· Herodotos der Geschichtschreiber war gekannt.
	· Themestokles starb, indem er Blut eines Stieres trank.		1550	37	19 ·	· Bakchalides[7] blühte; und Diagoras der Gottlose.
	· Sokrates ward geboren[6].		1551	38	20	
		79	1552	39	21 ·	· In Egiptos regnete es Flußstein vom Himmel[c][9].
					Artaran, Monate 7. Nach diesem:	
					Artašes Langhand, Jahre 40	
290	· Der Esther und des Murthche Dinge geben einige unter diesem an. Ich jedoch gebe es nicht zu. Denn nicht würde deren Taten verschweigen das Buch Ezr, welches unter diesem erzählt des Ezr und Neemia Auszug aus Babelon und die von ihnen geschehenen Werke, die in demselben Buche berichtet werden.		1553	40	1 ·	· In Sikilia herrschte[10] die Demokratie.
			1554	41	2 ·	· Die Sonne verfinsterte sich. Anaxagoras starb.
			1555	42	3 ·	· Kimon besiegte am Eurimedon[11] die Perser[12] in einer Seeschlacht, und der medische Krieg hörte auf.
		80	1556	43	4 ·	· Euenos war als Dichter mit Messungen der Worte gekannt.
				Perdikas, J. 28[13]		
	· Ezr, der Priester, war bei den Juden gekannt. Unter welchem Hoherpriester war Eliasib, Sohn Jóakims, dessen Vater Jesu des Jósedek war. Es war aber Ezr auch Schriftgelehrter des Heiligen Gesetzes und erlauchter Lehrmeister jener, die aus Babelon ins Judenland hinaufzogen.		1557	1	5 ·	· Heraklitos war gekannt.
			1558	2	6	
			1559	3	7	
		81	1560	4	8 ·	· Empedokles und Parmenides wurden als physische Philosophen bekannt.
			1561	5	9 ·	· Zenon und Heraklitos der Kritinäer[14] erschienen.
	· Pherek[l]ides der Zweite, Geschichtschreiber, war gekannt.		1562	6	10 ·	· Die Pythagorianer fielen in jene Zeiten.

a) Sync. Θερμοπύλαις, Hier. in Thermopylis. — b) T. gr. ἐν Πλαταιαῖς, Hier. in Plataeis. — c) Sync. Λίθος ἐκ τοῦ οὐρανοῦ ἔπεσεν ἐν Ποταμοῖς Αἰγός, Hier. Lapis in Aegis fluuio de caelo ruit.

A page of Karst's edition of the Armenian version, showing the format used throughout the work with continuous numbering of years from Abraham.

Codex Oxoniensis Bodleianus Auct. T. 2. 26, folio 84ʳ

A page of the Bodleian manuscript, showing the format used after the second year of Darius, with use of space dictated by the number and length of historical notices.

CODEX OXONIENSIS BODLEIANUS AUCT. T. 2. 26, folio 84ᵛ

PERSARUM   CONSULES   MACEDON

SOCRATESNAS   XX   SOCRATESNASCITUR   XXXUIII
CITUR POSTUR
b:m cenetra
men coccLxxxun
PERSARUM UI
ARTABANUS
MEN̅ UII   XXXUIII
POSTQUEMUIII
ARTARXERXES
QUILONGIMA
NUSCOGNO
MINABATURXL
Lxxuiiii oLymp'
EAQUAEDEHESTERETMARDOCAEO
SCRIBTASUNTQUIDAMADFIRMANT   XL
SUBHOCREGEGESTAQUODECONON
PUTO·NUMQUAMENIMEZRASDE
HESTERSILUISSETQUISCRIBITHOC
TEMPOREEZRAMETNEEMIAMRE   XLI
UERSOSEXBABYLONEETEADEINCEPSCONSE
CUTAQUAEABHISGESTAREFERUNTUR   XLII
SICILIAAPOPULOREGEBATUR
CYMONIUXTAEURYMEDONTEM
PERSASNAUALIPEDESTRIQUEGER   XLIII
TAMINESUPERATETMEDICUM   MACEDON XI
BELLUMCONQUIESCIT   PERDICCAXXUIIII
SOLISFACTADEFECTIO
Lxxx oLymp'
ANAXAGORASMORITUR
U   HERACLITUSCLARUSHABETUR   I
EZRASSACERDOSAPUDHEBRXOS
INSIGNISAGNOSCITURCUIUSAEta

EZRASSACERDOS
clarushabetur
etmagistereo
rumquidetas
Tiumxrenodea
Regressisunt

The overleaf of Plate 3.

HYPOTHETICAL RECONSTRUCTION OF AN ORIGINAL GREEK PAGE

Περσῶν   Μακεδόνων

Ολ οζ´ Σοφοκλῆς τραγῳδοποιὸς πρῶτος ἐπεδείξατο.

ιδ´   λβ´

ιε´   Θεμιστοκλῆς   ἐν Ῥώμῃ   λγ´
                εἰς Πέρσας   Σουνία παρθένος
ις´   φεύγει.   φθαρεῖσα   λδ´
                                        κατωρύγη ζῶσα.

ιζ´ Σοφοκλῆς καὶ Εὐριπίδης   Σωκράτης   λε´
        ἐγνωρίζοντο.   ἐγεννήθη.

Ολ οη´ Ἡρόδοτος ἱστοριογράφος ἐγνωρίζετο.

ιη´   Βακχυλίδης δὲ   Θεμιστοκλῆς   Λίθος ἐκ   λς´
        καὶ Διαγόρας   αἷμα ταύρου   τοῦ οὐρανοῦ
αφν´ ιθ´   ὁ ἄθεος   πιὼν τελευτᾷ.   ἔπεσεν ἐν   λζ´
        γεγόνασιν.   Ποταμοῖς Αἰγός.

κ´ Ζεῦξις ζωγράφος ἐγνωρίζετο.   λη´

Περσῶν ς´ Ἀρτάβανος μῆνας ζ´
μεθ᾽ ὃν ζ´ Ἀρταξέρξης   Σικελία   λθ´
ὁ λεγόμενος μακρόχειρ ἔτη μ´   ἐδημοκρατήθη.

Ολ οθ´ Τὰ κατὰ τὴν Ἐσθὴρ καὶ
Μαρδοχαῖόν φασί τινες
ἐπὶ τούτου γεγε-
νῆσθαι. ἐγὼ δὲ οὐ
α´ πείθομαι, οὐ γὰρ   Κίμων ἐπ᾽   ὁ ἥλιος   μ´
ἂν ἐσιώπησε τὰς   Εὐρυμέδοντι   ἐξέλιπεν.
κατ᾽ αὐτὴν πράξεις   Πέρσας ἐνίκα
β´ ἡ τοῦ Ἔσδρα γραφή,   ναυμαχίᾳ καὶ   μα´
ἥτις κατὰ τὸν Ἀρ-   πεζομαχίᾳ καὶ
ταξέρξην ἱστορεῖ   ὁ Μηδικὸς πόλεμος
γ´ Ἔσδραν καὶ Νεεμίαν   ἐπαύσατο.   μβ´
ἐκ Βαβυλῶνος ἀνελη-
λυθέναι καὶ τὰς
δ´ ἀναφερομένας αὐτῶν   μγ´
πράξεις γεγονέναι.

Hypothetical reconstruction for Olympiads 77 through 79, inferred from the extant texts shown in Plates 2, 3, and 4.

1

The Text of the *Chronicle*

The *Chronicle* of Eusebius does not survive in its original language and format. Eusebius completed the work shortly after its terminus at the Vicennalia of Constantine in 325. Within fifty years of his death in the late 330s, translations, epitomes, redactions, and extensions began to circulate. The work was consulted during the Middle Ages through these more accessible secondary versions. Consequently, it was the translations and epitomes, rather than the original Greek text, that were copied and transmitted through the medieval manuscript tradition to the modern world. Until the late sixteenth century, the work was known in the West only through the Latin translation incorporated into the *Chronicle* of St. Jerome. This version, presented as a showpiece to the Roman synod of 382, was a vulgate edition of the most substantial portion of Eusebius' work—the *Chronological Canons*. Jerome continued the chronicle to his own times, ending with the Battle of Adrianople in 378. He also expanded its scope to include more information of interest to Latin readers than Eusebius had, especially in the field of literary history. Jerome did not, however, include Eusebius' introductory chronographic excerpts. The erstwhile existence of such material was known only through the reference to a *prior libellus* (p. 8 Helm) in Jerome's translation of Eusebius' preface to the *Chronological Canons*.

Reconstruction of Eusebius' original, including that first book, has been a desideratum of modern scholarship since the sixteenth century, when Joseph Scaliger first directed historical criticism to the traditional chronology of antiquity as preserved by St. Jerome. Scaliger discovered several texts, including a

Greek manuscript of the *Chronographia* of the ninth-century Byzantine scholar known as Georgius Syncellus, which derived independently of St. Jerome from the *Chronicle* of Eusebius. Scaliger collected the testimonia and published them with critical commentary in his *Thesaurus Temporum* (Leyden, 1606) as the first step toward reconstruction of Eusebius' original. Since his time Armenian and Syriac witnesses have come to light, as well as critically important manuscripts unknown to Scaliger of St. Jerome's Latin version. Nevertheless, the extant translations and epitomes attest to the original in ways sufficiently different that each new discovery renders Scaliger's ideal of reconstruction ever more distant. An esoteric and often polemical debate has been carried on among specialists, most of them Eusebian editors, for almost two hundred years. The controversy centers on the original format of the *Chronicle* and the relative merits of the extant versions as witnesses to it. Neither Jerome's nor the Armenian translation has won a decisive victory. Reconstruction of the original remains an implausible project that would inevitably reflect primarily the bias of its author.

Sooner or later almost every classicist and historian of antiquity is confronted with evidence drawn from the *Chronicle* of Eusebius. Before he can properly pass judgment on its merits, he must deal with one of the most labyrinthine and controversial texts in the field. The modern editions are not always good representations of the manuscript traditions of the excerptors and translators, much less of Eusebius' hypothetical original. The scholar who draws upon Eusebian evidence is faced with the necessity of reconstructing for himself a hypothetical original for each entry of the *Chronicle* he encounters. Few are equipped to do so. Even in a printed text and even for an experienced scholar, using the *Chronicle* of Eusebius in the version of one of his translators—as interpreted by a modern editor—is a formidable task.[1]

An exposition of the problems involved, as clear and unbiased as possible, is the purpose of this chapter. In an effort to achieve some semblance of brevity without sacrificing completeness, the discussion is limited to the central issue of chronographic format. Illustrative material, including a sample page of the best modern edition of the Armenian version, several leaves of the Bodleian manuscript of Jerome's version, and a hypothetical reconstruction of an original Greek page, may be found in the collection of plates prefacing this chapter.

The *Chronicle* in Eusebius' Life and Works

Biographical information about Eusebius is unfortunately sparse, surprisingly so for one who was active in the public affairs of his time and influential in documenting its history.[2] References in the *Historia Ecclesiastica* to persons whom Eusebius considered his contemporaries suggest that he was born about 260. The account of the church historian Socrates (*H.E.* 2.4.), successor to Eusebius in that genre, of the events following the death of Constantine implies that Eusebius died between 337 and 340. Eusebius spent most of his life in Caesarea, the Roman provincial capital of Palestine, and it is likely that he was born there. He was not, however, a member of a prominent family. His elevation to the important episcopal see of Caesarea, probably in the year 314, he owes partly to the serious shortage of senior presbyters in the area in the wake of the vigorous persecutions so recently ended, partly to his reputation as a biblical scholar and exegete earned while in the service of the now-martyred bibliophile Pamphilus. His association with the learned Pamphilus was close. Much of his own intellectual growth and material comfort he owed to Pamphilus. Eusebius therefore regarded him as a father and perpetuated his memory by adding the distinctive ὸ Παμφίλου to his own name—*ob amicitiam Pamphili martyris ab eo cognomentum sortitus est.*[3]

Pamphilus was a native of Beirut, born of wealthy and noble parentage, who traveled to Alexandria to further his education. There he studied theology under Pierius and became acquainted with the work of Origen. He was profoundly impressed by the traditions of Alexandrian scholarship and Origen's application of its principles to biblical studies. Pamphilus decided to devote himself and his fortune to a life of scholarly asceticism after the model of Origen. Doctrinal disputes had resulted in Origen's banishment from Alexandria in 231. He reestablished himself in Caesarea and continued his work there for about twenty years until the Decian persecutions resulted in his own death, the scattering of his pupils, and the loss of much of his library. Pamphilus felt a divine vocation to reconstitute the Origenist scholarly tradition. He moved to Caesarea, was ordained to the priesthood, and established a school of biblical studies.[4]

With the help of younger scholars like Eusebius, Pamphilus sought to restore the work of Origen and to preserve it against any further catastrophe. His chief aim was to establish an

authoritative text of the Scriptures based on Origen's Hexapla
edition of the Old Testament and on such of his readings of the
New Testament as could be culled from his commentaries.
Origen's library had suffered badly during the Decian persecutions and Pamphilus set himself the task of salvaging what he
could of Origen's own manuscripts and collecting others from all
over the Christian world. Jerome (*Ep.* 34.1), in commenting
on Pamphilus' extraordinary diligence in gathering manuscripts
for the new library, likens his zeal as a bibliophile to that of
such renowned ancient scholars as Demetrius of Phalerum. The
library at Caesarea soon became famous and drew scholars from
other cities who wished to collate their own manuscripts with
those of Pamphilus. Eusebius was Pamphilus' closest collabo-
rator in this work and after the latter's death in 310 he undertook the direction of the library's efforts. Eusebius sought to
memorialize the work of his great patron in his *Life of Pamphilus*, a biography in three books to which he refers in the
Martyrs of Palestine (11.3). The *Life* is lost, and with it not
only the record of Pamphilus' significant achievements in biblical
scholarship but also a catalogue of the Caesarean manuscripts
mentioned, but not included in the *Historia Ecclesiastica* (6.32).[5]

It is from this lengthy period of scholarly activity at the
side of Pamphilus that most of Eusebius' own literary produc-
tion derives, including most of the *Chronicle* and much of the
Historia Ecclesiastica. He mentions the *Chronicle* in the first
book of the *Historia Ecclesiastica* (1.1.6) and in the tenth of the
Praeparatio Euangelica (10.9.11). The earliest reference is in
the *Eclogae Propheticae* (p. 1 Gaisford), where the only clear
indication of the work's original title also appears. According to
this citation, Eusebius entitled the product of his chronological
research Χρονικοὶ κανόνες καὶ ἐπιτομὴ παντοδαπῆς ἱστορίας
Ἑλλήνων τε καὶ βαρβάρων —"Chronological Canons with an
Epitome of Universal History both Greek and Nongreek."
Eusebius wrote the *Eclogae* at a time when Christian organiza-
tions were officially forbidden and the work must therefore be
dated sometime before 311. The *Chronicle* accordingly belongs
among Eusebius' earlier works. It is likely that the task of com-
piling so complicated a work had largely been completed before
the disruptions visited upon the Palestinian Christians beginning
in 303.

The most detailed reference to the *Chronicle* in Eusebius'

other works appears in the *Praeparatio Euangelica* (10.9. 1–11), a work that can be dated about 315.[6] The passage is worth summarizing in detail because it gives an indication of how the "Chronological Canons" were constructed and for what purposes the "Epitome of Universal History" might be used. Eusebius is investigating that favorite topic of the apologists, the relative antiquity of biblical history as compared with Greco-Roman history. He quotes Clement, Porphyry, Josephus, and Diodorus on the subject in general, then moves to the question of the date of Moses in particular. He notes that many writers have examined the issue, whose opinions he will present shortly (Porphyry, Africanus, Tatian, Clement, Josephus, 9.12–13.13). He too has examined the chronological question, and done so in a new way. Dating the ministry of Christ to the fifteenth year of Tiberius (Luke 3:1) and the rebuilding of the temple in Jerusalem to the second year of Darius (Ezra 4:24), he finds an interval between the two dates of 548 years. For the second year of Darius coincides with the first year of the 65th Olympiad (520/19) and the fifteenth year of Tiberius falls in the fourth year of the 201st Olympiad (28/29). From the second year of Darius to the first Olympiad is 64 Olympiads, or 256 years. Reckoning the same interval in the history of Judah he comes to the fiftieth year of Uzziah, in whose reign Isaiah and Hosea were prophets. Thus Isaiah was synchronous with the first Olympiad. The Greeks reckon 408 years from the first Olympiad to the fall of Troy. The same interval in biblical history reckoned from the fiftieth year of Uzziah brings Eusebius to the third year of Labdon as Judge of Israel. Four hundred years before that he finds Moses among the Hebrews, the giant Cecrops among the Greeks. Cecrops is recognized to have been earlier even than such mythological marvels of the Greeks as the flood of Deucalion, the rape of Europa, and the birth of Apollo. So Moses was earlier than all of these Greek gods and heroes and yet there are still 505 years of biblical history before he reaches the first year of Abraham's life. From Cecrops the same interval leads back to the Assyrian ruler Ninus. Eusebius concludes by stating that these facts have been demonstrated in his *Chronological Canons.*[7]

From this passage the following conclusions can be made about Eusebius' *Chronicle*:

1. Eusebius considered the work somehow innovative.

2. The *Canons* permitted relatively simple computations to be made using the Olympiad system.

3. The *Canons* included regnal lists of the biblical kings, judges, and patriarchs and some method of comparing them with the Olympiads and with the regnal lists of the Romans, Persians, Athenians, and Assyrians.

4. The chronological system was based on certain epochal dates including the fifteenth year of Tiberius, the second year of Darius, the first Olympiad, the fall of Troy, the Exodus, and the birth of Abraham.

5. The *Canons* together with the "Epitome of Universal History" permitted the dates of the Hebrew prophets and the Greek heroes to be compared.

6. The purpose of the work as a whole was partly to make clear the greater antiquity of Hebrew history relative to most others.

These inferences are confirmed and supplemented by Jerome's translation of Eusebius' preface to the *Chronological Canons* (7–19 Helm).[8] Eusebius refers to an ancillary volume (*in priore libello*) in which he says he collected as raw material for his chronological exposition the regnal lists of the Chaldeans, Assyrians, Medes, Persians, Lydians, Hebrews, Egyptians, Athenians, Argives, Sicyonians, Lacedaemonians, Corinthians, Thessalians, Macedonians, and Romans. In the present work he puts these lists side by side and enumerates the years of the several nations in a novel fashion through the use of a synchronistic format. There follows a chronological summary similar to that of the *Praeparatio Euangelica*, where he computes the same epochal intervals but with considerably more synchronistic detail.[9] To help simplify matters for the reader he has marked off the years by decades. The reader could thus see at a glance what synchronisms there are among the various kings and magistrates whose regnal years constitute the parallel lists. The usefulness of the work is increased, he says, by the appearance in the appropriate places of brief notices about things worthy of mention in the history of the several nations whose chronological systems have been inscribed. Thus it is easy for the reader to find out both the relative and absolute dates of the Hebrew prophets, kings, and priests on the one hand, and on the other the dates of the gentile gods and heroes, the founding of their cities, and the dates of their famous men, especially the philosophers, poets, and historians. He says that the *Chronicle* begins with a synchronism among Abraham, Ninus, Europs, and the Theban dynasty of Egypt, 2,044 years before the fifteenth year of Tiberius.

From Eusebius' own testimony a good description of the *Chronicle* can be inferred. Eusebius invented what he considered a method better than that used by his predecessors for comparing sacred and profane history and for demonstrating that Judeo-Christian history and literature was considerably older than Greco-Roman civilization. He composed a chronicle in two parts. The first was devoted to basic chronological research. Eusebius collected there brief historical chronologies of the different peoples of the world together with lists of their kings. These lists provided the raw material for the construction of the major work, the Χρονικοὶ κανόνες. Eusebius arranged the lists in parallel columns in such a way as to make the numbered years, as reckoned by each of the several nations in accordance with their own annual systems, appear as a horizontal synchronism on the page. Emphasizing the sacred, Eusebius decided to devise a universal chronological canon derived from biblical history. While his predecessors had attempted to compute the date of creation, Eusebius considered Abraham the most ancient figure whose date could be established with credible precision. He therefore began his *Canons* with the birth of Abraham and assigned to that year the number *1* in his universal standard. Every ten years he made some kind of distinctive mark, so that universal chronology was divided into convenient decades on the Abraham standard. With this chronological scale of his own devising Eusebius combined the standard literary method of reckoning dates by reference to the numbered Olympiads and their quartile subdivisions. For more recent times, although consular dates were still official, it was important that the *Canons* also permit easy extrapolation of dates according to the reigns of the Roman emperors.

Eusebius brought his two main chronological standards—years of Abraham and Olympiad years—into alignment by reference to his lists of the Persian kings. Certain of the epochs of Eratosthenes, who had perfected the Olympiad system, could be dated to a specific point in the Persian lists, notably the expedition of Xerxes. Roman chronology could not be associated directly with the Persian lists, but Dionysius of Halicarnassus (*Ant. Rom.* 1.71.4) had accommodated the annalistic tradition to Eratosthenes' system and dated the founding of Rome to the

first year of the seventh Olympiad. Biblical chronology could be
tied to the Persian lists through the history of the Babylonian
captivity. Specifically, resumption of work on the rebuilding of
the temple in Jerusalem is dated on scriptural authority (Ezra
4:24) to the second year of Darius. Eusebius made this epochal
year, 520/19 B.C., the fixed starting point for his chronological
constructions. The second year of Darius provided him an Archi-
medean Δός μοι ποῦ στῶ from which to generate a set of synchronisms among the four most fundamental chronological
scales—the Greek, Hebrew, Persian, and Roman. Reckoning by
intervals from the second year of Darius, Eusebius established
synchronisms among two or more of his chronological standards
at the epochs of the Exodus, the fall of Troy, the first Olympiad,
and the ministry of Jesus. He could then proceed to align his
regnal lists accordingly.

To the Χρονικοῖ κανόνες thus constructed Eusebius added
an Ἐπιτομὴ παντοδαπῆς ἱστορίας Ἑλλήνων τε καὶ
βαρβάρων. This phrase must not be construed as suggesting
that Eusebius inserted into his tables an epitome in the modern
sense—an abbreviated version of a single, but more nearly complete universal history. The essence of an epitome, in the ancient
sense, is its brevity. Many works of Greek history and chronography the ancient commentators characterized as epitomes by
virtue of their combination of brevity and completeness.[10] Eusebius did not incorporate into his *Canons* an abbrevated version of
someone else's universal history of the Greeks and the barbarians. Rather, he inserted at what he considered the appropriate
places concise notices of significant persons or events contemporary with the years designated in the tables. This arrangement
permitted the reader to determine at once, without having to
go through the necessary computations for himself, who among
the Greeks or barbarians was contemporary with whom among
the Hebrews.[11]

Eusebius was by no means a pioneer in the field of chronography. Indeed, so monumental a work as a universal chronicle
encompassing more than 2,000 years of human history would be
unthinkable except on the basis of a long chronographic tradition.
More than seven hundred years before Eusebius set to work on
his own chronicle, Hellanicus of Lesbos had already addressed
himself to the problem of adjusting different methods of chronological reference to a common standard. By the middle of the
second century B.C. such scholars as Eratosthenes and Apollo-

dorus had elevated chronography to the position of a science. More recently, Sextus Julius Africanus had put the science of chronography into the service of Christian apologetics and compiled five books of *Chronographiae* from the creation of Adam (5502 B.C.) to his own time (A.D. 221).[12] Yet both in the *Praeparatio Euangelica* (10.9.2: καινοτέραν ὁδεύσας) and in the preface (8 Helm, *curioso ordine coaptaui*), Eusebius lays claim to an innovation. The fundamental chronological information Eusebius could excerpt from elsewhere. His own contribution was the invention of a synchronistic format that graphically displayed both universal history and comparative chronology.[13]

The Early History of the Text (to 1875)

This much can fairly be inferred on the basis of Eusebius' own statements about the *Chronicle*. What his invention actually looked like can be judged only on the basis of the manuscript traditions of his translators. Here the difficulties begin, and it is necessary to treat the problem historically as well as descriptively.

JEROME (382)

The main division of the *Chronicle* of Eusebius, the *Canons*, has always been known to the West through the Latin version incorporated in the *Chronicle* of St. Jerome. Jerome says in his preface (5–6 Helm) that he transcribed as faithfully as possible the chronological tables of Eusebius, alternating red ink with black to help separate the *regnorum tramites* from one another. From the birth of Abraham to the fall of Troy the chronicle is *pura Graeca translatio*. Eusebius, being a Greek author, had not included a sufficiently extensive collection of Roman personalities and events to suit the needs and tastes of Latin readers. For the period between the fall of Troy and the Vicennalia of Constantine, therefore, Jerome says that he is adding some material excerpted from Latin authors.[14] Jerome continued the work from the Vicennalia of Constantine (325) to the sixth consulship of Valens (378), and that final portion, he says, *totum meum est*. Already there are difficulties in the way of equating Jerome's *Chronicle* with that of Eusebius. Jerome admits to having made some additions in order to adapt the work to a Western audience. More seriously, he indicates that his Greek exemplar extended to the year 325, the Vicennalia of Constantine.[15] Eusebius, however, cites the work in a passage that must be dated before the edict of toleration in 311. There are several ways to account for this anomaly, each of which has been used in support of one hypothesis or another about the transmission of the text:

1. The work was incomplete when Eusebius referred to it in the *Eclogae Propheticae*. After the Vicennalia of Constantine, he added the necessary pages to bring the *Chronological Canons* up to date, but made few (if any) changes in what he had already written.

2. Eusebius both continued the *Chronicle* and revised notices dealing with the outbreak of the persecutions in the light of happier events that had intervened.

3. Eusebius not only continued, but substantially revised the entire work, changing its character and format to reflect the new situation and giving the revised version a universal instead of an apologetic purpose.

4. The version used by Jerome is the work of an interpolator who completely altered the original.format and even substituted non-Eusebian *fila regnorum* for the genuine lists.[16]

Jerome's version of the *Chronicle* of Eusebius, composed little more than fifty years after the Vicennalia with which his exemplar ended, entirely supplanted the Greek Eusebius, at least in the Latin-speaking world, and rapidly became the standard encyclopedia of chronology in the West. Jerome's saintly example in continuing the *Chronicle* had many imitators. The work is extant today in over a hundred manuscripts, many of t'.em containing also the *Chronicles* of medieval continuators.[17]

SCALIGER (1606)

Modern research in the chronology of the ancient world begins with Joseph Justus Scaliger (1540–1609), whose work on the *Chronicle* of Eusebius remains of fundamental importance today. Scaliger spent most of his career in France, where he established an early reputation as a textual critic by emending and restoring texts through close examination of manuscript tradition. He then turned his attention to a thorough and systematic study of ancient history and became particularly concerned with the difficulties of establishing a sound and consistent system of historical chronology. In 1583 he published *De Emendatione Temporum*, emphasizing especially the necessity of broadening the scope of ancient history and chronology to include the Babylonians, Egyptians, and Persians, as well as the Greeks and Romans. This work secured Scaliger's reputation as Europe's leading Protestant scholar of antiquities. He won the senior professorship at Leyden vacated in 1590 by Justus Lipsius when he succumbed to the forces of the Counter-Reformation. At Leyden, Scaliger was freed not only from the disruptive religious politics of his native country, but also from the burdens of university lecturing. His new-found leisure and his vast stores of learning he devoted to the *Chronicle* of Eusebius, hoping to be able to extrapolate from it the primary chronological traditions of antiquity. The textual problems of Jerome's version had, of course, to be dealt with first.

Scaliger found that the manuscripts of Jerome's *Chronicle* fell into two distinct groups on the basis of chronographic format. The first group, represented for Scaliger by ten manuscripts of late date and often careless composition, nevertheless exhibits a consistent principle of organization, which led Scaliger to conclude that they all descended ultimately from a single, very old copy that preserved the original format of Jerome. In this arrangement, years of Abraham are entered by decades in the left margin of the page, the columns of regnal years appear grouped together in the middle, and on the right there is a broad margin in which the historical notices are inscribed. The format accommodates unusually long notices by interrupting the vertical flow of numbers and permitting the notice to be written along the entire width of the page. This space for historical notices Scaliger called the *spatium historicum*, and the family of manuscripts that exhibits it is often named accordingly. Scaliger, however, labeled the group *Priores*, since he considered the distinctive *spatium historicum* representative of the genuine arrangement of Jerome. Three older manuscripts Scaliger designated *Posteriores*, because they agreed in format neither with each other nor with the *spatium historicum* group. These manuscripts enter the notices in the middle of the page bracketed by the columns of numbers. In the earlier portion of the work, before the second year of Darius, the *Posteriores* sometimes enter two sets of notices between the *fila regnorum* of a single page. Sometimes they expand the entire chronological frame-

work to cover two pages instead of one, each page having text
in the midst of the numerals.[18]

In thus giving priority to the *spatium historicum* group,
Scaliger found himself largely in agreement with Arnaldus Pontacus, whose edition of the *Chronicles* of Jerome and Prosper
of Aquitaine appeared in 1604. Scaliger was, however, interested
less in studying the textual traditions of Jerome and his medieval
continuators than he was in reconstituting the chronological
traditions transmitted by Eusebius. The *prior libellus* mentioned
in Jerome's translation of Eusebius' preface to the *Chronological
Canons* led Scaliger to the conclusion that the *Chronicle* of Eusebius had originally been composed in two parts, of which
Jerome had translated only the second. Scaliger believed that the
lost portion had contained just such a collection of fundamental
chronological information as was needed for a study of archaic
tradition, especially for the ancient Near East. The goal he set
for himself was no less than the reconstruction of the Greek
text of both portions of the original *Chronicle* of Eusebius. In
this ambitious undertaking he was fortunate to have the assistance of his friend Isaac Casaubon who, although a Protestant,
received in 1599 a royal invitation to take up residence in Paris
and assist in the revival of learning there.

With access to the vast manuscript collections of Paris,
Casaubon provided Scaliger with transcripts of important chronographic documents. Fundamental was the discovery of the
world chronicle of the Byzantine monk Georgius, known as
Syncellus. In 1602 Casaubon sent a transcript to Scaliger, and
Scaliger was delighted to discover that it consisted of extracts
from Eusebius and from his predecessor in Christian chronography, Sextus Julius Africanus. Even where these authors were
not cited by name, Scaliger was sure that genuine Eusebiana
could be isolated. Under the rubric Σποράδην he found brief
notices often corresponding very closely to those of Jerome's
translation of the *Canons*. Under such headings as "Castor on
the Sicyonian kingship" he believed he had found excerpts from
the lost first book. Again Casaubon stirred Scaliger's excitement
by the discovery in 1605 of a manuscript containing some king
lists and a list of Olympic victors in chronological order from
the first to the 249th Olympiad. (Cramer, *Anecdota Graeca* 2,
115–63) Scaliger obtained a transcript of this document and
brought his vast knowledge of Greek language and literature to
bear on the problem of restoring it to its pristine state. This
manuscript Scaliger used as the basis for drawing up an Olym-

piad chronicle of his own, which many scholars mistook for an ancient document and were wont to cite as the "anonymous author of the Olympiads." The Olympic victor list itself Scaliger attributed to Africanus, hypothesizing that Eusebius had excerpted it from him for inclusion in the mysterious *prior libellus*. During his own residence in France Scaliger discovered an eighth-century Latin chronographic manuscript that he believed was based on excerpts from Africanus and the lost first book of Eusebius. He took a transcript of the work with him to Leyden. This document is known today as the *Excerpta Latina Barbara*, its author bearing the infelicitous title of "Barbarus Scaligeri." This entire collection of *testimonia Eusebiana* Scaliger included along with the *Chronicle* of Jerome and his own Ὀλυμπιάδων ἀναγραφή in *Thesaurus Temporum*, published in Leyden in 1606 (second edition published posthumously, Amsterdam 1658).[19]

Scaliger's hypotheses did not immediately receive universal acceptance. Many did not believe that the *prior libellus* had been as extensive as Scaliger's collection of Byzantine *Excerpta Eusebiana* suggested. Some even doubted that such a book had ever existed at all. Support came from Verona, the city of the ancient noble family of the Della Scalas, from whom the Scaligers claimed descent. In 1750 the Veronese scholar Girolamo Da Prato published a lengthy treatise *De Chronicis libris duo ab Eusebio scriptis et editis*. Da Prato produced exhaustive arguments in defense of the lost-book hypothesis and offered extensive suggestions as to the nature of the book's contents. He vigorously rejected the opinion of the most recent editor, Domenico Vallarsi (Verona, 1739), that Jerome had indeed translated both books and that the *Series Regum* and the *Exordium* exhibited in some of the manuscripts constituted that *prior libellus*. Da Prato argued that the *Series Regum* and *Exordium* were of late authorship and maintained that the Byzantine chronographers, especially Syncellus, preserved genuine Eusebian extracts from the lost first book. Da Prato's arguments were favorably received and in 1785 L. T. Spittler urged the scholarly community to accept the hypothesis.[20]

THE ARMENIAN VERSION (1787)

Spittler's comments had barely been published when all doubt was removed by the discovery in Jerusalem of an Armenian manuscript containing a translation of both portions of the *Chronicle* of Eusebius and including, among other things, an Armenian version of Scaliger's list of Olympic victors extending to the 249th Olympiad. There followed a disgraceful episode of scholarly rivalry and even piracy, which had the net result of delaying for more than a hundred years the publication of a sound, critical edition of the Armenian version.[21] The Jerusalem manuscript was conveyed to Constantinople and in 1787 the Lector Georg Johannesian communicated its existence to the Mechitarist community of Venice. In 1790, at the request of I. B. Aucher, Johannesian made a copy of the manuscript and sent it to Venice. This copy had been too hastily prepared and Aucher asked for another. Johannesian obliged and in 1793 gave a second copy to I. Zohrab to convey from Constantinople to Venice. By 1795 Aucher had an edition with Latin translation and commentary ready for the press, but he suppressed it in the hope of gaining an opportunity to examine the actual manuscript himself. Meanwhile he kept the second, improved transcript in his possession. Zohrab finally ran out of patience. In 1818 he stole the first transcript from Venice and took it to Milan. Before the year was out he and Angelo Mai had published a Latin translation of the Armenian version. Aucher, of course, was furious and immediately permitted his edition to be published in Venice. But it was the too-careful Aucher who was accused of plagiarism.[22]

SCHOENE-PETERMANN (1866–75)

In the 1820s, under the direction of Niebuhr and Dindorf, work was begun on the *Corpus Scriptorum Historiae Byzantinae*, which would contain new editions of Syncellus (Dindorf, Bonn 1829), the *Chronicon Paschale* (Dindorf, Bonn 1832), and such other works containing *testimonia Eusebiana* as that of Cedrenus (Bekker, Bonn 1838) and the chronicle attributed to Leo Grammaticus (Bekker, Bonn 1842). By 1860 Syriac versions of the *Chronicle* were known.[23] Alfred Schoene decided that the time had come to prepare a modern *Thesaurus Temporum* that would collect the most important testimonia together in one place. The work was projected in two parts, of which volume two appeared first.[24] This volume contained new editions of both the Latin and Armenian versions of the *Canons*, a Latin translation of the

Syriac epitome contained in Cod. Mus. Brit. Syr. Add. 14643, and the Greek fragments excerpted by Byzantine writers. The task of preparing a new edition of the Armenian version Schoene delegated to the orientalist H. Petermann.

In the hope of finding the original manuscript and vindicating the work of Aucher, Petermann betook himself in the fall of 1864 to Constantinople. To his dismay, the Armenian patriarch of Constantinople informed him that the manuscript was no longer there. It had been sent back to Jerusalem. Petermann believed that the manuscript was purposely being withheld. Instead of undertaking what he thought would be a fruitless search for the original, whether in Jerusalem or elsewhere, he went to the Mechitarist library in Venice to examine the 1793 copy. There he was delighted to find that the Venetian Mechitarists were not only eager to assist him but had also recently acquired yet another Armenian manuscript of the *Chronicle* of Eusebius. The director of the Armenian monastery at Musch had given the manuscript to P. Nerses, who brought it to Venice in the 1850s. It bears a note to the effect that it was written in 1696 in Tokat. This manuscript Petermann collated with the 1793 transcript, with a partial transcript in Aucher's own hand that Petermann believed Aucher had begun but not completed while in Constantinople between 1802 and 1809, with Aucher's edition, and with the edition of Zohrab.

Petermann's own edition was complete when he was informed that a recently (1865) published catalogue of the manuscripts in Etschmiadzin contained an entry (no. 1684) for an Armenian manuscript of the *Chronicle*. Nevertheless, Petermann remained content to base his 1866 edition of the *Canons* on that of Aucher, making what corrections seemed necessary on the basis of his own readings of the handwritten exemplars at the Venice monastery. His efforts during the next few years to gain access to the Etschmiadzin manuscript were unsuccessful. He was able to acquire just enough information to conclude that the manuscript was very similar to that of Nerses. When volume one of the Schoene-Petermann work was published in 1875, he was able only to express regrets. This volume contained Petermann's Latin translation of the so-called first book of the *Chronicle* with the extant Greek testimonia in a parallel column. The appendices included the *Series Regum* of both the Armenian (in Latin translation) and Latin manuscripts, a reprint of the χρονογραφεῖον σύντομον discovered and first published by Angelo Mai, and

Schoene's new edition of the *Excerpta Latina Barbara* discovered by Scaliger.

Meanwhile, Petermann's Latin translation of the Armenian version of the *Canons* had appeared in 1866. The Armenian version occupied the left-hand page together with a column of Greek testimonia. On the right-hand page was Schoene's new edition of the *Chronicle* of St. Jerome. In preparing this edition Schoene undertook an extensive reexamination of the very complicated manuscript tradition. Aucher's edition had given a good picture of the format of the Armenian version, and it did not agree at all well with the arrangement of Scaliger's *spatium historicum* group. Those late manuscripts of Jerome exhibit the synchronistic columns of numerals on the left of the page and inscribe historical notices on the right side of the page, permitting long notices to interrupt the chronographic framework and spread across the entire width of the page. The Armenian manuscript, on the other hand, sets the columns of numerals in the middle of the page and reserves a margin on each side for historical notices. In thus exhibiting two columns of historical text, the Armenian version agrees with the older manuscripts of Jerome. Schoene concluded that Pontacus and Scaliger had been wrong to give priority to the format of the *spatium historicum* group. He suggested that this arrangement had been introduced by one of the continuators, possibly by the anonymous author of the Gallic chronicle of 452 falsely attributed to Prosper. This continuator also interpolated into Jerome's preface a statement, not included in the older manuscripts, that explains the color code of the arrangement. It was that statement in particular which misled Pontacus and Scaliger. Jerome did alternate black ink with red to make the chronicle easier to read, but he had no need to key historical notices to numerals through the complicated use of various mixtures of the two colors.[25]

Schoene directed his attention to the format of the oldest manuscripts of Jerome, which Scaliger had paradoxically characterized as *posteriores*. For Scaliger this group was best represented by the Codex Bongarsianus, "B" (Cod. Bernensis 219) of the seventh century, the Freherianus, "F" (Cod. Leidensis, Scal. 14) of the ninth century, and the Petavianus, "P" (Cod. Leid. Lat. Voss. Q. 110) of the ninth century. To these Schoene added the seventh-century Amandinus, "A" (Cod. Amandinus Valentianus 495) and the Petavian fragments, "S." The last named constituted the oldest testimony to Jerome's *Chronicle*

of which Schoene was aware. It consisted of six pages appended
to the Petavianus (Voss. Q. 110 A). Schoene considered another
early fragment of only two pages in Rome (Vat. Reg. 1709) so
similar that he tentatively identified it as originally belonging to
the same manuscript. Subsequently, he discovered that another
fourteen pages of the same manuscript were extant in Paris
(Lat. 6400 B). The fragments are written in an Italian hand of
the fifth century. According to a note added by a later hand in
the Paris leaves, the manuscript once belonged to the great
Benedictine abbey at Fleury. It has accordingly come to be referred to as the Codex Floriacensis. Both "A" and "P" seem to
have been transcribed from this ancient manuscript. The exemplar of "F" was very similar, but the manuscript as it exists
shows evidence of a purposeful alteration of the original format.
These manuscripts constitute the "S" class. The Bongarsianus
is *sui generis* and, in the opinion of Schoene, of the highest
authority.[26]

These older manuscripts all agree in important respects.
They all have one format for the earlier portion of the *Chronicle*
and another beginning with the 65th Olympiad (520/19), the
second year of Darius. After the 65th Olympiad, the manuscripts
exhibit the columns of numerals toward the margins of the page,
with historical notices occupying a space in the middle. Only after
the destruction of the temple in Jerusalem in A.D. 70 do these
manuscripts resemble the *spatium historicum* group. The likeness
is purely coincidental, arising from the fact that hereafter only
the Roman column remains to be inscribed. The numerals representing the regnal years of the Roman emperors appear on the
left side of the page and the remaining space can be devoted to
historical notices. More significant for the history of the text is
the arrangement that these older manuscripts exhibit for the
earlier portion of the chronographic structure. Before the second
year of Darius there are sometimes as many as nine columns
of regnal years to be inscribed, in addition to the Olympiad
numbers and years of Abraham. The "S" class of manuscripts
uses two facing pages—verso and recto—to display the content
of the *Chronicle* from the first year of Abraham to the second
year of Darius (Olympiad 65.1, Abraham 1497). On each page
the format is similar to that used in the latter portion of the
Chronicle. Historical notices occupy the space in the middle of
the page and the columns of numbers appear on each side. But
since two pages are used for the chronographic display there are

two columns of historical text, two *spatia historica*, corresponding to any given set of years. After the second year of Darius
the contents of the *Chronicle* appear on a single page and there
is accordingly one *spatium historicum* in the middle. The Bongarsianus agrees with the "S" class in having two columns of
text before the second year of Darius and one thereafter. But
"B" does not use two pages for the doubled arrangement. The
entire content for a given set of years appears on one page. Thus
the single page of the Bongarsianus has two columns of text
bracketed on each side by the numerals of the *fila regnorum*.

Schoene noted how much easier it would be to generate the
spatium historicum format from that of the older manuscripts
than vice versa. He concluded that the doubled arrangement
represented the original format of St. Jerome. Furthermore,
since the Armenian version also has two columns of text, this
kind of format must have been in the Greek original and can be
attributed to Eusebius himself. The Armenian version adheres
to a single-paged arrangement consistently and does not, like
the "S" class of Jerome, use two pages for the content of a
single set of years. Schoene therefore concluded that the Armenian version agrees more nearly with "B" than it does with the
"S" class. He believed that Jerome's Greek exemplar must have
been organized, like the Armenian, by single pages and that
Jerome had preserved that arrangement. The ultimate common
archetype of both Jerome and the Armenian translator—that is,
Eusebius himself—must have used the same kind of format
with two columns of text appearing on a single page. The Bongarsianus manuscript of Jerome thus represented for Schoene a
purer tradition than the "S" class. He postulated that exigencies
of time and space had forced the ancestral scribe of the "S"
class to adopt a less demanding format for the crowded early
portion of the *Chronicle* by spreading the doubled arrangement
across two facing pages of the codex. The scribe of "B" or its
exemplar occasionally fell into the same aberration for similar
reasons.[27]

Schoene based his own edition of the *Chronological Canons*
on the combined authority of the Armenian version and the
Bongarsianus manuscript of Jerome. He organized the chronological tables of both versions by single pages, as he assumed
Eusebius must have done. This decision permitted Schoene to
publish the two versions side by side on facing pages for easy

comparison of the entries of the Armenian *Canons* with those of Jerome. The difficulties of printed publication, however, produced an unfortunate paradox. Although Schoene presented in his preface lengthy and conclusive arguments against the authenticity of the format of the *spatium historicum* group of manuscripts, his printed edition actually displays that kind of format for both versions of the *Canons*. The chronologcal framework is printed as a compact group filling much of the page, and the historical notices appear in a broad column occupying the right margin. Each notice is headed by a letter of the alphabet. The reader must find that same letter inscribed next to one of the numerals of the chronographic framework in order to determine where the notice actually stands. Much extrapolation is required of the user who wishes to form a picture of what the *Canons* actually look like in the manuscript tradition. The critical apparatus is very dfficult to use and adds to the effort required of the reader. Schoene indicated his own opinion of where the notice belongs by having the appropriate letter of the alphabet printed in bold type next to one of the numerals. The manuscript variants are indicated in small type. A capital letter stands for the manuscript, and a lowercase letter, printed in superscript, indicates which of the historical entries appeared at that year in the manuscript. Some of these notations have to be enclosed in parentheses, because the notice that stood at that year in the indicated manuscript appears on a different page in the edition. Furthermore, although the manuscripts show years of Abraham by decades, Schoene prints every year of Abraham for Jerome in order to make his version look more like the Armenian. Yet another aberration from the manuscript tradition results from the decision to print both versions as exact parallels. The requirements of the typesetter take precedence and there is no way for the reader to determine where the page divisions occur in the manuscripts. The Schoene-Petermann edition was reissued in 1967 through photomechanical reproduction with reduction in size from quarto to octavo by Weidmann Verlag of Zurich. This reprint is now widely available, so that it is more readily accessible to most scholars than the twentieth-century editions. It should be understood, however, that this edition must be used with caution. Schoene-Petermann does not present a fair picture of either version of the *Canons* as they exist in the manuscripts. Furthermore, Schoene's edition of Jerome's version was based on a wrong evaluation of the authority of the Bongarsianus manuscript, and Petermann's edition of the Armenian was based on an earlier modern edition and on late transcripts of the authoritative manuscript—not on the manuscript itself.

Scholars of the late-nineteenth century who used this edition with its provision for easy comparison among the Armenian, Jerome, and the Greek fragments generally assumed that the Armenian version was a better witness to the original *Chronicle* of Eusebius than was that of St. Jerome. Jerome in his preface admitted to making additions to the original. The Armenian presumably made no such changes. (But the translator's preface, if there was one, has been lost along with Eusebius' preface and the first few hundred years of the *Canons*.) Furthermore, the Armenian translator possessed and reproduced both books of the *Chronicle*. This version was accordingly based on a complete exemplar and scholars therefore supposed that the Armenian represents a purer, if younger, tradition than Jerome.

Curt Wachsmuth was explicit on the point. He maintained that the Armenian's format, which is consistent throughout and shows no change at the second year of Darius, represents the original format of Eusebius. The tables of numbers appeared in the middle of the page with historical notices in each margin. The outer margin, he suggested, was originally reserved for sacred history, the inner margin for profane. Jerome used a different and less authoritative Greek exemplar. The original format was altered to that preserved by the Bongarsianus with the two columns of text written between columns of numbers instead of in the margins. The scribe of the "S" class further altered the original by introducing the twin-page format in order to increase the available space. Jerome himself had changed the Eusebian arrangement after the second year of Darius, preferring to have one column of text instead of two, and allowing the space allotted to a given set of years to expand as much as necessary to accommodate this single column of text. This opinion about the priority of the Armenian version over the translation of Jerome was so widely accepted that it became common for scholars to cite even Jerome by years of Abraham instead of Olympiads and to refer in a misleading manner to the Armenian version as "Eusebius" and to the Latin version as "Jerome," as if the Latin translation were significantly less Eusebian than the Armenian.[28]

Modern Criticism of the Text

MOMMSEN (1889)

The Schoene-Petermann edition of *Eusebi Chronicorum Canonum Quae Supersunt* was dedicated to Theodor Mommsen, and it was Mommsen who made the fundamental discoveries that soon rendered the edition obsolete. In 1889 Mommsen reported on the discovery in the Bodleian Library at Oxford of a nearly complete manuscript of the *Chronicle* of St. Jerome of earlier date and better orthography than any other manuscript authority, with the possible exception of the fragments of the Floriacensis ("S"). The first few pages, containing 554 years of the *Chronicle*, are in a late hand. The remainder is written in an uncial hand that E. M. Thompson dated for Mommsen to the sixth century. According to Traube, however, the hand is contemporary with that of the Floriacensis and both can be dated to the fifth century. The Bodleian manuscript ("O") has the same double-page format for the earlier portion as "S" and its descendants. It was copied about the same time as "S" from a similar exemplar which cannot long postdate Jerome. "O" differs from "S" in some matters of text. The principal difference, however, is that "S" apparently preserved the page divisions of Jerome's 26-line original, while "O" conserved paper by writing 30 lines to the page. "O," "S," and their descendants together provide authoritative testimony to the antiquity of the double-sided format that Schoene had rejected for his edition. The discovery of "O," together with Schoene's own discovery somewhat earlier of a complete manuscript (Middlehillensis) that Mommsen considered a descendant of "O" and subsequently of the Paris fragments of "S," made it clear that the manuscript tradition of Jerome had to be examined anew and the *Chronicle* published again in an up-to-date edition.[29]

Mommsen also managed after many years of effort to gain possession of a partial transcript of the Etschmiadzin manuscript of the Armenian version, of which Petermann had been aware but unable to use for his edition. Mommsen obtained a transcript of the first fourteen pages together with the text and dates of certain entries that he considered critical for judgment of the manuscript tradition. He had the material examined and translated by F. Justi, then collated it with the readings of Peter-mann's manuscripts. Mommsen reported his conclusions in the 1895 issue of *Hermes*. He found the similarities between the readings of the Etschmiadzin manuscript and those of the manu-script that Nerses had brought to Venice in the 1850s sufficiently striking to confirm Petermann's conjecture that Nerses' manu-script had been copied from "E." The transcripts that Aucher and Zohrab used of the manuscript brought from Jerusalem to Constantinople in the late-eighteenth century Mommsen found preserved readings slightly different from "E," but sometimes better. The differences he believed could best be understood as editorial changes from an exemplar just like "E." Indeed, the descriptions of the now-lost Constantinople manuscript were very similar to the description Mommsen obtained of the Etschmiad-zin manuscript and both were said to have borne the seal of an Armenian Catholicus named Gregor. In fact, Mommsen con-cluded, Aucher's transcripts had been made from "E" itself.

The manuscript residing in Etschmiadzin was the same one that had been in Constantinople a hundred years earlier, the same from which Georg had made the 1790 and 1793 tran-scripts for Aucher. Petermann was unable to locate the original in Constantinople in 1864 because it had been removed for safe-keeping to the Etschmiadzin library near the Armenian capital. The same manuscript had been in Tokat in 1696 when Nerses' transcript was copied from it. The original could be dated paleographically to the twelfth or thirteenth century. But the modern editions were based on late-eighteenth-century copies with the readings of a late-seventeenth-century transcript ap-pearing in Petermann's apparatus. The entire critical apparatus could now be dispensed with. Mommsen urged that a new edition of the *Chronicle* with text and translation be prepared on the basis of the Etschmiadzin manuscript.[30]

Meanwhile, the Syriac representative of the *Canons* pre-served in Cod. Vat. Syr. 162 had been made widely available to historians and philologists through the edition with Latin translation published in 1884 by Siegfried and Gelzer. Peter-mann had suggested, contrary to the opinions of Zohrab and Aucher, that the Armenian version of the *Chronicle* was not a direct translation from a Greek exemplar but showed influence of a Syriac intermediary. Unlike the epitome that Roediger translated for Schoene's edition, this version, commonly attrib-uted to the Antiochene patriarch Dionysius of Tell-Mahre

(818–845), contains citation of the dates for the entries. The dates are expressed in years of Abraham, a fact that suggests an exemplar more closely akin to the Armenian version than to Jerome. Alfred von Gutschmid, however, sought to show that the Syriac epitome was entirely independent of the Armenian version and that the Syriac influences in the latter could be accounted for in the history of the Armenian language itself. The Armenian tradition ends with the sixteenth year of Diocletian, while the Syriac epitomator and Jerome had exemplars that reached to the twentieth year of Constantine. Furthermore, von Gutschmid found that the Syriac entries for the dates of the early bishops were closer to those of Jerome than to the entries of the Armenian version. Von Gutschmid's opinion was accepted and promulgated as dogma by Wachsmuth with the argument that Jerome and the Syriac epitome witness an exemplar of one type, while the Armenian translator used a Greek exemplar of another and better kind.[31]

SCHOENE'S WELTCHRONIK (1900)

The need for a new edition of so important a source as the *Chronicle* of Eusebius that would take into account the best Latin and Armenian manuscripts as well as the Syriac evidence was clear. Alfred Schoene considered undertaking the task himself, but had to abandon the project. He did publish a monograph detailing the results of his new inquiries into the manuscript tradition of St. Jerome and the implications for the textual tradition of the original *Chronicle* of Eusebius. Schoene argued on the basis of textual variants that the extant manuscripts derive from at least three very old exemplars written during the lifetime of Jerome himself. The "S" class of manuscripts with its double-paged organization for the earlier portion of the work and its change of format at Olympiad 65, the second year of Darius, represented the official and final version of St. Jerome prepared under his own direction by a skilled *librarius* who used a 26-line page. "O" was based on a somewhat earlier copy, which had a few uncorrected readings but exhibited the same format as the final version.

"O" and "S" and their descendants attest to what Schoene called the *Editio Romana*. This edition Jerome prepared as a showpiece for presentation at the Roman synod of 382. The

Greek *Canons* of Eusebius he studied while in Constantinople in 380–81. He dictated the Latin version rather hastily to his secretary, who had first transcribed the numerals of the chronographic framework. Jerome revised the work in preparation for the Roman synod and he continued to do so the rest of his life. A few private copies of the first, uncorrected effort were nevertheless in circulation. The Bongarsianus came from such a copy. The scribe did not understand the principles of organization and compressed the contents of two pages into one. The *spatium historicum* group of manuscripts, which all derive from the tenth-century London manuscript (Brit. Mus. 16974) containing the chronicles of St. Jerome, the anonymous continuation of 452, and Marius of Aventicum, preserved what must have been very old, uncorrected translation errors. This version must therefore have derived from another private copy, which came into the possession of the author of the anonymous continuation in the middle of the fifth century. It was he who completely transformed the organization of the *Chronicle*. Whoever set out to publish a new edition would face the unusual task, Schoene suggested, of recovering not the original text of Jerome but the improvements and corrections that he gradually made over the years in his own copies.

Schoene's arguments are too complicated to be summarized in detail. Two of the most noteworthy problems can serve as examples of the kind of evidence he used. At Olympiad 256 is the entry *Athlamos natali Romanae urbis cucurrit.* "B" has *Athlamos*; "O," "M," and the *spatium historicum* group have *Athalamos*. "A," "P," and "R" have *quadraginta missus natali Romanae urbis cucurrerunt.* The Greek must have read ἆθλα μʹ (40). Thus "B" has an uncorrected direct transliteration while "O" and the *spatium historicum* group have a variant of the same. The descendants of "S" ("A" and "P") have a more nearly correct translation. Schoene argued that the uncorrected version must be the earlier. "R" is not of the "S" class, since it does not preserve the doubled format. Schoene suggested that it derives from an uncorrected early private copy that was subsequently collated with a Greek version of Eusebius, perhaps Panodorus' chronicle. The other infamous example occurs at Olympiad 46, where all the older manuscripts have *Epimenides Athenas emundauit*, but the *spatium historicum* group has *Epimenides Athenas subuertit*. Schoene suggested that the Greek read καθαίρει (cleanse), which Jerome originally mistranslated as if it were καθαιρεῖ (destroy) but subsequently corrected. The younger manuscripts thus have the earlier, uncorrected reading.

Having established that "O" and "S" represent the authentic format and corrected text of St. Jerome, Schoene directed his attention to the question of the relative merits of the Latin and Armenian versions as witness to the original. He considered the format of Jerome considerably more complicated than that of the Armenian. He argued that it was absurd to think that Jerome could have made such striking changes, especially since he was working in haste and through the medium of dictation. The separation in the earlier portion of the *Chronicle* with sacred history on the left page and Greek history on the right corresponds well to Eusebius' comparative purposes as declared in his preface. The change in format at Olympiad 65 must also be ascribed to Eusebius himself, for whom the second year of Darius was an especially epochal year and a fundamental date for chronological computations. The same kinds of argument that tell against an alteration of format on Jerome's part Schoene applied also to the Armenian translator. The Armenian translator entered the Hebrew *filum* first; Jerome had the Assyrian column first. This change alone, quite apart from the other differences in format, would have introduced difficulties in transcription greater than a copyist or translator would want to assume. Furthermore, there are differences between the two versions, especially on the chronology of episcopal succession, that are irreconcilable. Jerome's entries are closer to the information contained in the *Historia Ecclesiastica* than are those of the Armenian translator. Interestingly enough, however, the *Series Regum* contained in the Armenian version agrees more nearly with Jerome's *Canons* and with the Syriac epitome than with the *fila* of the Armenian version itself. Schoene concluded that Eusebius had published two editions of the *Chronicle*. The earlier edition, published before 311, contained the chronographic excerpts of an introductory section as well as the *Chronological Canons*. The second edition contained only the *Chronological Canons,* revised, as was the *Historia Ecclesiastica,* after the Vicennalia of Constantine. The Armenian version represented the first edition; Jerome and the Syriac epitomator used the second edition. The Armenian *Series Regum* resulted from a collation of the two editions. Thus it was Eusebius himself who was responsible for the major differences in text and format between the Armenian and the Latin versions.

Schoene's arguments had important implications for judgment on the relative merits of the two versions. Since they represented two different editions, the Armenian and Latin versions had equal claim as authentic representatives of Eusebius. Nevertheless, the manuscript tradition of St. Jerome is considerably older than that of the Armenian version. Furthermore, "O" and "S" represented the corrected and official Editio Romana of St. Jerome, while Jerome in turn translated the revised edition of Eusebius. Schoene thus concluded that the modern preference for the Armenian version, which he had once shared and helped to promulgate, should be abandoned in favor of the much older manuscript tradition of Jerome.[32]

Schwartz (1907)

Mommsen's request for new editions of both versions of the *Chronicle* was reasserted after his death in 1903 by Eduard Schwartz. Schwartz was at work on a new edition of the *Historia Ecclesiastica* for which he and Mommsen had been commissioned by the committee on patristics of the Berlin academy for inclusion in a new collection of Greek patristics, *Die griechischen christlichen Schriftsteller* (GCS). Schwartz had earlier dealt with the *Chronicle* in an effort to reconstruct the king lists of Eratosthenes. His work on the *Historia Ecclesiastica* now required him to address the problems of the *Chronicle* more generally. Schwartz was constrained to use Aucher's edition of the Armenian version, which provides a clearer picture of the format than the Schoene-Petermann edition, and the photographic facsimile of "O" published in 1905 by J. K. Fotheringham (*The Bodleian Manuscript of Jerome's Version of the Chronicle of Eusebius*, Oxford 1905). In the *Berliner philologische Wochenschrift* (26 [1906] 744ff) Schwartz laid down the principles for a new edition of Jerome, and in his *Real-Encyclopädie* article on Eusebius (6 [1907] 1376, 1381) he called for a new edition of the Armenian version with translation into Greek, not Latin or German. New editions were commissioned for the *GCS*. Meanwhile Schwartz introduced an unfortunate and unnecessary complication into the debate about the textual tradition by suggesting that neither St. Jerome nor the Armenian version was an authentic representation of the original *Chronicle* of Eusebius.

Schwartz could not accept Schoene's theory of two Eusebian editions. Both Jerome and the Armenian translator worked, he thought, from the same kind of Greek exemplar. Although the Armenian manuscript breaks off at the sixteenth year of Diocletian, it was clear that the Greek exemplar reached the Vicennalia of Constantine. For an interval computed at the end of the discussion of Hebrew chronology in the introductory book uses that year as a terminus. Schwartz argued that Jerome's version was a more accurate representative of their common Greek exemplar than the *Canons* of the Armenian version, which was full of transcriptional errors. The Greek chronicle used by both translators was not, however, the genuine *Chronicle* of Eusebius, who had completed his work before the composition of the *Eclogae Propheticae* and therefore before 311. In his study of the king lists Schwartz had concluded that the extant versions of the *Chronicle* showed the influence of an interpolator who had continued the work to the Vicennalia of Constantine and also substituted for some of Eusebius' annual lists the much more popular chronology of Africanus. There were difficulties in his hypothesis, because he had to assume that the interpolator used a version of Africanus that was already corrupt.

Schwartz now took a much more extreme position. He maintained that Eusebius was too careful and serious a scholar, too circumspect in matters of absolute chronology ever to have imposed on his *Chronicle* a strict chronological framework such as that which appears in both the Latin and Armenian versions of the *Canons*. Eusebius never intended his historical notices to be read into a fixed absolute chronology. The *fila regnorum* of both versions of the *Canons* are often in disagreement with the chronographic excerpts so carefully collected in the prefatory book. Therefore it cannot have been Eusebius who composed those *fila*. The dates for Roman and Alexandrian bishops as they appear in both versions of the *Canons* contradict what Eusebius himself has to say about these successions in the *Historica Ecclesiastica*. He could not have fixed the succession of bishops in a strict chronological framework of *fila regnorum*, yet complain later in the introduction to his *Historia Ecclesiastica* about the lack of chronological reference points in such matters. Eusebius cites his *Chronicle* as early as 310, and Schwartz argued that the version that came into the hands both of Jerome and of the Ar-

menian translator had been continued to the twentieth year of
Constantine and drastically reworked by someone other than
Eusebius. His conclusion is devastating, and demands a transla-
tion rather than a paraphrase.

> One does not come to the hypothesis, as I earlier believed, of
> a systematic interpolation by which the *fila regnorum* were
> corrupted. One must take the decisive step and hypothesize
> that the system of continuous synchronistic chronological tables
> which Jerome took from his Greek original is a thoroughly
> unscholarly and unauthentic extension of the genuine tables.
> The apparent precision of the numerical system set up in such
> a way as to provide a date for everything betrays the work of
> a dilettante without the slightest understanding of scientific
> chronology.[33]

The issues that Schwartz raised are genuine. The problems
reflect rather on the difficulties that confront anyone, including
Eusebius himself, who attempts to construct a universal chronicle, than on the authenticity of the extant *Canons*. St. Jerome
comments explicitly on the difficulties of interpreting and transcribing the work in his translator's preface. The task of composition must have been much more difficult for Eusebius, who
had to start from the beginning. There is no reason to suppose
that Eusebius reproduced every detail of his chronographic excerpts when transforming them into numerical columns. Indeed,
it would be surprising if the *fila regnorum* did agree in every
respect with the preliminary material. The chronographic excerpts constituted the raw matter, as Eusebius says in the preface
to the *Canons*, for an innovative work. He collected the material
from a wide variety of authors who did not share a common
and consistent chronographic system. Some adjustments would
certainly be required to bring the diversity of sources into synchronistic harmony. If such a grandiose scheme betrays the
unscientific chronological dilettante, it must be admitted that it
was Eusebius who indulged in the dilettantism. The chronographic inconsistencies and the complications of synchronistic
composition begin with Eusebius. They were compounded by
errors and confusions of scribes in the Greek, Latin, Syriac, and
Armenian traditions. Whatever the faults of the *Canons* as we
possess it, whatever its inconsistencies with respect to the prefatory excerpts and Eusebius' own other works, it is not likely
that the basic format and organization derive from an interpo-

lator and not from Eusebius himself. Eusebius certainly did not
have to believe everything he wrote. He warns his readers
in the preface to the chronographic excerpts that they should
apply the dictum of the master—"It is not for you to know about
dates" (Acts 1:7)—to history as well as to eschatology. He
specifically says in the entry of the *Canons* at the first Olympiad
that nothing he has entered previously for Greek history is
credible. Eusebius transmits the chronographic tradition in
handy, synchronistic form. There is no reason that he should
have shrunk from fixing his entries with strict chronological
precision when his predecessors in chronography, both Hellenistic and Christian, had established precise dates for persons and
events of even the mythical period. Eusebius himself (*Praep.
Euang.* 10.12, 17–19, citing Clement) reports the precise intervals established by Apollodorus between the apotheosis of
Dionysus, the voyage of the Argo, and the apotheosis of Heracles.[34] One should not suppose therefore that Eusebius would
have eschewed such reckonings in the *Chronicle.*

It is just such an interlocking system of *fila regnorum* and
historical notices as appears in the extant versions of the *Canons*
that Eusebius seems to be describing in his own earliest and most
complete reference to the *Chronicle* (*Ecl. Proph.* 1, 27 Gaisford): χρονικοὺς συντάξαντες κανόνας ἐπιτομήν τε τούτοις
παντοδαπῆς ἱστορίας Ἑλλήνων τε καὶ βαρβάρων ἀντι παρα-
θέντες   ("arranging lines of dates and setting right alongside
them an epitome of every kind of history both of Greeks and
Nongreeks"). The system does not require every notice to be
referred "unscientifically" to one specific year in the chronological
framework. Such entries as the excerpts from Castor (27[a], 45[a],
64[a] Helm) and the lengthy discussion of the many different
dates assigned by the ancients to Homer (66[a] Helm) show by
their wording that they are not to be assigned to a specific year.
Other notices, beginning opposite the first regnal year of a
monarch, mention persons or events which are to be dated
within the reign of a particular king, but not to any one year.
A good example appears at the first year of Artaxerxes (110[g]
Helm): *ea quae de Esther et Mardocheo scripta sunt quidam
adfirmant sub hoc rege gesta.* But notices referring to the *floruit*
of persons, the foundation of cities, wars, treaties, and eclipses
would be meaningless unless the author intended them to be
read against a specific year of the chronological framework.

KARST (1911)

Schwartz' hypothesis of the unscientific interpolator is untenable. The Armenian and Latin versions of the *Chronicle* must be accepted as authentic representations of the original. A few years after Schwartz had attempted to absolve Eusebius from responsibility for creating the problematic work, the new editions that are the basis for modern research in Greek chronography began to appear. In 1906 Josef Karst undertook a new edition of the Armenian version using a photographic facsimile of the Etschmiadzin manuscript obtained by the Berlin academy. Karst translated the *Chronicle* into German, taking care to preserve as closely as possible the style and errors of the original. Karst's edition was published in the *GCS* in 1911. It is as close a representation of the format and arrangement of the manuscript as is possible in print, preserving both the pagination of the original and its disposition of the historical entries along the chronological framework. Alfred von Gutschmid and Eduard Schwartz had demanded that the Armenian version be published anew, this time with Greek translation. Karst pointed out that translation into Greek could be misleading. It was by no means clear that the Armenian version rested solely and directly on a Greek exemplar. Translation into Latin would have been insufficient, since it is impossible to preserve the style and color of the Armenian language in the narrow confines of Latin syntax. The editors of the *GCS* had therefore decided upon German as the most appropriate medium for the new edition.[35]

Karst supported Schoene's hypothesis that Eusebius had edited the *Chronicle* twice and that the Armenian version represented the earlier edition, the Latin version and the Syriac epitome the second. Karst based his arguments both on the format of the Armenian *Chronicle* and on the evidence of Syriac influence on the language. The Armenian version sets the chronological tables in the middle of the page with historical notices written in the margins. Most notices appear in the right margin, but Karst observed that the left margin was originally reserved for entries of sacred history. In this respect it agrees with the arrangement of the oldest manuscripts of Jerome in the earlier portion of the *Chronicle*. But the Armenian version observes the same format throughout the work and it exhibits the notices in the margins instead of between columns of numbers. It therefore agrees with none of the manuscripts of Jerome. Furthermore, the Armenian arrangement of the chronological columns sets the Hebrew *filum* first, while the older manuscripts of Jerome enter the Assyrian column first. The Armenian manuscript breaks off at the sixteenth year of Diocletian, and Karst found no reason to believe that the text originally extended further. He believed that the Armenian translator reproduced his exemplar with great care and would not have created major innovations in format. Karst concluded that the Armenian version faithfully preserved the arrangement of its exemplar. It represented Eusebius' first edition of the *Chronicle*, which he either completed or published as it was about the time that the great persecutions began in the later years of Diocletian's reign. At this time Christianity was not tolerated and Christians were often officially persecuted. This first edition of the *Chronicle* was therefore of chiefly apologetic character. It is for that reason that the Hebrew *filum* came first and that the division into two columns of text was continued for the entire work. The second edition was prepared after the Vicennalia of Constantine, when Christianity was not only tolerated but officially favored. The second edition emphasized the universality of history and historical chronology. Thus the regnal columns of the great empires—Assyrian, Persian, Roman— were entered first.[36]

The Armenian version preserves so many Grecisms literally translated or directly transliterated as to suggest that the translation was made directly into Armenian from a Greek exemplar. Petermann had shown, however, that there are also clear influences of Syriac. He concluded that the present Armenian version was the result of contamination between two earlier Armenian translations, one made directly from Greek and the other translated from a Syriac version of the *Chronicle*. Karst developed this hypothesis with a detailed analysis of the linguistic style. He found that the so-called first book, the chronographic excerpts, was a direct translation from Greek. There are very few Syriac influences that he could not account for in the history of the Armenian language. In the *Canons*, however, the situation is different. The Greek shows through less clearly and there are unmistakable Syriac influences that cannot be understood as ordinary loan words. There are also some elements that must derive from what Karst believed was the second edition of the *Chronicle*. The *Series Regum* in particular, and that passage of the first book (p. 62 Karst) which computes an interval to the

twentieth year of Constantine, show influence of the second
edition. The earliest evidence for the existence of the Armenian
version is found in the work of Lazar of Pharpi, who can be
dated to 600. About the same time a Syriac translation of the
Chronicle was made by Simeon. Karst suggested that the Armenian version, because of some imperfections especially in the
Canons, was collated very early with the Syriac version of
Simeon and reissued in a revised edition. In the eighth century
a Syriac translation was made of Eusebius' second edition, and
it was an epitome of this version that is included in the chronicle
attributed to Dionysius of Tell-Mahre. A ninth-century scribe
had this later Syriac translation at hand when he copied the
Armenian version. He made some changes in the Armenian text
on the basis of that Syriac version and also excerpted from it for
inclusion in the Armenian manuscript the king lists known as the
Series Regum. The contaminated version of the Chronicle that
resulted was copied again in the twelfth or thirteenth century
and after many peregrinations finally came to rest in Etschmiadzin. Thus, in Karst's opinion, the Armenian version as we know
it derives from three sources: 1) an Armenian translation made
about 600 of Eusebius' first edition, 2) a Syriac version of the
same edition made about the same time as the Armenian and
collated with it, 3) a Syriac version of Eusebius' second edition,
which influenced the Armenian text in the early ninth century.[37]

FOTHERINGHAM (1923)

Karst accepted and developed Schoene's hypothesis that both
the Armenian and Latin versions preserve the format of their
Greek exemplars—both arrangements derive from Eusebius himself, who revised the content and organization of the *Chronicle*
after 325. The new editors of St. Jerome, however, rejected the
theory of multiple editions. John Knight Fotheringham, in his
introduction to the collotype facsimile of the newly discovered
Bodleian manuscript of Jerome, showed that the textual variants
adduced by Schoene are not divided consistently among families
of manuscripts and do not lead to the conclusion that Jerome
prepared more than one kind of "edition" for his *Chronicle*. In
an article on the problematic list of thalassocracies that Jerome
and the Armenian exhibit in very different ways, neither one in
agreement with the text of Eusebius' excerpt from Diodorus in

the prefatory book (225 Petermann, 106–7 Karst), Fotheringham maintained that the evidence for more than one edition on
the part of Eusebius was equally unconvincing. He argued that
the Armenian and Latin versions must be considered as different
witnesses to the same text. In 1923 Fotheringham published an
edition of Jerome based on thorough examination of a large
number of manuscripts. He agreed with Schoene that the "O-S"
class of manuscripts, with the double *spatium* and two-page
composition for the earlier portion of the *Chronicle* and the
change of format at the second year of Darius, preserves
Jerome's own organization of the work and that Jerome in turn
found this kind of format in his Greek exemplar. He denied,
however, that Eusebius had published two substantially different
versions of the *Chronicle* with the extant Armenian translation
representing the earlier. It was clear that Eusebius had made
the work available before 311 and equally clear that he subsequently continued it to the Vicennalia of Constantine. But it did
not follow that Eusebius made any substantial changes in what
he had already written: *aliud est producere, aliud redigere.*[38]

Fotheringham's edition of St. Jerome, with its careful reconstruction of what must have been the arrangement of the 26-line
archetype, is an excellent one. Until recently, it was the only
convenient, modern, printed edition based on the oldest and best
manuscript tradition. With its full critical apparatus this edition
is, in that respect, still the best. Fotheringham's judgment on the
Chronicle of Eusebius, although essentially correct, he presented
in dogmatic fashion without the kind of detailed argumentation
necessary to account for the differences between the Armenian
and Latin versions on the basis of a single Eusebian edition.

HELM (1913–56)

Just such a study was then being prepared by Rudolf Helm.
Helm had been commissioned to publish a new edition of the
Chronicle of Jerome for inclusion along with Karst's edition of
the Armenian version in the *GCS*. The editors of the series
hoped eventually to be able to realize Schaliger's ideal of reconstructing the original *Chronicle* of Eusebius. The two scholars
commissioned to lay the foundations for the effort, however,
differed widely in their opinions about the relationship of the
extant versions to the original. Karst's translation of the Armen-

ian text with his arguments in support of the theory of multiple editions was published in 1911. Helm's edition of the Latin text was published in 1913, and in all essentials Fotheringham's 1923 edition was very little different. The world war had, however, interrupted the progress of Helm's work for the *GCS*. His edition was not set into print, but published through a photomechanical reproduction of Helm's own handwritten manuscript with the critical apparatus deferred for inclusion in a subsequent volume. Helm disagreed with Karst's assessment of the relationship of the Armenian version to the original of Eusebius and he was gratified to have his own opinions receive the support of Fotheringham, whose edition Helm had been able to examine in proof before it was formally published. He was himself then at work on the companion volume to his own edition of the text. This supplement would include critical apparatus, introductory arguments on the manuscript tradition and the relationship of Jerome's *Chronicle* to Eusebius and the Armenian version, as well as indices and an exhausive compilation of references to the testimonia bearing on the original Greek text and the interpretation of its entries.[39]

While this work was in progress Helm discovered that many of the differences between the Armenian and Latin versions could be accounted for on the hypothesis that the original *Chronicle* of Eusebius had been organized with several entries standing side by side in parallel columns of text contained within the space reserved in the middle of the page for historical notices. It was on this hypothesis in particular that Helm reported in *Eusebius' Chronik und ihre Tabellenform*. He demonstrated the weaknesses of Schwartz' "decisive thesis" that the synchronistic *fila regnorum* were the work of an interpolator and affirmed their Eusebian origin. Against Wachsmuth and Schoene, Helm defended Eusebius' assertion that his work was innovative. Not only must the synchronistic tables of the *Chronici Canones* be attributed to Eusebius, but it was Eusebius who invented and first used this kind of chronographic composition. There is no evidence that Castor of Rhodes, as Wachsmuth maintained, or Sextus Julius Africanus, as some believed, composed synchronistic tables. Eusebius' claim to the innovation must not be denied him.

The extant Armenian and Latin versions of the *Chronological Canons* attest to the outward appearance of Eusebius' invention in different ways. It is not necessary to posit two Eusebian editions, Helm argued, and two Eusebian variants of the same chronographic innovation in order to account for the differences. It must strike anyone who compares the Armenian and Latin versions with each other and with the σποράδην notices of Syncellus that the three witnesses preserve much the same material, but in different order. Commenting on the difficulties of his task as an editor and translator, Jerome notes in his preface (5 Helm) that he was burdened not so much by the problems of translation as by the difficulty of determining the correct *ordo legendi* of the entries. There could be no such difficulty in reading a single set of notices entered vertically one below the other in a discrete space, nor would Jerome have made such a comment if his exemplar had been organized like the Armenian *Canons*. The Armenian version has two columns of text, but they are entered in two discrete marginal spaces and can be reproduced with ease. The significance of Jerome's remarks can best be understood and the different order of entries in the Latin and Armenian versions most expeditiously explained by postulating a Greek archetype in which the notices were entered side by side in two or more parallel columns within a single space. The earlier portion of the *Chronicle* was written across two pages, with one such space on each page. In transcribing the work one had to read from left to right within the *spatium historicum* as well as from top to bottom, and problems of determining the *ordo legendi* might certainly arise. This hypothesis accounts for much, including the facts that the Armenian version exhibits more than one column of text throughout the work and that Jerome and the Armenian translator occasionally overlooked certain notices and failed to transcribe them. Helm demonstrated the value of his approach by applying the hypothesis to the entries on the episcopal succession in Rome and Alexandria, which had so troubled Schwartz. He showed that the Armenian and Latin versions could be derived from the same Greek exemplar, which was essentially in agreement with the *Historia Ecclesiastica*. In a separate study, Helm applied his approach to the list of thalassocrators and was able to account for many of the differences and omissions in the two versions of the *Canons*.[40]

CASPAR (1926)

The validity of Helm's hypothesis is beyond all reasonable

doubt. When published in the Berlin *Abhandlungen* and recapitulated in the second volume of Helm's edition of Jerome, the theory was greeted with a bitter review by Erich Caspar, whose own simultaneously published hypothesis about the format of the original *Chronicle* could not stand comparison with Helm's. Caspar had attempted to resurrect Schwartz' theory in a bizarre form. He argued that Eusebius never intended any of his notices to be read against a specific date. The most precise indication he cared to give was by decades counted from Abraham. He used different-sized letters and composed different shapes for the notices as an indication of how precisely they could be dated. An entry written in the form of a capital delta, for example, was an indication of relatively firm dating, while a notice written in the shape of a cross was to be understood as entered only approximately within the general time span of the page. In the original *Chronicle* there was a great deal of space for these loosely dated notices, since Eusebius used the twin-paged format throughout the work, reserving the left page for sacred history and the right for profane. Jerome did not understand his original. It was he who introduced the annalistic arrangement and he who decided upon a change of format after the second year of Darius.[41]

There is no evidence to support Casper's hypothesis except a few calligraphic adornments in the manuscripts that reflect Latin practice, rather than Greek. If Jerome had found the twin pages exhibited throughout his exemplar, he certainly would not have abandoned the arrangement. For many centuries the left page, reserved for sacred history, would have been virtually empty of historical notices and have provided just the space that Jerome needed to make his additions from Latin sources. He often used the left space for this purpose in the earlier portion of the *Chronicle* (e.g., 84[b], 88[a,b,c,d], 90[a,b], 94[a], 97[b], 99[b] Helm). After Olympiad 65 there are both fewer notices of sacred history to be inscribed and more Roman notices to be added. Had the original *Canons* contained an almost-empty left *spatium*, Jerome would have welcomed the space and retained the format. The task of transcription, translation, and augmentation would have been difficult indeed if he had both altered the format and reduced the space available to accommodate the larger Latin characters and the addition of notices relevant to Roman history and Latin literature. In a well-argued reply Helm laid to rest once and for all Schwartz' denial that Jerome preserves the essential format of the *Chronicle* of Eusebius and Caspar's new variation on that theme. Nevertheless, traces of the polemic remained nearly thirty years later in the introduction to Helm's second edition of the *Chronicle* of St. Jerome.[42]

Caspar's denunciation notwithstanding, the work of Fotheringham and Helm received the kind of welcome it deserved among scholars of Greek patristics in a review that Karl Mras published for *Wiener Studien* in 1928. Wachsmuth had been wrong to promulgate the doctrine that the Armenian version represents the genuine Eusebius while the translation of St. Jerome is significantly different. Schoene had shown that Jerome has an incontrovertible claim to authentic representation of the original format of the *Chronicle* of Eusebius. Fotheringham and Helm were also right to deny the theory of two Eusebian editions. Jerome and the Armenian translation attest to the same Greek archetype, and Jerome preserves the organization of the original more faithfully than does the Armenian version. The theories of Schwartz and Caspar are aberrant and should be abandoned. The older manuscripts of St. Jerome are the best witness to the form and arrangement of the original *Chronicle* of Eusebius. The chief difference lies in the pagination. Jerome used a 26-line page, while the pages of the Greek original contained 30 to 35 lines.[43]

Critical Conclusions

The Kommission für Spätantike Religionsgeschichte published a second edition of Helm's *Die Chronik des Hieronymus* in 1956, with introduction, 26-line text, critical apparatus, index, and full list of references to the testimonia both Greek and Latin included in one volume (*GCS* 47). The publication of this edition, a masterpiece of both scholarship and typography, marks the end, at least for the present, of the history of the text. It remains, even at the risk of becoming repetitious, to present a critical description of the text as we know it and to set forth the principles that guide the modern historian of antiquities in dealing with evidence drawn from the extant versions of the *Chronicle* of Eusebius. For illustrative material, see the collection of plates prefacing this chapter.

Eusebius composed his *Chronicle* in two parts. The first part, commonly called the *Chronographia* or first book, is extant only in an Armenian translation. It consists of a general preface followed by brief discussions of the chronological systems of the different peoples of the ancient Mediterranean world together with summary lists of their kings. The information is excerpted, with occasional comment and criticism, from a variety of sources: the Chaldeans according to Alexander Polyhistor, Abydenus, and Josephus; the Assyrians according to Abydenus, Castor, Diodorus, and Cephalion; the Hebrews according to the bible, Clement of Alexandria, and Josephus; the Egyptians according to Manetho, Josephus, and Porphyry; the Greeks according to Castor, Porphyry, and Diodorus; the Romans according to Dionysius of Halicarnassus, Diodorus, and Castor. To the Assyrian chronology Eusebius appended lists of the Median, Lydian, and Persian kings. He included in the Greek chronology a list of victors in the stadion course (stadionicæ) from the first to the 249th Olympiad (A.D. 217) and a list excerpted from Diodorus of those who ruled the seas (thalassocrats) from the time of the Trojan War to Xerxes' expedition against Greece. The Armenian translation ends abruptly with the Roman chronology apparently unfinished. Promised lists of the Roman emperors and consuls do not appear.

These chronographic excerpts provided the material for the second section of the *Chronicle*, which Eusebius referred to as χρονικοὶ κανόνες καὶ ἐπιτομὴ παντοδαπῆς ἱστορίας Ἑλλήνων τε καὶ βαρβάρων. The *Chronological Canons* presented the annual lists in synchronistic, tabular form along with brief notices mentioning important persons and events contemporary with the years of the lists. This main portion of the work is also extant in Armenian translation, but the manuscript does not include the first 343 years of the tables and the translation ends with the sixteenth year of Diocletian. A more nearly complete version of the *Chronological Canons* is extant in the Latin translation made by St. Jerome and preserved in a large number of manuscripts. Jerome's translation began with the first year of Abraham and ended at the twentieth year of Constantine. He continued the work to the sixth consulship of Valens (378). The Latin translation is preserved complete and it exhibits a chronographic format significantly different from that of the Armenian. The composition of a work containing synchronistic tables of dates as reckoned in several systems interconnected with historical text is extremely difficult. The more carefully a scribe or translator preserved the format and arrangement of his exemplar, the more accurately are the synchronistic lists and the positions of historical notices with respect to them likely to be transcribed.

JEROME

The earliest and best witness to the content, form, and arrangement of the *Canons* and therefore to the dates that Eusebius intended for his brief historical notices is the Latin translation included in the *Chronicle* of St. Jerome. This *Chronicle* closes with the sixth consulship of Valens (378) and it is likely, as Schoene suggested, that Jerome produced the work for presentation at the Roman synod of 382. This translation was thus composed about forty years after the death of Eusebius (ca. 340). The Greek exemplar that Jerome used could not have been far removed from Eusebius' original, and there is a distinct possibility that Jerome's exemplar was copied during Eusebius' lifetime from an archetype residing in Eusebius' great library at Caesarea. The extant manuscript tradition of Jerome's version of the *Chronicle* stands in similarly close chronological relationship to its author. According to the most nearly contemporary evidence, which happens to derive from the earliest of his continuators, Prosper of Aquitania, who wrote the so-called *chronicon consulare* in the mid-fifth century, St. Jerome died in 420.[44] The Floriacensis fragments ("S") of the *Chronicle* of Jerome are paleographically dated to the fifth century. The nearly complete Bodleian manuscript ("O") can also be dated to the fifth century. Where comparison is possible, "O" has text sufficiently different from "S" to show that one was not copied from the other. But both attest to the same chronographic format and the lacunae present in "O" can be accounted for only on the hypothesis that it was copied from a manuscript which, like "S," contained 26 lines to the page. The similarities are enough to suggest that the exemplars of "O" and "S" were copied from the same manuscript. "O" and "S" are themselves so ancient that their common ancestor must have been composed before the death of Jerome.

For antiquity and continuity alone, the early manuscript tradition of Jerome has a strong claim to authentic representation of the original format of the *Chronicle* of Eusebius. Although Jerome did augment the text by entering some additional historical notices drawn from Latin authors, he gives no indication that he

made any significant changes in the format of the original. On the
contrary, he says that apart from his additions to the historical
text he carried out the duties of the translator as faithfully as
possible. Curiously, he used the medium of dictation (*notario
uelocissime dictauerim*, p. 2 Helm). Synchronistic tables of numbers cannot easily be dictated. St. Jerome must have required his
bookman, at least for the earlier portion of the work, to prepare
for dictation of the text by first copying the columns of numbers
converted from the Greek alphabet system to Roman numerals.
Thus the scribe had to preserve with great care the format and
relative spacing of the original tables. Not only are significant
changes unlikely, but there is also much in the organization of the
tables as preserved in the oldest manuscripts that answers directly
to Eusebius' chronographic purposes and much that suggests that
it derives from Greek, rather than Latin, predilection.

"O," "S," and their close relatives "A," "P," and "N"
preserve one kind of arrangement in the earlier portion of the
Chronicle (60% of the whole) and a different format beginning
with the second year of Darius (520 B.C.). In the earlier portion
two facing pages are used to exhibit the synchronistic tables
(Plate 1). On each page the columns of numbers are inscribed
toward both the inner and outer margins with a relatively broad
space reserved in the middle of the page for historical notices.
The exact position of a given list depends on how many *fila* must
be entered in that section of the work. The Assyrians and their
successors, the Medes and the Persians, always occupy the extreme
left position on the left page. The Egyptian list is always the
filum most to the right on the right page. The positions of the
other lists shift as the total number of *fila* changes. In the first
section there are only two lists in addition to the Assyrians and
the Egyptians. The Hebrew list appears in the right margin of
the left page, and the Sicyonian is in the left margin of the right
page. The Argive list is added beginning with the 161st year of
Abraham immediately to the right of the Sicyonians. The addition
of the Athenian list in the 461st year in the position formerly
occupied by the Argives shifts the other lists left. The Argives
now appear in the left margin of the right page, the Sicyonians
in the right margin of the left page, while the Hebrews are
moved to the left of the *spatium historicum* and stand now immediately to the right of the Assyrian list. The Argives are replaced
by the Mycenaeans in the 711th year. At the epoch of Troy the
Mycenaean list ends, and the Athenians occupy the position at

the extreme left of the right page, with the Latins now appearing immediately to their right. The end of the Sicyonian list after the 888th year shifts the Athenian and Latin lists one position to the left. Shortly thereafter, the return of the Heraclids raises the total of *fila* to seven. The Lacedaemonians appear to the right of the Latins in the left margin of the right page, and the Corinthians are entered to the left of the Egyptians on the right side of that page. The division of the kingdom after Solomon results in the addition of a list of kings of Israel immediately to the right of the *spatium historicum* of the left page, while the kings of Judah occupy the position formerly held by the united Hebrews. The appearance of the Macedonian list raises the total to nine shortly before the first Olympiad, and it is entered immediately to the right of the Lacedaemonians in the left margin of the right page. With nine *fila* to be inscribed, there are now two in each margin of the left page, three in the left margin of the right page and two in the right margin of that page (2+2: 3+2; example: p. 84 Helm). As *fila* begin and end and their total number is gradually reduced again, similar shifts in position are made to suit.

This procedure, tedious to describe, is completely regular and fully rational. Jerome's bookman must have transcribed the framework with great care. The decision to enter the Assyrian list in the firm position of the extreme left, to be succeeded by the Medes, the Persians and, in the later portion of the work, the Ptolemies and the Roman emperors, lends continuity to the entire *Chronicle* and reflects a Greek conception of universal history as a succession of empires. The *spatium historicum* of the left page, on which the Hebrew *fila* always appear, contains notices of biblical history. The space reserved for historical notices in the middle of the right page, where the Greek lists begin and on which at least one Greek list is always inscribed, contains notices relevant to Greco-Roman history. This division into the sacred and the profane corresponds to Eusebius' announced intention in his preface (p. 18 Helm) to facilitate, by means of his format, synchronistic comparison between the Greeks and barbarians on the one hand and the Hebrews on the other. The arrangement is disturbed only by Jerome's Roman addenda, which often appear in the left space, where there was generally more room. Likewise, a notice of Eusebius is occasionally moved from the right into the left space because of overcrowding on the right side caused by the fact that the larger Latin characters used for the translation require more space relative to the *fila* than the original Greek characters (e.g., p. 87 Helm).

Every ten years there appears in the extreme left margin of the left page a numeral that is a multiple of ten and represents years elapsed since the birth of Abraham. The numeral is underlined, as are the corresponding numerals of the *fila regnorum* on both pages. Years of Abraham are not otherwise entered after his death at the age of one hundred. During his lifetime they had of course been entered in the Hebrew *filum* and not consecutively numbered in the extreme left margin, where the practice of inscribing multiples of ten is observed from the outset. This use of a continuous universal standard to mark off every tenth year of the *Chronicle* Eusebius specifically notes in the preface (p. 18 Helm): *omnem annorum congeriem in decadas cecidimus.*

The celebration of the first Olympiad marks a major epoch and thereafter the format is slightly, but significantly different. Olympiad numbers occupy a prominent position interrupting the vertical flow of numerals in all the *fila regnorum*. The number itself appears, like the decades of Abraham, just to the left of the firm imperial column (here, the Medes), while the word *Olymp* interrupts the numerals of that column. In all the other *fila* there is an empty space. The Olympiad numbers could have been written, like the decades of Abraham, in a space corresponding horizontally to one year in each of the *fila*. But they are not so entered. Olympiad numbers are given a clear horizontal space of their own, and the word *Olymp* appears as an interruption in the leading column. Thus the chronographic format is effectively organized by Olympiads and the numerals of the leading column serve to number the four years within the Olympiad. This arrangement is purely Greek and derives from the chronographic genre, well established by the time of Eusebius, of the Olympiad chronicle. Eusebius found persons and events in his sources dated by Olympiads, as did other late authors like Diogenes Laertius, Clement, and Tatian. This chronographic format made it possible for Eusebius easily to transfer that information to the *spatium historicum*. Furthermore, because the Olympiad numbers interrupt all the *fila regnorum* and are therefore not inextricably synchronized with a specific year, it was possible for Eusebius to begin historical notices on that line of the *spatium historicum* which corresponded horizontally only to an Olympiad number. He could thus accommodate information that he found dated in his sources only to an Olympiad and not specifically to one of the four years

within it. Thus the *Chronicle* should be cited by Olympiads and
one ought not to follow the misleading practice adopted for
Schoene's edition of numbering the years of Abraham consecutively and citing accordingly.[45]

The beginning of work on the construction of a new temple in
Jerusalem in the second year of Darius marks another major
epoch. Thereafter the early manuscript tradition of Jerome exhibits a chronographic format different in many respects from that
observed in the earlier portion (Plates 3, 4, and 5). Most striking is the change from a two-page format with its double *spatia*
and its clear distinction between the sacred and the profane.
Henceforward the relevant *fila* are inscribed toward the margins
of a single page, bracketing a single *spatium historicum*. That this
change in format was an innovation of Jerome can be denied on
logistical grounds alone. Jerome frequently used the left space for
the addition of his Roman notices, and he would certainly have
continued to make use of this space had the original retained that
format. There are also a number of positive considerations that
show that Eusebius made the change in format at precisely this
point in the *Chronicle* for very good reasons. The rebuilding of
the temple in the second year of Darius, a synchronism between
the sacred and the profane provided by Holy Scripture itself
(Ezra 4:24), was an especially epochal year for Eusebius and the
starting point of the fundamental computations that permitted
synchronization of the most important chronological scales. At
this epoch, the Hebrew list, last represented by the seventy years
of the Captivity, comes to an end and with it ends the biblical
account of history. Hence there is no reason to preserve a separate
space for biblical history. Eusebius does not actually announce
the end of the canonical account until Olympiad 83.3, 446/45
(113[a] Helm) : *Hucusque Hebraeorum diuinae scripturae annales
temporum continent.* But this anomaly is easily understood within
the context of the chronography. With the end of the seventy
years' Captivity the Hebrew *filum* comes to an end, and the history
of Israel is subsumed under the benevolent patronage of the Persian Empire. Four years earlier, Cambyses' conquest of Egypt
ends the *filum* that had occupied the extreme right position for
1492 years. Within eight years after the epoch of Darius, the
expulsion of Tarquinius brings the Roman column to an end.
Only two *fila* are left to be inscribed—the Persian and the Macedonian. There is no need to use two pages for reasons of space,
and the rationale for the division between sacred and profane no

longer applies. Although Eusebius does not enter a notice formally proclaiming the end of biblical history for several more pages, the epoch of the second year of Darius marked a logical and convenient point for the change in format. Interestingly enough, the first notice in the new format is on the tyrannicides Harmodius and Aristogeiton. This entry, since it seems purposely dated several years too early to bring it into synchronism with the epochal year, is a further indication that the change in format was in the Greek, the liberation of Athens being synchronized with that of Israel.

The similarities in format between the earlier and later portions of the work are such as to suggest to the uncritical eye that the abandonment of the twin pages was the only change. The *spatium historicum* is still in the middle of the page, with *fila regnorum* on each side until the final victories of Octavian over the kingdom of the Ptolemies and Titus over the Jews reduce the number to one—the list of Roman emperors inscribed beginning with Julius Caesar in the leftmost ("imperial") position. Years of Abraham are still entered by decades to the left of the corresponding number in the imperial *filum*, and Olympiad numbers continue to be inscribed in the middle of the leftmost *filum* and continue to interrupt all *fila*, occupying a horizontal line of their own in the chronological framework. But there is a significant change. In the earlier portion of the *Chronicle* the use of space is determined entirely by considerations arising from the *fila regnorum*. Jerome and a few of the extant manuscripts used 26 lines for the chronographic exhibition. In the one case that it is not necessary to interrupt the chronological framework with the announcement of a regnal succession, exactly 26 years are covered on the page (ironically, page 26 in Helm's edition). Otherwise, the number of years that can be included in the twin-page format depends on how many lines have to be left clear in the *fila* for the notation of the name, number, and regnal span of the new monarch. When one column is so interrupted, the same number of lines must be left blank in the corresponding space of all other *fila* in order to maintain the synchronization. Thus, at the other extreme (excluding those pages where important epochs like the fall of Troy require exceptional space), on page 102 of Helm's edition only twelve years can be included. Amasis and Croesus require two lines each, the accession of Cyrus requires seven lines, and there are three Olympiad numbers $(12+2+2+7+3=26)$. The historical notices have to be positioned appropriately with respect to the numerals so inscribed. Eusebius, like Jerome's bookman, must have worked on the chronological framework first, then added notices to the *spatium historicum*.

In the latter portion of the *Chronicle* the situation is different. The number of years that can be included on the page depends on the length of the historical notices. Eusebius had little to say about the third century B.C., and sometimes as many as sixteen years can be accommodated on one page (133 Helm). On the other hand, there is a great deal of comment to be made about the war between Octavian and Antony, therefore only one year is on that page (162 Helm). In this portion of the work, Jerome and his bookman must have worked in close partnership on chronological framework and text simultaneously. Jerome dictated the year of the imperial column (e.g., *Alexandrinorum septimus*); the bookman wrote the number in the left column and continued the series of numerals in the other columns. Jerome then dictated the historical notices belonging to that year, and the bookman inscribed them. Jerome announced the next year of the imperial column to which he desired to have notices dated. The bookman wrote the intervening regnal numerals and Olympiad numbers, if any, distributing them evenly in the gaps of the *fila* that corresponded to the space occupied by the previously dictated notices. As Fotheringham puts it, *non lemmata annis sed anni lemmatibus accommodati (praef. ed.* XXIII). It seems likely that Jerome found this kind of arrangement in the Greek original and that Eusebius had worked in a similar fashion, accommodating the *fila regnorum* to the text of the *spatium historicum*. The chief difference in chronographic format between Eusebius and Jerome in both portions of the *Chronicle* is the pagination. Eusebius' autograph probably had the 30 to 35 lines common among Greek manuscripts of the time. It thus contained more years to the page than Jerome's version. The difference is most significant in the latter portion of the *Chronicle*, where Jerome's additions greatly reduced the number of years that could be included on the page. The difference in pagination perhaps can help account for some of the displacements in Jerome's version from what must have been the original position of certain entries in the *spatium historicum*.

THE ARMENIAN VERSION

The manuscript tradition of St. Jerome provides by its antiquity and continuity a strong argument for the authenticity of the

chronographic format that it preserves. The tradition behind the
Armenian version makes the possibility that it is an accurate representation of the original format more remote. The Armenian
manuscript does preserve both sections of the work, the *Chronographia* and the *Chronographical Canons*, but that fact is by no
means an argument for the purity of the Armenian tradition. A
few pages of text are missing at the end of the *Chronographia*,
a few more from the beginning of the *Canons*, and at least one
from the end. The two sections must have been circulating separately and may therefore derive from quite different traditions.
At the time when the two books were brought together in a single
manuscript, several pages had already been lost from the end of
the one and from both the beginning and the end of the other.
The extant Armenian "tradition" derives from a single manuscript composed almost a thounsand years after the original
Chronicle of Eusebius, and it transmits an incomplete text. Furthermore, as Petermann and Karst have shown, the text does
not derive from a continuous Armenian tradition but is the result
of contamination between two earlier versions. The one was an
Armenian translation, the other a Syriac version of the *Chronicle*.

The format of the extant Armenian version can be seen partly
as a simplification of that preserved by Jerome, partly as a purposeful alteration. The format of the Armenian *Canons* is essentially the same throughout the work, with the chronographic display always contained on a single page (Plate 2). The *fila regnorum* are grouped together in ruled columns in the middle of
the page. The Egyptians occupy the extreme right position, as they
do in Jerome's version, but the extreme left column is reserved
for years of Abraham, which are numbered consecutively throughout the work. To the right of the years of Abraham stand not the
Assyrians and their imperial successors, but the Hebrews for as
long as there exists a Hebrew list. When the Olympiads begin, the
numbers do not occupy a special horizontal space that divides the
fila into tetrads. They are entered like all other numerals in a
ruled vertical column. It stands to the left of the years of Abraham. The columns are also ruled horizontally, but not always by
decades or any other consistent system. Years *ab urbe condita*
are, however, entered by decades beginning with the seventh
Olympiad. The decades are not incorporated into the ruled system of *fila*, but stand in the extreme left margin. Historical notices
are entered to the left and to the right of the system of numerals.

On the whole, sacred history generally appears in the left and secular in the right. But the separation is not consistent.

One cannot posit two Eusebian editions to account for the differences in format between the Latin and Armenian versions. The Armenian *Chronographia* computes an interval to the twentieth year of Constantine (62 Karst), the same terminus to which Jerome attests for the Greek original. Although the Armenian *Canons* end with the sixteenth year of Diocletian, the Syriac epitomes attest to an original extending to the Vicennalia of Constantine and there is no reason to believe that the lost pages of the Armenian version did not reach the same terminus. Indeed, the Armenian chronographer Samuel Aniensis (12th century), who began his work with the birth of Christ and used Eusebius as a principal source for the early period, has a note at the twentieth year of Constantine to the effect that this year was the terminus of Eusebius' work.[46] It is certain that Eusebius had composed the *Chronicle* before 311, but it is equally certain that he subsequently continued it to the Vicennalia of Constantine. There is no evidence that the earlier version was transmitted unfinished to any of the extant translators or excerptors. In any case, a major change in format between the two versions is not likely. Eusebius had only to add a few pages to the *Chronicle*, not rework the whole. The earlier text did not necessarily extend as far as the extant Armenian translation. The only evidence of a joint, and it is by no means conclusive, appears in Olympiad 264 (277–80), where there is a chronological summary that has no parallel except at the very end of the work: *secundo anno Probi iuxta Antiochenas •CCCXXV• ann• fuit, iuxta Tyrios •CCCCII• iuxta Laodicenos •CCCXXIIII•, iuxta Edessenos •DLXXXVIII•, iuxta Ascolonitas •CCCLXXX•* (223[k] Helm). Wallace-Hadrill argued that the entry about the beginning of the great persecution in Olympiad 270 (301–4) looks forward to better days under Constantine and could not have been written until well after 311, perhaps not until after Constantine's final victory over Licinius: *XVIIII• Diocletiani anno mense Martio in diebus paschae ecclesiae subuersae sunt. Quarto autem persecutionis anno Constantinus regnare orsus* (228[b] Helm).[47] Such evidence seems dubious at best.

AN ALEXANDRIAN REDACTION

The Armenian and Latin versions must be considered independent witnesses to the same original *Chronicle*. The *fila regnorum* of the two translations are fundamentally the same. Minor differences can be accounted for as transcriptional variants. The Armenian version gives the Lydian king Ardys 38 years of rule (185 Karst), while Jerome assigns 37 (94 Helm). The list of the *Chronographia* (33 Karst) agrees with Jerome. Where there are major differences, for example the omission of the first four Median kings in the Armenian *Canons*, Jerome is more nearly in agreement with the chronographic excerpts of the prefatory book than is the Armenian version of the *Canons*. The fact that the Armenian *Series Regum* agrees better with Jerome and with the lists of the *Chronographia* than it does with the extant version of the Armenian *Canons* is not evidence of a collation between two editions with different sets of *fila regnorum*. Rather it suggests that the *Series Regum* were excerpted from a better transcription of the *Chronicle* than the extant Armenian and inserted into the manuscript as a corrective. The Latin *fila* are a better representation of the excerpts in the prefatory book and they are more accurately synchronized than the Armenian *fila*. The shortcomings of the Armenian *fila* arise partly from the centuries of transmission and contamination that separate Eusebius from the Armenian manuscript and partly from the fact that the Armenian translator or, rather, an intermediary redactor, significantly altered the form and arrangement of the original.

The format of the Armenian version can be derived from that exhibited by the oldest manuscripts of St. Jerome, but not vice versa. The basic change was the decision to compact all the *fila* into ruled columns in the middle of the page. This alteration made it possible for the copyist or redactor to work on one column of numerals for as long as he wished, then go back and carry a second column to that point, and continue in this fashion until all the columns were filled. For this kind of composition it was necessary to have one column of numerals that was continuous throughout the work, could be entered first, and could serve as a control. Hence the decision was made to number years of Abraham consecutively in the left column. The redactor worked on this column first and was able to ignore all the other numerals in the exemplar. He had only to observe where there were gaps in the *fila* of the exemplar for the entry of regnal successions and skip a corresponding number of lines in the master column. It was natural to set the Hebrew column immediately to the right and enter it next, because for the first hundred years of the *Canons* the Hebrew *filum* was in fact years of Abraham. Moreover, this placement of the column helped in the positioning of historical notices in the new format. In the original, the historical notices stood in the middle of the page with the Hebrew column either immediately to the right or immediately to the left. Thus the copyist could read the notices against the numerals of the Hebrew column. When he entered them in the left margin of the transcription, the Hebrew numerals standing to the left in the *fila* served as a guide for the positioning. On the right page of the original, the notices were in the middle, not always adjacent to the same *filum*. But the Egyptian column was always on the extreme right. Thus the redactor retained that position for the Egyptian numerals, read the historical notices against them, and entered the text in the right margin of his page alongside the Egyptian column. The redactor had no desire to change his format after the second year of Darius and attempt to follow the original by entering text and numerals simultaneously, with text in the middle and numerals toward the margins. He retained his basic procedure, entering all the numerals first, beginning with the column of Abraham. He entered years of Abraham first, ignoring the other numerals of the exemplar but observing the space allowed for them. He then filled in the other columns before transcribing the text. He continued to use two text columns, partly for reasons of space and partly because the original text was arranged with two or more entries standing side by side in the *spatium historicum*.

The only Syriac epitome that carries dates, that attributed to Dionysius of Tell-Mahre, cites the *Chronicle* by years of Abraham. Karst (Einl. 54) demonstrated that both the Armenian and Syriac versions were first translated from Greek exemplars in the late sixth century. Since both the Armenian and Syriac derivatives are organized by years of Abraham, this arrangement must have been in the Greek exemplars. It is not an innovation of either translator. Thus the change in format was exhibited in a Greek version of the *Chronicle* composed before 600. The most likely candidate for the authorship of this purposeful redaction—which must originally have observed a more careful synchronization of the *fila*, with the distinction between sacred and profane in the left and right margins of the earlier portion more consistently maintained than in the extant Armenian—is the early-fifth-century Alexandrian monk Panodorus. Syncellus says of him (617) that he was a historian of unusual critical skill in chronology. It was through Panodorus

and his contemporary Annianus, who carefully scrutinized the
work of their predecessors in Christian chronography, that the
excerpts from Africanus and Eusebius came to Syncellus. According to Syncellus (62–65) the two monastic chronographers were
concerned with the computation of the Easter cycle and with the
correct dating of Christ's Incarnation and Resurrection relative
to the date of the Creation. Africanus and Eusebius had disagreed in this matter. Africanus dated the birth of Christ 5,500
years after Creation (Syncellus 62). Eusebius (36 Karst) objected to the attempt to provide a precise, continuous chronology
from the Creation to the birth of Abraham, because of differences in the genealogies among the different versions of the book
of Genesis and because no one could know how long Adam had
been in Paradise. Nevertheless, to satisfy the inevitable curiosity
of some petulant reader, he did provide a computation of the
interval between Adam and Abraham as being 3,184 years (15,
250 Helm). The birth of Christ he dated to Olympiad 194.3
(169[c] Helm) or the year 2015 on the Abraham scale (cf. 211
Karst). The interval between Adam and Christ is thus 5,200
years in Eusebius' opinion, 300 years less than in Africanus'
system. To organize Eusebius' *Chronicle* by years of Abraham
made it more suitable as a monastic text and permitted Panodorus and Annianus to compare directly the chronographic systems of Eusebius and Africanus. According to Syncellus (62),
the two chronographers were contemporaries and flourished in
the time of Theophilus, bishop of Alexandria (388–416). He
adds (617) that Panodorus also flourished in the time of the
emperor Arcadius (383–408). Thus it was about the year 400
that Panodorus used the *Chronicle* and reorganized it to suit
his own purposes.[48]

If this suggestion is correct, the Armenian version of the
Chronicle derives from a Greek redaction prepared about a
quarter of a century after St. Jerome composed the Latin version. Jerome retained the essential format of the original, and
the manuscript tradition of his version is nearly contemporary
with Jerome himself. The Greek redactor altered the format of
the original and thereby no doubt introduced some errors in the
synchronization of the tables and some displacements in the positioning of the historical notices with respect to them. This redaction was circulated widely in the Eastern empire, where it was
used by Byzantine chronographers and translated into Armenian
and Syriac for the use of scholars working in those languages.[49]

The errors of the original redactor were compounded when this version of the *Chronicle* was translated into Armenian, collated with the Syriac, and transmitted through the scribal culture until it reached the writer of the extant twelfth- or thirteenth-century manuscript.

GENERAL ANIMADVERSIONS

Most notorious among the differences in synchronization between the Latin and Armenian translations is the displacement of the Olympiad numbers with respect to years of Abraham. The Armenian version sets the first Olympiad number against Abraham 1240, while in St. Jerome's version the first year of the first Olympiad is Abraham 1241. Jerome's tables yield the traditional equation of the first Olympiad with 776 B.C., as can be seen, for example, in the entry of Solon's archonship to the third year of the 46th Olympiad (594/93) and the last year of the decennial archons to the first year of the 24th Olympiad (684/83). It is easier to explain the Armenian's error than Jerome's accuracy. The text of the *Chronicle* says that the first Olympiad was celebrated in the second year of Aeschylus' life-archonship at Athens (86^b Helm, 181 Karst), and the Armenian format synchronizes the first Olympiad with that year. Jerome's text says the first Olympiad was celebrated in the second year of Aeschylus, but the *fila* synchronize the first year of the first Olympiad with the third year of Aeschylus. Eusebius presumably did likewise. It was Eratosthenes who perfected the chronographic system of the Olympiads. He reckoned intervals from the year before the first Olympiad, since that year marked the end of the quasi-historical period. Thus in Eratosthenes' version of the Athenian list, which Eusebius received through Castor (85 Karst), the second year of Aeschylus marked what Clement (*Strom.* 1.138) in his excerpt from Eratosthenes (*FGrHist* 241 F 1) called προηγούμενον ἔτος τῶν πρώτων Ὀλυμπίων [*sic!*]. For Eratosthenes, then, the third year of Aeschylus was indeed synchronous with the first Olympiad. It is possible that Eusebius understood this curious distinction, but the wording of the text (*secundo anno Aeschyli prima Olympias acta*) makes it unlikely. For purposes of chronographic synchronization, Eusebius had to equate all his years with one standard calendar, either the Syro-Macedonian year beginning in the fall or the Julian year beginning in the winter. Eusebius of course knew that the

Olympic games were celebrated in the summer; but the chronographic Olympiad year began several months later in his system,
synchronous with all other years. Thus the first Olympiad was
celebrated in the second year of Aeschylus, but the first Olympiad
year began several months later, synchronized in Eusebius' tables
with the third year of Aeschylus.[50]

The fact that St. Jerome preserves this synchronization is a
further indication that his bookman carefully transcribed the
chronological framework before Jerome dictated what was in this
case his translation of an apparently contradictory text. This
difficulty with the positioning of the Olympiad year in the two
versions of the *Chronicle* poses a problem for the modern user.
It is customary to correct the Armenian version in this matter
and to cite it by years of Abraham, using Jerome's equation of
Abraham 1241 with Olympiad 1.1 and thus our 776/75 B.C.
This practice is wrong. Eusebius organized his tables by Olympiads and it was possible for the user to read it that way, as we
do Jerome. There is no way of knowing exactly what procedures
the redactor of the new format used in reading the notices of
his exemplar and transcribing them to the margins of the reorganized work. He may have observed the numeral of the
nearest *filum* in the original and attempted to transcribe the
notice against that numeral of the reorganized *fila*. Or he may
have read the exemplar by Olympiad years and transcribed accordingly. Probably he did both. Thus any method of translating
into Julian years B.C. is likely to be misleading. The modern
reader is better advised, however, to adhere to the Armenian's
own principles of organization than to attempt to correct it.
Before the first Olympiad it is customary to cite by years of
Abraham and translate with the equation 1241=776 B.C. It
would be pedantic to try to alter that convention. Beginning with
the first Olympiad, however, the Armenian version should be
cited by years of Abraham and converted to Julian years B.C.
through its own equation of Abraham 1240 with Olympiad 1.1
and thus with 776/75 B.C.

The format and organization of the *Chronicle* of St. Jerome
as preserved in the oldest manuscripts is essentially that of
Eusebius. The redactor of the Greek edition from which the
Armenian and Byzantine traditions descend altered the plan of
the work significantly. Even this alteration is not likely to be
well preserved in the twelfth-century manuscript, which has

transmitted a copy of incomplete and once-independent versions of both portions of the *Chronicle* under the influence of yet another, Syriac, version of the work. As far as the *Chronological Canons* is concerned, the Armenian version is of considerably less value as a witness to the chronological traditions preserved by Eusebius than is the *Chronicle* of St. Jerome. But neither version can be used independently of the other. Jerome made additions to the contents of the *spatium historicum*, and the text of the Armenian version helps show what the additions were. The Armenian version also supplies the text and at least the approximate position of some notices that Jerome inadvertently omitted. Furthermore, Jerome departed from the arrangement of the original in one important respect. The different order of the entries in the Armenian from that in Jerome can best be accounted for on Helm's "nebeneinander" hypothesis. Eusebius' *spatium historicum* accommodated notices entered horizontally side by side as well as vertically one below another. Thus Jerome had difficulty determining the *ordo legendi* (5 Helm). He and his bookman had much more difficulty determining the *ordo transcribendi*, since the decision had been made to enter the translated notices in a single vertical column.[51] Errors in positioning and complete omissions therefore inevitably arose. The redactor of the Greek exemplar underlying the Armenian version had the same problem and made errors and omissions of his own.

The text, order and position of the notices relative to the chronological framework as they appear in both versions of the *Chronicle* must be carefully compared in an effort to determine the probable position of the entries in the original—that is, the date to which Eusebius assigned each notice and the date that he presumably found in his own sources. Excerpts from Eusebius in the late Byzantine chroniclers can be helpful in reconstructing the Greek of the text and sometimes in identifying a disputed notice as Eusebian. It must be remembered that these are excerpts and that they may have come to the late chroniclers at second hand. In particular, it is likely that Syncellus and the other Byzantine excerptors used the *Chronicle* in the redaction of Panodorus and Annianus. The Greek testimonia are therefore not to be considered as witnesses completely independent from the Armenian and Syriac versions. Dates are cited on a system of reckoning from the Creation, a method more nearly akin to that of Africanus than to Eusebius' Abraham standard.[52]

HYPOTHETICAL RECONSTRUCTION

This discussion of the textual tradition is best concluded by offering just such a comparison of the extant testimonia leading to a hypothetical reconstruction of a small portion of the work. The illustration shows how the *Chronicle* might have been organized for Olympiads 77 through 79 (472/71–461/60), accounting for the differences in the position of the entries that Jerome and the Armenian version exhibit for those Olympiads. The illustration also shows how the downward shifts in the dates for Socrates, Cimon, and the ʾolar eclipse of 464 were introduced into the *Chronicle*. Plates 3 and 4 contain reproduction of those leaves of the Bodleian manuscript which contain Olympiads 77 through 79 of Jerome's version. On Plate 2 the corresponding page of Karst's edition of the Armenian version is reproduced. Karst retains the pagination and arrangement of the manuscript and it is therefore not necessary to reproduce an Armenian text that would be intelligible to few. Plate 5 contains the hypothetical reconstruction of the original Greek *Canons* that results from comparing the Latin and Armenian versions with each other and with the Greek excerpts.[53]

The arguments on which the reconstruction is based are as follows. In Olympiad 77, both St. Jerome (J) and the redactor of the Armenian format (R) read first the notice that stands farthest left near the top, "Themistocles." R then moved right for "Sunia," while J read down for "Sophocles." J moved up and right for "Sunia," then left again for the second of the two tragedian-notices that appeared in that Olympiad. Both redactors moved down immediately to Olympiad 78, overlooking "Socrates," which stood to the right in Olympiad 77. In Olympiad 78 both entered first "Herodotus," then, in different order, "Themistocles" and "Bacchylides-Diagoras." This difference is accounted for by assuming that "Herodotus" was entered against the Olympiad number, while the other two notices stood side by side immediately below. Both redactors then moved right and before proceeding any further entered the overlooked "Socrates" from Olympiad 77. "Zeuxis" was entered below "Bacchylides-Diagoras" in the original. J read the notice before moving right for "Themistocles," but R, in haste to rectify the omission of "Socrates," now failed to notice "Zeuxis." After "Socrates," J moved down for "lapis," then left to enter "Artaxerxes" in the

Persian *filum* and immediately down to Olympiad 79 and "Esther," before reading right for "Sicilia" in Olympiad 78. R moved down from "Socrates" to "lapis," then down and left to read "Esther" and right for "Sicilia," "Sol," and "Cimon." After entering "Sicilia," J moved down and read left to right for "Cimon" and "Sol." Since J had only one column of notices and entered the lengthy "Esther" first, "Cimon" and "Sol" appear several years too late. Because of the natural tendency to read down before right in a chronicle, notices that stood the farthest right in the original appear one to three years too late in the strictly vertical transcription. Conversely, notices that stood most to the left might now be entered too early. Displacements in either direction by two or three years are therefore not surprising.

SUMMARY

Whatever errors, displacements, and omissions the redactors introduced in the positioning of the entries with respect to the chronological framework have been compounded by the scribes of the manuscript tradition. In the case of the Armenian version, a translator, a collator, and many generations of copyists stand between the redactor and the extant manuscript. No single entry in any one of the manuscripts, or even the consensus of them all, constitutes chronological evidence in itself. The manuscripts attest only approximately to the placement that the redactors assigned the entries. The redactors in turn altered the format— one slightly, the other significantly—and used exemplars one generation removed from Eusebius. Eusebius had chronographic problems of his own and was in any case several centuries removed from the best traditions of Greek chronography. Each entry constitutes a threefold problem of its own—a textual problem, a problem of source criticism, and a problem of chronological method in the ultimate source. The notices must be evaluated not only with respect to their textual position in the chronological framework of the *Canons*, but also in comparison with independent testimony relevant to the date of the person or event in question. Only when the text, possible source, and probable ultimate rationale of a notice (and its date) have been thoroughly investigated can the *Chronicle* of Eusebius, as preserved by his translators, become a meaningful and useful chronographic document.

2

Greek Chronography

The dates Eusebius intended for historical entries of his chronological tables present textual difficulties. The significance of a Eusebian date as evidence for historical chronology raises "chronographic" problems. The distinction is critical. Transcriptional error is inevitable in the transmission of so complex a text. The extant manuscripts often disagree with each other and can therefore attest only approximately to an original Eusebian date. Even where there is consensus among the best manuscript authorities, we must concede the possibility of a three- or four-year difference between the date at which the manuscripts enter a notice and the original date of Eusebius. The user is accordingly tempted to assume that the date that he can explain on one hypothesis or another is the date Eusebius knew, provided that at least one of the manuscripts exhibits the relevant notice at approximately that year. Such a procedure is hazardous and one must manage the evidence carefully. Arguments based solely on the manuscript evidence, however, are tenuous indeed. Given the textual difficulties, one cannot treat the extant evidence as an independent or primary witness to the chronographic tradition. Not all of the intervals and relationships among the dates of the extant texts are significant. If one assumes that they are and endeavors to explain them as chronographic devices, he may find himself solving an arithmetical puzzle of his own creation that has no relevance to the genesis of the tradition. When using Eusebian evidence, the historian must distinguish between textual difficulties and chronographic problems, while recognizing the importance of both for his argument.[1]

The terms *chronography* and *chronographic* are widely used among historians of antiquity, but not always well understood. The terminology is employed in two quite different senses. In the broadest sense, chronography is any record of historical events precisely dated by reference to an absolute chronological system. Thus, as has often been remarked, the *Chronicle* of Eusebius represents the highest development of Greek chronographic tradition. Encompassing more than 2,300 years of human history, the work enabled the reader to determine by reference to Olympiad years or years from Abraham the absolute date of a person or event within a wide variety of national histories. Simple addition or subtraction yielded precise intervals of relative chronology. Such a chronographic record presupposes the ability to associate events with dates in the first place. The term *chronography* has therefore taken on a second meaning, referring to the process by which precise dates were established for persons and events not yet included in an absolute chronology.

Eusebius was a chronographer only in the first sense. His immediate chronographic purposes did not require him to undertake a primary investigation into problems of historical chronology. His sources provided the means of extrapolating dates for persons and events in accordance with one system of chronology or another. Where there was disagreement among the sources, Eusebius either recorded a representative selection of the variant opinions, as he did in the case of Homer (66[a] Helm), or he chose one authority over another, as he did for early biblical chronology (*Chron.* 1, 34–62 Karst). Eusebius' purpose was to harmonize already existing chronological systems in order to display the universality of history in a concise, synchronistic form. His own chronographic methods pose no serious historical problem.[2] Chronographic difficulties do arise, however, when one approaches the dates Eusebius transmits for persons and events of the period before absolute chronological standards existed. The problem is most acute for archaic Greece (traditionally, 776–480 B.C.). Eusebius and other late sources preserve precise, absolute dates. Yet there existed no contemporary archival practice for recording dates. Indeed, it is not too extreme to say that there was not yet a sense of historical time at all. The problem associated with evaluating these early dates is how and when they were established. From what sources and by what methodology could the Greeks assign an absolute chronology to persons and events whose dates could not possibly have been known?

It is in connection with early Greek chronology that the terms *chronography* and *chronographic* are now most frequently used. Chronography in this special sense can be defined as the reconstruction of an absolute chronology for a period from which no such dates had been transmitted. Hence the traditional dates of archaic Greek history are often called "chronographic," while the persons supposed to have established them are "chronographers." The terminology may be unfortunate, but the distinction between two kinds of dates is important. Whatever label we apply to them, the dates our sources give for persons and events of the archaic period are of a completely different order from those which could have been contemporaneously recorded by reference to an already-existing chronological standard.

Greek chronography is among the most controversial (and arachneal) problems in archaic Greek history. A properly annotated survey of all the contributions on the issue would require a volume in itself. No definitive solution of the chronographic problem is in sight. Indeed, none is possible or even desirable. What follows therefore is a brief discussion of certain fundamental questions, intended to provide perspective—not a solution. Early Greek chronology is not a problem to be "solved," but a tradition to be understood and respected.

The Establishment of Chronological Standards

The prerequisite of chronography is a standard of reference upon which a historical chronology can be built. The point of division in the nature of our evidence is accordingly approximately at the time when such standards began to be used. Eusebius' own chronological standard, the numbered Olympiad year, is a relative latecomer. The earliest evidence for the existence of a numbered system of Olympiads appears in a fragment of Philistus (*FGrHist* 556 F 2), a Syracusan historian of the late fifth or early fourth century. Since the fragment derives from a late author (Stephanus of Byzantium ca. 500) to whom the system of numbered Olympiads was a commonplace, and because the numeral in the fragment is in fact a conjectural emendation, we cannot be sure that the attribution of numbered Olympiads to an authority as early as Philistus is correct. According to Polybius (12.11.1), it was the early third-century Sicilian historian Timaeus who first used the list of Olympic victors as a synchronistic tool for historical chronology (*FGrHist* 566 T 10). It may therefore have been Timaeus who introduced the system of referring to the Olympiad by a number as well as by naming the victor in the stadion course. By the end of the third century, the Alexandrian scholar Eratosthenes (*FGrHist* 241) had made Olympiad reckoning the basis of a consistent chronological system that was subsequently widely adopted. Since the Olympic festival was celebrated only every fourth year, a numbered Olympiad actually included four years. Erastosthenes obtained a more precise reference by subdividing the Olympiad. An exact date required two numbers—that of the Olympiad and one of the numbers from 1 through 4.

A numerical system has obvious advantages for chronographic purposes over a list of eponyms, since it makes possible an arithmetical computation of the intervals between events. For strictly chronological (as opposed to chronographic) purposes, however, a distinctive name serves just as well as a number for the precise identification of a year. The Greeks had long used systems of eponymous years and were comfortable with dates expressed as proper names rather than as numbers. Chronographic convention reflected this conservatism by including the name of the stadion victor, considered eponymous for the Olympiad, as well as the number. Numbering the list was a relatively minor, specialist innovation, and it does not matter how late the innovation was introduced. It was the establishment of the list of eponyms that made the Olympic festival a potentially useful chronographic tool. According to Plutarch (*Numa* 1.6) it was the late-fifth-century sophist Hippias of Elis who first drew up a list of Olympic victors. It was therefore he who established the convention of identifying the Olympiad by stadion victor, rather than the victor in some other contest, and it was he who first made a complete list of stadion victors publicly available. Whether or not Hippias numbered the list, whether or not he intended the list to be used for chronological purposes, the redaction he carried out defined the point at which consistent chronological references based on the Olympic festival became possible. A system of chronology based on the Olympic festival would therefore not have been possible before the end of the fifth century.[3] When we turn to other dating systems, we find much the same result.

For official purposes, each state had its own calendar and its own system of naming the years. The local systems of Athens and Sparta, however, became widely recognized standards for obvious reasons, and they remained fundamental in the chronographic genre. The earliest known archon list is the one whose fragmentary remains have been discovered at the Athenian agora. The fragments contain names of archons who must be dated as early as the 590s. The list itself, however, is dated to the 420s.[4] Several considerations combine to suggest that this list was the first of its kind. Most important, at least for the study of Greek chronography, is that the first use of the archon list for historical chronology occurred some twenty years after the inscription of the known list, when Hellanicus published his *Attic History* organized annalistically by archons (*FGrHist* 323a). Such a work stood in stark contrast to the earlier *Histories* of Herodotus, completed during the Archidamian War, or shortly thereafter, about the time the epigraphic list was established.[5] Herodotus' subject was not specifically Athens and to his general audience the use of archons' names as dates would have been inappropriate, if not unintelligible. Herodotus mentions an archon's name only once (Calliades, 8.51.1). The very unusualness of this citation suggests that for Herodotus annalistic history based on the archons' list was impossible.

An archon's name can be a date to a historian only if events are regularly associated with archons' names, if it is possible to count the interval between one archon and another, and if there is some assurance that anyone who wishes to verify the interval will make the same count. The computations cannot be made except on the basis of a complete and authoritative list. Herodotus was well aware of the importance of chronology in the telling of history, and he used the annalistic lists that were available for kingdoms of the Near East. He had recourse to no such device in dealing with early Greek history, and the most probable explanation for this difference in treatment is that no such lists were available. The fact that Herodotus could not or would not set Athenian history in an absolute chronological framework, while Hellanicus (also a foreigner) could do so with sufficient influence to warrant an attack by Thucydides (1.97) suggests that the list erected in the agora in the 420s was the first official, public list.[6] The use of archons' names as chronological references, both informally and in public documents, was certainly older. Nevertheless, only when an authoritative list had been published did it become possible to construct an absolute historical chronology from traditional statements like "Salamis was in the year of Calliades," autobiographical remarks such as Simonides' "I was in my eightieth year when Adeimantus was archon" (fr. 77 Diehl), or documents associated with an archon's name, like the law against torture voted under Scamandrius (Andocides, *Myst.* 43).

At Sparta the name of the chief ephor was used officially for the dating of documents by the last third of the fifth century, as Thucydides' (5.24) transcription of the treaty concluded between Athens and Sparta in 422/21 attests. According to late sources the first college of annual ephors was constituted during the reign of King Theopompus and headed by Elatus, who held office during a year corresponding to 754/53 or 753/52, depending on the method of computation used in interpreting the sources.[7] Many scholars believe that this date is historical, based on a complete list of eponymous ephors analogous to that of the Athenian archons, continuously maintained from the time of Elatus. Others suggest that an official list begun at some later point in the development of the ephorate, perhaps the time of Chilon in the middle of the sixth century, was extended back to Elatus. In the latter case the redactor is sometimes identified with Charon of Lampsacus, whose catalogue of works in the *Suda* includes a πρυτάνεις τῶν Λακεδαιμονίων.[8] This debate focuses on the wrong issue. For early Sparta, dating by reference to the kings would be more appropriate than ephor dates, even if there did exist a list of eponymous ephors from the time of Elatus. For Athens, the evidence is incontrovertible that by the end of the fifth century there was an official list of annual archons beginning with Creon in the early seventh century. For Sparta, we can say only that the ephor was eponymous for official dates beginning sometime in the fifth century. There is no evidence that a list of early ephors ever existed, whether genuine or "constructed." The only early names, three in all, that have been transmitted to us are of ephors closely connected with the history of the institution itself. Elatus was the first ephor, said to have established the office during the reign of Theopompus (Plutarch, *Lycurgus* 7). Chilon, who was one of the seven sages and considered an important political figure

(Herodotus 7.235) was ephor during the 56th Olympiad, 556/53 (Diogenes Laertius 1.68). The third name is that of the mysterious "star-gazer" Asteropus who, according to the third-century king Cleomenes III (Plutarch, *Cleomenes* 10) lived long after the establishment of the ephorate in its original form and was in some way responsible for the institution's upstart power. The few events of early Spartan history that carry chronological references in the sources are dated by Olympiads or king years, never eponymous ephors. This is true even in the fifth century of the famed earthquake and helot revolt (Thuc. 1.101), which Plutarch (*Cimon* 16.4) says occurred in the fourth year of King Archidamus.

The annual ephorate was a powerful political institution in classical times. When the necessity of incorporating official dates into documentary records was recognized in the fifth century, the Spartans, like the Greeks of most other states, decided to name the year after the chief magistrate, so that each date would have a distinctive name. It was important for those who were interested in Spartan history to try to date the establishment of the ephorate. It was not necessary to draw up a complete list of supposedly "eponymous" ephors either to date the institution itself or for the reconstruction of a chronology for early Spartan history in general. At Sparta, unlike most Greek states of the time, the kingship remained a living institution. Spartan tradition remembered the names of the kings associated with important events of the past, including the establishment of the ephorate in the reign of King Theopompus. The development of a historical chronology therefore required a recension of the king lists, giving the number of years each king had served and assigning events associated with his reign to appropriate regnal years. Such a recension of the king lists perhaps appeared in Charon's *Lacedaemonian Prytanies*—a work that the *Suda* specifically states was a chronicle.[9]

For official purposes eponymous dates based on an annual office had their advantages. For chronographic purposes an office held for life can be more convenient. The regnal lists permit intervals between events, at least within an individual reign, to be computed arithmetically instead of by counting off the different eponyms for every year. At Sparta local chronology could be based on an office held for life, so a chronographer did not need to reconstruct a list of eponyms reaching back to the eighth century. No more is to be made of the practice of ephor dating than that it arose in the fifth century in response to the need for official, documentary dates. When in the late-fifth century Charon undertook a chronicle of Spartan history, he recognized that Spartan tradition was inextricably associated with the royal families and that king lists were potentially more useful for chronology than a list of eponyms.[10]

The conclusion for Sparta, then, is that, as at Athens, official dates did not come into currency until sometime in the fifth century. For the "chronographic" problem as it relates to early Spartan history, however, it is not the official dating system with which we must be concerned, but the king lists. The first redaction of the king lists was carried out by Charon of Lampascus, a few decades after the publication in Athens of an official archon list reaching back into the seventh century. The evidence from other states is meager. What evidence there is does not suggest that chronology, either official or historiographic, appeared any earlier than at Athens or Sparta. Argive chronology first makes its appearance in the late-fifth century with Hellanicus' redaction of the list of the priestesses of Hera (*FGrHist* 4 F 74–84). At Delphi the publication both of a list of annual archons and of a list of Pythian victors was carried out in the late-fourth century by Aristotle and Callisthenes.[11] At Miletus a list of stephanephoroi was established, beginning with the eponymous priest for 525/24, but the list itself was not first published until 335/34.[12]

Reconstructing the Prechronographic Past

The fundamental prerequisite for chronography, a standardized scale of reference, first appears in the Greek world in the last third of the fifth century. The Athenian archon list was first published in the 420s, and about the same time eponymous dates were adopted at Sparta for use in official documents. The beginnings of some kind of archival practice that henceforward made possible a chronographic record based on contemporary sources can now be assumed. The Athenian archon list, however, also included more than 250 entries before that of the incumbent whose name identified the year of its publication. The establishment of an archon list reaching back more than two centuries before the date of its publication was surely intended to serve an archival function, rather than to provide a framework for early Athenian chronology. Nevertheless, the publication of such a list made historical chronology possible, while the sense of history that Herodotus had brought to the Greek world made such work desirable. Literary chronology soon was born and suddenly fluorished. Hellanicus used the archon list as the framework for an annalistic history of Athens. His *Argive Priestesses of Hera*, published during the Peace of Nicias, was a Panhellenic chronicle reaching far back into antiquity. Hellanicus also carried out a redaction of the list of victors at the musical contests of the Spartan festival of the Carnea (*FGrHist* 4 F 85–86), beginning with Terpander, but we do not know whether he published the list in a chronographic setting or merely as the framework for a history of music. Hippias undertook a redaction of the Olympic victor list on behalf of his native Elis. It may not be approprite to characterize this work as "chronographic" or to impute to Hippias a desire to promote Olympic dating as a Panhellenic chronology, but the work was at least a chronicle of the Olympic games, and it did make Olympic dates possible for the first time. Charon of Lampsacus turned his attention to Spartan history and published a recension of the Spartan king lists, a work specifically called a chronicle in the *Suda*.

Implicit in this kind of work, especially that of Hellanicus, is the reconstruction of an absolute historical chronology for persons and events of the unsystematized past. All the dates of our sources prior to the Peloponnesian Wars are, in varying degree, products of reconstruction. For the fifth century, of course, most dates rest on secure tradition, accurate memory, and literary and documentary evidence easily accommodated to the newly established chronological systems. As one reached deeper into the past, more and more inference was required to associate dates with events. The lists published in the late-fifth and in the fourth centuries provided the framework for chronographic reconstruction. Events firmly associated in the tradition with an archon's name—Cleisthenes with Isagoras, Pisistratus with Comeas, the Panathenaea with Hippocleides—could now be dated precisely, relative to each other and to the present, through inclusive count of the intervening eponyms in a complete, official list. There is, however, a prior question. The lists set in order the names of magistrates and priests, kings and victors who lived two hundred years or more earlier than the time these lists were published. The earlier portions of the lists must themselves be regarded as the product of reconstruction. The possibility cannot categorically de denied, and we should not become tendentiously dogmatic. Nevertheless, no archival practice of state or temple that might have maintained earlier versions of the lists is demonstrable, despite the best efforts of modern scholars.[13] On the other hand, the repeated attempts to move to the opposite extreme and bring down in ruins the entire structure of early Greek chronology cannot be approved.[14] Our skepticism about the existence of early lists that would have been suitable for official or historiographic chronology and from which the later lists could have been copied or excerpted must be tempered by the realization that there is a difference between chronology and history, between archons as eponyms and archons as archons, between lists and their contents—a difference as fundamental as that between the yardstick and the line.

Of Olympic chronology Plutarch says (*Numa* 1.6), "it is difficult to be precise about dates, especially those reckoned by the Olympic victors, for Hippias of Elis published the list late, they say, beginning from nothing to compel confidence."[15] The most extreme conclusions have been drawn from these remarks, casting doubt on the historicity not only of the Olympic victor list but on the earlier portions of all eponymous lists, whether of magistrates, kings, victors, or priests. It is hazardous indeed to infer too much from such a passage. Plutarch's comments must be considered in context. The first comment, that Olympic chronology is imprecise, is Plutarch's own, and he is referring specifically to the difficulty of dating early Roman kings like Numa on the Olympiad system. The imprecision derives not from difficulties in Hippias' list but from the fact that so many different Olympic dates had been assigned to the foundation of Rome. Plutarch's comment reflects the same problem that Dionysius of Halicarnassus (*Ant. Rom.* 1.74) specifically discusses. The exact meaning of Plutarch's second remark is unclear. We do not know who his authority was ("they say"), and it is quite possible that his lack of confidence here too applies not to the list itself, but to its application to Roman chronology. We must agree that Hippias published the list late; but even if the skeptical remark applies to Hippias' sources for the list, extreme conclusions should be avoided. Plutarch does not say that Hippias started from nothing, but from nothing absolute. The most that we should conclude, therefore, is that there was no official, archival record to impose inflexible constraint upon the redactor. We cannot, however, maintain that there was no evidence whatsoever for Hippias' list, for the list of Athenian archons, or even for the clearly "chronographic" lists of Hellanicus for Argos and Charon for Sparta.

Official records of state or temple kept for the purpose of maintaining a continuous and contemporary documentation of institutional activity did not exist. The late-fifth-century lists were the first of their kind. On this point we must insist. Other kinds of records did exist, however, and we must be equally firm in stating that the late official lists were based on an abundance of solid evidence. There is unequivocal testimony for the existence of certain documents, and we can be sure that those attested are but a tiny fraction of what was available in the late fifth century. Fragments of the *axones* of Solon, for example, remained for even Plutarch to see (*Solon* 25.1). There were at Olympia private or dedicatory records attesting to the glory of bygone victors. The epigram to the Samian boxer Pythagoras (not necessarily the philosopher) attests to the existence both of such records and of a source of memorized traditions: "I am Pythagoras: ask of the Eleans what were my feats" (*Anth. Plan.* 3.35; Diogenes Laertius 8.48). The epigram itself derives from an ancient inscription, while its contents suggest that the Eleans were a storehouse of memory about victors like Pythagoras (entered in the extant list at the 48th Olympiad, 588/87). Thus such records as there were could be supplemented not only by scattered literary references such as the poems of Solon and Tyrtaeus, but also by living tradition. The tradition no doubt included memorized lists. Even so, the task of redaction must have been monumental indeed, and the exact lists produced were not in every detail the only ones possible on the available evidence. These lists were not the product of purely archival research—an activity that would not have been possible. They were just as certainly not forgeries either. The Athenian archon list was clearly the product of official redaction, and Hippias no doubt carried out his work on the list of stadion victors under the supervision, as well as with the approval, of Elean officials. Even Hellanicus in Argos and Charon in Sparta must be regarded as redactors of an "authorized version," which could not have won currency if it contravened the received tradition.

The earlier portions of the list were products of reconstruction. Various theories have been adumbrated as to how the construction was accomplished. These theories tend to suppress the complexities of hard reality, as if the authors of the lists were geometers constructing symmetrical figures with compass and ruler. According to one hypothesis, the Olympic victor list is historical only from the 50th Olympiad (580/79), when the beginnings of an archival system are postulated. The previous 200 years are alleged to be an artful construction, representing an interval of six generations, with little if any basis in traditional material.[16] The Spartan king lists are supposed to result from chronographic construction based on a genealogical count, and many theories have been offered.[17] Until recently, the Athenian archon list has been relatively sacrosanct. Most discussion of the early list concentrates on the problem of reconstructing the official list from the fragmentary literary and epigraphic remains.[18] Now, however, the historicity of the official list established in the 420s has been cast into doubt. The assumption has been made that many names were positioned in the early list according to numerical ratios, genealogical counts, and other such artificial methods of construction. According to one theory, the archonship of Solon, officially positioned in the list at the year corresponding to 594/93, was computed by reference to the 42-year cycle of heroes (*Ath. Pol.* 53). Solon was set two such cycles before the expulsion of the tyrants in 510/9. The construction was wrong, since in the early sixth century the cycle was (so it is suggested) only 21 years long, and the compilers of the list should therefore have placed Solon at the year corresponding to 573/72. Other names in the early list were allegedly positioned by genealogical calculations. Pisistratus, the archon of 669/68, was set three-and-two-thirds generations of 39 years each before the archonship of Hippias in 526/25. The Miltiades of 659/58 stands five generations of 27 years each before the Miltiades of 534/23.[19] Another commentator has pointed out that the interval between the first Olympiad (776/75) and the beginning of the decennial archons (753/52) is 23 years, while the interval between the beginning and the end of the period of decennial archons (684/83) is thrice 23 years—thus suggesting that these dates were computed by a genealogical count based on an average generation length of 23 years.[20]

Such hypotheses are at once too simplistic and too abstract, modern solutions to problems of modern invention. Even if we concede that it was difficult to reconstruct the earlier portions of these lists, we must also recognize that there was an abundance of evidence available that could never have been synthesized by mathematical equations. There was documentary evidence, public and private, literary evidence like the poems of Solon, and family tradition. We can never know exactly what combinations of what kinds of evidence produced lists like that of the Athenian archons or the Olympic victors. Surely it was the received tradition that dominated, not an abstract model of chronographic theory. We must not concede too much. The Greeks remembered more than we give them credit for. There are people today who can recite the names and dates of all the American presidents. Some can even recite from memory the list of Roman emperors! We can of course check such lists against published ones. If we could not, we would cultivate the art of memory much more seriously. That was the situation of the Greeks. Precisely because there existed no official, continuous archival record, people took pains to remember the sequence of magistrates and victors. Again, we must not become too simplistic. For there may have been gaps in one person's memorized list that had to be supplemented by another's, and people doubtless sometimes disagreed about the exact sequence. It was important, therefore, to publish official lists, especially when historiography and the beginning of state archives started to render the art of memory obsolete. We are dealing with reconstruction, not construction. As best they could, the redactors published lists that corresponded with what people remembered. Perhaps the official lists were not absolutely "correct" in every detail. Since we cannot do better, however, we had best leave them alone. The number of regnal years assigned to Spartan kings is, of course, a situation somewhat different from a list of eponyms. There is room for more "error." Still, it was the local memorized tradition that Charon of Lampsacus endeavored to crystallize, not a theory about how long a royal generation should be or how it could be subdivided and factored.

The conclusion, then, is that we must combine skepticism about the existence of early lists with confidence in the authenticity of the first lists that finally were published. The annual lists of magistrates, kings, priests, and victors on which early Greek chronology is based are structurally sound. They will bear no fundamental alteration for as far back as the redactors themselves thought the evidence allowed—a point that varies from the middle of the sixth to the middle of the eighth century, depending on the list in question. This combination of skepticism with confidence must be extended to the traditional dates of archaic Greek history in general. The evidence of texts like the *Chronicle* of Eusebius must be analyzed in scrupulous detail.

Sometimes it must be rejected as being corrupt or distorted. The objective, however, is not to undermine the tradition, but to discover what the tradition was, how it was systematized, and through what media it was transmitted to the extant sources. Different devices were required for the solution of different problems, and the received tradition took precedence over methodological consistency. An acceptable systematization of the material resulted, but not in such a way as to embody an abstract model of chronographic theory whose underlying assumptions can be subjected to modern "correction."

The Chronographic Tradition

Greek chronographic tradition is as complicated as the material that chronographers sought to systematize. The effort to introduce chronological system into the multifarious traditions of the prechronographic past was begun in the late-fifth century, both officially by persons like the unknown redactors of the Athenian archon list and, in literature, by antiquarians like Hellanicus of Lesbos, Hippias of Elis, and Charon of Lampsacus. Such works were used, criticized, continued, and combined by historians and chronographers of the Hellenistic and Alexandrian periods to produce the dates that eventually reached the epitomizing sources of Eusebius. Greek chronographic literature today lies in a fragmentary ruin. It is often difficult even to say who was a chronographer and who was not. Antiochus of Syracuse, for example, is a likely candidate for identification as the source of the chronological intervals included in Thucydides' history of Western colonization (6.1–5). The extant fragments, however, are not such as to suggest that he was a "chronographer" who dealt systematically with such questions.[21] Seven centuries separate Hellanicus from Eusebius. With the sole exception of the *Marmor Parium* (264 B.C.), which was inscribed on stone, the *Chronicle* of Eusebius is the earliest product of Greek chronographic literature that survives in a continuous text. Even in Eusebius' case it is necessary to work through his translators and continuators. It is therefore not possible to trace step by step the evolution of Greek chronographic tradition or to analyze in definitive detail the methodology that the ancient chronographers brought to bear on the problem of reconstructing the past. The number of contributors was legion. More impor-

tant, the development of the tradition was not uniformly systematic. No kind of historical writing can do without some sort of
chronological framework. Many writers not primarily chronographers were obliged to date persons and events of the distant
past. To the chronographer systematic chronology is an end in
itself. To others, dates are only incidental to the primary effort.
Thus, the tradition transmitted to the sources of Eusebius could
combine dates deriving from one or more chronographic systems
with chronological data based on no "system" at all.

Many genres of Greek literature contributed to the
growth of chronographic tradition. After the example of Hellanicus, local histories abounded. The *Corinthiaca* of Eumelus
(*FGrHist* 451), the *Megarica* of Dieuchidas (*FGrHist* 485),
and the *Sicelica* of Antiochus (*FGrHist* 555) are but illustrative
of a long list. The genre is best known through its Athenian
representative, the *Atthides* of Cleidemus, Androtion, Phanode-
mus, Melanthius, Demon, and Philochorus (*FGrHist* 323–
28). Aristotle's *Constitution of Athens* included a section on
historical development with a chronology based on that of the
Atthidographers. His study of political institutions required the
collection of 158 such *Constitutions*. Although all but the Athenian *Constitution* are lost (except for scattered fragments), we
may suspect that many of the 157 others included historical
chronologies. Of Aristotle's students and colleagues, two are
known beyond doubt to have written chronicles of their native
states. Demetrius of Phalerum composed an *Anagraphe* of the
Athenian archons (*FGrHist* 228), and Phainias of Eresus is
credited with a *Prytaneis* of his native city (F 17–19 Wehrli).
Aristotle and Callisthenes drew up a list of Pythian victors.
Such work clearly has chronological implications, and the Pythian
list is closely associated with Callisthenes' account of the establishment of the games and the history of the First Sacred War.[22]

While Ephorus undertook to write a universal history reaching into the very distant past, other writers of the fourth century
turned their attention to subjects of more limited scope, yet
with more important implications for the reconstruction of early
Greek chronology. Histories of literature, music, philosophy, and
science began to appear. Biographies of poets and politicians
were written. The industry of the Peripatetics is especially noteworthy. The doxographic work of Theophrastus, tracing the
development of philosophical teachings, was enormously influential. Lives of the philosophers were written by Ariston and

Aristoxenus. Menon wrote a history of medicine. Chaemeleon, Phainias, and Praxiphanes studied lyric and dramatic poetry. Biographical work is attributed to Dicaearchus, Heraclides Ponticus, and Hieronymus of Rhodes. Aristoxenus studied the history of music, while Eudemus wrote histories of the sciences. Treatises on discoveries (περὶ εὑρημάτων) were included among the works of Heraclides Ponticus and Strato.[23] Among the works of Ephorus was a περὶ εὑρημάτων and a universal history beginning with the return of the Heraclids. He made some kind of statement (*FGrHist* 70 F 223) that permitted Clement of Alexandria to report that Ephorus' date for the return of the Heraclids was 735 years before the crossing of Alexander into Asia. Ephorus' role in developing a chronology for Greek antiquity has been much discussed—no doubt overrated.[24] We must realize that the monographs of the Peripatetics dealt more specifically with antiquities and therefore contributed much to the growth of chronological traditions. That Phainias, for example, suggested a date for the return of the Heraclids is specifically attested (F 19 Wehrli).

In the third century the historian Timaeus, the polymath Eratosthenes, and Sosibius, the chronicler of Spartan antiquities, adopted Olympiad dating; the Olympic era provided a convenient numerical scale for chronologcal references. The influence of this innovation was enormous. Still, the mass of synchronisms, intervals, hypotheses of doxological succession, and other data with chronological implications that had been produced by the literature of the preceding two centuries could neither be entirely accommodated to the Eratosthenic system nor completely supplanted by it. The earlier authors continued to exert an influence of their own, and they are frequently cited in chronological contexts by authors like Pausanias, Strabo, Plutarch, Diogenes Laertius, and Clement of Alexandria. Just as the early traditions that had once been sifted and combined to produce the first chronographic efforts could continue to be transmitted, albeit transformed through contact with their systematized versions, so now the literary efforts of antiquarians produced a multifarious chronographic vulgate ready in its turn to be sifted, combined, and newly synthesized. The system of Eratosthenes itself passed through many hands and was adapted to many purposes. It was to become especially influential on biography and literary history through the *Chronicle* of Apollodorus and his epitomators. Slightly different versions of Eratosthenes' system could, however, be combined with each other and with quite independent data to produce yet another element of the growing tradition.

The rise of the Roman Empire broadened the scope of chronography. Polybius felt that the time was at last ripe for a truly universal history, and attempts to build a truly universal chronography soon followed. During the first century B.C. scholars like Alexander Polyhistor (*FGrHist* 273) began collecting data from all the nations of the Empire. The chronographer Castor of Rhodes (*FGrHist* 250) sought to harmonize the eponym lists of East and West with each other and with the chronological system of Eratosthenes. In the time of Augustus Dionysius of Halicarnassus (*FGrHist* 251), in his work περὶ χρόνων, united the chronology of Greece and Asia Minor, especially for the mythical period, with that of Rome and the West. Olympiad chronicles offering an epitome of universal chronology from the first Olympiad to the author's own time became popular. The best known is that of Phlegon of Tralles (*FGrHist* 257), composed in the time of Hadrian. One such Olympiad chronicle transmitted the now tangled nexus of chronographic traditions to Eusebius. A century earlier Sextus Julius Africanus (A.D. 221) brought Greek chronography into the service of Christian apologetics and chiliastic expectation, adding an entirely new dimension to the tradition that he selected for inclusion in his *Chronographiae*.

This brief, selective survey, by no means exhaustive, indicates the scope of the problem that faces anyone who confronts the *Chronicle* of Eusebius either as evidence for early Greek chronology or as a thesaurus of the Greek chronographic tradition. The work of these and many other authors too numerous to mention who interested themselves in matters of early Greek chronology and thus contributed directly or indirectly to the traditions that reached late sources like Eusebius exists only in scattered fragments. In many cases no more than bare names and titles are preserved, listed in lexica like the Byzantine *Suda*. The late authors who are preserved were, like Eusebius, interested only in the dates—not in the evidence and methodology underlying them. They sometimes cite their sources, but they rarely mention and never discuss the methodology of their chronographic authorities. The statement of Diodorus (1.5.1) and Plutarch (*Lycurgus* 1.3) that the succession of the Spartan kings was fundamental to the computations of Eratosthenes and Apollodorus is an important shred of evidence. It also illustrates

how little information such authors pass on to us. Whatever the
methodology of an individual authority may have been, the
methods employed by his precessors must also be taken into
account in any attempt to uncover the rationale behind a particular date, as must the medium through which the information
was subsequently transmitted.

The Methodological Problem—Genealogical Chronology

Not a single one of the chronographic works, properly so
called, that were influential in constructing an absolute chronology for early Greek history has been preserved to us whole.
Data deriving from them, extant in later sources, stand at the
end of a long history of transmission. Systematic modification,
contamination from other sources, and transcriptional error are
possible at every stage. Analysis of chronographic method should
therefore be conducted through study in meticulous detail of the
tradition underlying a particular set of dates. A few generalizations are nevertheless in order. In particular, there is a widely
held thesis that much of early Greek chronology is a construction
based on the counting of generations. This theory is useful; but
it cannot in itself explain the traditional chronology, and it
should not be allowed to dominate investigation of these
problems.[25]

The material available for constructing a chronology for
Greek history of the archaic period and earlier included a broad
range of epic and lyric poetry, folk tradition and myth, the
orally transmitted memory of family tradition, and local history,
often colored by tendentious propaganda of various hues. Included, of course, was the genealogical tradition of the leading
families. Some of them, like members of the Spartan royal
houses, traced their pedigrees back into the heroic age. The
chronological implications are clear. One could, theoretically,
obtain a relative date for a hero like Heracles or for any intermediate name in the line by counting the number of names in the
pedigree between the ancestral figure and his putative contem-
porarary descendant, then multiplying the result by the length
of a generation supposed average for that family. Stories told
about one's ancestors could provide a means for the relative
dating of events by a similar computation. Intermarriage broad-
ens the possibilities by permitting a synchronistic link to be

established among pedigrees. Cylon the Athenian had married into the family of the Megarian tyrant Theagenes. The Alcmeonids had a marriage link with the Sicyonian Orthagorids. The Athenian Philaids had married into the Corinthian family of the Cypselids, who were in turn related by marriage to the Bacchiads. The Bacchiads could be connected to the Spartan royal houses through their claim of common descent from Heracles. Chronological constructions could be made by placing interconnected sets of the synchronisms explicit in intermarriage and implicit in the traditional material in a genealogical framework until contact was made with a known pedigree whose genealogical structure could be given arithmetical expression. It is doubtful, however, that such procedures really were the fundamental basis of the chronographic tradition.

Genealogical information could be obtained *viva voce* from members of the noble families. We know that much of it was collected (some no doubt invented) and crystallized in writing during the fifth century by professional genealogists and mythographers like Hecataeus of Miletus, Acusilaus of Argos, and Pherecydes of Athens (*FGrHist* 1–3). There are, however, serious difficulties with the evolutionary theory that chronography was the child of genealogy. The steps involved in making the transition from pedigrees to dates strain credulity. Two families claiming descent from the same hero may have a different number of names in their pedigrees, implying a different number of generations between the hero and the contemporary descendants. For the sake of chronological consistency names will have to be added and subtracted, or different generational lengths posited, or some combination of both adjustments employed, without somehow disturbing any of the synchronisms implied by the tales associated with various ancestors. Furthermore, a generation is a relatively long time compared to the four years of an Olympiad or the single year of an annual magistracy. An especially illustrious ancestor had many accomplishments for his descendants to boast of, and presumably a long career of glory. A generational computation produces the same vague, relative date for different events associated with the ancestor and with his contemporaries in supposedly cognate genealogies. If generational chronology is to be considered the fundamental tool of chronographic construction, then additional devices must be posited to account for the achievement of precise, discrete dates. The illustrious ancestor's career must be subdivided, giving rise to the anomalous notion of fractions of generations. The generational chronology itself must be converted to an annalistic system. This means that an annalistic system must be found or constructed to reach as far back as the genealogical line in question. Events of the subdivided generation must then be arbitrarily assigned to regnal years or eponyms to produce a precise, absolute chronology. As if these were not problems enough, the basic idea—the average length of a generation—is itself difficult to define. It might be the actuarial average of human life spans somehow empirically derived, a theoretically ideal life span, the average age at procreation, or the average differences in ages between fathers and sons. The average will vary from time to time, from family to family.

Generational chronology is a natural device and an appropriate one for computing approximate intervals between persons and events separated by long periods of time, especially if no evidence other than genealogical tradition is available. But a precise, absolute date requires a possibly fictional, certainly constructed annalistic list coupled with arbitrary fractions of a supposedly average generation length within a pedigree that may have been tampered with for the sake of mutual consistency among genealogies. Generational chronology mechanically converted to an annalistic system can easily lose its link to genealogy and become a purely artificial mathematical device. With the introduction of the chronographically logical, but biologically absurd idea of fractions of generations, the question of when a person does or should produce offspring has little to do with the intervals computed. To divide life into seven stages, as Solon did, or four, as Pythagoras did, is natural. Subdividing generations, so as to say that something happened five-and-seven-ninths generations ago is quite another matter. Once generations have been subdivided, the principle of generational chronology has in fact been abandoned. The numbers originally devised to represent generations have become instead chronographic periods. There can be little doubt that genealogical chronology played some role in the effort to systematize the received material about the undated past. The difficulty lies in determining how the theory was actually applied and to what extent genealogical chronology and its counterpart in chronographic periodization dominated the construction. If genealogical chronology with fractional generations to represent short intervals is in fact the fundamental tool in the chronographic armamentarium and if the dates of our sources are simply arithmetical representations of family pedigrees, then the structure of early Greek chronology can be quantified and subjected to sophisticated sociological analysis so as to yield for us the primitive material from which the now-traditional dates were derived. If it can be determined how many generations and fractions of generations, computed at what average length and applied to what absolute base, underlie a given date, we can evaluate the historicity of the date by examining the appropriateness of the generational length used and then make whatever adjustments might seem necessary.

The difficulties that would be involved in perfecting such a methodology are enormous. Let us not try, for the effort would rest on fundamentally false assumptions. Early Greek chronology is not the product of a single systematic effort abstractly carried out in a scholar's chamber on the basis of a consistent body of evidence that would yield to a theoretical model. Genealogical chronology may well have been useful, especially for the heroic age. But different estimates of the time of the same or closely related events based on slightly different genealogies computed from different base dates with different generational lengths assumed would exist side by side both with each other and with chronological material based on other than genealogical considerations. Generational chronology is a device for introducing system into the available evidence. That material often included chronological indications in the form of synchronisms and intervals as well as generations. The well-known statement of Tyrtaeus (as quoted by Pausanias 4.6.5, 4.13.6, 4.15.2) that the Messenian War lasted for twenty years and was fought by "our fathers' fathers" in the time of King Theopompus is a noteworthy example. The time of the war could be variously estimated, depending on the length of the generation posited and on whether Messenian or Spartan pedigrees were used. Theopompus is also associated with other events, including the establishment of the ephorate and the institution of the Olympic festival. It is not likely that all estimates of his time would converge, and the differences in opinion could produce compromises that would become independent data of their own. Such tensions certainly existed already before the so-called chronographers set to work on the systematization of the material and introduced new tensions leading to new compromises. The point is too obvious to belabor further and must be reduced to a dictum. While genealogical chronology and other systematizing devices certainly played a role in the development of early Greek chronology, they were only a part of a rich, complex, living, and growing tradition to which arithmetic can never do justice.

Herodotus and Early Greek Chronology

Interest in historical chronology among the Greeks is clearly evident in the *Histories* of Herodotus. The work of Herodotus is fundamental to the study of Greek chronography for a number of reasons. His career intervenes between those of the genealogists and the first appearance of chronography in the work of Hellanicus. Some scholars have therefore supposed that the work of Herodotus can reveal the missing links between genealogy and chronography—that Herodotus borrowed and improved upon the methods of a Hecataeus and that a Hellanicus made the further refinements necessary to adapt the methodology to annalistic chronology. Furthermore, since the work of all the chronographers has perished, but the *Histories* of Herodotus have not, modern scholarship perforce turns to Herodotus for both historical and chronographic information. We should indeed turn to Herodotus for help. What we shall find, however, is not confirmation of the evolutionary hypothesis, which moves from genealogy to chronography. Instead, we shall find proof (provided that we read Herodotus and do not manipulate the text) that Greek chronological tradition rests on a wonderful mixture of ingredients no one of which can be distilled out without destroying the rest.

The chronology underlying the work of Herodotus has been discussed time and time again with litttle agreement. Much of the discussion concentrates on certain passages taken as being based on genealogical chronology, as proof that such reckoning is indeed the fundamental chronographic tool, and as suggestive of what generational lengths were in fact employed for various kinds of pedigrees. What these passages and all the discussion about them really show is that it is impossible to reduce Greek chronological structures to genealogical equations. Herodotus says at 2.142 that three generations of men is 100 years. This should mean that Herodotus, if he used such devices, would compute genealogical lines at 33 years a step. At 2.144, however, he says that the interval from his own time to that of Heracles

is about 900 years. That should be 27 generations. But Herodotus elsewhere (7.204, 8.131) gives the Heraclid genealogies
of Leonidas and Leotychides, the Spartan kings at the time of
the Persian Wars. Both pedigrees include 21 names, from Heracles to Leonidas and Leotychides. About fifty years separate
the Persian Wars from Herodotus' time of writing. On one
hypothesis these 21 generations therefore cover about 850 years
and suggest an average generational length in the Heraclid line
of 40 years, rather than 33. Another commentator allows one
generation for Heracles to grow up and produce offspring and
another generation for the interval between the Persian Wars
and Herodotus. The 900-year interval now represents 23 generations of 39 years.[26] Herodotus reports the regnal years for
the Mermnad kings of Lydia (1.15, 16, 25, 86), and the total
for the five generations from Gyges to Croesus is 170 years.
This suggests a generation length of 34 years. But since Croesus
had supposedly been granted three years of grace by Apollo
before his final fall, the Mermnad line should really have ruled
for only 167 years—five generations at 33 years each. On yet
another interpretation, the fourteen years of Croesus are left
out of the count as being historical rather than "chronographic."
The 156 years of his four predecessors yield an average generation of 39 years.[27] Gyges usurped the Lydian throne from the
Heraclids, who had passed it without interruption from father
to son, Herodotus says, during 22 generations and 505 years
of rule (1.7). The 22 generations average 23 years each, with
one year for some reason missing from the total. Herodotus
says (1.95) that the Assyrians ruled over upper Asia for 520
years before the Medes set the example of revolution. The
number of generations is not stated, but if one compares these
Assyrians with the Heraclid Lydians and supposes the 520 years
to be genealogically based, he might conclude that the Assyrians
ruled for about 20 generations. A generational length of 26
years is thus added to the collection. But the 520 years could also
be 13 generations of 40 years, 13⅓ generations of 39 years,
15⅔ generations at three to a century with the total rounded
to the nearest ten, or 22½ generations averaging 23 years each
with the sum again rounded off.

We now have a list of possible generational lengths to attribute to Herodotus or to his authorities that includes 23, 26,
33, 34, 39, and 40 years. Some of them are factorable and there-

fore potentially useful for computations requiring the arithmetical representation of fractional generations. But not one of them is either proved or provable as the Herodotean generational length, with the exception of the general estimate of three to a century—an estimate that Herodotus uses only once for a singular problem. The study of Greek chronography runs the risk of being reduced to an exercise in arithmetical gymnastics, with the prize going to that contestant whose reasoning forms the most nearly perfect circle. Greek chronography is not simply a branch of Greek mathematics, nor is it a monogamous and harmonious "marriage of genealogy and arithmetic," to use the metaphor of one student of the subject.[28] Genealogical information was useful, to be sure, and arithmetical devices were often required to systematize the data and establish intervals. The arithmetic was not always based on theoretical considerations. A genealogical computation might be applied in combination with an interval already included in the tradition—the twenty years of the first Messenian war, the thirty-six years of Pisistratid tyranny, the eleven years of the Lydo-Milesian war—to produce a datum not itself reducible to a genealogical equation. Arithmetical symmetry in the construction was not a requirement, nor must it be supposed that consistency among computations used to systematize different kinds of material for different purposes was a primary desideratum. It was much more important to "save the phenomena," and the phenomena were a complicated literary, oral, and political tradition whose content was always subject to growth and change. In reconstructing a king list, for example, many factors other than the genealogy of the line would have to be taken into account. Synchronisms between the kings of various lists traditionally associated in war or diplomacy would not all be preserved by simple generational computations. It might be deemed appropriate to use one kind of computation in one part of the list and a quite different periodization in another, depending on the nature of the material to be synthesized and the prevailing political winds.[29] The result was not a specimen of mathematical beauty, but a pragmatic tool for historical reconstruction.

The attempt to discover a mathematically consistent chronological structure in the fabric of Herodotus' *Histories* or to demonstrate that his chronological indications are genealogically based is a gross oversimplification. Herodotus should not be characterized as a chronographer at all. It was his job to report and instruct, not to force the information into chronological system. For precisely that reason, what Herodotus reports is indeed instructive of chronological tradition. He inherited from his informants a wide diversity of information, including chronological estimates that already incorporated the tension between one tradition and another, between one kind of estimate and another. The material included in Herodotus' work shows how different ways of confronting historical time could and did exist side by side in a meaningful way. The *Histories* of Herodotus bring together traditional genealogies, reported intervals, the chronological constructs of some authorities (e.g., Lydian king lists), the synchronisms implied in the tales of other sources, and simple statements to the effect that one event had taken place a generation or two before another. System in an abstract, modern sense there is not, but history and historical chronology are abundantly present in a well-wrought narrative.

Herodotus' statement that there are three generations of men to a century is a good general estimate, which he brought to bear on a particular problem. The Egyptian priests had contended that during 341 generations no god ever appeared in human form. Herodotus converted this statement to an interval of years in order to give the reader some idea of how long a period of time was involved in this tradition as compared to the relative youth of such Greek traditions as the 900 years since Heracles. Three to a century is a reasonable estimate of the average generational length and a very convenient one for dealing with as large a number of generations as 341. Now, 341 times 33⅓ equals 11,366⅔, while Herodotus gives the total as 11,340. The most diverse kinds of conclusions have been drawn from this discrepancy: Herodotus meant to count 33 years to a generation throughout his book, but he was too clumsy at arithmetic to make it work. Or, because he made a mistake in the computation, Herodotus must have borrowed the method from somebody else—a somebody else who can therefore be presumed to have made the 33-year generation influential on a large number of chronological constructions both in the work of Herodotus and elsewhere. Or, on the contrary, since Herodotus made an error, this length for a generation must not have been in common use at all and can be absolutely excluded from fifth-century chronographic construction.[30] The truth is that Herodotus made no mistake in the arithmetic at all. He did not say that a generation was 33 or 33⅓ years long. He said that he could deal with the 341 generations by estimating three generations to correspond to a hundred years. His reasoning from there is very straightforward if we grant to Herodotus the kind of shortcut arithmetic still commonly and appropriately used for the estimation of a large sum. Herodotus is dealing in 3s and 100s, and raising each side of the equation by the power of ten very quickly produces a result. Three generations is 100 years, thirty generations 1,000 years, and 300 generations is 10,000 years. Thus 333 generations is 11,100 years. That leaves a remainder of eight generations to be estimated (still by 10s and 3s) at 30 years each, producing a grand total of 11,340 years. Herodotus need not be presumed to have used this estimate of a generation anywhere else in his history, because he never again had to deal with a huge raw figure like that included in the tradition of the Egyptian priests.

The intervals that Herodotus sets alongside the Egyptian traditions—1,600 years since Dionysus, 900 since Heracles, 800 since Pan—derive from an unknown Greek mythographic tradition that certainly used genealogy as a basis for the computation of the intervals. But that tradition may have been quite independent of the Heraclid genealogy of the Spartan kings, which Herodotus reports in an entirely different context without applying genealogical chronology to the line. The 22 generations of Heraclid rule in Lydia is certainly independent both of Spartan tradition and of the mythographic computation of the date of Heracles. The 22 generations of Lydian Heraclids is an integral part of the tradition that made a close link between Lydian and Greek culture. The 505-year interval during which these kings ruled does not result from the application of an average generational length to these 22 kings, but derives from the complex problem of determining the length and successions of imperial rule in Asia Minor. The 520 years of Assyrian rule is linked to the same general problem of succession of empires. To suppose that either number can be reduced to a genealogical equation, with or without fractional multipliers and chronographic dividends, is to oversimplify both the historiographic problem and the nature of Herodotus' reports.[31]

In writing of early Near Eastern history, Herodotus reports definite regnal lengths for the kings of certain dynasties. The a priori suspicion that these lists are partly fictional constructs is confirmed by the discovery of Assyrian and Babylonian records that contradict them.[32] There is no way of knowing what mixture of documents, tradition, and arithmetical construction produced the erroneous lists. In his treatment of early Greek history, Herodotus uses no such devices of absolute chronology, presumably because none were yet available. Genealogical reckoning could produce approximate intervals for distant persons and events like Heracles and the Trojan War (2.145). The method is too imprecise to be useful for more recent history, and Herodotus' narrative of events shows no trace of genealogical chronology. He relies instead on local tradition and introduces a relative chronology that can provide a link from one tradition to another through the use of synchronisms. Where the tradition included generational indications of time, Herodotus reported them as such without applying numbers to compute an interval. The Alcmeonid stories of 6.125–26 provide an example. Sometimes the tradition included intervals of years and Herodotus reports them—the thirty years of rule in the Corinthian tradition on Cypselus, for example (5.92)—with no suggestion that the intervals are the arithmetical representation of some other kind of information.

Herodotus' narrative is instructive indeed of how richly diverse the materials were that could be collected and interwoven for the reconstruction of the past. The annalistic lists of different kingdoms of the East, for the construction of which different materials and methods must be presumed on the part of Herodotus' authorities, stand alongside each other as a framework for the reporting of traditional stories that had a life quite independent of the formal lists. With this material the local traditions of the Greeks can be intertwined through the use of the synchronisms implied in international relations. This kind of mixture with all the potential tensions implicit in it—meaningful in its totality, but difficult and controversial in matters of detail —is the real characteristic not only of Herodotus' sense of time, but of the traditional structure of early Greek chronology in general. The systematization of genealogically based family traditions, the redaction of eponym lists, the construction of historical narratives local or universal, the composition of annalistic chronographies, the growth of local chronicles, the establishment of broadly based systems of historical time like that of Eratosthenes, and the chronographic tradition that transmitted them— all derive from a diversity of materials and methods as rich and irreducible as life itself. That is why there can never be agreement on Herodotus' chronological "methods," nor ever a definitive solution to the chronographic problem.

Summary

Herodotus left his early Greek chronology vague and unsystematized, perhaps refusing to try to wring from his sources more precise data than the evidence allowed.[33] Later authors, living now in an age of annalistic dating, were not satisfied. They demanded precision, and they were willing to use any device necessary. The material to be systematized now included Herodotus—a point that cannot be overemphasized. The process of combination and recombination began simultaneously with the birth of annalistic chronography itself among Herodotus' younger contemporaries. The establishment of annalistic lists like that of the Spartan kings or the Athenian archons facilitated the reconstruction of historical chronology and the establishment of absolute dates for persons and events of the past. Precision in chronology was now demanded not only in the relatively solid traditions of the fifth and sixth centuries, which literary and documentary sources could supplement, and the vague memories of the seventh century, but even for the dark ages that memory and tradition could barely touch. Arithmetical devices had to be used to systematize the material and help fill in the gaps. The chronological construction had to be consistent with the traditional material, but the devices employed did not have to be consistent with each other. Herodotus' synchronistic relativism had been abondoned. But chronography remained a mixture of popular history, literary tradition, and arithmetical construction. Even as Herodotus had incorporated in his work different kinds of temporal measurement to suit different kinds of material, so too would his successors.

As the tradition grew, it became ever more complex (even garbled), ever less reducible to axiomatic fundamentals. The course of history continually produced more events that could be regarded as epochal and used as base dates for one kind of estimate or another—the battles of Leuctra and Chaeronea, Alexander's crossing of the Hellespont, the establishment of the successor kingdoms, and so on. Until late in the development of Greek biography, chronography, and historiography, the work of one's predecessors had to be taken into account. This scholarly information, itself the result of compromise and contamination, was combined and recombined with popular tradition and political propaganda. To that mixture the author added his own stylistic tastes and literary purposes. The writer might wish to glorify his homeland, to establish artful connections between political and literary history, to certify the claim of one contemporary sect over another that it was the true and direct spiritual heir of one of the famed early philosophers. He might wish to synchronize the early histories of all the provinces of the Roman Empire to display the irresistible workings of some mysterious force. Or he might have a quite bizarre chronographic purpose like that reflected in the title of a work attributed to Castor (*FGrHist* 250 T 1)—an *Anagraphe* of Babylonian and thalassocratic history in a single work. The chronographer and his arsenal of tools were sometimes called upon to perform such formidable tasks as the construction of a world chronology true to historical fact that could also be set in the framework of the prophet Daniel's vision (9.24) of "seventy weeks of years."

The result was a flood of verbiage and a mass of conflicting data. The situation prompted Eusebius specifically to admonish his readers in the introduction to his *Chronicle* (pp. 1–2 Karst) that the famous words of the Master should be applied not only to eschatology, but to historical chronology as well—"It is not for you to know about dates or times; the father has set them within his own control" (Acts 1:7). Greek chronography had become too much for mere mortals to cope with. This fact had long since begun to exert a new kind of influence on the tradition. The process of combination and the proliferation of books was then, as always, paralleled by a process of selection and condensation. Information was collected, distilled, and made readily accessible in concise handbooks, encyclopedias, and lexica. It was through such media that Eusebius collected his own data. Eusebius made the final selection and arranged the data in a chronicle so universal and so convenient that, right or wrong, it rendered all others obsolete and became the chronological textbook of the Middle Ages. What the Father of History had unintentionally begun, the Father of Church History unintentionally canonized and laid to rest.

3

Excursus: The Chronological Method
of Apollodorus

The traditional dates of early Greek history result from a centuries-long effort among historians, antiquarians, and chronographers to construct an absolute chronology for persons and events of the undated past. Some degree of artificiality is inevitable in any such effort. In particular, arithmetical devices must sometimes have been employed in order to adapt the primary data to the new annalistic systems of dating. The problem for the modern historian is to determine what kinds of systematizing devices were employed, what combinations of traditional material and theoretical construction underlie the extant dates. Genealogically based indications of time were included in the traditional material, but it is by no means clear either that genealogical tradition dominated the evidence or that chronographic method was an evolutionary development from genealogical chronology. While the modern theory of genealogical chronology is relatively straightforward, applying the theory to explain the genesis of dates transmitted in our sources is not. The evidence seldom allows a final determination of what arithmetical devices were actually employed or why the so-called chronographers deemed them appropriate.

The modern historian is obliged to look for possible arithmetical interpretations of the evidence in order to separate the fundamental tradition from the artificial overlay of construction. Estimates of the average length of a generation are not the only possible source of chronographic intervals, however, and we must take care not to force the evidence into conformity with a chronographic model of our own creation so as to validate an a priori theory of genealogical chronology. The same body of evidence allows different and equally viable arithmetical interpretations. Compernolle, for example, observed that some of the intervals in Thucydides' history of the Sicilian colonization (6.1–5) are multiples of 35, and he accordingly ascribed them to a genealogically based chronographic system in which the average generational length was computed at 35 years. Hence, traditional statements that one city had been founded a certain number of generations before another or that a certain number of generations had elapsed between the foundation of the city and some recent epochal event in its history could be accommodated to annalistic chronology by the application of 35-year generational lengths to the tradition. From the same data in Thucydides, however, Miller adduced a 36-year generation with fractional subdivisions of 9 years. Miller hypothesized that Eusebius' date for the foundation of Syracuse in 736/35 (89^g Helm) derives from the same chronographic system as Thucydides' intervals, representing seven generations of 36 years each before Gelon's conquest of Syracuse in 485/84. Miller sought confirmation of the hypothesis in the date of the *Marmor Parium* (*FGrHist* 239 A 31) for the foundation of Syracuse in the year corresponding to 758/57, this date representing the same genealogical count, but with an average generational length of 39 years instead of 36. That is, the tradition had included a statement to the effect that Syracuse was founded seven generations before Gelon's conquest of the city, and the two extant dates are but different arithmetical representations of that genealogical tradition.[1]

The possibility of using different generational lengths could certainly have produced different absolute dates from the same genealogically based information. Too many generational lengths are possible, however, too many base dates can be posited, and there is no ancient tradition to support any of the generational lengths hypothesized (35, 36, and 39 years). The theory of subdivided generations to account for the intervals in Thucydides that are not exact multiples of the generational length posited is especially hazardous. Hypothetically, it is possible that fractional generational lengths could be used to convert to absolute dates a traditional statement to the effect that one event had taken place at about the same time (or within the same generation) as an-

other event, but a little bit earlier or later. It is difficult to know
what short intervals (if any) should actually be interpreted that
way; and it is circular to construct tables of dates based on the
application of a generational length and its fractions to some
epochal base and then conclude that any date in our sources that
happens to coincide was originally based on just such a construction.[2] Clement of Alexandria (*Strom.* 1.131) says, for example,
that Eumelus, although older, overlapped chronologically
(ἐπιβεβληκέναι) with Archias, the founder of Syracuse.
Theoretically, such a statement might derive from a Corinthian
tradition that Eumelus had lived in the same Bacchiad generation as Archias, but was already famous for his poetry by the
time that Syracuse was founded. Absolute dates could be computed by setting Eumelus a fraction of a generation earlier than
Archias. The fact that Eusebius has a date for Eumelus a few
years before his entry on the foundation of Syracuse (89 Helm)
might be interpreted as supporting such a hypothesis. On the
other hand, it is equally plausible that Clement's statement does
not represent primary tradition at all. He simply deduced the
relative chronology of Eumelus and Archias from his chronological source and stated that one was older than the other. The
dates may well derive from entirely independent computations—
Archias being dated by reference to the foundation of Syracuse,
Eumelus by his position in the history of literature, neither date
related to Bacchiad genealogy.

The possibilities are unlimited. The evidence is meager and
must be handled with great care. The only "generational length"
or chronographic interval that is well attested is that based on a
forty years' count. The use of a 40-year generation has been
attributed to Hecataeus, who is said to have applied it to the
Heraclid genealogy of the Spartan royal houses to arrive at a
relative date for Heracles himself.[3] The intervals Thucydides
uses in the "Archeology" (1.1–23)—sixty years from Troy to
the Boeotian migration, twenty years more to the return of the
Heraclids, 300 years from Aminocles to the "end of this war,"
260 years since the naval battle between Corinth and Corcyra,
400 years of Spartan constitutional stability—can be interpreted
as calculations based on generations and half-generations of 40
years each.[4] Chronographic construction based on the 40 years'
count is well attested, however, only in the fragments of the
Chronicle of Apollodorus, composed in the middle of the second
century B.C. Interestingly enough, in this case—the only one that

can adequately be tested—the forty-year interval does not derive from a historiographic practice of estimating the length of a generation, but from a philosophical model of the stages of life.

Hermann Diels demonstrated a hundred years ago that many of Apollodorus' biographical dates derived from chronographic construction rather than from primary evidence.[5] If a person's birthdate was not known, Apollodorus computed one for him by synchronizing his intellectual maturity with an event that could reasonably be associated with the height of his career and assigning to him the age of forty at the time. Felix Jacoby studied Apollodorus' chronographic method in detail in *Apollodors Chronik*, a now classic work.[6] Apollodorus, because of the enormous influence of his *Chronicle*, provides the only concrete illustration of how Greek chronographic methods were in fact applied. Apollodorus' influence permeated the later chronographic tradition, sometimes manifesting itself by specific citation of his name, frequently suggested only by distinctive features of Apollodorus' method. The latter is especially true for the historical notices of Eusebius' *Chronicle*, where the Apollodoran influence is strong but only once acknowledged (84[f] Helm). A discussion of the chronographic tradition represented in the sources of Eusebius necessarily requires an introductory description of Apollodorus' method. Any such account is heavily indebted to Jacoby, and his work must be consulted for the detailed examination of the evidence that it would be superfluous to repeat here. Nevertheless, there are interesting features of chronographic method present in the Apollodoran system that Jacoby did not recognize and that show that Apollodorus' procedures did not evolve from genealogical chronology. Furthermore, the work of Apollodorus represents a synthesis of the chronographic tradition as it had developed during the 250 years since Hellanicus and provides a specific illustration of the processes outlined in chapter 2.

Greek chronography developed as a mixture of remembered tradition, literary and documentary evidence, and arithmetical construction. By the time of Apollodorus, memory was obsolete and such traditions had been transformed by chronographically systematized versions of the past. The literary evidence had become enormous by the addition to the primary sources of secondary treatments of the same events. The literature now included the prodigious output of Apollodorus' predecessors in the Alexandrian school, the work of the Peripatetic biographers, critics, and antiquarians, as well as the chronological constructions of scholars working in the tradition of Hellanicus. Apollodorus often used this secondary material. As is well known, he adopted the chronographic system of Eratosthenes, a systematic redaction of the most fundamental annalistic standards—the Spartan king lists, the Athenian archon list, and the list of Olympic victors now converted to a numbered system of Olympiads with annalistic subdivisions. Local chronicles like those of the Atthidographers offered a valuable store of already-dated information. Most important was the antiquarian work of the Peripatetics.[7]

Apollodorus' predecessors expressed their opinions about relative chronology, they established synchronisms between persons and events, and sometimes they gave absolute dates. They did not, of course, always agree with each other. Glaucus of Rhegium (Plutarch, *de Mus.* 4), to take a well-known example, said that Terpander was older than Archilochus, while Phainias of Eresos (fr. 33 Wehrli) stated that Terpander was the younger. Eratosthenes (*FGrHist* 241 F 11) identified the philosopher Pythagoras with the Olympic victor of 588, but Aristoxenus (fr. 16 Wehrli) synchronized Pythagoras with Polycrates about 530. The chronographic tradition was not uniform, and Apollodorus could not make a credible synthesis simply by sifting through the scholarly literature and making excerpts. Therefore he based his own chronology not only on the work of his predecessors but also on the original sources of information. In other words, Apollodorus used the primary evidence to judge the adequacy of his predecessors' work, so that, in effect, he made a new combination of the unsystematized data with the chronographic tradition as it had developed thus far. For the archaic period Apollodorus, like his predecessors, could find contemporary evidence in the work of the lyric poets. The *Histories* of Herodotus was a fundamental repository of tradition about the period. Neither the primary sources nor Herodotus provided dates. For absolute chronology, Apollodorus turned to the scholarly tradition. He needed either to find absolute dates on good authority that agreed with his understanding of the issues or else to construct a chronology of his own.

A system of chronological reference was prerequisite, and Apollodorus adopted that of Eratosthenes. Eratosthenes had established an authoritative version of the Spartan king lists that he aligned with the Olympiad system, thus providing a continuous annalistic system from the return of the Heraclids to the present. Being both a patriot and an archaizer, however, Apollodorus preferred to express the dates as Athenian archon years beginning with the archonship of Creon in 683/82, as intervals for the earlier period. Eratosthenes himself provided the synchronistic tools. With this system of absolute chronology either Apollodorus or, perhaps, Eratosthenes combined what he thought to be the chronological system inherent in the *Histories* of Herodotus. The regnal years of Herodotus' Lydian reports he combined with the Olympiad system by synchronizing the fall of Sardis with the second year of the 58th Olympiad, 547/46. The date was based on Berossus' Greek version of the Babylonian literary chronicles that detailed the career of Cyrus.[8] The conversion of Herodotus' Persian and Median material to an absolute chronology he achieved by much the same method as that of modern historians who systematize Herodotus—a combination of the Babylonian evidence on Cyrus with Herodotus' own statements (7.20, 8.51) that the Persians invaded Europe in the fifth year of Xerxes' reign and reached Attica when Calliades was archon.[9] The Greco-Oriental synchronisms of Herodotus—for example, Periander and Alyattes, Pisistratus and Croesus, Polycrates and Cambyses—could then be made to yield at least approximate dates on an absolute scale of reference. Apollodorus imposed this systematized version of Herodotus on the primary evidence by attempting to connect persons and events mentioned in the early sources, especially the lyric poets, with something also mentioned by Herodotus. If, as was the case for the early period that Herodotus did not cover, it was not possible to introduce approximate dates by reference to Herodotus, Apollodorus sought for plausible synchronisms between his sources and Eratosthenes' recension of the early lists of kings and magistrates.

Both the early eponym lists and, more especially, the lists of Spartan and Corinthian kings were the product of redaction and reconstruction carried out long after the purported beginning of the lists. The Oriental lists reflected in Herodotus' reports derive, at least in their earlier portions, from a similar effort at reconstruction. Eratosthenes no doubt had to do a certain amount of manipulation to bring the Greek lists into harmony with each other, and further manipulation was required to align the Greek system with the various oriental lists that could be extracted from Herodotus. The result, finally, had to be brought into

reasonable agreement with the relative chronology implied in
Herodotus' treatment of early Greek history as well as with his
Greco-Oriental synchronisms. The dates that Apollodorus attached to events mentioned in the early sources therefore derived
already from a reconstructed chronological system that was the
product of a long scholarly tradition. Even by reference to this
system of absolute chronology, however, Apollodorus could often
introduce only approximate dates into the material with which
he was working. The combination of the chronographic system
of Eratosthenes with the synchronisms of Herodotus and with
the chronological implications of the primary material produced
an interval within which an event could be presumed to have
happened, but not a precise date. In order to obtain the required
precision and, in particular, to fix within the chronological
structure the vital statistics of famous persons of antiquity,
Apollodorus had recourse to mathematical devices. Apollodorus
did not, however, base his own constructions on any notion of
the average biological generation. He turned instead to a theoretical model of the stages of life. Apollodorus gave primacy for
his chronological purposes to a philosophical question rather
than to a statistical consideration. What was important to him
was the theoretical age of intellectual maturity (acme), not the
average age of biological procreation.

Solon (fr. 19 Diehl) divided life into ten stages of seven
years each, with intellectual maturity falling between the ages
of 43 and 56. For Apollodorus, however, one reached intellectual maturity at the age of 40. Jacoby argued that Apollodorus borrowed this idea from Pythagoreanism. For according
to Diogenes Laertius (8.10), Pythagoras regarded the full life
as one of eighty years and divided it into four stages corresponding to the seasons of the year. The age of 40 is the half-way
point and marks the division between the summer and the autumn
of life. According to this theory, then, the age of 40 is the time
when the fruit of life is ripe, a metaphor suggested by the word
ἀκμή itself. The connection between Pythagoreanism and Apollodorus is provided by the Peripatetic biographer and musician,
Aristoxenus of Tarentum. Aristoxenus (fr. 16 Wehrli) synchronized the 40th year of Pythagoras with the tyranny of Polycrates. Apollodorus (*FGrHist* 244 F 339) did likewise.[10]

This Pythagorean teaching provided the model for Apollodorus' chronological constructions using the interval of 40 years.
His predecessors may well have used the same interval and de-

rived it from the same source. The evidence requires us to concentrate on Apollodorus, but it is by no means certain that he
was the first to apply the Pythagorean doctrine to chronography.[11] For Apollodorus, the age of 40 marked the ἀκμή
("bloom") of a person's life. He accordingly considered a person whose dates were not otherwise known to have been forty
years old at the time of some appropriate event that Apollodorus
could somehow date by reference either to his general chronological scheme or to events for which he had already established
dates. Thales, for example, was assigned the theoretical age of
40 at the time of the great solar eclipse he had supposedly predicted (*FGrHist* 244 F 28), while Thucydides reached his acme
at the beginning of the great war that he both witnessed himself
and recorded for all posterity (*FGrHist* 244 F 7). Apollodorus
dated the events by tying the chronological implications of the
material to his general structure of annalistic chronology. Then
he computed a birthdate for the person the 40th year earlier. If
the date of death was known, Apollodorus computed the total
life span directly. If the date was not known, Apollodorus
either assigned the person a theoretically perfect life of eighty
years or, more frequently, he used synchronisms to establish
what he considered an appropriate date. The death of Thales,
for example (*FGrHist* 244 F 28), he synchronized with the fall
of Croesus, because Herodotus (1.75) last mentions Thales in
connection with his alleged participation in the war of Croesus
against Cyrus. The death of Stesichorus he synchronized with
the birth of Simonides (*FGrHist* 244 F 337) at a date that
could be inferred from the latter's own statement (fr. 77 D)
that he was eighty years old when Adeimantus was archon
(477/76).

Apollodorus applied the doctrine even when he was able to
establish actual dates of birth or death by other means. The
date of Socrates' death, for example, was well known, and Plato
said (*Apology* 17 d) that he was about seventy years old at the
time of the trial. Apollodorus therefore dated his birth to the
70th year before the trial and condemnation, the Attic year corresponding to 469/68. Although the acme method was not necessary to compute the birthdate, it was nevertheless important
to state when Socrates had flourished. Having established the
birthdate, Apollodorus used it to fix the acme of Socrates in the
fortieth year thereafter, 430/29.[12] The date of one's acme was

important, quite apart from its significance for the person at issue. It also served as a starting point for further chronographic computations.

A second fundamental principle in the system of Apollodorus, well documented in Jacoby's study, was the establishment of a 40-year interval between the acme of master and pupil or between the acmes of successive sets of practitioners in the same field. The interval in this case perhaps represents an intellectual "generation," for the forty-year acme suggests the age at which the fruit of intellectual life is ripe for dissemination. Thus if the dates of one person could be determined either through the acme method or by other means, the dates of that person's teachers, pupils, and each member of an entire succession could be inferred by setting their respective acmes forty years apart. The method entails the chronographically aesthetic synchronism of the master's acme with the pupil's birth. The birth of Democritus, for example (*FGrHist* 244 F 36), Apollodorus synchronized with the acme of Anaxagoras (*FGrHist* 244 F 31). We do not find open-ended series of such successions, however, for the introduction of other dates (known or computed) associated with the persons involved complicates the scheme.

The acme method and its corollary were used in conjunction with the kinds of synchronistic treatment typical of Greek chronography and in combination with certain epochal dates considered appropriate starting points for computation. Apollodorus often dated the birth, acme, or death of a person by reference to one of these epochs, and he sometimes assigned compound sets of synchronisms to them. Some of these epochal dates were part of the chronographic system that Apollodorus inherited from Eratosthenes. In addition, Apollodorus established new chronographic epochs in the context of his own computations. The acme of Thales in 585/84 was a starting point for the dating of Arion and of Archilochus at forty-year intervals.[13] To the epochal year of the fall of Sardis he assigned a complicated synchronism among Thales, Anaximander, Anaximenes, and Pythagoras.[14] The date he knew for the battle of the Eurymedon, 468/67, marked the deaths of Themistocles and Aristides, the acme of Cimon, and a synchronism of the death of Simonides with the acme of Bacchylides and the birth of Diagoras.[15] The year of Aeschylus' death in 456/55 was the starting point for computing important dates in the careers of the three great tragedians, while at the epoch of the beginning of the Peloponnesian War there was a synchronism among Herodotus, Hellanicus, and Thucydides.[16]

The interval of 40 years is well attested for Apollodorus, well documented in Jacoby's study. Problems arise when we ask if that was the only interval that Apollodorus used. If so, distortions in the chronology may be suspected, since intervals of 40 years were sometimes too long. Jacoby hypothesized, on the basis of Diogenes' division of the perfect life into four stages of 20 years each, that Apollodorus used the "half-acme," the age of 20, to date a person's first entry into professional life.[17] Such a hypothesis would also suit the theory that Apollodorus' method derives from genealogical chronology with the basic generational length of 40 years divided in half. There is in fact very little evidence to support such a division. The only clear case is that of Anaxagoras, who began to study philosophy at the age of 20; but this statement derives from an autobiographical remark rather than from chronographic theory (*FGrHist* 244 F 31 and Komm.). There is, however, evidence to suggest that Apollodorus used theoretical ages of 25 and 64, as well as 40. This larger set of intervals permitted more flexibility in the method, accommodating a variety of traditional relationships. Furthermore, the numbers cannot be seen as deriving from genealogical chronology, but they can plausibly be connected with Pythagoreanism.

The evidence is, as usual, not so full as one would like. In at least two cases, however, it is clear that the Apollodoran chronology grouped three closely related persons together at a synchronistic epoch with ages of 25, 40, and 64.[18] The first group, significantly enough, includes Pythagoras. Apollodorus (F 339) is the source of the vulgate date for the *floruit* of Pythagoras in 532/31. He specifically stated (F 29) that Anaximander was 64 years old in 547/46, and he synchronized the acme of Anaximenes with the fall of Sardis (F 66). Now 547/46 was Apollodorus' date for the fall of Sardis, so that Anaximander's 64th year was synchronous with the 40th of Anaximenes. With an acme in 532/31, Pythagoras was 25 years old in the epoch of the fall of Sardis. The second group is the three tragedians. Apollodorus is cited by name for the dates of the tragedians only once in the extant texts, but he is probably the source of the vulgate chronology. Diodorus (13.103.4–5) says that Apollodorus (F 35) synchronized the death of Euripides with that of Sophocles in 406/5, stating that Sophocles was 90 years old when he died. Thus, Sophocles flourished at the age of 40 in 456/55. That was the date of Euripides' first presentation according to one *vita* (134 West.), and another (139 West.) says he was 25 years old at the time. This age at that date accords with Eratosthenes' opinion (*FGrHist* 241 F 12) that Euripides was 75 years old when he died and with the vulgate synchronism of Euripides' birth with the Persian Wars in 480/79 (e.g., Diogenes 2.44–5). The year 456/55 was also the date of Aeschylus' death (*Marmor Parium FGrHist* 239 A 59), and a synchronism between his acme and the birth of Euripides at the epoch of the Persian Wars would result in an age of 64 for Aeschylus when he died. Thus, Aeschylus, Sophocles, and Euripides were at the ages of 64, 40, and 25 in the year 456/55.

A third such instance cannot be reconstructed from the extant tradition. It does not seem likely, however, that the appearance of these ages at a synchronistic epoch in two such important cases as these is adventitious. That these relative ages are in fact significant follows from consideration of the numerology itself. In the first place, the interval between 25 and 64 is the same as the interval between 1 and 40, so that this set of numbers fits well with the method of the acme. A person born in the year of another's acme reaches the age of 25 when his elder is 64. The age of 25 is appropriate for dating a first entry to fame, such as Euripides' first presentation. The age of 64 can be used to date an event presumed to have occurred after the acme—Aeschylus' death, in Anaximander's case the publication of a summary of his life's teachings (Diogenes 2.2). The synchronistic possibilities are well illustrated by the tradition about the tragedians. With an acme in 456/55, Sophocles was born in 495/94, when Aeschylus was 25 years old, and this is the age attested for his first presentation in the *Suda*.[19] In 480/79 Euripides was born, Aeschylus flourished at the age of 40, and Sophocles was a youth of 16. The central synchronism is that at 456/55—death of Aeschylus at age 64, acme of Sophocles at age 40, first presentation of Euripides at age 25.

Furthermore, the very numbers 25, 40, and 64 have a remarkable arithmetical relationship, which suggests that their use in the chronographic tradition is not coincidental. The ratio 25:40 is the same as 40:64, reducible to the ratio 5:8. The factors of 40 are 5 and 8, which are also the square roots of 25 and 64. In other words, the set of numbers 25, 40, and 64 forms a geometrical proportion of the type $a^2/ab = ab/b^2$, where $a = 5$ and $b = 8$. Now, proportion was at the heart of Pythagoreanism, and these numbers are most salient in the chronographic tradition about Pythagoras and persons associated with him.[20] Further-more, we know that it was from Aristoxenus (fr. 16 Wehrli) that Apollodorus adopted the synchronism between the acme of Pythagoras and the tyranny of Polycrates. Aristoxenus was, among other things, a doxographer personally acquainted with eminent Pythagoreans of the fourth century.[21] It may therefore have been he who introduced to the chronographic tradition, especially to Apollodorus, a Pythagorean model for the division of life into proportional stages. The perfect life is one of 80 years divided at the arithmetical mean of 40 and subdivided into unequal but proportionate parts such that the arithmetical mean of the whole is the geometrical mean of the segments. Apollo-dorus knew of this teaching in its original form through Aris-toxenus. Diogenes or his source had received an epitomized version reporting only that there were four segments and wrongly making them equal.

We must not press too hard and try to show that a theory of proportionals underlies the entire Apollodoran system, much less the entire chronographic tradition. The evidence will not allow it and we should not, in any case, expect the traditional chronology to yield to any one theoretical model. Nevertheless, it is important to recognize that Apollodorus' method was rooted in a philosophical model, not a strictly historiographic practice. The acme at age 40 was a philosophical ideal. The interval of forty years representing an intellectual "generation" derives from that ideal, through the synchronism of the master's acme with the pupil's birth. It does not derive from genealogical chronology. Furthermore, where the use of theoretical ages and intervals other than 40 years can be demonstrated, the numbers employed are not simple fractions or fractional multiples of the basic interval. They represent a philosophical model for the stages of life, but they have no connection with the notion of subdivided generations. In short, the theory of genealogical chronology with fractional generational lengths is a modern in-vention that cannot be attributed to the ancient chronologists.

It is, of course, insufficient merely to note that Apollodorus used theoretical intervals and ages other than 40 and that they derive from the Pythagorean preoccupation with square numbers and mean proportionals. We must also ask how Apollodorus applied his method in specific cases and why he thought it appropriate to do so. We need to know, in other words, whether Apollodorus' method was arbitrary. In the case of the tragedians, the 64-40-25 model applied to the year 456/55 systematizes the tradition according to which Aeschylus was a mature man at the time of the Persian Wars, Sophocles a youth, and Euripides an infant. It represents a final synthesis of the chronographic tradition on these persons, with little departure from the opinions of earlier authorities and fully consistent with what facts were known about their careers. The case of the philosophers is much more interesting, allowing us to see how Apollodorus used a mathematical device to construct an absolute chronology from the relative chronology inherent in the tradition.

Apollodorus adopted from Aristoxenus the synchronism of Pythagoras' 40th year with the tyranny of Polycrates. That synchronism as such does not yield a precise date. Both Herodotus (3.39) and Thucydides (1.13.3), however, had synchronized Polycrates with Cambyses, so that Apollodorus could infer an approximate date for the acme of Pythagoras at the time of Cambyses—that is, about 530. In the doxographic tradition, Pythagoras was considered the student of Anaximander who in turn was the student and younger contemporary of Thales, the teacher and elder contemporary of Anaximenes.[22] Apollodorus had dated the acme of Thales independently to 585/84 and his death to 547/46, the time of the fall of Sardis (F 28). Anaximander and Anaximenes had to be dated between Thales and Pythagoras, maintaining the relative chronology, and a precise date for the synchronism of Pythagoras with Polycrates had to be established. Apollodorus accomplished all of this by assigning to Anaximander, Anaximenes, and Pythagoras the ages of 64, 40, and 25 at the epoch of the fall of Sardis. Thus Anaximander flourished in 571/70. He was 14 years younger than Thales, 24 years older than Anaximenes—an acceptable systematization of the traditional relationships. Furthermore, Pythagoras, one full intellectual generation younger than Anaximander, could now be precisely dated to 532/31, and a date for the beginning of Polycrates' tyranny about that time follows—again an acceptable systematization of the tradition that Polycrates' coup took place shortly before Cambyses' expedition to Egypt.

One more example is instructive of this kind of methodology, now using only the 40-year interval in connection with traditional material such as that reported by Herodotus and with independently computed dates. Apollodorus dated Archilochus partly through references in his poems to the Cimmerian invasions. Herodotus associated the Cimmerian invasions with the reign of Ardys, so that Apollodorus could infer an approximate date through his systematized version of the Lydian lists about 660. Herodotus synchronized Arion with Periander, and Apollodorus dated Periander to 627. Arion's famous ride took place a few years after the accession of Periander, according to Herodotus, so that Apollodorus could infer an approximate date about 620. He established precise dates for Archilochus and Arion by counting off intervals of 40 years from a base date such that the resulting calculations would accord with the approximate dates. In this case, the date of Thales' acme was a base that produced the desired result. Arion flourished in the fortieth year before Thales, 624/23, and Archilochus in the fortieth year before that, 663/62.[23]

Apollodorus' use of the method, then, was not arbitrary, and we may note one well-known case where Apollodorus refrained from applying the 64-40-25 set, although it would have produced very nearly the desired result. For the historians Herodotus, Hellanicus, and Thucydides, Apollodorus wished to express the relative ages of approximately contemporaneous persons, but he had (or at least thought he had) better evidence, which made the application of the 64-40-25 theorem unnecessary. Thus, computing separately the acme dates of the historians, he expressed their relationship at the epoch of the Peloponnesian War (F 7) with the ages 40 (Thucydides), 53 (Herodotus), and 65 (Hellanicus) These numbers are very close to the 40-55-64 that would result from the addition of a 15-year interval to the first two numbers of the theoretical set. Nevertheless, Apollodorus believed that the application of the theory was not appropriate. When he did apply the theory, he did so only to compute precise dates within approximate intervals that he had already established. That is, the application of the numbers is the last step in a well-reasoned process; arithmetic alone cannot explain the dates. The chronographic process required arithmetical devices yielding precise dates. It was nevertheless firmly rooted in the tradition and therefore fundamentally reliable.

One technical detail must be appended relevant to the interpretation of Apollodoran evidence. It is essential to remember, in dealing with the acme method of Apollodorus, his computation of epochs, and his establishment of synchronisms, that for the historical period at least, Apollodorus expressed his dates in Athenian archon years. Throughout his chronological system he therefore followed the convention natural for those who count by eponym years and reckoned his intervals with both end points included. Thus an acme at the age of 40 must be interpreted as meaning "in the fortieth year of life," and intervals of 25 and 64 years are counted in the same way. An interval of 40 years reckoned inclusively corresponds to an interval of 39 years in our numerical system of dating. Most of our late sources, including those used by Eusebius, express the Apollodoran dates in the Olympiad system, so that the interval frequently has the appearance of being ten Olympiads. The appearance is deceptive, and the difference of one year between ten Olympiads and forty archon years inclusively counted is often crucial for interpreting the genesis of an Apollodoran date. Anyone who compares Diels's treatment of Apollodorus, reckoning intervals numerically either on the Olympiad system or by Julian years B.C., with the more precise analysis of Jacoby's inclusive count will see how significant the difference can be.[24] We must not conclude, however, that Apollodorus in fact reckoned by "generations" or chronographic periods of 39 years. A 39-year interval is the modern equivalent of the ancient 40-year interval inclusively counted. For Apollodorus the chronographic interval was 40, and not 39 in disguise. The distinction is important. Modern commentators have attempted to attribute a generational length of 39 years to the Greeks, subdividing it into fractional intervals of 13 years.[25] Apollodorus would have been appalled.

4

The Sources of Eusebius

Eusebius' evidence for early Greek chronology derives from a many-faceted chronographic tradition representing seven hundred years of development. There are textual problems associated with any Eusebian entry, and the traditional chronology for the period from before the middle of the fifth century is itself controversial. A third complication is introduced by the question of how the information was transmitted to Eusebius. Each notice must be considered from these three standpoints so as to distinguish the information of early tradition from the sometimes distorting influence of centuries of transmission.

Source criticism of entries collected in a late chronicle has severe limitations. Eusebius seldom cites his authorities in the *Chronological Canons*, and independent evidence is hard to find. What evidence does exist is also late and beset by its own problems of text and source. One must nevertheless seek to identify or, at least, to characterize the intermediate sources if the notices of Eusebius and other late authors are to be understood in the context of the tradition that produced them. Some of Eusebius' information is of the highest antiquity. The entries on Themistocles, for example, preserve in both date and content the popular tradition (right or wrong) about his career as it existed for Athenians of the late fifth century.[1] Other notices reflect a confused combination of traditions about a date that was the subject of learned controversy. Of the three entries on Lycurgus, for example, two are different expressions of the same computation of the lawgiver's time, while the third combines the information about one Lycurgus with the date associated with another.[2]

Still other entries derive from once-solid traditions reduced to incoherence in successive stages of transmission. The Pisistratid notices, for example, derive from the Atthidographic vulgate of Philochorus, but the entries have little semblance either in date or in content to the Atthidographic version, much less to the original nexus of information.[3] Some notices can be understood only as resulting from the contamination of scholarly computation by often whimsical popular tradition. The impossibly early date for Hipponax in Olympiad 23 (688/85) derives from false synchronism of Hipponax with Archilochus on the basis of a chronologically absurd invention that the two had vied for the attentions of Sappho. Moreover, the entry is attached to a date that originally represented an attempt to date Homer, not Archilochus.[4] Only an examination of the tradition that influenced Eusebius' immediate sources permits us to make the necessary distinctions among the extant notices.

Chronographic Composition and the Sources of the *Spatium Historicum*

The *Chronicle* of Eusebius was composed in two distinct parts—the *Chronographia*, or "first book," and the *Chronological Canons*. This fact is familiar to all users of the work. One must also realize that the *Canons* itself consists of two parts. The parallel columns of numerals, or *fila regnorum*, constitute the chronological framework, while historical information associated with the inscribed numerals is found in the *spatium historicum*, a broad space in the middle of the page. This distinction is important for source criticism of the work. Eusebius rarely cites his authorities for the information included in the *spatium historicum*, but the sources used for the *fila regnorum* are presented in the prefatory *Chronographia*. We must begin by asking how the composition of a chronicle including both a synchronistic display of numerals and an epitome of historical information influenced the selection of sources and how much of the information included in the historical epitome could have been excerpted from the same authorities who provided the annual lists.

SOURCES OF THE CHRONOGRAPHIC EXCERPTS

In the notices of the *spatium historicum* relevant to Greek history of the archaic period, Eusebius cites an authority only twice. One of the dates for Hesiod he attributes to Porphyry (84ᶜ Helm), and one of the entries for Lycurgus carries the authority of Apollodorus (84ᶠ Helm). For a full list of possible sources we must turn to the *Chronographia*. In this introductory portion of the *Chronicle*, Eusebius presents excerpts from his main authorities for the fundamentals of Greek chronology (80–124 Karst). The section begins with something like a table of contents: Athenian kings, Argive kings, Sicyonian kings, Lacedaemonian kings; those who controlled the sea and for how long they did so; the Olympiad reckoning of the Greeks; early kings of the Macedonians; the successors of Alexander who were kings of the Macedonians and Thessalians, the Syrians, and the Asians. The material itself follows in slightly different order, with specific citation of the authorities in all but two cases. From Castor (*FGrHist* 250 F 2–4) Eusebius excerpts lists of the Sicyonian, Argive, and Athenian kings. At the end of each list is a statement indicating the relative chronology between the given list and the main standard of reckoning, the Olympiad system. The essential structure of that system duly follows—a numbered list of the eponymous stadion victors from the first through the 249th Olympiad. He does not name the authority for this fundamental list, which contains within it a list of Roman emperors from Julius Caesar to Antoninus Pius Caracalla, each entered in the Olympiad of his accession. After the Olympiad list Eusebius presents excerpts from Diodorus (bk. 7, fragments 8, 9, and 11) on the lists of Corinthian kings, Lacedaemonian kings, and rulers of the sea (thalassocrats). A Macedonian list follows for which the authority is not specifically cited in the extant Armenian text. That this list too comes from Diodorus (bk. 7, fragment 15) is attested by the presence of a similar list in Syncellus (498–99) preserved under the name of Diodorus. The section on Greek chronology closes with lists of the successors of Alexander excerpted from the *Chronicle* of Porphyry (*FGrHist* 260 F 3, 31, 32).

Eusebius' main authorities for the fundamentals of Greek chronology, then, are Castor, Diodorus, Porphyry, and an as-yet-unidentified source for the Olympic victor list. Castor's chronicle dealt with the period from Ninus of Assyria (2123 B.C.) to the ratification of the Pompeian reorganization of Asia (61) in only six books (*FGrHist* 250 T 2). The early lists that Eusebius excerpts were probably all included in the first book. There is accordingly no reason to suppose that Eusebius used an epitomized version of this book. The excerpts from Diodorus, however, certainly reached Eusebius in an epitomized form. The immediate source may have been the *Chronicle* of Porphyry, a work that began with the fall of Troy and one for which the lists of Corinthian, Lacedaemonian, and Macedonian kings would therefore have been appropriate. It was Porphyry, then, who provided the citation of Diodorus as authority for these lists. From Porphyry, too, Eusebius excerpted the lists of the successor kingdoms. Castor may not have included lists of the Corinthian, Lacedaemonian, and Macedonian kings but he certainly dealt with the successors of Alexander (*FGrHist* 250 F 12).[5] The fact that Eusebius used Porphyry rather than Castor for this material suggests that Eusebius excerpted only from Castor's first book, finding the subsequent books progressively too full of detail to permit the regnal lists to be excerpted with ease. Porphyry no doubt consulted Castor in drawing up his version of the lists, but the fact that he does not attribute them to Castor suggests that Porphyry made his own redaction on the basis of several authorities.

Eusebius' immediate sources for the Greek king lists are therefore only two: the first book of Castor, dealing with the mythical period, and the *Chronicle* of Porphyry, exhibiting material beginning with the fall of Troy and continuing to Roman times. He also used the *Historia Philosophica* of Porphyry, as the excerpt prefaced to the Olympic victor list shows. Of all the material included in the section on Greek chronology, it is the Olympic victor list that is most crucial to the question of what sources Eusebius used for the notices of the *spatium historicum* relevant to archaic Greek history. An author who listed the names of all the stadion victors from the first through the 249th Olympiad may have done so in the context of a general chronicle epitomizing Greco-Roman history by Olympiads. The author of this list cannot so easily be identified as has generally been supposed, and the centrality of the issue must be made clear. The relationship between the chronographic authorities—Castor, Porphyry, and the author of the Olympic victor list—and the sources of the *spatium historicum* depends to a great extent on the format of the *Canons* and the methods used in its composition.

TECHNIQUES OF COMPOSITION

The Greek lists and the other matter collected in the first book of the *Chronicle* constitute what Eusebius refers to as "a kind of timber for a future project."[6] From these raw materials he constructed the chronological framework of the *Canons*. Eusebius had first to enter the annual lists running vertically down the margins of each page. He must have composed so large a work in a number of sections, the divisions being dictated by the length of the various lists and the positions in them of important epochs and synchronisms. He began with the birth of Abraham, which he synchronized with the 43rd year of the Assyrian Ninus, the 22nd year of Europs of Sicyon, and the beginning of the 16th dynasty in Egypt. The first section of work was probably the 160 years during which only these four lists had to be entered. He then went back through these pages and entered the appropriate historical notices and chronographic comments. The next section began with the first year of Jacob and the start of the Argive list (27 Helm). It probably ended with the death of Joseph and the beginning of the servitude in Egypt (36 Helm). The beginning of the Athenian list 150 years later (41 Helm) would be the next appropriate point of division. The death of Joshua and the beginning of the period of the Judges ended a section of about 120 years (47 Helm), and the next division of work ran to the end of the Argive list and the beginning of the Mycenaean (53 Helm). Another 125 years brought Eusebius to the fall of Troy, an epoch that marked a major division (61 Helm). The next section included the 150 years to the building of Solomon's temple (70 Helm), perhaps divided again where the Latin, Lacedaemonian, and Corinthian king lists began (66 Helm). The number of annual lists to be entered was now eight. The next division came about 200 years after Solomon's temple, at the point where the beginning of the Macedonian list raised the total of regnal lists to nine (83 Helm). The first Olympiad (86 Helm) and the fall of Israel (88 Helm) marked major epochs and rather small sections of work. The next section of about 150 years ran to the fall of Judah (100 Helm), and at the second year of Darius there was a major division with a change in format after the first year of Olympiad 65 (105 Helm).

For the period before the second year of Darius, Eusebius entered the king lists first, leaving the space in the middle of the page blank. He then added notices in that space. In the section beginning with the 65th Olympiad, Eusebius worked on the annual lists and the historical notices simultaneously. Divisions in labor were henceforth dictated more by important historical events requiring large amounts of space rather than by chronographic considerations arising from the annual lists. Six such divisions are apparent both in Jerome and in the Armenian version. In Olympiad 86 (114 Helm) the rebuilding of the walls of Jerusalem requires a lengthy comment on the interpretation of Daniel's 70 hebdomads. The death of Alexander and the beginning of the Ptolemaic kingdom in the 114th Olympiad marks another division (125 Helm). The remaining divisions were provided by important epochs of sacred history—the leadership of Judas Maccabaeus in Olympiad 155 (141 Helm), the kingship of Herod the Great in Olympiad 186 (160 Helm), the crucifixion of Jesus in Olympiad 202 (175 Helm), and Titus' sack of Jerusalem in Olympiad 212 (187 Helm).

In both of the major divisions of the *Chronicle* Eusebius had to work with historical sources as well as with his strictly chronographic authorities. In the first portion he dealt with the chronography first, then turned to history. In the second, where chronographic composition was difficult only for the period during which lists of the Hellenistic kingdoms had to be entered, he worked on the chronological framework and excerpted his historical sources simultaneously. In both portions he divided the labor into manageable sections for ease of composition and to minimize the number of different source books that had to be used at once. The discovery of the Armenian version has shown what Eusebius' strictly chronographic source looked like. He had before him either his own first book or a convenient summary of it similar to the collection of king lists that appears in the Armenian version (144–55 Karst) and some of the manuscripts of Jerome (1, app. 1 Schoene). What kinds of historical sources he used can be inferred only from the notices themselves.

CHARACTERISTICS OF THE HISTORICAL SOURCES

The *Chronicle* exhibits through the entries that appear alongside the annual lists a formidable variety of material that Eusebius appropriately characterizes as a "digest of every kind of history."[7] Only once does he state what kinds of sources in general (as opposed to attributing a specific notice to a specific authority) he used to compile the digest. The historical books of the Old Testament recorded Israelite history up to the time of the Persian king Artaxerxes I (465–425). Thereafter, Eusebius says (113[a] Helm), he follows the books of Maccabees,

Josephus, and Africanus. The last-named authority is the one Eusebius actually had before him, Africanus himself having incorporated epitomes of Maccabees and Josephus into his *Chronographiae*.[8] Eusebius says that these writings included a *uniuersam historiam* up to Roman times. The *Chronographiae* of Sextus Julius Africanus is discussed in greater detail below. For the present it must be noted that Eusebius' remark here does not necessarily imply that Africanus wrote a comprehensive world history or that he was Eusebius' sole source for historical notices from the middle of the fifth century B.C. Eusebius' statement is made in the context of sacred history, at the point where the biblical account ends. Africanus concerned himself primarily with sacred history. He was Eusebius' main authority for sacred history after 445 B.C., but only because there existed no complete and concise canonical account. The reference to universal history means no more than that Africanus made explicit certain synchronisms between important events of sacred history and Greco-Roman history. In other words, Africanus dated sacred history by reference to external standards as well as to years since Creation. His purpose was both to be intelligible and to show how the whole of history was moving toward a common divinely ordained end.

Africanus was Eusebius' principal source for sacred history after the time of Ezra and Nehemiah. For our immediate purposes, the most important characteristic of Africanus' work was its combination of scope with brevity. The *Chronographiae* of Africanus began with the creation of the world and ended with the year corresponding to A.D. 221. The last event mentioned was probably the participation of Africanus himself in the colonization of Nicopolis in Palestine during the reign of Elagabalus (OL 250.1, 221/22, p. 214[h] Helm). The work encompassed 5,723 years in five books.[9] The period of more than 600 years from Nehemiah's rebuilding of the walls of Jerusalem in the time of Artaxerxes to the establishment of Nicopolis during the reign of Elagabalus was all included in the end of the fourth book and in the fifth.[10] The exigencies of chronographic composition suggest that Eusebius' other sources for notices included in the *spatium historicum* were similarly concise. For early Greco-Roman history those sources included a chronological compendium of important persons and events in Greek and Roman history expressed either in Olympiads or in years *ab Vrbe condita*, or both.[11] He also had a handbook of legendary history, both Greek and Italian, and, if it was not already included in the chronological compendium, a list of colony foundations.

The source for legendary history was Castor. His chronicle covered the period from Ninus to 61 B.C. in six books (*FGrHist* 250 T 2, F 5). The first book, which Eusebius expressly cites for the Assyrian regnal list (26 Karst), included at least the 1,280 years from Ninus of Assyria and Egealeus of Sicyon to the end of the Assyrian empire (2123–843). It probably ran to 754—the last year of the life archonship at Athens, the last year of unlimited regal power at Sparta, and the last year before the foundation of Rome.[12] Thereafter Castor devoted more and more space to events as he neared his own time, and his account thus became less useful as a chronological handbook sufficiently concise to meet Eusebius' needs. The first book of Porphyry's *Historia Philosophica*, from which Eusebius excerpted the epochal intervals between the fall of Troy and the first Olympiad (89 Karst), treated the history of philosophy from Homer to Pythagoras. It was therefore of sufficiently large scope and appropriately small size to be a useful handbook for notices of the *spatium historicum*. That Eusebius did use it is attested by the specific attribution of one of the dates for Hesiod to Porphyry (84[c] Helm). The second book was of somewhat smaller scope, dealing with the philosophers between Pythagoras and Socrates. Eusebius could easily have excerpted the dates to produce a convenient list of *floruits* for that period. The third and fourth book were of no use as chronological compendia. Each dealt with a single philosopher, the third being devoted to Socrates and the fourth to Plato.[13]

Some of Eusebius' notices for persons and events of early Greek history come from Castor and Porphyry, who were also among his main authorities for the chronographic fundamentals. Other notices come from very short, specialized lists like that of the thalassocrats attributed to Diodorus (106 Karst) and perhaps, like Diodorus' king lists, transmitted to Eusebius through the chronicle of Porphyry. The difficulties involved in the composition of a chronographic work as complex as the *Chronicle* of Eusebius required its author to use concise epitomes of historical information as well as of annual lists. He had to minimize the number of such epitomes that it was necessary to use at the same time. It is therefore most likely that Eusebius excerpted the majority of his notices on archaic Greek history from a single source, which (like Castor's first book) covered long periods of history in very few pages.

THE SOURCE FOR GREEK HISTORY

The *Chronicle* was originally organized with several columns of notices lying side by side in the middle of the page. Eusebius had to use more than one source to record the histories of so many different peoples. He kept the number of sources to a minimum, and a correspondence between columns and sources may have helped to simplify the task.[14] The source for Greek history must have expressed the dates in the Olympiad system. For after the first Olympiad, which he regarded as the beginning of the historical period for Greece, Eusebius made Olympiad numbers the most outstanding feature of the chronographic framework. Olympiad numbers occupy a horizontal space of their own, interrupting all other annual lists. The regnal years in those lists thus appear in such a way as to serve for both author and reader as a means of numbering the four years within an Olympiad. This organization of the *Chronicle* suggests that Eusebius' main source for Greek history was an Olympiad chronicle that offered a concise epitome of a relatively long period in a rather short space.

Like the chronicle of Thallus (*FGrHist* 256), the book Eusebius used had an introduction dealing with the period from the fall of Troy to the first Olympiad. It must have been much more compact than Phlegon's Olympiad chronicle (*FGrHist* 257) and perhaps was similar in format and scope to the extremely abbreviated Oxyrynchus Chronicle (*FGrHist* 255; *P. Ox.* 12). The contents of the *spatium historicum* suggest that, for the early period at least, Eusebius' author focused on the dates of famous persons and the events associated with them. A change is evident beginning with the late-fifth century. Starting with Olmypiad 87 (432/29) and the beginning of the Peloponnesian War, the *Chronicle* contains significantly more political and military history than previously. Nevertheless, notices similar to those contained in the earlier period remain prominent, epitomizing literary and philosophical history. The last two entries of this style note the *floruit* of Eratosthenes in Olympiad 141.1 (213/12) and that of Aristarchus the grammarian in Olympiad 156.1 (156/5).

This stylistic evidence based on the contents of the *spatium historicum* allows two conclusions. The first is that Eusebius used two Olympiad chronicles. One was a literary-philosophical compendium that covered the entire period down to the time of Eratosthenes and Aristarchus. The other epitomized political-military history, and either it began with the Peloponnesian War or only became detailed from that date. In that case Eusebius was making excerpts from two different books at once for Greek history of the Classical and Hellenistic periods. The second conclusion is the more economical and therefore the more likely: Eusebius used the same Olympiad chronicle for Greco-Roman history both before and after the Peloponnesian War. It dealt with ancient history from the fall of Troy at least to the time of the Roman conquest. The work contained a preface listing events and intervals between the fall of Troy and the first Olympiad. Subsequently, it epitomized Greco-Roman history by Olympiads. The author's source material was fuller for Greek history than it was for Roman. Beginning with the Peloponnesian War the author either used or inherited a wider variety of sources than he did for the earlier period. But the same basic epitome of literary and philosophical history underlay the entire work to the time of the Roman conquest. It began with the fall of Troy and ended with the *floruit* of Aristarchus (Olympiad 156) and the final subjugation of Macedon: *Romani interfecto Pseudofilippo Macedonas tributarios faciunt* (Olympiad 157.3, 150/49, p. 143ᶜ Helm).

This biographical epitome which, together with excerpts from the first two books of Porphyry's *Historia Philosophica*, dominated Eusebius' material for the archaic period of Greece came to him through a source organized by Olympiads, so that the information was immediately adaptable to the format of the *Canons*. With the Olympiad numbers dominating the chronographic framework of the *fila regnorum*, the page was prepared in such a way as to permit an Olympiad chronicle to be transcribed into the *spatium historicum*. In other words, the *Chronological Canons* of Eusebius incorporates an Olympiad chronicle with the dates appearing as numerals in the framework instead of as words in the text. The next question is whether this source can plausibly be identified with any of the authorities whom Eusebius excerpts in the *Chronographia* for the fundamentals of Greek chronological convention. A few fragments of Olympiad chronicles are extant. There are two anonymous papyrus fragments—*P. Ox.* 12, "The Oxyrhynchus Chronicle" (*FGrHist* 255), and *P. Ox.* 2082, commonly attributed to Phlegon (*FGrHist* 257a). Photius (*Bibl.* cod. 97) preserves an excerpt from Phlegon (*FGrHist* 257 F 12). These fragments show that it was in the nature of the genre to begin each section of text with the ordinal number of the Olympiad in the regular series followed by the name of the victor in the stadion course. The text is then subdivided through the use of the numbers 1 through 4 to identify the years within the Olympiad. In the *Canons* of Eusebius the Olympiad numbers interrupt the *fila regnorum*; and the numerals of the *fila* mark off the four years of the quadrennium, making it unnecessary to inscribe the numbers 1 through 4 for each Olympiad. The names of the stadion victors are not given in the *Canons*, but they do appear in the *Chronographia*. It is therefore possible that the same work from which Eusebius transferred information dated by Olympiads to the *Canons* also included the list of Olympic victors excerpted in the *Chronographia*.

The Authorship of the Olympic Victor List

In the prefatory book of the *Chronicle*, where Eusebius collected the raw materials for the chronographic structure of the *Canons* he presents (89–103 Karst) a numbered list of the Olympic victors in the stadion course through the 249th Olympiad (A.D. 217). Such a list is essential in this collection of material, because Greek chronographic convention required the identification of an Olympiad by reference to the eponymous victor in the stadion course as well as by number. Eusebius' list appears to be an excerpt from a larger work. It includes a preface about the institution of the Olympic games, a few comments about the history of the festival (e.g., establishment of the Pancration in Olympiad 33), occasional synchronisms of fundamental chronographic importance (e.g., accession of Cyrus in Olympiad 55, beginning of the Peloponnesian War in Olympiad 87), and the names of the Roman emperors from Julius Caesar to Caracalla in the Olympiad of accession. The authority for this list is not specified in the Armenian text. A Greek version of the list (Cramer, *Anecd. Par.* 2, 141–53) came to the attention of Joseph Scaliger long before the discovery of the Armenian *Chronographia*. Scaliger recognized the list as a fragment of

Eusebius' lost *prior libellus*, whose erstwhile existence he had hypothesized. He further suggested that Eusebius had excerpted the Olympic victor list from the also-lost *Chronographiae* of Sextus Julius Africanus, a Christian chronographer whom Scaliger believed the fundamental source of Eusebius' own *Chronicle*.[15] This identification of the author of the Olympic victor list with Sextus Julius Africanus has since become dogma, and it is repeated without argument in standard works.[16] The identification is based on the fact that the Olympic list extends to the time of Africanus and no further. The list ends with the 249th Olympiad. Africanus is said to have closed his five books of *Chronographiae* with the year 5,723 since Creation. That year in the chronographic system of Africanus corresponds to A.D. 221 in our system and to the first year of the 250th Olympiad in Eratosthenes' system. The usual conclusion is that Africanus published his work in the Roman consular year corresponding to A.D. 221, before the celebration of that year's Olympic festival.[17]

The argument is based on a chronological coincidence that seems conclusive. The discovery of the Armenian text, however, makes the identification of the author of the Olympic victor list with Africanus problematical, although this fact has not been recognized. These last extant pages of the Armenian *Chronographia*, dealing with the fundamentals of Greek and Roman chronology, are difficult. The text nevertheless suggests the attribution of the list to an author more likely to have worked within the established genre of the Olympiad chronicle than was Africanus, with his system of years numbered from the era of creation (5,500 B.C.) and his eschatological perspective. Eusebius cites his authorities for the chronographic fundamentals, but he does not cite Africanus for this list or for any of the matter included in the prefatory volume on Greco-Roman chronology. It cannot be maintained that all of the material in the Greek portion of this first book came to Eusebius through Africanus and that Eusebius either suppressed that fact to prevent the magnitude of his own accomplishments from being diminished or felt it unnecessary to acknowledge a debt that should have been obvious to his readers.[18] Much of the material in this section Eusebius excerpted from Porphyry, who was a contemporary of his and wrote after Africanus did. The Olympic victor list with its preface about the institution of the festival follows immediately upon an excerpt from Porphyry. The Greek section ends with lists of the successor kingdoms excerpted from Porphyry. The intervening lists of Corinthian and Lacedaemonian kings, thalassocrats and Macedonian kings are excerpts from Diodorus but came to Eusebius through a chronological epitome that we have identified as the *Chronicle* of Porphyry. The unidentified Olympic victor list may well be part of the material that Eusebius excerpted from Porphyry. Such a hypothesis is supported by the appearance of a bibliographic footnote to the entire section that concludes with the name of Porphyry. In the Armenian text the note looks like a prescript to the Roman section. It is in fact, as Schwartz recognized, a subscript to that large portion of the *Chronographia* which deals with the pre-Roman secular history of the Greco-Oriental world.[19]

The text as it appears in Karst's German edition of the *Chronographia* (p. 125; cf. Petermann's Latin edition, 263–65) can be translated as follows:[20]

Having assembled this universal compendium from the following records, which are here listed in order—

Alexander Polyhistor;
Abydenus, who wrote histories of the Assyrians and the Medes;
Manetho's three books of Egyptian memorabilia;
Cephalion's nine books of the Muses;
Diodorus' library of 40 books, an epitome of history up to Gaius Caesar;
Cassius Longinus' 18 books, a compilation of 138 Olympiads;*
Phlegon, the freedman of Caesar, 14 books, an epitome of 229 Olympiads;
Castor's 6 books, an epitome from the time of Ninus to the 181st Olympiad;
Thallus' three books, a brief compendium from the fall of Troy to the 167th Olympiad;
Porphyry, our contemporary philosopher, an epitome from the fall of Troy to the reign of Claudius—

let us present the chronology of the Roman Empire, which first got its name in the seventh Olympiad, when Romulus founded the city of the Romans; both the city and the empire subject to it were named from him; before that time they are called sometimes Latins, sometimes Aborigines, with still other names at other times.

Eusebius here lists the main authorities whom he had cited previously for the chronologies of all ancient peoples except the

*CCXXVIII olompiades, *Petermann*; CXXVIII, *Aucher*.

Hebrews. His authorities for Hebrew history he summarizes elsewhere (34 Karst): the historical books of the Old Testament, Josephus, and Africanus. Eusebius does not actually cite Africanus in the Hebrew section except to chastise him for error (47–48 Karst), but he acknowledges in the bibliography for that section and in one of the chronological discussions (61 Karst) that it was through Africanus that he used material from Josephus. These are the only places in the entire prefatory book where Africanus is mentioned. His name does not appear in the bibliography for the Greco-Oriental section. Three names do appear of authors who are not actually cited in that section— Cassius Longinus, Phlegon, and Thallus. There are no extant fragments of Cassius Longinus. The citations of Thallus are not such as to permit an inference about the contents or format of his chronicle. A lengthy fragment of Phlegon (*FGrHist* 257 F 12), however, shows that he wrote an Olympiad chronicle that listed the names of the victors in the various games (not just the stadion victors) and epitomized the important historical events of each year of the tetrad. It is likely that Cassius Longinus and Thallus were also Olympiad chroniclers.

The names of Cassius Longinus, Phlegon, and Thallus are to be taken as a group and can have relevance, as Schwartz suggested, only as authorities for the Olympic victor list. Schwartz followed Scaliger in identifying the author of the list as Africanus and argued that Eusebius also took over the names of these authorities for the Olympiads from Africanus. Schwartz identified Cassius Longinus with the Cassius mentioned by Minucius Felix (21.4) in order to have an author earlier than Africanus.[21] Such an argument begs the question, for Schwartz assumed Africanus to be the author of the list. The discovery of the Armenian evidence challenges that assumption, and the earlier hypothesis should not be allowed to exercise an undue influence on the interpretation of the additional evidence. Eusebius does in another work (*P.E.* 10.10.4) give a quotation from Africanus that includes an Olympiad date on the authority of Diodorus, Thallus, Castor, Polybius, and Phlegon. That fragment does not lead to the conclusion that Africanus was an Olympiad chronicler or that Eusebius knew of Olympiad chroniclers only through Africanus. The date in question is the accession of Cyrus, synchronized with the 55th Olympiad. Africanus gave the date as a part of a discussion of Cyrus, the Liberator of Israel. The date of Cyrus' accession to the throne was pivotal to Africanus' chiliastic chronography, and it is only natural that he cited external authority for the validity of the date. He did not, however, follow the usual practice in Greek chronology of identifying the eponymous victor. Africanus gave an Olympiad date in the context of his discussion of sacred history and the passage does not support the hypothesis that Eusebius had his list of stadion victors through Africanus. The presence of the name of Cassius Longinus at the head of the group of Olympiad chroniclers listed in the bibliographic note suggests that we consider him as a possible authority for the list.

This Cassius Longinus is certainly the same as the influential scholar and rhetorician of the third century A.D. to whom the famous treatise *On the Sublime* used to be attributed. The *Suda* (3, p. 279 Adler) summarizes his career, stating that he was a philosopher, a polymath, and a critic, who was the teacher of Porphyry. He wrote a wide variety of works, some of which the *Suda* lists. The *Chronicle* is not included in that list, but the identification of Eusebius' Cassius Longinus with that of the *Suda* is none the less secure.[22] Photius (*Bibl.* cod. 265) dates his acme to the time of Claudian (268–70), while the *Suda* and Syncellus (721) differ only slightly in stating that he flourished in the time of Aurelian (270–75). The *Suda* adds that Aurelian had him executed for conspiring with the rebellious Zenobia of Palmyra.[23]

Cassius Longinus, the teacher of Eusebius' contemporary Porphyry, lived and wrote in the late third century. His Olympiad chronicle therefore cannot have been known to Eusebius through the *Chronographiae* of Africanus published some fifty years earlier. Africanus is not even mentioned in the bibliography of authorities for secular chronology. Cassius Longinus, however, is included in the list at the head of a group of Olympiad chroniclers who are not mentioned in the main body of the text. The only extract in Eusebius' section on Greek chronology for which the authority is not clearly stated either in the Armenian text or in the excerpts of Synchellus is the list of Olympic victors. That list is also the only extract to which the names of the Olympiad chroniclers can have any relevance. The list is preceded and followed by material excerpted from Porphyry. Eusebius' main authority for Greek regnal lists was Porphyry, and he was a student of Cassius Longinus. Both Longinus and Porphyry were philosophers. Both also wrote chronicles. Both are included in the bibliographic notice.

The evidence is circumstantial, but no less so than that on which the attribution to Africanus is made. It is a reasonable hypothesis that the list of Olympic victors derives from Cassius Longinus and was transmitted to Eusebius by Porphyry. A note to that effect may have preceded the preface to the list and been inadvertently omitted by a scribe because of the presence of Porphyry's name a few lines earlier. Cassius Longinus had himself probably used the chronicles of Phlegon and Thallus. Even if he did not follow them slavishly the debt was duly acknowledged, so that the presence of their names in the text derives from him. The preface about the institution of the festival is slightly different from that attributed to Phlegon (*FGrHist* 257 F 1). More significantly, it is also different from the one fact about the institution of the festival that can specifically be associated with the name of Africanus. Syncellus cites the third book of Africanus for the statement that the first Olympiad when Coroebus won in the stadion, was really the fourteenth celebration of the games.[24] The preface to Eusebius' list cites Aristodemus of Elis for the fact that the victory of Coroebus was the 28th from the establishment of the games by Iphitus. Variant opinions are also noted, which is not the case with Phlegon's introduction. The preface to Eusebius' list, then, was composed by Cassius or by Porphyry on the basis of more thorough research into the question than had been done by Phlegon or Africanus.

Eusebius' list of Olympic victors runs from the first to the 249th Olympiad. At its head, however, stands a title indicating that the list includes only 247 Olympiads: "The Greek Olympiads, from the first to the 247th, in which Antoninus son of Severus ruled over the Romans." The usual conclusion is that the author of the list began his work in 209 (Ol. 247), but did not finish until after 217 (Ol. 249), when he added the additional two names.[25] It is odd that the author would not in that case also have changed the heading of the list prior to its publication. There are other difficulties if Africanus was the source. The list includes the names of the Roman emperors in the Olympiads of their accession. A list composed just before the celebration of the 250th Olympiad in 221, when Africanus supposedly published his *Chronographiae*, should include Macrinus and Elagabalus in Olympiad 249. Eusebius' list does not include these names, and that omission is fully consistent with the title. It is a list both of Olympic victors and of Roman emperors. According to the title the list runs from the first Olympiad to the time of Antoninus Caracalla, son of Severus, who became emperor in Olympiad 247 (209–12). Caracalla acceded to the principate in 211 and became sole emperor in 212. He was murdered in the Roman year corresponding to 217 which the chronographers equated with the first year of the 249th Olympiad.[26] The author of the list included the name of Caracalla in the title and ended the list with the year 217, the 249th Olympiad, when Caracalla died. This terminus may have been dictated by political considerations in the turmoil of the third century. On the other hand, the author perhaps abandoned work on his chronicle when he reached the year 217. If the author was Cassius Longinus, it was his untimely death that brought the work to a close. The fact is indisputable, however, that this list ends in 217 with the death of Caracalla—not in 221, when Africanus published his *Chronographiae*.

The list of Olympiads and emperors ends with the second victory of Heliodorus, the 249th Olympiad. Scholars have concluded that Africanus drew up the list. The bibliographic note suggests that it derives through Porphyry from Cassius Longinus, Phlegon, and Thallus. According to Karst's text, however, Cassius Longinus' chronicle included only 138 Olympiads, Phlegon's 229, and Thallus' 167. Thus Longinus' work ended 111 Olympiads short of the extant list, and the hypothesis that he was its author seems impossible. As it happens, however, the issue is not that clear. There are serious textual difficulties with the numerals transmitted in this portion of the Armenian manuscript. Thallus is credited with 167 Olympiads in the Armenian text, but Syncellus (609) cites him as reporting an eclipse of the sun at the time of the crucifixion. That must be the eclipse of November 24, A.D. 29, which took place during the 202nd Olympiad.[27] The corruption in the number of Olympiads attributed to Thallus forced his name into a lower position in the bibliographic list than the name of Castor. Castor with his 181 Olympiads thus interrupts the list of those who were Olympiad chroniclers in the strict sense—Cassius Longinus, Phlegon, and Thallus. To attribute 181 Olympiads to Castor, however, is also wrong. His chronicle ended in the consulship of Piso and Messalla (*FGrHist* 250 F 5), the fourth year of the 179th Olympiad (61/60). The 138 Olympiads of Cassius Longinus is a modern corruption, a printing error in Karst's edition. Petermann's edition reads 228, Aucher's edition has 128. The correct reading of the Armenian text is 228.[28] But this number, like those for Castor and Thallus, may also be corrupt. Cassius Longinus appears first in a list that runs in descending order by the number of Olympiads included in the several chronicles. Thallus' number was corrupted early, and his name was accordingly entered after Castor's. Cassius Longinus is entered before Phlegon, who included 229 Olympiads. In the exemplar used for the extant Armenian text, Cassius Longinus must have been credited with a number of Olympiads greater than Phlegon's 229. Only so would his name stand at the head of the list. Cassius Longinus is credited with 18 books, compared with Phlegon's 14. The four additional books seem appropriate for the inclusion of the twenty additional Olympiads up to the 249th.

It is difficult to imagine that Eusebius, in collecting the data for the chronographic fundamentals of the first book, leafed through 18 books of an Olympiad chronicle in order to extract a list of stadion victors. As has already been suggested, the excerpt was probably made by Porphyry. His chronicle was not, however, an annalistic history organized by Olympiads, and Eusebius does not indicate that it contained more than one book. He cites the work last in the bibliographic notice as "Porphyry from the fall of Troy to the reign of Claudius." The emperor is Claudius Gothicus, whose short reign (268–70) was in the time of Longinus and Porphyry. Porphyry's chronicle is known only through the extracts in Eusebius.[29] It was a work similar to Eusebius' own first book, a collection of information about chronology.[30]

Porphyry's book covered the period from the fall of Troy to the emperor Claudius Gothicus. Eusebius cites the epochal intervals of Apollodorus from the fall of Troy to the first Olympiad from the *Historia Philosophica*. The *Chronicle* must therefore have covered this period in a different way. As a native of Tyre, Porphyry perhaps used Oriental regnal lists for the early period. It is therefore he who is responsible for the fact that Eusebius' Assyrian list, supposedly an excerpt from Castor, has been altered to make the fall of Troy synchronous with Teutamus (31 Karst).[31] The Median, Lydian, and Persian lists, which follow the Assyrian list in the Armenian version without specific citation of authority, thus also derive from the *Chronicle* of Porphyry. That is, Porphyry exhibited lists of the Assyrian, Median, Lydian, and Persian kings from the fall of Troy to Alexander's conquest of Persia. He then listed the successors of Alexander. Eusebius presents these lists of the successors with specific attribution to Porphyry (74–80, 109–24 Karst). All of this material Porphyry excerpted from Castor with some modifications. For the Greco-Roman world Porphyry excerpted from Cassius Longinus a list of Olympic victors from the first to the 249th and a list of Roman emperors from Caesar to Caracalla. He extended the list of emperors another 50 years to reach his own time, that of Claudius Gothicus. It does seem odd that he did not also extend the list of Olympic victors. That difficulty exists, however, whether it was Eusebius or Porphyry who made the excerpt and whether Cassius Longinus or Africanus was the source. Each successive Olympiad chronicler took over and extended his predecessor's list of victories and history of the festival—for example, Cassius Longinus from Phlegon, and Phlegon from Thallus. Porphyry, however, was not an Olympiad chronicler and neither, strictly speaking, was Eusebius. Porphyry's chronicle, like Eusebius' first book, presented chronographic excerpts from earlier authorities. For both, an extension of the list of emperors was all that was necessary to reach the contemporary period.[32]

Scaliger hypothesized on the basis of a near (not exact!) coincidence between the end of the list (217) and the completion of Africanus' *Chronographia* (221) that the extant list of Olympic victors was transmitted to Eusebius by Africanus. The Armenian text of Eusebius' chronographic excerpts suggests the equally viable alternative that Eusebius' list derives from Cassius Longinus, whose student Porphyry, one of Eusebius' principal authorities, excerpted the list from the eighteen books of Cassius' Olympiad chronicle. Decision between the two hypotheses depends on whether Africanus in fact composed a work from which such a list could have been excerpted. Since the two questions are closely related, the investigation also tests the hypothesis that Africanus was a major source of Eusebius for the Greek historical notices included in the *spatium historicum* of the *Canons*.

Sextus Julius Africanus and Chiliastic Chronography

The lost *Chronographiae* of Africanus we know primarily through the fragmentary citations of Eusebius and Syncellus. In addition, Photius (*Bibl.* cod. 34) gives a brief description of the work. Photius (ca. 850) says that Africanus began with the creation of the cosmos, following the Mosaic narrative; continued to the birth of Christ; and closed with a rapid survey of events from the birth of Christ to the time of the emperor Macrinus, encompassing 5,723 years in five books. Syncellus (609–14 Dindorf), in a long excerpt from that portion of the work dealing with the Passion, cites an interval of 5,531 years from the creation of Adam to the time of the Resurrection and 192 years from the Resurrection to the end of the work in the 250th Olympiad. These figures and the traditional 32 or 33 years of the Incarnation show that Africanus computed his era of creation by synchronizing the birth of Jesus with the cosmic year 5500.[33] This is a chronographic system that builds from the seven days of creation and from Daniel's (9:24) apocalyptic "seventy weeks of years" to produce an eschatological interpretation of the entire span of history as encompassing seven millennia. The first five thousand years embrace the biblical period from the creation of Adam to the end of the Babylonian captivity, the sixth millennium includes 500 years of preparation for the Christ and 500 years more of human history, while the seventh millennium would bring to pass the thousand years of the Kingdom of Heaven.

The contents of this work must be judged from the fragments that carry Africanus' name. Much of Gelzer's reconstruction rests on tenuous evidence.[34] He ascribes to Africanus much of the information contained in late-Byzantine sources that express dates by Africanus' system of years from Adam. Africanus' system of numbering the years from the creation of the Cosmos was widely used in Byzantine chronography, although the Kingdom of Heaven had not arrived on schedule. Information derived from other sources and dated by other standards was accommodated to Africanus' era. In particular, Annianus and Panodorus in their chronicles (Syncellus 62–63) adapted Africanus' scale of time, computing the difference between Eusebius' reckoning of early biblical chronology and that of Africanus. They transmitted to Syncellus and other authorities information that they found in the *Chronicle* of Eusebius dated by Olympiads and years from Abraham, but they expressed the dates in a chiliastic scale of years since Adam. To facilitate such conversions Annianus and Panodorus prepared a redaction of Eusebius' *Chronological Canons* with years of Abraham continuously numbered in a prominent column instead of entered by decades in the margin. From this redaction, both the extant Armenian text and the Byzantine excerpts derive.[35] Thus, these Byzantine dates do not derive from Africanus. Most of them in fact derive from Eusebius. His system of years from Abraham was converted to Africanus' system of years from Adam. The era is Africanus'; the chronology, Eusebius'.

Photius says that Africanus' work was extremely concise, but with nothing essential left out. Photius, who became the Patriarch of Constantinople in 858, means "nothing essential for salvation," since the extant fragments show sacred history always to be the focus. There is nothing in the fragments that cite his name to suggest that Africanus wrote a universal narrative of sufficient scope to encompass the details of Greco-Roman history or that he composed annalistic chronography such as to require notation and comment for each of the 5,723 years that had elapsed since the beginning of time. Eusebius objected strongly to any attempt to impose historical time on Paradise or to provide a precise chronology for the antediluvian period on which even the texts of Genesis did not agree (34–62 Karst). He describes Africanus' chronographic purposes and methods in an important passage of the *Praeparatio Euangelica* (10.10.1–2), which is a direct quotation from Africanus' third book:

> Until the Olympiads there is nothing precise in the stories of the Greeks. Before this time everything is confused and there is mutual agreement on nothing. The Olympiads provide precision in many respects, because the interval is not large and the Greeks kept a quadrennial list of them. Therefore I shall treat the period before the first Olympiad very lightly, selecting only the most noteworthy of the mythical tales. Afterwards, for events of especial interest, I shall synchronize Hebrew to Greek, treating of the Hebrews in detail (ἐξιστορῶν μέν), while touching upon the Greeks (ἐφαπτόμενος δέ), and I shall fit them to one another in the following fashion. Taking one Hebrew event of the same time as an event included in the history of the Greeks, bearing both in mind, I shall by a process of selection and juxtaposition (ἀφαιρῶν τε καὶ προστιθείς) make clear what event, Greek, Persian, or other, was synchronous with the Hebrew event and so perhaps achieve my purpose.

This passage suggests that Africanus juxtaposed Greek Olympiad dates, when he reached that period, with his scale of biblical chronology beginning with Adam. The passage also shows that Africanus concentrated on Hebrew history and selected only such events of secular history as happened to be approximately synchronous with the biblical events on which he was focusing. Africanus says that he will take hold first of a Hebrew action, then look for a Greek or Persian event with which to synchronize it. His own description of his purposes and method is not such as to suggest that he would in the course of his narrative take note of the celebration of every Olympiad, give the name of the stadion victor, and proceed to report what events of Greek history could be assigned to those four years. For Africanus, sacred history is the main subject, and the coming of the Kingdom of Heaven in the seventh millennium of human history is the true meaning and purpose of chronological research. Greek history is only incidental to the main subject and, for most of its course, entirely irrelevant to chiliastic chronography.

Africanus wished to make clear to a Greek-speaking world the synchronisms between important epochs of sacred history and contemporaneous events in the Greek world. He needed also to provide the reader a means of converting his scale of years from the Creation to established contemporary standards. Hence he stated that the first Olympiad was celebrated in the first year of king Ahaz of Judah (Syncellus 371) and that the 5,723rd year from Adam, with which his work closed, corresponded to the consulship of Gratus Sabinianus and Vitellius Seleucus (725 years after the expulsion of the kings and the beginning of the annual consulship), to the archonship of Philenus (903 years since Creon), and to the year of the 250th Olympiad (Syncellus 400). Africanus may have adduced similarly complete synchronisms elsewhere. He clearly used the Greek and Oriental king lists drawn up by Castor, among others, and the lists of archons, consuls, and Olympiads. In the very early portion of the work, when stating that so-and-so was patriarch, judge, or king of Israel for so many years, he also stated who was king and for how long at that time elsewhere in the world. Eusebius quotes Africanus as saying, for example, that when Joatham was king in Jerusalem, Aeschylus was archon for 23 years in Athens (*Canons*, 86[k] Helm).

Africanus used these lists for synchronistic statements, but it does not follow that he reproduced them in their entirety in a form similar either to Eusebius' collection of lists in the *Chronographia* or to the tabular display of the *Chronological Canons*. Africanus wished to show who of the Greeks was synchronous with the famous persons of the Bible. He did not, however, write Greek history, much less Greek chronography, for its own sake or with the detail of Eusebius' annual lists and *spatium historicum*. Indeed, by the time of the first Olympiad the biblical story was coming to a close. Only a few events remained: the fall of Israel to Assyria, the conquest of Jerusalem by Nebuchadnezzar, the liberation effected by Cyrus, the rebuilding of the temple in the time of Darius, and the refortification of the city during the reign of Artaxerxes. Thus Africanus' treatment of the period from the middle of the eighth century to the end of the fifth dealt more with Assyrian, Median, Babylonian, and Persian synchronisms than with the largely irrelevant details of the developing Greek world.

The five books of Africanus' *Chronographiae* are lost beyond reconstruction, and this is not the place to essay an exhaustive survey and synthesis of the debris.[36] Judgment on whether or not Africanus had composed the kind of work from which Eusebius could have excerpted either the Olympic victor lists or a significant number of the Greek historical notices included in the *spatium historicum* depends on the interpretation of a very small body of evidence. The influence of Africanus on late Byzantine writers is undeniable. Some of these authors have historical notices that they either attribute to Africanus or date by reference to what looks like Africanus' biblical chronology for the kings of Israel, Judah, and Persia. Some of these notices are also strikingly similar to the notices of Eusebius' *Canons* for archaic Greek history. The problem is that these authors also used the *Chronicle* of Eusebius through one medium or another. Thus the notices of Eusebius and the regnal years he associated with them could be combined with Africanus' biblical chronology in such a way as to produce dates in agreement with neither authority.

Largely on the basis of this ambivalent Byzantine material, Scaliger characterized Eusebius as the excerptor of Africanus.[37] Heinrich Gelzer, *Sextus Julius Africanus und die byzantinische Chronographie* (Leipzig 1880, 1898), reexamined the evidence in detail. Gelzer's study as a whole shows that Africanus' influence on Eusebius was marginal. In his attempt to reconstruct the fourth book of Africanus, however, Gelzer attributed to Africanus not only the Olympic victor list but also a collection of late material sufficiently large as to suggest that Africanus was Eusebius' main source for the historical entries that appear in the

Canons relevant to Greece in the archaic and early classical periods. This impression of Eusebius' overwhelming debt to his predecessor in Christian chronography is widely shared. Rudolf Helm, for example, whose appreciation of the singularity of Eusebius' work was strong, published a study of Eusebius' sources in the *spatium historicum* that concentrates on Africanus. Helm warns against attributing too much of the Byzantine material to Africanus. He confines himself almost exclusively to the information from Josephus which Eusebius found in the text of Africanus for the history of Palestine in the Hellenistic period. The article nevertheless concludes with a generalization so broad as to strengthen (unintentionally, no doubt) the general impression that the lost contents of Africanus' work are to be found throughout Eusebius' *spatium historicum*:

> It seems therefore that Eusebius in the historical notices which he entered alongside his years followed very closely in the footsteps of Africanus. This fact will hardly surprise us. For it was a novel and until that time unheard of thing that one should while displaying a long series of years also note for individual years what things seemed worthy of mention in the histories of the several nations. That he collected material from someone else and turned it to his own use in a new form is therefore no matter for scorn.[38]

Eusebius' tabular display of universal history and chronology was certainly no mean accomplishment. There can be no doubt that most of the material included was excerpted from elsewhere and that Eusebius' own contribution was primarily the synchronistic, annalistic format. Eusebius was thoroughly familiar with the work of Africanus. He cited some of his synchronisms for the mythical and transitional periods.[39] He used Africanus as a principal source for the history of Palestine and Syria in the Hellenistic period.[40] Nevertheless, the view that Africanus was among the main authorities for Greek historical notices of the archaic and classical periods cannot be substantiated. The evidence that Africanus in his fourth book included precise dates for a significant number of specific persons or events in Greek history is slight and derives from sources that excerpted both Africanus and Eusebius. The fact that Africanus' era of creation was popular among Byzantine writers is irrelevant. Judgement on this issue in fact depends on just two obscure passages, and we must therefore abandon generalizations and focus attention on them. Both cite Africanus by name, and both have entries that parallel those of Eusebius' *Canons*.

The chronicle preserved in a Paris manuscript of the eighth century and known since the time of Scaliger as the *Excerpta Latina Barbara* contains on folio 31 the following:[41]

Post haec et Africanus dinumerans ipsam prophe
tiam septem ebdomadarum et septuagesimum
numerum extendens ad XRI aduentum. Post
Artaxerxem autem regnauit Xerxes filius eius
menses ·V· et occisus est. Et post hunc regnauit
Ogdianus menses ·VII· Fiunt simul anni V milia XXXVII.
Post istos regnauit Darius iuuenis qui uocatur
Memoratus annos XVIIII· Fiunt anni V milia LVI·
Fuit autem sub istos in Hierusalem princeps sacerdotum
Joachim· filosofi autem cognoscebantur illi circa agoram.
Post Darium autem regnauit filius eius Artar
xerxis secundus qui uocatur Memoratus
annos XLII· Fiunt simul anni V milia XCVIII· Fuit au
tem sub istum princeps sacerdotum in Hierusa
lem Heliasibus. Filosofi autem cognosceban
tur temporibus Artaxerxis· Sofoclus
et Traclitus et Anaxagoras et Hirodotus
et Melissus
et Euripidus
canto conpositor
et Protagorus
et Socrator
    ritor
et Fideas statu
as conpositor
et Theetitus
artifex.
et Dimocritus
Abderitus
et Ippocratis
medicus
et Thucudidus ritor. et Empedocles et Gor
gias et Zinon et Parmenidus et Socratus Athi
neus et Periclus et Eupolus et Aristofanus
architector· Hii omnes cognoscebantur. unde
et Africanus sub Artaxerxe rege dinumerat
filosofos. Post Artaxerxem autem Memo
ratum regnauit filius eius Ochus in Babylonia
annos XXI· Fiunt simul anni V milia CXVIIII· Fuit
autem in Hierusalem princeps sacerdotum Jodae.

The persons listed in this passage as flourishing in the time of Artaxerxes appear in the same order in the *spatium historicum* of Eusebius, all except the first (Sophocles) dated to years within the reign of Artaxerxes. Gelzer attributed the list to Africanus and concluded that Eusebius excerpted from Africanus the corresponding entries, including the celebrated notice about Herodotus' declamation of his books before the Athenian boule (113ᶜ Helm).⁴² On the contrary, the author of this strange chronicle inserted into an excerpt from Africanus about the succession of the Persian kings some more detailed material that he found in Eusebius. All that Africanus needed to have said was that in the time of Artaxerxes the philosophers of the agora flourished. The author of the *Excerpta* turned to Eusebius for detailed proof of the synchronism. He listed some of the Greek authors whom he found in Eusebius on those pages of the *Canons* which also included the regnal years of Artaxerxes. The author concludes "all of these people were flourishing and that is why Africanus synchronizes the philosophers with king Artaxerxes."⁴³

The other set of notices that Gelzer believed common to both Eusebius and Africanus appears in Syncellus (489 Dindorf). The passage is contained within one of the collections of miscellaneous notices that Syncellus exhibits under the rubric Σποράδην. This particular collection appears in that section of the work which deals with the years 5082 to 5170 of the cosmos (419–331 B.C.). Only the portion that Gelzer attributed to Africanus is reproduced here.⁴⁴

(488.19)   Σποράδην
Πλάτων πρὸς Σωκράτην ἐφοίτα.
Σιμίας καὶ Κέβης καὶ οἱ λοιποὶ Σωκρατικοί.
(489.1)   Ἀφρικανοῦ
Ὀλυμπιὰς πζ΄.
Ὁ Πελοποννησίων καὶ Ἀθηναίων πόλεμος ἑπτακαιεικοσαετής,
ὃν Θουκυδίδης συνέγραψε, δι᾽ Ἀσπασίας πόρνας δύο καὶ
στήλας κατὰ Μεγαρέων ἀστυγειτόνων Ἀθηναίοις συνέστη.
Ὀλυμπιὰς πη΄./
Βακχυλίδης μελοποιὸς ἐγνωρίζετο./
Ἀθηναίους ἐπίεσεν ὁ λιμός./ Σωκράτης φιλόσοφος
καθαρτικὸς ἤνθει./ Εὔπολις καὶ Ἀριστοφάνης κωμικοί,
Σοφοκλῆς τε ὁ τραγῳδοποιὸς ἐγνωρίζετο./ Γοργίας καὶ
Ἱππίας καὶ Πρόδικος, ὡς δέ τινες, καὶ Ζήνων καὶ
Παρμενίδης κατὰ τούτους ἤκμαζον.

(489.14) Πῦρ ἐκ τῆς Αἴτνης ἐν τοῖς κατὰ Σικελίαν τόποις ἐρράγη.

There follow thirty-two more such entries in this collection of miscellany. All but seven of them have a counterpart in the *Canons* of Eusebius. The first two notices in the collection, which precede the name of Africanus, do not appear in Eusebius. Of those which Gelzer attributed to Africanus, all but the first (Peloponnesian War with mention of Aspasia and the Megarian Decree) have an exact counterpart in Eusebius (114[h], 115[a], 114[e], 114[b], and 115[d], 114[d], 115[e] Helm).

Syncellus frequently cites both Africanus and Eusebius, and it is clear that he excerpted from both or used a source that had already done so. Most of the miscellaneous notices in the rest of this passage and in other lists of Σποράδην elsewhere in the work are excerpts from Eusebius. The one thing unusual about this particular collection is the appearance of Olympiad numbers. The Olympiad numbers 87 and 88 bracket a notice that has no direct parallel in Eusebius, and the name of Africanus precedes that set. We should conclude that the unusual entry, not paralleled in Eusebius and not of the ordinary Σποράδην type, is the one that comes from Africanus, while the rest derive from the *Canons* of Eusebius. The material from Africanus accordingly includes notation of Olympiad 87 (432/31), summary discussion of the outbreak of the Peloponnesian War closing with notation of the next Olympiad (OL 88, 428/27).[45] The notices that follow the citation of Olympiad 88 (Bacchylides, the plague, Socrates) appear in Eusebius at Olympiads 86 and 87, not Olympiad 88. This fact too suggests that there is a change of source at Syncellus 489.7.

This fragment of Africanus with its Olympiad dates and its annalistic appearance is nevertheless the one fragment that bears most directly on the crucial question of whether Africanus included in his *Chronographiae* an annalistic Olympiad chronicle of Greek history that might have been Eusebius' source for the list of stadion victors and for the notices of the *Canons*. Africanus was interested, on the present hypothesis, primarily in the chiliastic chronology of sacred history. He dealt with the Greeks only incidentally for the purpose of making explicit the synchronisms between important events of sacred history and contemporary happenings in the secular world. This fragment citing Olympiads and discussing briefly the outbreak, length, and causes of the Peloponnesian War seems to constitute a decisive counterexample. That appearance is superficial. The fragment can be understood in the context of sacred history and by reference to the succession of Persian kings whose regnal years provided the backbone of sacred chronology for this period.

The appearance of Olympiad dates in the fragment is not in itself particularly significant. Dating by reference to Olympiads was a virtually universal practice among Greek historians and chronographers by the time of Africanus. It was the most widely understood chronological reference, and it would be surprising if Africanus had not used such dates in order to make his scale of years from Adam understandable to his readers. A lengthy excerpt from Africanus shows that he did use Olympiad dates and other secular standards in conjunction with years from Adam for dating his narrative of sacred history. The passage appears in Syncellus, 581–84, where he cites Africanus for the story of how Herod the Great, in the midst of the chaos generated by Octavius' war with Antony and Cleopatra, gained for himself the throne of the client kingdom of Judea. The story is not told year by year, but Africanus inserts into the narrative at what he considers the appropriate places the statements that the 185th (40/39) and 186th (36/35) Olympiads were celebrated. Toward the end of the passage there is a chronological summary stating that the fall of Alexandria and death of Cleopatra happened in the 11th year of the Roman monarchy, the fourth year of the 187th Olympiad (29/28) and the 5,472nd year since Adam. The section closes with the statement that the 188th Olympiad (28/27) was celebrated after the fall of Alexandria, a summary of the colonizing activity of Herod, and a confused comment to the effect that regular bissextile leap-years were finally established beginning with the 189th Olympiad (24/23), the 24th year of the Caesarean era in Antioch.

Syncellus 581–84 shows that Africanus did use Olympiad dates in dealing with the history of Palestine, but that he did not organize his narrative within the framework of a strict annalistic format. Although he dated events by reference to Olympiads as well as to regnal years and years from Adam, he did not follow the practice customary among Greek Olympiad chroniclers of identifying the Olympiad by reference to the name of the stadion victor as well as the ordinal number. The outward appearance of the excerpt at Syncellus 489, which looks like a fragment of an Olympiad chronicle, is deceptive. The tabular appearance arises from the fact that Syncellus incorporated the excerpt in one of his itemized lists of miscellany. The content of the fragment, although of Greek reference, can be understood as an excerpt from a narrative dealing primarily with the chronology of sacred history. Africanus wished to make clear what synchronisms obtained among the Greeks, Persians, and Hebrews. The outbreak of the Peloponnesian War was one of the epochs of Greek chronographic reckoning established by Eratosthenes.[46] It is therefore not surprising that Africanus included it. Even in this case, however, it is likely that Africanus mentioned the great war only in the context of Hebrew history. He adduced this well-known Greek epoch in synchronism with epochal events that took place in the Holy Land during the reign of Artaxerxes.

The refortification of Jerusalem was accomplished by Nehemiah through the benevolence of Artaxerxes. The event was pivotal for Africanus' interpretation of the seventy hebdomads mentioned in the vision of Daniel (9:24).[47] According to the chronicler whose account of this period became canonical, Nehemiah began the work in the twentieth year of Artaxerxes and brought it to completion in the thirty-second year of Artaxerxes (Nehemiah 2:1, 5:14). He then returned to the court of Artaxerxes for an unspecified period of time before obtaining permission once again to try to settle the affairs of the holy city (Nehemiah 7:2, 13:6). Africanus synchronized the beginning of Nehemiah's work in the twentieth year of Artaxerxes with the fourth year of the 83rd Olympiad (445/44).[48] The completion of the work twelve years later accordingly fell in the fourth year of the 86th Olympiad (433/32).[49] It was therefore in Olympiad 87 (432/31) that Nehemiah returned to the court of the king. It is at this point in the narrative that the excerpt that Syncellus included in the list of p. 489 appeared. A likely reconstruction of the narrative is as follows:

> After twelve years as governor Nehemiah completed the rebuilding of the walls. It was the 32nd year of King Artaxerxes, the fourth year of the 86th Olympiad, and the 5,070th year since Adam. Nehemiah returned to the court of the king. It was the 87th Olympiad. In Greece the twenty-seven-year war of the Peloponnesians and Athenians, which Thucydides wrote about, broke out because of the two harlots of Aspasia and the decrees issued against the Athenians' neighbors the Megarians. It was the 88th Olympiad. Nehemiah returned to Jerusalem to purify the city. Artaxerxes died after 40 years of

rule in the fourth year of the 88th Olympiad, which was the 5,078th year since Adam.

What is known about Africanus' *Chronographiae* and what fragments can with certainty be attributed to that work suggest that Africanus did not chronicle Greek history with sufficient detail or precision to have been a major source of Eusebius for the notices of the archaic and classical periods. Africanus adduced a Greek synchronism for each important person or event in Hebrew history that he discussed. Eusebius treated his predecessor with due respect and included many of these synchronisms. Thus, for example, Africanus synchronized Homer and Hesiod with Solomon.[50] At the year corresponding to Abraham 1000, the 20th year of Solomon, Eusebius entered: *Quidam Homerum et Hesiodum his temporibus fuisse aiunt* (71[b] Helm). The number of such notices that can be connected with a synchronism of Africanus is small.

Eusebius' Main Source—An Unidentified Olympiad Chronicler (Cassius Longinus?)

The attribution to Africanus of Eusebius' list of Olympic victors must be abandoned. Africanus did not write a work to which such a list would have been appropriate. The Olympiad chronicler Cassius Longinus is therefore a better candidate. We must also eliminate Africanus as a principal source for the Greek historical notices of the *spatium historicum*. A few notices can be connected with the Greco-Hebrew synchronisms of Africanus. Some can plausibly be ascribed to Eusebius' main authorities for the chronographic fundamentals—Castor and Porphyry. None of these sources can be identified as Eusebius' main authority for the notices of the archaic period. The organization of the *Chronicle* and the difficulties involved in its composition suggest that the main source was an Olympiad chronicle that made the information available in a concise form easily transferred to the *spatium historicum* of the *Canons*.

Eusebius' source may have been the same from which the list of stadion victors was excerpted—the Olympiad chronicle of Cassius Longinus in eighteen books. The Olympic victor list was perhaps an excerpt transmitted to Eusebius by Porphyry. That is, for the complete list Eusebius was not using the chronicle of

Cassius Longinus at first hand. He did, however, use some such Olympiad chronicle directly for the notices of the *spatium historicum*. It does not seem likely that Eusebius combed through all eighteen books to compile the list. He may have found the list already excerpted for him in the *Chronicle* of Porphyry. Nevertheless, such works tended to be extremely concise for the earliest periods, covering vast intervals in a single book and becoming gradually more detailed as the Olympiad chronicler reached more recent times. Eusebius may very well, therefore, have found the first book or two of Cassius Longinus of sufficiently large scope and small size to be a convenient source from which to make excerpts. Unfortunately, the identification cannot quite be made final. While it seems probable that the same Olympiad chronicle, that of Cassius Longinus, underlies the Olympic victor list indirectly and the Greek historical notices directly, the immediate source will henceforth be identified only as "Eusebius' Olympiad chronicler."

The result of all this verbiage may seem small. We have still the same Olympic victor list with all its problems, still the same confused *spatium historicum*. The conclusion is nevertheless well worth the tortuous argument and the necessary digressions into obscurity. For Eusebius is now placed solidly within the Greek chronographic tradition and so too is the extant Olympic victor list. It is on that tradition, rather than the aberrant Africanus, that attention must focus. If the temptation to identify Eusebius' immediate source with Cassius Longinus must be resisted, it is nevertheless clear that much of the information included in the *Canons* derives through the genre of the Olympiad chronicle from the best traditions of Alexandrian scholarship. In fact, the majority of Eusebius' notices relevant to the history of the Greek world in the archaic and classical periods reflect the influence of Apollodorus. To Apollodorus we must therefore return, focusing now not on his own chronological methods but on the characteristics of the late tradition that transmitted the Apollodoran vulgate—the tradition to which Eusebius' Olympiad chronicler belonged.

Apollodorus adopted the chronographic system of Eratosthenes, converting Olympiad dates, for a combination of patriotic and metrical reasons, to Athenian archon dates. The influence of the Eratosthenic chronology and the catholic embrace of Apollodorus' scholarly interests made his *Chronicle* a standard work of reference superseding all earlier efforts. Ironically enough, Apollodorus' synthesis of chronological information was so good that it even superseded itself. Prose excerpts of the work were made for a variety of purposes. The Olympiad system of Eratosthenes, which had become an internationally recognized standard, at least for literary purposes, was reimposed on the archon dates of the original *Chronicle* of Apollodorus. Chronological handbooks based on Apollodorus circulated widely, and it is therefore by no means surprising to find his influence strong in the *Chronicle* of Eusebius.

The *Chronicle* of Apollodorus represented the culmination of generations of chronological tradition. His dates, together with the chronographic system of Eratosthenes in which they were embedded, quickly became standard in literature and traditional in the popular vulgate. Epitomes of Apollodorus provided the chronological framework for most subsequent works of history and biography, as well as for those who wrote chronicles in the strict sense. Diodorus, for example, combined his narrative sources with a chronological source of unknown authorship which transmitted to him the Athenian archon list as well as the dates for persons and events established by Eratosthenes and Apollodorus. Diogenes Laertius reported the Apollodoran dates in his *Lives* of the philosophers. He used a chronological handbook that was circulating under the name of Apollodorus and that he frequently cites as Ἀπολλόδωρος ἐν τοῖς Χρονικοῖς. This version of Apollodorus expressed the dates in the Olympiad system, specifying the precise year within the quadrennium. Other Apollodoran dates came to Diogenes through Sosicrates of Rhodes, a contemporary of Apollodorus who adopted the Apollodoran acmes for persons included in his *Successions of the Philosophers*. Sosicrates expressed the dates both in the Olympiad system and by naming the Athenian archon. Yet a third source transmitted Apollodoran dates to Diogenes, without, however, citing the authority and expressing the dates only with an Olympiad number.[51] This third source is the one most nearly akin to the sources of Eusebius' Olympiad chronicler.

Later chronographers like Castor of Rhodes and Dionysius of Halicarnassus mounted their own work on the Apollodoran system. Through such intermediaries the Apollodoran dates found their way into the works of Clement, Tatian, and other Christian apologists. Porphyry's *Historia Philosophica* transmitted the chronology of Apollodorus not only to Eusebius but also, through a Syriac translation, to later Arabic sources. The influence of Apollodorus was strong among Latin writers, too. The three-volume world chronicle of Cornelius Nepos included Apollodoran dates expressed both in Olympiads and in years *ab Vrbe condita*. Cicero's friend T. Pomponius Atticus consulted a version of Apollodorus in drawing up his *Liber Annalis*. Through Nepos and Atticus the Apollodoran dates were transmitted to Cicero, Pliny the Elder, Gellius, and Solinus.[52]

Although the system of Eratosthenes and Apollodorus was standard and their influence on the later sources is unmistakable, Greek chronographic tradition did not thereby become uniform. The work of earlier authors remained in existence to be consulted in one form or another by antiquarians like Plutarch. Variant traditions about important and controversial dates were transmitted in the chronological handbooks that late authors had at their disposal. Clement of Alexandria, for example (*Strom.* 1.139), reports the several dates for the fall of Troy and the return of the Heraclids attributed to Phainias, Ephorus, Timaeus, Clitarchus, and Duris, as well as Eratosthenes. In discussing the relative chronology of Moses and Homer, Tatian (*ad Graecos* 31) cites for the date of Homer the variant opinions of Crates, Eratosthenes, Aristarchus, Philochorus, and Apollodorus. Undated synchronisms also continued to circulate. In the same passage Tatian reports synchronisms between Homer and Archilochus and between Archilochus and Gyges.

The chronographic system of Eratosthenes and the literary chronology of Apollodorus became a part of that vast store of tradition which Greek chronography at every stage of its development could excerpt, manipulate, and systematize. Writers like Clement and Tatian sometimes delighted in parading their authorities. In general, however, neither citation of sources nor discussion of chronological difficulties was a characteristic feature of the encyclopedic literature of the period. The authors of chronological and biographical handbooks were interested rather in distilling as much information as they could in the smallest possible vessel. The chronographic system of Eratosthenes was the standard of reference, but with it could be combined fragments of variant traditions transmitted apart from the chronological system that made them intelligible. The acme dates of Apollodorus constituted the biographical vulgate, but they too could be combined with dates derived by a different methodology or with vague synchronisms that belonged to no consistent chronological scheme at all. Tatian's discussion of the date of Homer is again instructive. He regards as standard the date of Eratosthenes and Apollodorus for the fall of Troy, about 400 years before the first Olympiad. With the Homer-Archilochus synchronism, however, he combines dates that are independent both of Eratosthenes and of each other. He states that Archilochus flourished in the 23rd Olympiad at the time of Gyges, about 500 years after the Trojan War. The interval of 500 years after Troy is not a date for Archilochus or for Gyges, but Theopompus' opinion about the relative dates of Troy and Homer (*FGrHist* 115 F 205). What absolute date, if any, Theopompus used for the Trojan War is unknown. Tatian's date in Olympiad 23 (688/87) is 500 years (wrongly counted) after the Eratosthenic date for Troy, an adaptation of Theopompus' interval to the standard.[53] The Gyges-Archilochus synchronism was proverbial, and it did not necessarily carry any absolute date.

Those elements of the Apollodoran chronology which can be identified in the pages of Eusebius' *Canons* had passed through many hands by the time they reached the Olympiad chronicler who was Eusebius' major source for the notices of the *spatium historicum*. At every stage of transmission there was opportunity for the inevitable scribal errors and interpretative confusions to corrupt the tradition. The Apollodoran tradition that reached this late author was not only corrupt, but it was also often contaminated almost beyond recognition. The *Chronicle* of Apollodorus had early been epitomized; and only the strictly chronological information, with dates converted to Olympiads, was being transmitted. Since there was no continuous narrative text in a chronological epitome, it was easy to combine in a single encyclopedic work of reference the dates of Apollodorus, variant opinions of other chronographers, and the proverbial synchronisms of the vulgate. Passages like Clement's discussion of the interval between the return of the Heraclids and the campaigns of Alexander and Tatian's discussion of the date of Homer suggest that such handbooks were based on Eratosthenes and Apollodorus but also contained a mass of data from other traditions. Olympiad chroniclers like Eusebius' source made a representative selection and transmitted only the date, not the authority. In the process of selection and transmission, Apollodorus' chronology was combined not only with independent traditions but also with other versions of Apollodorus that might themselves be corrupt or contaminated. Such is the case, for example, with Diogenes' dates for Thales. Diogenes (1.37–

38) cites the *Chronicle* of Apollodorus for the date of Thales' birth in the first year of the 35th Olympiad (640/39). He says that Thales died at the age of 78 in the 58th Olympiad (548/45), but that Sosicrates reports his age to have been 90. The 78-year life span is computed on the basis of the Apollodoran acme for Thales in 585/84. But the birth date had been corrupted from Olympiad 39 to Olympiad 35. Sosicrates therefore recomputed the life span.[54] Eusebius himself combines different versions of the Apollodoran system. His Olympiad chronicler worked within the Apollodoran tradition. Porphyry's *Historia Philosophica* also transmitted the dates of Apollodorus, and Castor's system was based on Eratosthenes and Apollodorus.

A few examples will suffice to show what kinds of error and contamination were typical of the information transmitted by Eusebius' major source. Even in those notices which are clearly of Apollodoran origin, Eusebius preserves a tradition full of confusion. The most frequent error is the report of a person's *floruit* at a date to which Apollodorus had assigned the birth. This confusion occurs in Eusebius' notices for Thales (96^b Helm), Simonides (102^h), Diagoras (110^b), and Anaxagoras (107^e). The error is a common one in the late sources and has its origin in the use of the ambiguous γέγονε. The word can be taken in the sense both of ἦν (*floruit*) and ἐγεννήθη (*natus est*). A similar error is the occasional substitution of *floruit* at a date that originally referred to the death of a person. This curious exchange appears in one of the notices for Bacchylides (114^h). Apollodorus synchronized the birth of Democritus with the acme of Anaxagoras in 460/59. Eusebius enters the *floruit* of both in the Olympiad of Anaxagoras' birth and adds Hellanicus and Heraclitus to the synchronism (107^e). He notes the *floruit* of Xenophanes at Apollodorus' date for the birth of Simonides (103^d), while the *floruit* of Simonides appears at the Apollodoran date for the acme of Xenophanes (103^p).[55]

There is evidence also that Apollodorus' dates were combined with the dates and synchronisms of other traditions. Eusebius records three dates for Lycurgus (79^c, 83^d, 84^f). The first is the epochal date of Eratosthenes and Apollodorus. The second derives from an authority who combined the Apollodoran epoch with a version of the Assyrian king lists. The third entry, which Eusebius attributes to Apollodorus, derives from the tradition that associated Lycurgus with Iphitus in the official establishment of the Olympic festival. By the time they reached Eusebius the three dates had been combined in such a way as to give the appearance of a single tradition according to which Lycurgus' life and political activity extended over a very long period of time. The first notice records his *floruit* in 883/82, the second dates his formulation of laws to 820/19, and the third notes the completion of his legislation in 796/95.[56] Eusebius combines with Apollodorus' date for the end of the first Messenian War (89¹) the date of Sosibius for its beginning (89ᶜ). Eusebius records Apollodorus' date for the acme of Archilochus in 664 (94ᵉ). He also knew Tatian's date for Archilochus in Olympiad 23 (688/85). But he does not enter Archilochus in that Olympiad. Hipponax appears instead, dated much too early through false synchronism with Archilochus (93ᵉ).[57]

Eusebius' entries in Olympiad 42 (612/19) are particularly interesting. Here he notes the *floruit* both of Alcman and of Stesichorus (98ᵈ,ᵉ). Apollodorus synchronized the birth of Stesichorus with the death of Alcman in one of the years of Olympiad 37 (632/29). Eusebius preserves the Alcman-Stesichorus synchronism, but he substitutes *floruit* for the death of the first and the birth of the second. He places the synchronism in Olympiad 42 instead of Olympiad 37. Olympiad 42 was the Apollodoran acme of Pittacus, with whom both Sappho and Stesichorus were sometimes synchronized. Eusebius' source combined the Alcman-Stesichorus synchronism of Apollodorus with the Sappho-Stesichorus synchronism of another tradition, which had itself been combined with the Apollodoran acme of Pittacus. The notices in Olympiad 42 show the influence of the Apollodoran chronology, but they do not actually preserve Apollodorus' date for either of the persons mentioned.[58]

The examples could be multiplied, but the detailed treatment of the combination of traditions that produced Eusebius' dates belongs to the commentary on the individual entries. The maze of error, contamination, and false synchronism that Eusebius transmitted shows that the original *Chronicle* was no less a *tumultuarium opus*, to use Jerome's phrase (p. 2 Helm), than the translations of it that the extant manuscripts preserve. Some of Eusebius' notices are excerpts from his main chronographic authorities for Greek history, Castor and Porphyry. Others attest to the Greco-Hebrew synchronisms of Africanus, and a few derive from the chronological discussions that Eusebius read in the works of Clement and Tatian. Both Castor and Porphyry based their work on the Alexandrian standard of Eratosthenes and Apollodorus. Whatever changes they introduced had a definite chronographic or historical purpose. Eusebius' main source, however, was a chronological compendium whose only purpose was encyclopedic brevity. Clement, Tatian, and Africanus found their information about ancient Greek chronology in similar handbooks. In Eusebius' case the encyclopedic compendium took the form of an Olympiad chronicle, which epitomized the important persons and events assigned to a given Olympiad with little or no mention of the reasons or authorities for the date. The chronicle had a preface summarizing the chief events of the period from the fall of Troy to the first Olympiad, with the dates expressed as intervals from one epoch or the other. These late chronological handbooks were ultimately descended from one or more of the epitomes of the *Chronicle* of Apollodorus and therefore based on the chronographic system of Eratosthenes. Four hundred years separated the Alexandrian tradition from Eusebius' immediate source. During these centuries of transmission the encyclopedic distillers of knowledge had attempted to adapt the entire tradition to the Apollodoran standard. The chronographic system of Eratosthenes and the historical chronology of Apollodorus were gradually combined with the dates of other traditions and with the unsystematic synchronisms of popular opinion. The result was an indiscriminate mix such as that transmitted by Eusebius.

Apollodorus is best attested in fragments of his chronology for famous persons. Eusebius' biographical dates thus permit inferences to be made about the manner in which the Apollodoran chronology was transmitted to Eusebius' source. What can be said about the Apollodoran influence on Eusebius' biographical dates is applicable by extension to his Greek chronology in general. Apollodorus wrote a universal chronicle. Most of the extant named fragments derive from epitomes made for biographical purposes. But Ps. Scymnus, *Orb. descr.* 16, preserves a kind of table of contents for the original *Chronicle* of Apollodorus (*FGrHist* 244 T 2). According to this author it contained dates for conquests, military expeditions, migrations of peoples, barbarian incursions, naval movements, festival foundations, alliances, treaties, battles, deeds of kings, lives of famous men, exiles, wars, dissolution of tyrannies. The named fragments attest to the existence of an epitome containing the "lives of famous men." There were doubtless epitomes made for purposes other than biographical that were no less influential on the later literature. It is therefore a reasonable hypothesis that the dates that Eusebius found in his sources for the political and military history of the ancient Greek world are of the same type as his biographical dates. That is, they derive ultimately from the Alexandrian standard of Eratosthenes and Apollodorus but have been significantly affected by the contaminating influence of other traditions.

The paucity of independent testimonia makes it impossible in most cases to analyze in detail the chronographic pedigrees of Eusebius' dates for events, as distinct from persons, of the archaic period. Eusebius' main source apparently concentrated on biographical information for this period and included considerable political and military detail only beginning with the Peloponnesian War. This phenomenon suggests that, at some stage in the transmission of information included by Eusebius' Olympiad chronicler, two chronological handbooks of somewhat different emphasis were combined. The first was descended from an epitome of the entire *Chronicle* of Apollodorus, but it excerpted primarily the biographical dates. This handbook included only a few dates of political and military history. The second handbook was based on a detailed epitome of Apollodorus' chronology of political and military history, but that epitome did not include the material of Apollodorus' first book. Like the biographical epitome, the political-military handbook was much influenced by elements of other traditions. With this material either the chronicler or his sources combined a list of colony dates. It is likely that this list also derived from what can be called an Alexandrian recension of the Κτίσεις literature, but it too had no doubt been contaminated by dates at variance with those of Eratosthenes and Apollodorus. The result is a complicated network of combination and recombination, error and adaptation. Sometimes what can be learned about the pedigrees of Eusebius' biographical dates through comparison with other late sources has implications for the understanding of the political and military dates. The information preserved by the *Suda* is especially useful in discovering possible connections between Eusebius' biographical and political notices. Many of Eusebius' biographical dates can be understood only in the light of evidence contained in the *Suda*. The combination of Eusebius' notices with those of the *Suda* produces a fuller version of the tradition. Similarities between the two are so striking as to suggest that the *Suda*'s main chronological source, Hesychius of

Miletus, either used the same Olympiad chronicle that Eusebius did or one that derived from the same literary tradition.

The massive chronographic literature produced in the Hellenistic period was systematized by Eratosthenes and Apollodorus. They made a prudent and reasoned selection aiming for internal consistency within the chronography and external consistency with the literary tradition. They also sought to bring their chronographic system into reasonable agreement with the mainstreams of Greek historiography, using for the archaic period the *Histories* of Herodotus as a touchstone. Nevertheless, much of the existing chronographic and historiographic material had to be rejected. This work of Eratosthenes and Apollodorus was epitomized in several forms for a variety of purposes, and the epitomes soon replaced the originals. These epitomes were transmitted to late antiquity by chroniclers and encyclopedists who combined with the Alexandrian standard fragments of the chronographic and literary traditions that Eratosthenes and Apollodorus either had not bothered to include or had in fact rejected. Eusebius himself of course represents the last and historically the most significant stage in this process of combination and contamination. His own sources—Castor, Porphyry, Africanus, Clement, Tatian, and the important but not finally identified Olympiad chronicler—transmitted information derived in different ways from Apollodorus and corrupted in varying degrees by other traditions. Eusebius recombined this material yet again in the context of his own universal chronicle. The fundamental core of Eratosthenes and Apollodorus present one way or another in all of Eusebius' sources for early Greek chronology makes it difficult and often impossible to identify either the immediate source of the information or the avenue of transmission. This confusion gives to the *Chronicle* a paradoxical kind of unity that confers upon it the dominant characteristics of Greek chronographic tradition in general: The chronological traditions that Eusebius received, excerpted, combined, and transmitted represent in form and outward appearance the best of Alexandrian scholarship. In detail, however, the individual notices are of vastly different significance and veracity.

Summary

Eusebius' immediate sources for notices of the *spatium his-*

toricum relevant to Greek history of the archaic period can be summarized, in the order of their relative importance, as follows:

1. Eusebius' Olympiad chronicler (Cassius Longinus?)—a chronicle similar in format and scope to the Oxyrynchus Chronicle. With a preface covering the period from the fall of Troy to the first Olympiad, a stylistically distinct portion of this chronicle that may have been its first book epitomized Greco-Roman history to the time of the Peloponnesian War. What was perhaps a second book continued the annalistic account to the time of the Roman conquest of Greece. The product of centuries of excerpting and combination, the work was dominated in its earlier portions by what had originally been an epitome of Apollodorus' biographical dates. With this biographical information the work combined a list of colony foundations also based on the chronographic vulgate of Eratosthenes and Apollodorus, derived ultimately from the κτίσεις ἐθνῶν καὶ πόλεων of Hellanicus, but corrupted and contaminated during centuries of transmission. The sources underlying the chronicle were cognate with the sources of the *Suda*.
2. Porphyry—an excerpt, which Eusebius made himself, from the first two books of the *Historia Philosophica*, listing *floruit*'s and philosophical successions from Homer to Pythagoras. These dates too descended from Apollodorus.
3. Castor—the first book of the *Chronological Epitome,* summarizing legendary history from Egealeus of Sicyon to the foundation of Rome within a chronological structure accommodated to the chronographic system of Eratosthenes.
4. Sextus Julius Africanus—Greco-Hebrew synchronisms (e.g., Homer and Solomon) excerpted from the third and fourth books of the *Chronographiae.*
5. Clement and Tatian—a few notices taken from discussions of notorious chronological controversies, notably the relative dates of Homer and Moses. Clement and Tatian themselves depended on encyclopedic sources similar to those underlying Eusebius' Olympiad chronicler.
6. List of thalassocrats excerpted from Diodorus and transmitted to Eusebius through the *Chronicle* of Porphyry. The presence of this list in the prefatory books suggests that Eusebius considered it part of the chronographic framework. His translators and redactors brought the entries into the *spatium historicum*, producing such serious

distortions as to prevent the reconstruction of the list. Other Diodoran material—e.g., lists of the Corinthian, Lacedaemonian, and Macedonian kings—came to Eusebius through Porphyry. These lists were among the raw material for the *fila regnorum*, but Diodorus was not a source for the entries of the *spatium historicum*.

Part 2

Selected Studies
in Early Greek Chronology

Prolegomena

The purpose of the following collection of studies is twofold. First they illustrate the general problems discussed in Part 1, serving as test cases for the hypotheses and specific examples of the conclusions presented there. Second, they provide detailed demonstration of the critical techniques appropriate for interpreting the evidence of Eusebius and cognate texts for early Greek chronology between the eighth century B.C. and the end of the Peloponnesian War. The studies are directed to analysis of the chronographic tradition as complete as the evidence allows. The results have implications for absolute chronology, but solution of the historical question as to the "correct" date of the persons and events discussed is not among the immediate purposes. Both the argument and the bibliographical citations are therefore limited to issues bearing directly on the chronographic tradition. The focus—biographical chronology—is required by the nature of the evidence. Both the *Chronicle* of Eusebius and the late chronographic tradition in general are dominated by this kind of information. Since it is the biographical dates that are best attested in a variety of sources, it is through them that the tradition can best be understood.

Each study is prefaced by a collection of the relevant Eusebian notices to facilitate cross-reference between the argument and the evidence at issue and to minimize the need to leaf through two other volumes while using this one. The notices appear in pairs as in the following example:

OL 70.4 (497/96) : Pythagoras philosophus moritur. (107^t)
AA 1517 (499/98) : Pithagoras der Philosoph starb. (191)

The first member of the pair represents Jerome's version of the notice as published in Rudolf Helm's edition (*GCS* 47, Berlin 1956). The number in parentheses following the text is the page of Helm's edition that contains the entry, while the superior letter corresponds to Helm's system of reference for the historical notices of the page. Preceding the notice is a date expressed in numbered and subdivided Olympiads or, for the period before the first Olympiad, in years of Abraham (AA). This date is that at which the entry is to be read in Helm's edition. An Olympiad number without subdivision indicates that the notice is to be read on the line corresponding to the Olympiad number that interrupts the chronological framework. Such a notice is accordingly not dated to a precise year within the Olympiad. In parentheses are the corresponding Julian years B.C., converted by the formula AA 1 = 2016 B.C. and OL 1.1 = 776/75 B.C.

The second member of each pair is the Armenian text of the notice as published in Josef Karst's edition with German translation (*GCS* 20, Leipzig 1911), followed by the appropriate page number. The date is expressed in years of Abraham (AA), where the notice is to be read in Karst's edition. The date is converted to Julian years B.C. by two different formulae. Dates prior to AA 1240 are converted by the equation AA 1 = 2016 B.C., as with Jerome's dates. This practice has long been the standard. Beginning with AA 1240, however, the year at which the Armenian version sets the first Olympiad number the equation is AA 1240 = 776/75 B.C. As explained in chapter 1, Jerome and the Armenian differ by one year in the alignment of Olympiad numbers to years of Abraham. It has been a standard practice to "correct" the Armenian version in this matter and to convert to Julian years with the formula AA 1241 = 776/75. The Armenian version's own equation of AA 1240 with Olympiad 1.1 and therefore with 776/75 should be used instead. The reason for this departure from earlier practice is that the exemplar underlying the Armenian version was organized by Olympiads, and Olympiad numbers are prominent in the extant text. In the alignment of historical notices, therefore, the redactor of this version was influenced as much by the Olympiad numbers of the exemplar as by any other element of the chronographic framework. If he read a notice against the first year of an Olympiad, we should not move the entry into the last year of the preceding Olympiad by using Jerome's alignment of years of Abraham.

References to Syncellus follow the pagination of Dindorf's 1829 edition, still the most recent.

5

Lycurgus

a) AA 1134 (883) : Lycurgus insignis habetur. (79ᶜ)
   No corresponding Armenian entry.
b) AA 1197 (820) : Lycurgus Lacedaemoniis iura
   componit. (83ᵈ)
   Lacuna in the Armenian version.
c) AA 1221 (796) : Lycurgi leges in Lacedaemone iuxta
   sententiam Apollodori hac aetate susceptae. (84ᶠ)
   AA 1221 (796) : Des Likorgos Gesetze zu Lakedmonia,
   nach Apolodoros im 18ᵗᵉⁿ Jahre des Alkemines. (180)
   Syncellus 349 : Ἀπολλόδωρος Λυκούργου νόμιμα ἐν
   τῷ η′ Ἀλκαμένους.

Eusebius' entries for Lycurgus provide an appropriate first
case in this selection of studies for several reasons. The dates
fall within the period that conservative chronographers regarded
as no longer mythical but not yet historical, and that they therefore approached with caution.[1] A study of Eusebius' evidence on
Lycurgus is accordingly a useful medium for discussing chronographic tradition relevant to that difficult transitional period
between the fall of Troy and the first Olympiad. Furthermore,
the tradition on Lycurgus and the "Lycurgan" reforms is especially controversial and most students of antiquity have some
familiarity with the issues involved. Analysis of Eusebius' notices
about Lycurgus offers one of the most striking demonstrations
of how complex the tradition can be that underlies the late
chronographic texts upon which we depend for so much information about early Greek chronology. The intricacies of text,
source, tradition, and redaction emerge in a network of interrelationships that shows how much care must be exercised in

dealing with evidence drawn from the *Chronicle* of Eusebius. The argument can therefore serve as a general introduction to the set of critical techniques that should be applied whenever Eusebian evidence for early Greek chronology is at issue.

Superficially, Eusebius' three dates for Lycurgus seem to impute to him an extraordinary length of life and legislative activity. If Lycurgus was "famous"—that is, about forty years old—in 883, as the first entry states, he was over a hundred years old when, in 820, according to the second notice, he formulated his laws, and yet another quarter of a century elapsed before the legislation was completed, on the evidence of the third entry, in 796. In the older tradition on Lycurgus as we know it there is no parallel for so prodigious a life span or so long an interval for the Lycurgan reforms. The collection of notices does not, however, constitute a chronographic fantasy of late invention. The three entries derive from the best traditions of Hellenistic scholarship, albeit by a tortuous route.

The 883 Date

Eusebius' first notice, dating the *floruit* of Lycurgus to the 880s, derives from the well-known epoch computed by Eratosthenes. Apollodorus adopted the date and through the popular epitomes of his *Chronicle* it soon became standard. The principal evidence for the Apollodoran date (*FGrHist* 244 F 61b) is preserved by Eusebius himself (89 Karst) in an excerpt from the first book of Porphyry's *Historia Philosophica* (*FGrHist* 260 F 4):

> Apollodorus says that there is an interval of 80 years from the fall of Troy to the Heraclid invasion of the Peloponnesus. From the return of the Heraclids to the Ionian colonization the interval is 60 years, and from that time to Lycurgus there is an interval of 159 years. The total from the fall of Troy to the first Olympiad is 407 years.

Clement of Alexandria (*Strom.* 1. 138) attributes a similar passage to Eratosthenes (*FGrHist* 241 F 1a):

> Eratosthenes records the chronology as follows. From the fall of Troy to the return of the Heraclids is 80 years, from that time to the Ionian colonization 60 years, an additional 159

years to the regency of Lycurgus, and 108 years to the year preceding the first Olympiad, from which there is an interval of 297 years to the expedition of Xerxes.

Together, the two passages show that Apollodorus followed Eratosthenes for the chronology of the period between the fall of Troy and the first Olympiad, counting the intervals from the year before the first Olympiad, 777/76. The fall of Troy is therefore 1184/83, and the date of Lycurgus is 885/84.[2]

Eusebius reports this date for Lycurgus in an excerpt from Porphyry included in the prefatory book. The immediate source for the entry of the *Canons* was the selection of epochal intervals and *floruits* that Eusebius made from Porphyry's first two books for use in composing the *spatium historicum*.[3] Eratosthenes and Apollodorus had dated Lycurgus by counting an interval of 108 years before the beginning of the Olympiads. The date was reported, however, as an interval of 299 years after the fall of Troy, and Eusebius positioned his notice accordingly. The entry appears two years later than the date attested for Eratosthenes and Apollodorus. The reason for this discrepancy is that the *Canons'* version of the Lacedaemonian king lists results in a date two years too low for the return of the Heraclids, and that date in turn lowered Eusebius' epoch of Troy by two years. Eusebius used the Apollodoran intervals as reported by Porphyry to date Lycurgus, but he counted the years from his own date for the fall of Troy ($1182 - 299 = 883$).[4]

According to Plutarch (*Lyc.* 1.2), Eratosthenes and Apollodorus computed an early date for Lycurgus by reference to the lists of the Spartan kings. Jacoby reconstructed the Eurypontid list of Apollodorus, using the list included among Eusebius' chronographic excerpts (106 Karst), attributed to Diodorus. According to the excerpt, the first Olympiad was celebrated in the tenth year of Theopompus. Although there is a lacuna in the earlier portion, the list from Prytanis to Theopompus is in order, except that the list assigns 38 years of rule to Nicander. The result is a date for the first year of Charilaus in 883/82, the same that appears in the list of the *Canons*. The Apollodoran date should be 885/84, and Jacoby therefore increased Nicander's years to 40:

Prytanis	49 years:	979/78	— 931/30
Eunomus	45 years:	930/29	— 886/85

Charilaus	60 years:	885/84 — 826/25
Nicander	40 years:	825/24 — 786/85
		(38 years *cod.*)
Theopompus	47 years:	785/84 — 739/38
		(10th year = 776/75).

Thus the date of Lycurgus in 883, 885/84 in the emended text, was the first year of Charilaus.[5]

The synchronism between Lycurgus and the first year of Charilaus represents the standard tradition about Lycurgus' place in the genealogy of the Spartan kings. Herodotus (1.65) reports that some believed Lycurgus to have been an Agiad.[6] The vulgate tradition, which Plutarch (*Lyc.* 1.4) traces to the poet Simonides, considered Lycurgus a Eurypontid who effected his reforms while serving as regent for his nephew Charilaus. Disagreement did exist, however, as to the filiation. Simonides had said that Lycurgus was the son of Prytanis. According to Plutarch, all other authorities considered Lycurgus the son of Eunomus and the brother of Polydectes, whose premature death brought his infant son Charilaus to the throne. Charilaus' uncle Lycurgus was therefore designated regent. According to Jacoby's reconstruction, Apollodorus synchronized Lycurgus with Charilaus. Plutarch cites Apollodorus for an early date for Lycurgus based on the Spartan king lists. Apollodorus was an authority of such stature that Plutarch should have taken note of the fact if he did not share the vulgate opinion about Lycurgus' parentage. The difficulty is that Polydectes' name does not appear in the Eurypontid list of Apollodorus. Jacoby therefore assumed that Apollodorus must have followed Simonides in considering Lycurgus the son of Prytanis, and he interpreted the Apollodoran epoch of Lycurgus accordingly. Prytanis died in 931 and was succeeded by his son Eunomus, the brother of Lycurgus and the father of Charilaus. Apollodorus adopted Eratosthenes' date for Lycurgus in 885/84, but he could not associate that year with the lawgiver's acme. In the system of Apollodorus one reached his acme in the fortieth year of life. With an acme in 885/84, Lycurgus would have been born in 924/23, several years after Prytanis' death. Jacoby dated the acme instead to 914/13. For according to Clement (*Strom.* 1.117) Apollodorus dated the acme of Homer to 944, so that Homer was still alive when Lycurgus was young: ὥστε ἐπιβαλεῖν αὐτῷ Λυκοῦργον τὸν νομοθέτην ἔτι νέον ὄντα. Jacoby took 914/13 as Apollodorus' date for the death of Homer at the age of seventy and the acme of Lycurgus at the age of forty. If Lycurgus reached his acme in 914/13, he was born in 953/52, well within the lifetime of his putative father, Prytanis. Jacoby computed his age as 68 in 885/84, when he assumed the regency for Charilaus. With this computation he combined the lifespan of 85 years reported in the *Macrobioi* (85). Thus Lycurgus was 85 years old when he stepped down after 18 years of regency, and he died shortly thereafter.[7]

Jacoby's computations are not all in order. If Lycurgus was 40 years old in 914/13, he was 69 in 885/84, 86 in the 18th year of regency, and 87 when he resumed private life or died. Jacoby put an unnecessary strain on the evidence in order to account for the failure of Polydectes to appear in Eusebius' version of Apollodorus' Eurypontid list. It is logical to suppose, as Eusebius' entry implies, that the epoch of Lycurgus marked the lawgiver's acme. However one computes the intervals, there is no special significance for the Apollodoran chronology in the 85-year life span reported by the *Macrobioi*. It was one of the author's favorite ages.[8] We should therefore try the alternate course: 885/84 does mark the Apollodoran acme of Lycurgus; Apollodorus is included among Plutarch's "all other authorities" and he considered Lycurgus the son of Eunomus and the brother of Polydectes. But there is something wrong with Jacoby's interpretation of Eusebius' Eurypontid list. The coincidence between the epoch of Lycurgus in the Apollodoran system and the first year of Charilaus in the list suggests that the list derives from Apollodorus. There is no difficulty in assuming that 885/84 was the acme. If Lycurgus was in his fortieth year in 885/84, his birth in 924/23 fell within the reign of Eunomus according to the list, and Eunomus was the father of Lycurgus in Plutarch's vulgate genealogy. Clement's remark also fits well. Clement (e.g., *Strom.* 1.131) uses ἐπιβαλεῖν to indicate a chronological overlap. His statement about Apollodorus' dates for Homer and Lycurgus therefore does not necessarily mean that Apollodorus reported a personal meeting between the two. It does mean that Apollodorus' date for the death of Homer was later than his date for the birth of Lycurgus. Clement adds the qualification that the chronological overlap was at an early point in Lycurgus' life (ἔτι νέον ὄντα). If Lycurgus fluorished in 885/84, his birth in 924/23 was twenty years after Homer's acme and ten years before Homer's death—just the sort of chronological overlap that Clement's phraseology suggests. The failure of Polydectes to appear in Eusebius' Eurypontid list does not require reinterpretation of the other evidence. Eusebius' list is a record of regnal years for chronological purposes, not a report of Eurypontid genealogy. Polydectes was the son of Eunomus and should have succeeded him. But he died prematurely and left the infant Charilaus as heir to the kingship. Polydectes is thus part of Eurypontid genealogy, as Plutarch says. But he is not part of Eurypontid chronology, as far as Eusebius and his immediate sources are concerned: he did not occupy a year. Those few authorities who say that Lycurgus was son of Prytanis are either quoting Simonides (e.g., schol. Plat. *Rep.* X. 599d) or making, like Jacoby, the wrong inference from Charilaus' appearance in the chronographic list as immediate successor of Eunomus (e.g., Phlegon *FGrHist* 257 F 1).

The fragments transmitted by Eusebius and other late authors permit the partial reconstruction of the Apollodoran chronology. Some refinements in our understanding of the Apollodoran dates are possible. Some modifications in the reconstruction are necessary, as has been suggested, especially with respect to Eusebius' version of the Lacedaemonian kinglists. Even when the Apollodoran chronology has been satisfactorily reconstructed, serious problems remain. How Eratosthenes computed the epoch of Lycurgus at the year corresponding to 885/84 is by no means clear. Plutarch's belief that the date was an inference from the king lists does not settle the issue. The king lists are themselves, at least in part, the result of chronographic construction.[9] The date of Lycurgus may have been a starting point for the construction of the Eurypontid list rather than an inference from the list once made. Eratosthenes was at work some 150 years after the efforts to establish a chronology for early Greek history were begun. During this century and a half the variant opinions about the date of Lycurgus and differing versions of the Spartan king lists had an opportunity to exert a mutual influence on each other such that neither retained clear priority. Eratosthenes and Apollodorus inherited a chronological controversy about Lycurgus based on at least three different methods of chronographic construction. The position of Lycurgus' brother Polydectes in the genealogy of the Eurypontid kings could produce a variety of chronological estimates, depending on which version of the pedigree was followed, at what point in the list a count was begun, and what numerical average was assigned to a generation. A second method of construction is through synchronism with famous persons whose dates had already been estimated.

According to Plutarch, Lycurgus was commonly synchronized with Homer. Herodotus' estimate (2.53) places Homer in the ninth century, 400 years before Herodotus' own time, and this interval may well have exerted an early influence on attempts to date Lycurgus. Indeed, it is conceivable that Thucydides' (1.18.1) interval of slightly more than 400 years for Spartan constitutional stability derives from Herodotus' interval for Homer through synchronism with Lycurgus. Thucydides' vague addition of a few more years would then represent the interval elapsed since Herodotus wrote. Such a suggestion is no more conjectural than the common belief that Thucydides' interval derives from a genealogical count. Thus Eurypontid genealogy and the dates for Homer and Lycurgus could exert mutual influences on one another as the tradition grew. The third method employs computation based on epochs or era dates. The most common of these, especially important for Eratosthenes and Apollodorus, was the Olympic era, corresponding to 776/75. Aristotle, among others (Plutarch, *Lyc.* 1.1), believed Lycurgus to have been associated with the institution of the Olympic festival. Those who wished to date Lycurgus earlier were constrained to consider the first numbered Olympiad a formalization of an already-established festival. Lycurgus could thus be associated with the earlier establishment, but his date had to be set on the four-year cycle. Eratosthenes' date, for example, is 108 years, 27 Olympiads, before 777/76, the year during which preparations for the first numbered Olympiad were being made. Those who used Olympiad dating for the historical period and dates expressed in Lacedaemonian regnal years for the earlier period had to establish a point of contact between the two. The Olympic era thus exercised an influence on the Spartan king lists. Generation counting, traditional synchronisms, and chronographic construction are inextricably interrelated.

The conversation of Eurypontid genealogy to Eurypontid chronology could not be accomplished by a simple generational calculation and an apportioning of years to kings to produce a date for Charilaus and therefore by simple inference a date for the acme, regency, and legislative activity of Lycurgus. Genealogical chronology, if it ever existed pure, was influenced by synchronistic traditions, by rough estimates like Herodotus' of the interval between a famous person and the present time or Thucydides' estimate of the antiquity of Spartan constitutional stability (1.18.1), and by the introduction of chronographic systems like that based on the Olympiads. The year 885/84 in the Eratosthenic system for the epoch of Lycurgus was some sort of compromise that attempted to reconcile as many of the traditions and as many of the variant dates as possible. The date was influenced in part by Eurypontid genealogy, but the need to establish a credible date for Lycurgus, retaining a synchronism with Homer, may have required some alterations in the genealogical tradition. Once established, the epoch exerted an influence of its own on the construction of Eurypontid chronology. Even so, there can have been no rigid formula to convert generations to dates and to allocate regnal years by the application of arithmetical devices with a base date of 885/84. Synchronisms between Eurypontids and Agiads and between kings and events required manipulation and reconciliation at every step. Each new attempt to establish a chronology had also to take into account the results of previous efforts.[10]

The 820 Date

Eusebius enters the *floruit* of Lycurgus in 883, a notice that transmits the Apollodoran acme of Lycurgus 299 years after the epoch of Troy. In a second notice he dates the Lycurgan legislation to 820. Since the time of Scaliger, scholars have generally associated this entry with the statement of Thucydides (1.18.1) that by the end of the recent war the Lacedaemonians had been under the same political order for just over 400 years. Now, Thucydides makes no mention here of Lycurgus, but that fact would not have bothered the chronographers. It is certainly possible that some chronicler computed a date for the Spartan "constitution" somewhat more than 400 years before the end of the Peloponnesian War, connected it with Lycurgus, and transmitted to the sources of Eusebius the statement that Lycurgus prepared his laws in a year corresponding to 820 B.C. On the other hand, there is no evidence that anyone did so. It would be surprising if a computation based on no less an authority than Thucydides did not carry with it Thucydides' name and exert more of an influence on the chronographic tradition. The search to find traces of such an influence has therefore been duly conducted.

Both Thucydides' interval and Eusebius' date have been associated with an alleged date of Callimachus for Lycurgus in 828.

According to the preface to Eusebius' list of Olympic victors (90 Karst), Aristodemus and Polybius said there were 27 unlisted Olympiads between the time that Iphitus and Lycurgus established the festival and the first regularly numbered Olympiad, when Coroebus was listed as victor. The preface adds that Callimachus counted 13 such unlisted Olympiads and Coroebus was victor in the 14th. The 27 Olympiads of Aristodemus and Polybius reflect Eratosthenes' and Apollodorus' interval of 108 years between the epoch of Lycurgus and the first Olympiad. Similarly, Callimachus' 13 Olympiads represent 52 years, yielding a date of 828 for Lycurgus. Callimachus is supposed to have computed the date on the basis of Thucydides' interval, using the end of the Archidamian War (421) as a terminus.[11]

Such a hypothesis attributes to Callimachus chronographic scholarship that seems quite out of character. Callimachus was interested in such things as the early history of the national festivals, but not in making new calculations to challenge the chronographic system of his contemporary Eratosthenes. Callimachus accepted Eratosthenes' date for Lycurgus but believed that the Olympic festival had originally been celebrated every eight years. Thus the thirteen Olympiads represent an interval of between 104 and 112 years, but not a date for Lycurgus different from that established by Eratosthenes.[12]

Gelzer ascribed Eusebius' date to Africanus and believed that it was computed from Thucydides' interval.[13] He did not, however, argue the case, and the evidence for such a date in Africanus is in fact very weak. The Byzantine chronographers synchronize the Lycurgan legislation with Azarias, king of Judah, and they give dates for Azarias' reign in Africanus' system of years from Adam that correspond to the years 843–792. Even if it is correct that Africanus dated Lycurgus within that interval, we do not know that the precise year was 820. But the synchronism between Lycurgus and Azarias may not derive from Africanus at all. The Byzantine chronographers used both Eusebius and Africanus. The synchronism between Lycurgus and Azarias can be read in the *Canons* of Eusebius at the years 887–83 (79[a,c] Helm). With this synchronism the Byzantine chronographers combined Africanus' dates for Azarias. Their date for Lycurgus is therefore that of Eratosthenes as transmitted by Eusebius' first notice.

There is insufficient evidence for the widely held belief that Eusebius' date for Lycurgus in 820 derives from Thucydides through Callimachus, Africanus, or any other intermediary. The route toward a correct understanding of this entry is tortuous, but rewarding. Eusebius' entry appears at the year of Abraham 1197. Eusebius dates the death of Sardanapallus and the end of the Assyrian empire to the same year. In the chronographic excerpts Eusebius cites Abydenus, Castor, Diodorus, and Cephalion on Assyrian chronology and closes with a list of Assyrian kings compiled from what Eusebius calls "reliable books" (25–32 Karst). The last name in the list is Sardanapallus, to which is appended the statement "Unter diesem gab Lakoriges Gesetze den Lakedmoniern." The synchronism between Sardanapallus and Lycurgus cannot be an interpolation from Africanus or from the *Canons*. It appears much earlier in Velleius Paterculus 1.6.1: *quippe Sardanapalum . . . Arbaces Medus imperio uitaque priuauit. ea aetate clarissimus Grai nominis Lycurgus Lacedaemonius*. The common source of Velleius and Eusebius for this synchronism was probably the *Chronological Epitome* of Castor.

Castor's date for Sardanapallus cannot be extrapolated directly from Eusebius' Assyrian list. The list was based on Castor's, but the "reliable books" from which Eusebius made the excerpt was Porphyry's *Chronicle*.[14] Porphyry made adjustments in the list for reasons of his own, perhaps on the basis of evidence he considered better. Nevertheless, an approximate date for Castor's Sardanapallus-Arbaces-Lycurgus synchronism can be derived on the assumption that Castor followed Ctesias for the list of Median kings and accepted the date of the chronographic vulgate for Cyrus' revolution against Astyages, the last of the Median kings, in 560. According to Ctesias (*FGrHist* 688 F 5 = Diodorus 2.32–34), the Median kings from Arbaces to Astibarus ruled for a sum of 282 years until the accession of Astyages. Ctesias does not give the regnal years of Astyages, but the average of the eight preceding kings is 35 years and that, according to Herodotus (1.130), was the length of Astyages' reign. The total from Arbaces to Astyages is thus 317 years. This interval, computed from 560 as the date of Cyrus' rebellion, yields a date of 877 for Arbaces' revolt from Sardanapallus. According to Eusebius' list (32 Karst) Sardanapallus himself ruled for 20 years. Thus the synchronism between Sardanapallus and Lycurgus falls within the years 896–77.

Castor's date for Lycurgus is accordingly none other than the Eratosthenic date (885) expressed as a synchronism. Because Eusebius accepted (probably from Porphyry) a shorter version of the Median list allowing only 256 years (32 Karst, 258 years in Jerome's Assyrian *filum*) from Arbaces to Astyages, the synchronism between Lycurgus and Sardanapallus appears about sixty years too late in the *Canons*. Eusebius' alignment of the Assyrian and Athenian lists so that the Assyrian list ends in the time of Thespieus (32 Karst, 83[a] Helm) results also in the transfer of Castor's synchronism from Sardanapallus to Thespieus. Eusebius inserts the synchronism into his excerpt of Castor's Athenian list (88 Karst) : Unter diesem [Thespieus] gab Likurgos Gesetze den Lakedämoniern.[15]

Eusebius' date for the Lycurgan legislation in 820 does not derive from Africanus and it cannot be connected with Thucydides' 400-year interval of Spartan constitutional stability. The date derives from Eratosthenes' epoch of Lycurgus in 885/84, a date that Eusebius knew and recorded from another source, the *Historia Philosophica* of Porphyry. This second notice derives from Castor's expression of that date as a synchronism with Sardanapallus. Eusebius converted the synchronism to a date by reference to a version of the Assyrian and Median king lists that no longer preserved Castor's original date for Sardanapallus. Eusebius read the synchronism in the *Chronographical Epitome* of Castor, but he used the shortened version of the king lists that appeared in the *Chronicle* of Porphyry (the "reliable books"), so that the entry came to be dated to 820.

The 796 Date

Eusebius' first two notices derive from Eratosthenes' epoch of Lycurgus in 885/84—the first through Apollodorus and Porphyry's *Historia Philosophica*, the second through Castor and the redaction of Castor's Assyrian chronology that appeared in Porphyry's chronicle. The third entry, in which Eusebius specifically cites Apollodorus, raises more serious difficulties, both for the reconstruction of the Apollodoran system and for the interpretation of Eusebius' Agiad list of Lacedaemonian kings. St. Jerome enters the legislation of Lycurgus *iuxta sententiam Apollodori* at the year of Abraham 1221 (796 B.C.), the 18th year of Alcamenes in the Lacedaemonian *filum*. In the Armenian version the 18th year of Alcamenes appears in the text of the notice as well as at the position in the Lacedaemonian *filum* that corresponds to AA 1221. Syncellus' excerpt of the text also includes the regnal year and, like Jerome and the Armenian version, he specifically mentions Apollodorus. Syncellus specifies the 8th year of Alcamenes, rather than the 18th. This is a textual corruption of a common sort and it does not affect the interpretation of the notice. Syncellus' ἐν τῶι η΄ is haplography for an original ἐν τῶι ιη΄.[16]

Apollodorus dated the acme of Lycurgus to 885/84, the first year of his regency. The eighteen years of regency must have been the period during which Apollodorus considered the Lycurgan constitution to have been imposed upon the Lacedaemonians. The 18th year associated with the Eusebian notice cannot, however, represent Apollodorus' date for the end of Lycurgus' regency. Apollodorus would have synchronized the completion of the legislation with the 18th year of Charilaus, not Alcamenes. Eusebius both knew and transmitted the date of the Apollodoran acme of Lycurgus. His subsequent statement that the laws of Lycurgus were enacted almost a hundred years later in the system of Apollodorus must be wrong. The error may be in the citation of Apollodorus, in the mention of the laws, in the synchronization of the date with the 18th year of Alcamenes, or some combination of all three.

Problems begin with the interpretation of the absolute date associated with the 18th year of Alcamenes. Alcamenes' 18th year corresponds to AA 1221 and the year 796/95 in the Lacedaemonian (Agiad) *filum* of the *Canons*. According to Eusebius' excerpt from Diodorus (106 Karst), the first Olympiad was celebrated in the tenth year both of the Agiad Alcamenes and of the Eurypontid Theopompus. Jacoby attributed the synchronism to Apollodorus, because Diodorus (1.5.1) cites Apollodorus for the chronology of the period between the fall of Troy and the first Olympiad as reckoned by reference to the Lacedaemonian kings. This synchronism, together with the regnal intervals of Eusebius' Eurypontid list, produces, as has already been shown, a date for the first year of Charilaus that agrees with the date of Eratosthenes and Apollodorus for Lycurgus. The evidence is circumstantial and there are difficulties in Jacoby's efforts to reconstruct the original lists of Eratosthenes and Apollodorus from Eusebius' excerpt of Diodorus. Nevertheless, Jacoby is right at least in taking the synchronism of the first Olympiad with the tenth years of Alcamenes and Theopompus as a starting point for the reconstruction of the lists.[17]

Eusebius abandoned this synchronism between the first Olympiad and the tenth year of Alcamenes when he transferred

Diodorus' Agiad list to the chronographic framework of the *Canons*. In this version of the list, both in the excerpts and in the *Canons*, the Agiads from Eurysthenes to Alcamenes rule for a total of 325 years, the sum including 37 years of Alcamenes. Apollodorus synchronized Alcamenes' 10th year with the first Olympiad and he computed an interval between the return of the Heraclids and the first Olympiad of 328 years. For Apollodorus the sum of the Agiads from Eurysthenes to Alcamenes' 37th year must therefore have been 354 years. Whatever the reasons for this 30-year discrepancy between Apollodorus' intervals and those of the list that reached Eusebius, he either had to abandon Apollodorus' dates for the fall of Troy and the return of the Heraclids or to reject the synchronism between the first Olympiad and the tenth year of Alcamenes. Eusebius chose the latter course. The 325-year sum of the list attributed to Diodorus was suggestive of Apollodorus' 328-year interval between the return of the Heraclids and the first Olympiad. The difference of three years was negligible, and Eusebius decided to interpret the 325 years of the list accordingly. He reduced the interval between the fall of Troy and the year 777/76 from 407 years (88 Karst) to 405 years (86ᵃ Helm), resulting in a date for the epoch of Troy of 1182. The date of the return of the Heraclids, eighty years later in the *fila*, was thus 1102, and Eusebius ran the 325 year Agiad *filum* from 1101 to 777.

Such a hypothesis gains additional force from the presence of similar phenomena in the Corinthian list. According to the excerpt from Diodorus (104 Karst), there is an interval from the return of the Heraclids to the tyranny of Cypselus of 447 years, during 90 years of which annual prytanies ruled. The total of regnal years for the kings should be 357. But the sum of regnal years in the excerpt is only 325. Again, Eusebius had either to abandon the Apollodoran date for the return of the Heraclids or reject the 357-year interval between the Heraclids and the beginning of the annual prytanies, and again he chose the latter course. The date of the *Canons* for the return of the Heraclids had already been established by the decisions made in dealing with the Lacedaemonian list, so the Corinthian list also begins in 1101. Either there is a textual corruption in the excerpt or Eusebius himself made a transcriptional error in entering 35 years for the first king instead of the excerpt's 37 years. The Corinthian *filum* of the *Canons* actually runs for 323 years, ending in 779 instead of 777.

The reasons for these discrepancies between the chronographic intervals of the excerpts and the actual regnal lists are to be sought in the source material. They do not result from corruption in the text of the *Chronicle*, although some such errors compound the confusion. One must not, with Schwartz, posit an interpolator who purposely altered the structure of the original.[18] The amount by which the lists fall short of the intervals suggests that either Diodorus or some intermediate authority attempted to reconcile the chronological system transmitted by Diodorus' chronographic source (who followed Eratosthenes and Apollodorus) with a system based on Ephorus. The sum of the regnal years both in the lists of the prefatory excerpts and in the *Canons* falls short of the chronographic intervals cited in the excerpts by just over thirty years. Apollodorus dated the return of the Heraclids to 1104 and the first year of Heraclid rule to 1103. Ephorus did not deal with chronology so precisely. But he made some kind of statement that permitted one to infer an Ephoran "date" for the return of the Heraclids corresponding to 1070 or 1069.[19] The difference between the two dates for the return of the Heraclids is just over thirty years. Diodorus (or his authorities) reduced the number of regnal years allotted to the various kings in order to adapt the Apollodoran lists to the Ephoran "date" for the return of the Heraclids, without disturbing the traditional (Apollodoran) dates for Theopompus and Alcamenes in Sparta and the end of monarchical rule in Corinth. Eusebius received the shortened lists, and he attempted to readjust them to the Apollodoran date for the return of the Heraclids. In reconstructing the original Apollodoran list it is not sufficient, with Jacoby, to add a name (Menelaus) to the Agiad list or to add 29 years to the last name of the Corinthian list. The shortened list that reached Eusebius may have been produced by the subtraction of a few years from each name.[20]

Thus the 18th year of Alcamenes came to occupy a position corresponding to 796/95 in Eusebius' Lacedaemonian *filum*. For Apollodorus, however, whom Eusebius cites as the authority for the notice at that date, the 10th year of Alcamenes was 776/75 and his 18th year should therefore correspond to 768/67. Apollodorus adopted the Lacedaemonian lists of Eratosthenes. The Laconian chronographer Sosibius, a contemporary of Apollodorus, had a version of his own. A passage in Clement (*Strom.* 1.117) permits a partial reconstruction of Sosibius' chronology for the Eurypontid line (*FGrHist* 595 F 2). The passage appears in the context of a discussion of the date of Homer. Clement says that Sosibius dated Homer to the eighth year of Charilaus. He adds enough of Sosibius' Eurypontid chronology to make this date intelligible to his readers with respect to the Olympic era:

βασιλεύει μὲν οὖν Χάριλλος ἔτη ἑξήκοντα τέσσαρα, μεϑ' ὃν υἱὸς Νίκανδρος ἔτη τριάκοντα ἐννέα. τούτου κατὰ τὸ τριακοστὸν τέταρτον ἔτος τεϑῆναί φησι τὴν πρώτην ὀλυμπιάδα.

Charilaus ruled for sixty-four years, followed by his son Nicander for thirty-nine years. In his thirty-fourth year, according to Sosibius, the first Olympiad was established.

For Sosibius, Nicander 34 corresponds to 776/75 and his last year was 771/70. The next name in the list must have been Theopompus, who follows Nicander both in Herodotus' (8.131) Eurypontid genealogy and in Diodorus' version of the Eurypontid list. Theopompus' first year was therefore 770/69 in the Sosibian chronology and his 18th was 753/52. If Sosibius agreed with Eusebius' and Diodorus' ultimate authority (presumably Eratosthenes) in synchronizing the beginning of the reigns of Theopompus and Alcamenes, then in Sosibius' system the 18th year of Alcamenes was also 753/52.

Now, the year 753/52 (or 754/53, depending on the method of counting used in interpreting the evidence) is the traditional date for the establishment of the Spartan ephorate.[21] Some authorities (e.g., Herodotus 1.65) associate the ephorate with the reforms of Lycurgus. The traditional date in 753 may have been the 18th year of Alcamenes in Sosibius' chronology. Eusebius' third entry says that Apollodorus assigned the laws of Lycurgus to the 18th year of Alcamenes. For Apollodorus Alcamenes' 18th year was 768/67, not 753/52. In an effort to reconcile the difference, Eduard Schwartz suggested that Spartan tradition associated the ephorate with Lycurgus and with the 18th year of Alcamenes, but that there was disagreement among the chronographers as to the absolute date. He argued that Apollodorus, although he dated Lycurgus himself much earlier, considered the Lycurgan reforms to have been completed with the establishment of the ephorate and that Apollodorus used a version of the ephor list that began in the year corresponding to 768/67. The traditional date in 753/52 is Sosibian, but both

dates represent the 18th year of Alcamenes. Schwartz believed
that this hypothesis of a 15-year difference in the length of rival
versions of the ephor list, together with a solid tradition associating the institution with the 18th year of Alcamenes, accounts
for the existence of two different Alexandrian recensions of the
Lacedaemonian king lists and for Eusebius' notice at Alcamenes'
18th year: *Lycurgi leges in Lacedaemone iuxta sententiam Apollodori hac aetate susceptae.*[22]

The principal objection to Schwartz' view is that it is not
likely that the tradition, before it passed through the hands of
the chronographers, associated events with a specific year of a
king's reign. Such statements are extrapolations from the chronographic lists and it is wrong to take them as constituting the
primary evidence from which the lists were constructed. Eusebius'
notice makes no mention of the ephorate. Whatever date Sosibius had for the ephorate, his date for Homer (with whom Lycurgus was often synchronized) in the reign of Charilaus suggests that he followed the chronographic vulgate in dating the
Lycurgan reforms to the time of Charilaus—not the time of
Theopompus and Alcamenes. Furthermore, we do not even know
that Sosibius associated the year 753/52 with the 18th year of
Alcamenes: we possess no fragments of his Agiad list. The assumption that Sosibius agreed with Eratosthenes in synchronizing
the first years of Theopompus and Alcamenes cannot be proved.
Sosibius may have accepted Eratosthenes' version of the Agiad
list, but disagreed about the Eurypontid list. Or he may have
attempted to replace the Agiad list as a chronological tool and
win priority instead for the Eurypontid list. In that case he did
not date anything by reference to Agiad regnal years.

It is dubious at best that Sosibius ever said that the ephorate
was established in the 18th year of Alcamenes. But it is certain
that Apollodorus said no such thing. The traditional date, 754
or 753, is in fact the Apollodoran date.[23] Jacoby therefore
rightly rejected Schwartz' hypothesis, although he was too insistent that there could have been no disagreement about so
fundamental a date as the beginning of the ephor list.[24] But
Jacoby's solution to the problem posed by the Eusebian notice
at Alcamenes' 18th year is also unsatisfactory. Jacoby argued
that Apollodorus followed Timaeus (Plutarch, *Lyc.* 1.1) in
positing the existence of two persons named Lycurgus. On this
view, the elder was the Lacedaemonian lawgiver who lived
early enough to make a synchronism with Homer credible, while

the younger was that Lycurgus who assisted Iphitus to establish
the first of the regular series of Olympic festivals. Thus Eusebius' third entry refers to the younger Lycurgus and his mention
of the laws is an error. But the 18th year of Alcamenes is still
problematic. Apollodorus' younger Lycurgus should have flourished in the tenth year of Alcamenes, because Apollodorus synchronized that year with the first Olympiad. Jacoby therefore
had to posit a textual error in Eusebius' source. An original
"tenth year" was corrupted to "eighteenth year" and the notice
was entered at that year of an already corrupt version of Apollodorus' Agiad list.[25]

Jacoby was right that the Apollodoran system included a
younger Lycurgus who flourished at the time of the first Olympic
festival, but this hypothesis cannot, as it stands, account for the
Eusebian notice. The kind of corruption present in Syncellus—
"8th" instead of "18th"—can easily be understood as a scribal
error. But a corruption from "10th" to "18th" is not likely in
Greek. While confusion between two homonymous Lycurgi
would be understandable there is no trace of confusion in Eusebius' notice. It is definitely the Lycurgan legislation that he
enters, and there is no hint of association with the Olympic
festival. The 18th year is, of course, reminiscent of Lycurgus'
regency in the vulgate tradition and the notice would make excellent sense if it read Charilaus instead of Alcamenes. But how
such an error could have occurred strains the imagination. We
would have to suppose that an intermediate source had preserved
Apollodoran excerpts in some such fashion as the following.
"According to Apollodorus the laws of Lycurgus were enacted
in the 18th year of Charilaus and there was also another Lycurgus who flourished in the time of Alcamenes." Compression of
the statement so as to omit the second clause and substitute Alcamenes for Charilaus is possible, but such a hypothesis is no
more convincing than Jacoby's emendation of the number.

Franz Kiechle reexamined the problematic notice in detail
and concluded that it must somehow derive from the Sosibian
chronology. He argued that it is highly probable that Sosibius
did agree with Eratosthenes and Apollodorus in synchronizing
the first years of Theopompus and Alcamenes, because both systems allow about the same interval between Theopompus' first
year and the outbreak of the Messenian War, during the course
of which Alcamenes died. Furthermore, a reckoning of twelve
generations and 400 years from the death of the Agiad Cleom-

brotus at the battle of Leuctra in 371 would yield a date for his ancestor Alcamenes of 771. The date is within one year of that implied by Clement as the Sosibian date for the first year of Theopompus. Beginning with this date (771 or 770), having before him an ephor list beginning in 754 or 753, aware of Timaeus' suggestion that there was a second Lycurgus, and confronted with the vulgate tradition associating Lycurgus with the ephorate, Sosibius dated a second Lycurgan legislation to the 18th year of Alcamenes. This opinion was transmitted to Eusebius, but falsely attributed in the sources to Apollodorus.[26]

Kiechle's hypothesis is not implausible, but the weaknesses in the argument must be recognized. The only association between Eusebius' notice and the ephorate is the fact that in Syncellus the notice is immediately followed by mention of the ephorate. Both Schwartz and Kiechle depended too heavily on this juxtaposition. The notices of Syncellus are just what the rubric σποράδην implies: miscellaneous excerpts culled from scattered references. Syncellus can sometimes be useful for recovering the Greek wording of a notice or attesting to the Eusebian origin of a disputed notice. But the miscellanies of Syncellus cannot be used as evidence for the order, arrangement, or placement of the notices in the Eusebian *Canons*. Furthermore, we do not know Sosibius' Agiad chronology or even whether he used Agiad regnal years for chronological purposes. We do not even know what date (if any) Sosibius computed or accepted for the establishment of the ephorate. It cannot be assumed that the chronographers uniformly agreed on the date corresponding to 754 or 753, because it is by no means certain that this date was based on an actual list.[27] Sosibius' date for Homer in the reign of Charilaus implies that he also dated Lycurgus and the Lycurgan reforms to the time of Charilaus. Although Timaeus and Apollodorus hypothesized the existence of a younger Lycurgus in order to account for the tradition that a Lycurgus was associated with the establishment of the regular Olympic festival, there is no trace of any suggestion that there was a second Lycurgan legislation. Finally, we must deal with the possibility that the problematic citation of the 18th year of Alcamenes was not originally in the Eusebian text at all. It does not appear in Jerome's text, our earliest and best witness. The fact that the regnal year is mentioned by Syncellus as well as by the Armenian version does not constitute two independent witnesses. Syncellus' excerpts ultimately derive from the same Greek redaction of the

Chronicle from which the Armenian translation was made.[28] The redactor altered the format of the original. When entering the notices he might have read the disputed Lycurgus entry against the 18th year of Alcamenes in the Lacedaemonian *filum* and wrongly introduced the regnal year into the text. If so, we must account for an Apollodoran date in the year corresponding to AA 1221, 796 B.C., where the notice appears in the text, and disregard the 18th year of Alcamenes. The only possible association is the younger Lycurgus whom Apollodorus dated to 777/76, 108 years after the Lacedaemonian lawgiver. Such an opinion is reflected in Cicero (whose information derives through Nepos from Apollodorus), *de rep*, 2.18: *centum et octo annis postquam Lycurgus leges scribere instituit, prima posita est olympias, quae quidam nominis errore ab eodem Lycurgo constitutam putant.* In the process of transmission, the sources of Eusebius, like Cicero's *quidam*, confused the two Lycurgi, and the accomplishments of the elder were attributed also to the younger. Furthermore, the interval was corrupted from 108 years to 88, an easy error in Greek (PH to ΠH). Eusebius counted off the 88 years in his *Canons*, beginning with his date (883) for the elder Lycurgus as 1, and so coming to the year 796 as 88. That the year happened to be the 18th of Alcamenes in the Lacedaemonium *filum* is coincidence.[29]

Summary

The conclusions may be represented schematically (necessarily oversimplified) as follows:

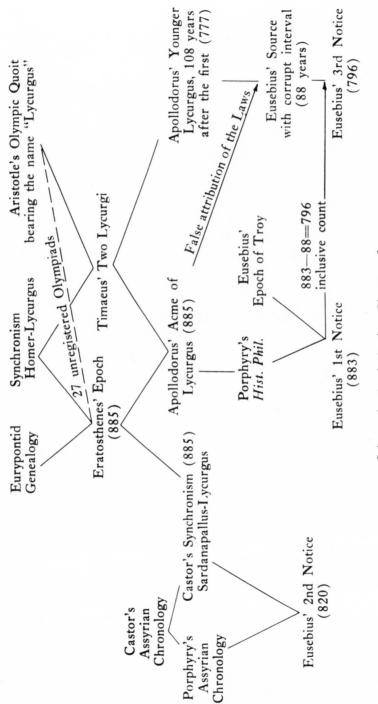

Schematic Analysis for Chapter 5

6

Hesiod

a) AA 1208 (809): Hesiodus insignis habetur, ut uult Porphyrius. (84^c)
   Lacuna in the Armenian version.
b) OL 3.2 (767/66): Hesiodus secundum quosdam clarus habetur. (87^f)
   No corresponding notice in the Armenian version.

Eusebius' notices for Hesiod provide an excellent and relatively simple example of how cross-contamination within a growing system of traditions can produce different absolute dates from the same primary elements. Eusebius cites Porphyry, one of his principal immediate authorities on early literary history, for the *floruit* of Homer in the year corresponding to 809. Much the same reasoning that led Porphyry to this date also produced the later date for Hesiod, which Eusebius reports at the year corresponding to 767/66.

The articles of the *Suda* for Homer and Hesiod confirm in every detail Eusebius' attribution of the 809 date for Hesiod to Porphyry. According to the *Suda*, Porphyry (*FGrHist* 260 F 20) dated Hesiod 100 years after Homer and 32 years before the first Olympiad. The *Suda* specifically cites the *Historia Philosophica* (*FGrHist* 260 F 19) for the date of Homer, stating that Porphyry dated him 132 years before the first Olympiad. The article adds that Porphyry computed 407 years between the fall of Troy and the first Olympiad and that his date for Homer is therefore 275 years after the fall of Troy. Since most dates for Homer were expressed as intervals reckoned from the epoch of Troy, the *Suda*'s additional information allowed the reader to make easy comparisons between Porphyry's date and the opinions of others.

Eusebius (89 Karst) cites Porphyry's *Historia Philosophica* for Apollodorus' intervals between the fall of Troy and the first Olympiad, and here too the total is stated as 407 years. As has been noted in chapter 5, the count backward from the first Olympiad rather than forward from the epoch of Troy was the original method, and one started from the year corresponding to 777/76 as ·"1." Porphyry's intervals for Homer and Hesiod should be interpreted accordingly. The absolute dates are therefore 909 (777 + 132 = 909 = 1184 — 175) for Homer and 809 (777 + 32 = 809 = 909 — 100) for Hesiod, according to the intervals that the *Suda* attribues to Porphyry.

The precise computations are important. Since Eusebius synchronized the first Olympiad with the second year of Aeschylus (86[b] Helm), he preserved the year 777/76 as the starting point for counting (cf. chapter 1). He therefore correctly arrived at the year corresponding to 809 in the *Canons* in interpreting the interval of 32 years before the first Olympiad that he excerpted from the *Historia Philosophica* of Porphyry for the *floruit* of Hesiod. Furthermore, Apollodorus, who was Porphyry's usual authority on literary history, dated the acme of Hesiod to 807—not 809. Apollodorus also set Homer 100 years after the Ionian colonization (*FGrHist* 244 F 63), dating his acme to 944, while Porphyry dated Homer to 909. One must therefore ask why Porphyry disagreed with Apollodorus on the dates for Homer and Hesiod and what authorities he followed instead.

The evidence for the Apollodoran dates of Hesiod appears in Solinus 40. 16–17 (*FGrHist* 244 F 332): *inter quem* (Homer) *et Hesiodum poetam, qui in auspiciis olympiadis primae obiit, centum triginta octo anni interfuerunt.* The phrase *in auspiciis olympiadis obiit* suggests that Apollodorus dated the death of Hesiod to 777/76. The interval of 138 years computed inclusively from that date yields 914 for Homer. That is the year to which Apollodorus dated the death of Homer, although some authorities mistook the date as a *floruit.*[1] The same 138-year interval reckoned from Apollodorus' date for the acme of Homer in 944 yields an Apollodoran acme for Hesiod in 807.

Apollodorus' reasoning is clear. Eratosthenes (*FGrHist* 241 F 9) had dated Homer to 1084. Having adopted the dates of Eratosthenes for the fall of Troy, the Ionian migration, and Lycurgus, Apollodorus nevertheless dated the acme of Homer to 944, 100 years after the Ionian migration in order to allow a chronological overlap with Lycurgus. The death of Homer he dated to 914, the poet's 70th year of life. Eratosthenes' epoch

of Lycurgus in 885/84, interpreted as an acme, yielded a birthdate for Lycurgus in 924/23. Thus Apollodorus was able to
preserve the old synchronism between Homer and Lycurgus by
producing the chronological overlap that Clement (*Strom.* 1.117)
attributes to him (*FGrHist* 244 F 63b), instead of by dating
the acme of each to the same year.[2] Hesiod's poems show no
awareness of the Olympic festival. The latest possible date for
Hesiod's death was therefore 777/76. It was reasonable to assign to him, as to Homer, a life span of seventy years. Thus
Hesiod's acme at the age of forty was in the year 807.[3]

Since Porphyry frequently follows Apollodorus, Jacoby believed that his date for Hesiod preserves the Apollodoran acme.
Eusebius enters Porphyry's date at 809. A two-year shift in the
Canons of St. Jerome is not uncommon, given the difficulties of
the textual tradition. Jacoby counted the 32-year interval of the
Suda inclusively from 776 to yield 807 as Porphyry's date for
Hesiod. But Jacoby's computation is based on misinterpretation
of the *Suda*. As has already been demonstrated, Porphyry's date
for Hesiod 100 years after Homer and 32 years before the first
Olympiad was 809 and not the Apollodoran 807.

The dates of Homer and Hesiod are usually interdependent.
It is necessary, therefore, to account first for Porphyry's disagreement with Apollodorus on the date of Homer before explain-
ing the slight difference in their dates for Hesiod. Porphyry's
date for Homer is very nearly the same as that reported by the
author of the *Marmor Parium* (*FGrHist* 239 A 29): 634 years
before the *Marmor's* base date in 264/63 is the year corresponding to 907 or 906. The *Marmor* dates Hesiod (A 28)
about 30 years earlier than Homer, and the *Marmor's* date for
the fall of Troy precedes Homer by about 300 years. The influence of Ephorus on these dates has long been recognized.
Ephorus maintained that Hesiod was older than Homer
(*FGrHist* 70 F 101). His genealogy of the two poets places
Homer in the generation after Hesiod (F 1). The *Marmor's*
interval of about 30 years between the two poets corresponds
to Ephorus' interval of one generation. The interval between the
Marmor's dates for the fall of Troy and those of the two poets
suggests that Ephorus set Hesiod eight and Homer nine generations after the Trojan War. The *Marmor's* interval between
the fall of Troy and the first Olympiad is 433 years, or 13 generations. Ephorus dealt with early Greek history through synchronisms and genealogy, not absolute dates. Whoever converted
his scheme to an absolute chronology said that Homer lived four

generations before the first Olympiad, the generations computed at three to a century.[4]

Porphyry's date for Homer derives from this interval of four generations before the first Olympiad. His date in 909 is 132 years before the terminus for counting (777/76), but 133 years before the era itself. The interval corresponds to the "Ephoran" four generations. In Poryhpry's source the date was no doubt expressed only as an interval of years, without reference to generations and without attribution to Ephorus. It would be vain to speculate on the identity of that source, but Porphyry preferred this somewhat later date for Homer over the Apollodoran 944. He reported it in the *Historia Philosophica* along with the epochal intervals of Apollodorus for the fall of Troy, the return of the Heraclids, the Ionian colonization, and Lycurgus. The *Historia Philosophica* began with Homer, and Porphyry apparently desired a closer synchronism between Homer and Lycurgus than that implied by the Apollodoran acmes, 944 and 885. Porphyry knew the Apollodoran acme of Hesiod in 807, and he accepted it as expressing an approximately correct estimate of Hesiod's date. But having decided to follow another authority in dating Homer to 909, Porphyry decided to express the interval between Homer and Hesiod as an even 100 years. The combination of the "Ephoran" date for Homer with the Apollodoran date for Hesiod suggested the interval of about 100 years. A slight adjustment in the date of Hesiod, from the Apollodoran 807 to Porphyry's 809, resulted.[5]

Eusebius' later date for Hesiod in Olympiad 3.2 (767/66) is different from all others specifically attested. But the date can be explained as resulting from the application of this same 100-year interval between Homer and Hesiod, which the *Suda* says was the opinion of Porphyry and ἄλλοι πλεῖστοι, to another computation of the "Ephoran" date for Homer. Jerome (77ᵉ Helm) quotes the *Latina Historia* for the statement that Ephorus (Euforbus, *codd.*, *corr. Scal.*) dated Homer to the 124th year before the foundation of Rome or, as Nepos would have it, 100 years before the first Olympiad (Ephorus F 102b). The date in the 870s is, as Jacoby pointed out in commenting on the fragment, the nine Ephoran generations computed from Eratosthenes' date for the fall of Troy. These nine generations become significant for the Eusebian entry on Hesiod when combined with Sosibius' date for Homer (*FGrHist* 595 F 2).

According to Sosibius, Homer flourished in the eighth year of Charilaus. Charilaus ruled for 64 years and was succeeded

by Nicander, in whose 34th year the first Olympiad was celebrated. Sosibius' absolute date for Homer was therefore 867/66
or 866/65, depending on whether 777 or 776 was used as the
terminus. Sosibius' date for Homer in the reign of Charilaus
must be connected with his version of the Lycurgus legend, for
it was during the first years of Charilaus that Lycurgus served
as regent and lawgiver. In Sosibius' account, the synchronism
between Homer and Lycurgus must have been exact. During the
term of his regency Lycurgus went on his travels and in the eighth
year he met the poet Homer. For the synchronism expressed as
a personal meeting during the period of regency, Sosibius is
following Ephorus (F 149, 19). The date in 866 is approximately nine generations, 300 years, after the fall of Troy, reckoned now from Sosibius' date for the fall of Troy in 1172 (F 1).
The precise date in the eighth year of Charilaus, 867 or 866 is
of course Sosibius' own.

There is no way of knowing what date, if any, Sosibius had
for Hesiod. But Eusebius' sources, who elsewhere preserve remnants of Sosibian chronology, applied to Sosibius' date for
Homer the commonly held opinion that 100 years separated
Hesiod from Homer.[6] The result was the date in 767/66 recorded in the *Canons*. Eusebius' immediate source was his
Olympiad chronicler, and no special significance should be attached to Jerome's *secundum quosdam*. A similar phrase (*ut
quibusdam uidetur*) appears in the entry for Dracon (97[g]). Eusebius shows no awareness of another date for Dracon and there
can be no doubt that his date, which was the vulgate Olympiad
39, came to him through the Olympiad chronicler.

Eusebius' date for Hesiod in 767 can be accounted for as the
product of the kind of combination and contamination typical
of his source material. There is no basis for any attempt to
connect this date with what little is known about early Boeotia.
Most improbable is the recent effort to associate the date through
the story of the Homer-Hesiod *agon* in Euboea with the colonizing activity of Chalcis and Eretria or with the war between them
on the Lelantine plain. Like other dates for Hesiod, this one is
connected with the debate about the relative ages of Homer and
Hesiod and the alleged meeting between Homer and Lycurgus.
It is not the product of any chronographer's attempt to count
the number of generations between, say, the defeat of Chalcis
by Athens after the expulsion of the Pisistratids and Chalcis'
victory over Eretria in the Lelantine War.[7]

7

Arctinus and Eumelus

a) OL 1.2 (775/74): Arctinus Milesius uersificator floren-
tissimus habetur. (86[1])
   AA 1241 (775/74): Arktios der Milesier blühte als
   Sagendichter. (181)
b) OL 5.1 (760/59): Eumelus poeta, qui Bugoniam et
   Europiam, et Arctinus, qui Aethiopidam conposuit, et Ilii
   persis agnoscitur. (87[e])
   AA 1255 (761/60): Eumelos, der Poet, der die Bugonie
   schuf und die Europie; und Artinos der die Ethiopika und
   die "Einnahme Ilions," war bekannt. (181)
c) OL 9.1 (744/43): Eumelus Corinthius uersificator agnoscitur. (89[b])
   AA 1271 (744/43): Eumeles, der Korinthier, blühte als
   Sagendichter. (182)

These entries for the poets Arctinus and Eumelus are useful
for exploring the possible interrelationships between the dates
of persons transmitted in the chronographic tradition and those
of events. Eusebius' notices on Arctinus and Eumelus also help
show that the sources of his Olympiad chronicler were similar
to those from which the chronological information of the *Suda*
derives. The tradition common to both had been affected by
cross-contamination between earlier traditions and therefore
transmitted combinations of elements once separate.

Only Eusebius preserves absolute dates for Eumelus, and
only Eusebius and the *Suda* have dates for Arctinus. Eusebius
enters Arctinus and Eumelus twice. There are separate notices
in the first and the ninth Olympiads, and the two appear in
synchronism in the fifth Olympiad.[1] The *Suda* has no entry for

Eumelus, but there is a confused chronological notice for Arctinus that can be explained by reference to the Eusebian dates: The *Suda* dates the *floruit* of Arctinus to the ninth Olympiad (744/41), 410 years after the fall of Troy: γεγονὼς κατὰ τὴν θ᾽ ὀλυμπιάδα μετὰ υι᾽ ἔτη τῶν Τρωϊκῶν. The manuscripts of the *Suda* do not agree on the interval between Arctinus and the epoch of Troy. "V" reads υι᾽ (410) with a correction to υλ᾽ (430) noted above. Neither of these intervals reckoned from the *Suda's* (Eratosthenes') epoch of Troy 408 years before the first Olympiad (1184) yields the *Suda's* Olympiad date (744) for Arctinus. Furthermore, the *Suda's* Olympiad date agrees with neither of Eusebius' Olympiad dates for Arctinus. Attempts to solve the problem by emending the text have of course been made. One suggestion brings the notice of the *Suda* into agreement with Eusebius by reading υη᾽ (408) instead of υι᾽ (410) and emending θ᾽ (9) to α᾽ (1). Thus Arctinus would have flourished 408 years after the fall of Troy at the time of the first Olympiad, where Eusebius enters him. A corruption from υη᾽ to υι᾽ is possible, but the emendation from θ᾽ to α᾽ is hazardous, especially since the manuscripts are unanimous in reading θ᾽. Rohde therefore emended the epochal interval to υμ᾽ (440), in order to make the notice of the *Suda* internally consistent without doing violence to the authority of the manuscripts. With this emendation, Arctinus flourished in the ninth Olympiad (744), 440 years after the fall of Troy (744).[2]

No emendation in the text of the *Suda* is necessary. The 30-year discrepancy between epochal interval and Olympiad date in the article on Arctinus is paralleled by Eusebius' entries for Arctinus and Eumelus. The 410-year interval from the fall of Troy yields a date in the second or third year of the first Olympiad and that is where Eusebius' entry for Arctinus appears. Eusebius synchronizes Arctinus with Eumelus in the fifth Olympiad, then enters Eumelus himself in the ninth Olympiad—the *Suda's* Olympiad date for Arctinus. Clearly, the sources of the *Suda* conflated the dates of two nearly contemporaneous poets who sometimes were synchronized. The epochal interval referred originally to Arctinus (410 years after Troy = 774), while the Olympiad date belonged to Eumelus (Olympiad 9, 744/41). In the process of transmission separate notices on Arctinus and Eumelus were combined because both were poets of the epic cycle whom some authorities synchronized. By the time the information reached the *Suda*, however, some such phrase as σύγχρονος ἦν Εὐμέλου had disappeared from the combined notice entered in the encyclopedic handbooks under the name of Arctinus. There is a similar case in the dates of Eusebius and the *Suda* for Phocylides and Theognis. Of Phocylides the *Suda* says: σύγχρονος Θεόγνιδος. ἦν δὲ ἑκάτερος μετὰ χμζ' (647) ἔτη τῶν Τρωϊκῶν, ὀλυμπιάδι γεγονότες νθ' (OL 59, 536/35). The 647 year interval from Troy corresponds to the last year of the 60th Olympiad (537/36), not to Olympiad 59. Eusebius enters Phocylides in Olympiad 60 and Theognis in Olympiad 59 (103[l,p] Helm). Again, the sources of the *Suda* combined two notices into one, synchronizing Phocylides with Theognis. The epochal interval was excerpted from a notice on Phocylides, the Olympiad date from a notice on Theognis, and the two were combined into a single chronological note. The common source of Eusebius and the *Suda* for these dates was a handbook of literary history based on the biographical vulgate deriving from Apollodorus. Eusebius' immediate source was an Olympiad chronicler and he therefore preserves the Olympiad dates better than the *Suda*, whose immediate sources were organized alphabetically.

Arctinus flourished in the first Olympiad, Eumelus in the ninth. Since only Eusebius and the *Suda* have absolute dates for the two poets, there is insufficient evidence to determine exactly how these dates were established. Some plausible conjectures may, however, be hazarded. For Eratosthenes and Apollodorus the first Olympiad marked the beginning of the historical period.[3] As has been shown in chapter 6, Apollodorus' chronology for literary history brought the transitional period between the fall of Troy and the first Olympiad to a close with the death of Hesiod *in auspiciis olympiadis primae* (Solinus 40. 16–17 = Apollodorus *FGrHist* 244 F 332). It is reasonable to suppose that he marked the beginning of the historical period with the *floruit* of the eldest of Hesiod's successors in epic, Arctinus of Miletus. Such an opinion is in fact reflected by Dionysius of Halicarnassus (1.68.2), who refers to Arctinus as the most ancient poet within reliable knowledge (παλαιότατος ὢν ἡμεῖς ἴσμεν ποιητὴς 'Αρκτῖνος). Arctinus may have been considered the earliest poet within historical knowledge simply because he was from the ancient and famous city of Miletus. Or perhaps such a conclusion could be drawn from the geographical knowledge reflected in the poems attributed to him. The first Olympiad was chosen as a date for Arctinus because of this opinion about his antiquity. The precise date in 775 or 774, if the *Suda*'s interval of 410 years from Troy is definitive, must have been dictated by other considerations. If the date is connected with early Milesian history, the first foundation of Sinope is an event with which the poet might have been synchronized. For Eusebius dates the foundation of Trapezus to the 750s (AA 1260, p. 182 Karst; omitted by Jerome), and Trapezus was a colony of Sinope (Xen. *Anab.* 4.8.22). In this system of chronology, then, the Milesians must have founded Sinope before 750. The year 774 may have been the chronographic date, but we have entered the realm of empty speculation. Whatever event (if any) the chronographers associated with Arctinus in order to produce a more exact date, his *floruit* within the first Olympiad derives from a preconceived notion about his antiquity.

For Eumelus the evidence is better. According to Pausanias (4.4.1), Eumelus wrote his hymn to Delian Apollo in the time of King Phintas, when the Messenians sent a chorus to Delos. Thus Eumelus could be synchronized with Phintas, apparently on the basis of a reference to him in the poem. Now, Pausanias says (4.4.4) that Phintas lived in the last generation before the first Messenian war, and he dates the beginning of the war (4.5.4.) to the second year of the ninth Olympiad (743/42). The last possible date for the synchronism between Eumelus and Phintas is therefore the first year of the Messenian war.[4] Eumelus was accordingly dated to the ninth Olympiad (744/43), in synchronism with the outbreak of that war. Eusebius' entry on the beginning of the Messenian war appears in Jerome just before the notice on Eumelus and in the Armenian version immediately after Eumelus. This difference in the order of the entries suggests that in the original *Canons* the two notices were entered side by side at the same year. The date in the ninth Olympiad derives from Sosibius. We do not know that Sosibius himself was concerned with literary history. But the synchronism between Eumelus and the last years of free Messenia (i.e., the outbreak of the first Messenian war) was part of the biographical vulgate and Eusebius' sources combined it with a date for the Messenian war deriving from Sosibius.[5]

The synchronism between Eumelus and Arctinus that led to the confusion in the *Suda's* chronological note about Arctinus appears in the *Canons* of Eusebius at the fifth Olympiad (760/57). The date happens to mark the mid-point between the individual dates given for Arctinus and Eumelus. But the notice does not represent a compromise between the other two dates. It derives from a separate computation. Clement of Alexandria (*Strom.* 1.131) concludes a discussion of the relative ages of Archilochus and Terpander with a remark pertaining to Eumelus: Εὔμηλος δὲ ὁ Κορίνθιος πρεσβύτερος ὢν ἐπιβεβληκέναι Ἀρχίᾳ τῷ Συρακούσας κτίσαντι (Eumelus of Corinth, being of earlier date, overlapped with Archias the founder of Syracuse). A synchronism between Eumelus and Archias is reasonable. Both were Corinthian Bacchiads and both were associated with ancient events—Eumelus with the first Messenian war, Archias with the foundation of Syracuse. The foundation of Syracuse afforded a date for Archias and through Archias that date could also be assigned to Eumelus. Eusebius dates the foundation of Syracuse to Olympiad 10.3, 738/37. The date does not agree with either of his dates for Eumelus (760/59, 744/43). But the *Marmor Parium* (*FGrHist* 239 A 31) dates Archias' expedition to Syracuse in the 21st year of Aeschylus, king of Athens. The interval on the stone cannot be read, so that the date intended by its author must be inferred through the Atthidographic lists. In the Athenian king lists transmitted from the Atthidographers to Eusebius by Castor (85–89 Karst) and reproduced in the *Canons* of Jerome the 21st year of Aeschylus corresponds to Olympiad 5.3, 758/57. Thus Eusebius' date for Eumelus in the fifth Olympiad is the same as the *Marmor*'s date for the foundation of Syracuse.

Eusebius' sources for literary history dated persons by Olympiads, not regnal years. But the coincidence between Eusebius' date for Eumelus and the date of the *Marmor* for Syracuse in the 21st year of Aeschylus is striking. It is not likely that Eusebius found Eumelus dated in his sources to the 21st year of Aeschylus or synchronized with the foundation of Syracuse, which he dates much later. Eusebius found Eumelus dated to the fifth Olympiad, which happens to include the 21st year of Aeschylus. The rationale, unknown to Eusebius, was the synchronism of Eumelus with Archias and the foundation of Syracuse. His sources followed one system of chronology for the Sicilian colony foundations, but remnants of other systems appear in connection with literary history. The fifth Olympiad includes the year to which Apollodorus dated the outbreak of the first Messenian war, 757/56. It is possible therefore that this date for Eumelus derives from Apollodorus, that Apollodorus shared with the

author of the *Marmor Parium* a common source for the date of
Syracuse, and that Apollodorus united the synchronism between
Eumelus and Archias' foundation of Syracuse with the synchronism between Eumelus and Phintas' free Messenia. That is,
Eumelus flourished in 758/57 when Archias was colonizing Syracuse, and this date was also the last year of free Messenia, for
the Spartan attack began in the next year, 757/56.[6]

Arctinus also appears in the fifth Olympiad, but only through
synchronism with Eumelus. In both versions of the *Chronicle*
Eumelus and Arctinus are combined in a single notice, with Eumelus appearing first. The date refers strictly to Eumelus, and
Arctinus is included simply because the fact that both were
ancient cyclic poets suggested a synchronism. One should not
therefore search in early Milesian history (or elsewhere) for a
separate computation leading to a date for Arctinus in the fifth
Olympiad.

In summary, then, Eusebius' date for Arctinus in the first
Olympiad derives from an unknown authority who dated him
to that time on the grounds that Arctinus was the earliest poet
of the "historical" period. His date for Eumelus in the ninth
Olympiad represents a combination of the synchronism between
Eumelus and Phintas of Messenia, an inference from a poem,
with Sosibius' date for the first Messenian war. The same dates
underlie the confused notice of the *Suda* on Arctinus. Eusebius'
date for Eumelus in the fifth Olympiad represents a synchronism
with Archias, oecist of Syracuse, and possibly also with Apollodorus' date for the first Messenian war.

8

Tyrtaeus and the Messenian Wars

a) OL 8.3 (746/45): Lacedaemonii contra Messenios vicennale certamen habebant. (89^c)
   AA 1274 (742/41): Die Lakedämonier führten Kriege mit den Messeniern. (182)

b) OL 11.2 (735/34): Messena a Laced́aemoniis capitur. (89^i)
   AA 1282 (734/33): Sirakuse und Katane in Sikilia wurden gegründet. Messene ward von den Lakedämoniern eingenommen. (182)

c) OL 15.1 (720/19): Bellum quod in Thyrea inter Lacedaemonios et Argiuos gestum est. (90^g)
   AA 1297 (719/18): In Thyrea der Kampf der Argiver und Lakedämonier. (183)

d) OL 35.4 (637/36): Messena a Lacedaemoniorum societate discedit. (96^g)
   AA 1380 (636/35): Messene fiel von den Lakedämoniern ab. (185)

e) OL 36.4 (633/32): Myrtaeus Atheniensis poeta cognoscitur. (96^i)
   AA 1383 (633/32): Timeos der Athener war gekannt. (185)

The mainstream of the tradition that reached Eusebius' sources represented the chronographic vulgate deriving from Eratosthenes and Apollodorus. The tradition had, however, been affected by other influences in such a way as to transmit information that derived now from one source, now from another, and that sometimes combined elements so as to produce a new chronological datum true to none of the earlier traditions. The influence of the Laconian scholar Sosibius (*FGrHist* 595) has

already been noted in chapters 5, 6, and 7. The clearest evidence
of cross-contamination between traditions deriving from Apollodorus and Sosibius appears in connection with Eusebius' notices
on Tyrtaeus and the Messenian wars. These entries have re-
peatedly been subjected to close scrutiny in the continuing debate
over the chronology of the Messenian wars, so that there is
little to be added to the present understanding of the chronographic tradition on the issue.[1] Nevertheless, since the evidence
of Sosibian influence on Eusebius' sources is most striking in these
notices, they demand inclusion in this collection of studies.
Furthermore, close analysis of the Eusebian evidence in comparison with other extant testimonia suggests that Sosibius'
version of early Spartan chronology was but a variant of Eratosthenes' system. By combining Sosibian and Apollodoran influences, Eusebius' sources produced a tradition representing
cross-contamination between two versions of the same original
system.

The starting point for chronographic computation of the
dates of the first Messenian war was Tyrtaeus' statement (preserved by Pausanias 4.6.5, 4.13.6) that Ithome fell in the
twentieth year of the war and that King Theopompus was responsible for the victory. Tyrtaeus also said (Pausanias 4.15.2–
3) that the war had been fought by "spearmen fathers of our
fathers." Pausanias interpreted this remark as meaning that
Tyrtaeus lived in the third generation after the first Messenian
war. If the dates of Tyrtaeus himself had been known, chronographers could have dated the first Messenian war by reference
to this generational indication. But Tyrtaeus' date was not independently known; and, as Pausanias points out (4.15), Tyrtaeus did not name the kings in power when the Messenians
revolted and precipitated the second Messenian war, the conflict
in which Tyrtaeus himself participated. It was therefore necessary to date the first war by reference to King Theopompus'
position in the king lists, then to compute a date for Tyrtaeus and
the second war in the third generation thereafter.

There were two traditions concerning the time of Theopompus' death relative to the end of the war. Two different calculations of the war's date with reference to Theopompus' regnal
years were therefore possible. According to one tradition—that
reported by Pausanias, 3.7.5, 4.6.5—Theopompus survived the
war and was still alive, although aged and in pain, at the time
of the battle of Thyrea. Pausanis (4.3.7) dates the end of the

war to Olympiad 14.1, 724/23. In the Eurypontid list of Eratosthenes and Apollodorus (above, chapter 5) Theopompus' 10th year was 776/75, and he ruled for a total of 47 years. Theopompus' last year was therefore 739/38, fifteen years before Pausanias' date for the end of the war. Clearly, Pausanias' date is not Apollodoran. In the Eurypontid list of Sosibius (*FGrHist* 595 F 2), Nicander ruled for 39 years, and his 34th year was synchronized with the first Olympiad. The 47th year of Nicander's successor Theopompus was therefore 724/23, Pausanias' date for the end of the war. Since it was Theopompus who, according to Tyrtaeus, was responsible for the victory, Pausanias' date must be Sosibian. According to Pausanias, Theopompus survived the war, and this version may also be Sosibian. In that case it is Sosibius who was Plutarch's Lacedaemonian source for the statement (*Agis* 21) that Theopompus was only wounded by Aristomenes, not slain as the Messenians maintained.

In the version of Sosibius, then, Theopompus brought the war to an end in his 47th year, Olympiad 14.1, 724/23. Since the twenty-year duration of the conflict was firmly established through Tyrtaeus, Sosibius must have dated its outbreak to Olympiad 9.2, 743/42. Pausanias (4.5.10) transmits this date for the beginning of the war, and it was this date that also reached the sources of Eusebius. The manuscripts of Jerome vary in the placement of the entry from Olympiad 8.3 to Olympiad 9.1, while the Armenian version dates the twenty-year war to 742/41.[2]

According to a second version, which Pausanias (4.6.4) attributes to Myron, Theopompus was slain by Aristomenes shortly before the death of the Messenian king Aristodemos. Pausanias says (4.13.6) that the war continued for another five months and that the Messenians surrendered at Ithome toward the end of the year. In this account Theopompus' death falls in the last year of the war. Jacoby demonstrated that Apollodorus followed this latter version. The usual practice in dealing with part of a year at the end of a king's reign was to assign those last few months to the chronographic first year of the successor, in this case Theopompus' grandson Zeuxidamos (Pausanias 4.15.3). Thus Theopompus' last full year, his 47th in Apollodorus' list, was 739/38. Theopompus died and the war ended in 738/37, Olympiad 10.3.[3] This is the date for the end of the war that Eusebius' source reported, the extant manuscripts varying from 740/39 to 734/33.

The *Canons* allow an interval of only about ten years between the beginning and the end of the war. Yet Eusebius' first notice reports the war as being of twenty years' duration. This anomaly cannot be accounted for in manuscript variations. Eusebius or, rather, his source combined two different computations in reporting dates for the war. The date for the beginning of the war derives from Sosibius (OL 9.2, 743/42), while the date for its end is Apollodoran (OL 10.3, 738/37). In the original *Canons* there was accordingly an interval of only six years. Eusebius was taking excerpts from his Olympiad chronicler for inclusion in the *spatium historicum* of the *Chronological Canons.* He epitomized the content, but did not trouble himself with the implications.

According to Sosibius, Theopompus survived the war and was still alive at the time of the battle of Thyrea. Since his date for the end of the war was the 47th year of Theopompus, he must have given to Theopompus more than the 47 years of Eratosthenes' list. Nevertheless, it is clear that for both Apollodorus and Sosibius, the 47th year of Theopompus was a key date. In Sosibius' version, Theopompus brought the war to an end in the 47th year of his reign. For Apollodorus, Theopompus died in the last year of the war after 47 years of rule. The two versions are variants of Eratosthenes' Eurypontid chronology. In the version of Apollodorus, Theopompus died and the war ended several months after the completion of his 47th year. Sosibius also dated the end of the war by reference to Theopompus' 47th year. In his version, Theopompus was wounded in his 47th year. He brought the war to an end several months later, but during the same chronographic year— περὶ τὸν ἐνιαυτὸν λήγοντα (Pausanias 4.13.6). If Sosibius agreed with Eratosthenes on the date of Theopompus' accession, this variant would result in a difference of only one year in the dates for the war. But Sosibius aligned the Eurypontid list with the Olympiad system differently from what Eratosthenes had. Hence what was originally an Eratosthenic date for the end of the war was lowered some fifteen years.

Further evidence that the Sosibian chronology is but a variant of that of Eratosthenes is to be found in the reported dates for the battle of Thyrea. In the version common to Sosibius and Pausanias, Theopompus was still alive, after the end of the Messenian war, at the time of the battle of Thyrea. Eusebius dates the battle, according to the Oxford manuscript of Jerome, to 720/19, four years after the Messenian capitulation by Sosi-bius' reckoning. Solinus (7.9) dates the battle to the 17th year of Romulus. The date corresponds to 735/34 by Cato's era for the founding of Rome and is therefore three years after Apol-lodorus' date for the end of the Messenian war. Jacoby noted that both dates for the battle of Thyrea are one Olympiad later than the two dates for the end of the Messenian war.[4] The re-lationship can be expressed more precisely. The two dates for the battle of Thyrea mark the same relative position in the two versions of the Eurypontid lists. Sosibius dated the end of the Messenian war to the 47th year of Theopompus. Apollodorus dated it to the year after Theopompus' 47th, the first of Zeuxi-damos. The dates both of Eusebius and of Solinus for the battle of Thyrea therefore correspond to the fourth year after Theo-pompus' 47th in the Eurypontid lists of Sosibius and Apollo-dorus, respectively. That is, Eusebius' date is Sosibian and Sosi-bius' date is that of Eratosthenes and Apollodorus (Theopom-pus' 47 + 4, for Sosibius = Theopompus 51) applied to a differ-ent alignment of the Eurypontid list with respect to the absolute chronology of the Olympiads. Sosibius' Eurypontid list is ac-cordingly a variation of the Eratosthenic list, with changes like the increase in Theopompus' years made for a number of rea-sons. Eusebius' sources, by combining Sosibian and Apollodoran dates, in fact combined one version of the Eratosthenic system with another.

    Eusebius enters Tyrtaeus at the 36th Olympiad (636/33). Tyrtaeus had to be dated relative to the first Messenian war, although he himself had fought in the second. Tyrtaeus did not state who was king at the time of the second war, but he indi-cated that the rebellion took place in the third generation after the conquest. That was Pausanias' inference from the phrase "spearmen fathers of our fathers." Jacoby argued that Apollo-dorus made the same inference and computed the generations at 40 years each.[5] Since Apollodorus dated the end of the first war to 738/37, his date for the rebellion and for Tyrtaeus must have been Olympiad 30 (660/59), counting the intervals in-clusively, and that was the year of the Pisatan Anolympiad in Eusebius' list (p. 92 Karst). Sosibius also adopted an interval of 80 years between the two wars. From Sosibius' date for the end of the first war in 724/23 two intervals of 40 years each yield a date between 646 and 644 for the rebellion, depending on the method of counting used. To the 34th Olympiad, 644/43,

Pausanias (6.22.2) assigns the Anolympiad of the Messenians' Pisatan allies. The *Suda* dates Tyraeus' acme (s.v.) to Olympiad 35. These must be Sosibian dates. To date Tyrtaeus a few years after the outbreak of the war is logical enough, since it was after an initial defeat that the poet assumed command of the troops. It is not likely that the Spartan Sosibius called Tyrtaeus an Athenian, however, as did Pausanias (4.15.6) and the sources of Eusebius. The Sosibian date was combined with the popular tale that the Spartans required the assistance of a lame Athenian poet to deal with the situation (Philochorus *FGrHist* 328 F 215). Jerome and the Armenian translator date both the Messenian rebellion and the acme of Tyrtaeus one Olympiad later than the Sosibian dates. Since the *Suda*, with similar source material, dates Tyrtaeus to Olympiad 35, Eusebius probably did also. The downward shift in the extant *Canons* is an instance of transcriptional error, deriving in this case, perhaps, from difficulty in reading the correct Olympiad dates associated with entries on the beginning or the end of an original Eusebian page (cf. above, chapter 1).[6]

9

Archilochus

a) p. 67ᵃ Helm: licet Archilochus •XXIII• olympiadem et
quingentesimum Troianae euersionis annum supputet.
p. 174 Karst: und andere unter Archilochus um die
dreiundzwanzigste Olympiade, 500 Jahre nach den Ili-
schen Dingen.
Syncellus 340: ἕτεροι κατὰ 'Αρχίλοχον περὶ τὴν
κγ΄ (23) ὀλυμπιάδα μετὰ ἔτη φ΄ (500)
που τῆς ἀλώσεως Τροίας

b) OL 23.1 (688/7): Hipponax notissimus redditur. (93ᵉ)
No corresponding Armenian notice.

c) OL 29.1 (664/3): Archilochus et Simonides et Aristoxenus musicus inlustres habentur. (94ᵉ)
AA 1351 (665/4): Archilochus und Simonides wurden
gekannt. (184)

The chronographic tradition gives us two absolute dates for
Archilochus. Both are of great interest for the study of tradition
in the broadest sense and, more particularly, for the evaluation
of the texts that preserve the fragmentary remains of the Greek
chronographic tradition. The first date, that in the 23rd Olympiad, Eusebius shares with other authorities. Enough fragments
from earlier stages in the tradition are extant to permit its
development to be traced. The date in the 23rd Olympiad
(688/85) derives from a very complex set of unsystematic combinations, and it has no value as chronological evidence. The
second date, in the 660s, is preserved only in the *Chronicle* of
Eusebius. There is, however, enough independent evidence to
show that the date derives directly from the best traditions of
Hellenistic scholarship and that it was based on reasoning similar

to that still adduced in debates over the date of Archilochus. Analysis of these two dates shows the tradition at its worst and at its best, demonstrating that every date preserved in the extant texts must be approached with caution and judged on its own merits after thorough investigation with every available critical technique.[1]

The Date in the 23rd Olympiad

Archilochus' reference to Gyges and his riches (fr. 22 Diehl) became proverbial and led naturally enough to a synchronism between the two. The synchronism and the rationale behind it are best known through the remark that appears in the text of Herodotus (1.12): τοῦ (Gyges) καὶ ᾽Αρχίλοχος ὁ Πάριος κατὰ τὸν αὐτὸν χρόνον γενόμενος ἐν ἰάμβῳ τριμέτρῳ ἐπεμνήσθη. That ancient scholars used this synchronism to estimate the date of Archilochus is attested indirectly. Archilochus is supposed to have participated in the colonization of Thasos, and the dates for the foundation of Thasos are the same as those reported for the beginning of Gyges' reign in Lydia. Clement (*Strom.* 1.131) cites Xanthus for the date of the foundation of Thasos in the 18th Olympiad (708/5), and he cites Euphorion (*Strom.* 1.117) for the beginning of Gyges' reign in the same Olympiad. A variant date for Thasos in the 15th Olympiad (720/17) he attributes to Dionysius (*Strom.* 1.131, presumably Dionysius of Halicarnassus) and this earlier date is based on a date for Gyges inferred from Herodotus' Mermnad chronology. Yet a third date for Gyges appears in the *Canons* of Eusebius, according to which Gyges' reign began in the second year of the 20th Olympiad (699/8). It is perhaps this date for Gyges that led Clement to say (*Strom.* 1.131) that Archilochus must have flourished after the twentieth Olympiad.[2]

Despite the obvious synchronism between Archilochus and Gyges, based on a direct inference from the poems, neither of the dates preserved for Archilochus agrees with any of the chronographic dates for Gyges and the beginning of Mermnad rule in Lydia. In fact, only Tatian (*ad Graec.* 31) offers an absolute date for the Archilochus-Gyges synchronism as such:

ἕτεροι δὲ κάτω τὸν χρόνον ὑπήγαγον, σὺν Ἀρχιλόχῳ γεγονέναι
τὸν Ὅμηρον εἰκόντες. ὁ δὲ Ἀρχίλοχος ἤκμασε περὶ
ὀλυμπιάδα τρίτην καὶ εἰκοστήν, κατὰ Γύγην τὸν Λυδόν,
ὕστερον τῶν Ἰλιακῶν ἔτεσι πεντακοσίοις.

Others date him much later and synchronize Homer with
Archilochus. Archilochus flourished in the 23rd Olympiad,
at the time of Gyges of Lydia, 500 years after the Trojan
War.

Even in this case the Olympiad date cannot be associated directly
with the synchronism between Gyges and Archilochus. Tatian's
statement is included in his discussion of the date of Homer, and
the date follows upon a synchronism between Homer and Archilochus. The authority for that synchronism (Tatian's ἕτεροι)
is Euphorion. The 500-year interval represents Theopompus'
opinion about the relative dates of Homer and the Trojan War.
These facts are clear from Clement's discussion (*Strom.* 1.117)
of the date of Homer:

ναὶ μὴν Θεόπομπος　　　(*FGrHist* 115 F 205) μὲν ἐν τῇ
τεσσαρακοστῇ τρίτῃ τῶν Φιλιππικῶν μετὰ ἔτη πεντακόσια τῶν ἐπὶ
Ἰλίῳ στρατευσάντων γεγονέναι τὸν Ὅμηρον ἱστορεῖ. Εὐφορίων δὲ
ἐν τῷ περὶ Ἀλευαδῶν κατὰ Γύγην αὐτὸν τίθησι γεγονέναι, ὃς
βασιλεύειν ἤρξατο ἀπὸ τῆς ὀκτωκαιδεκάτης ὀλυμπιάδος, ὃν καί
φησι πρῶτον ὠνομάσθαι τύραννον.

In the 23rd book of *The Philippics* Theopompus says that
Homer lived 500 years after the expedition against Troy.
Euphorion in his book about the Aleuads (*sic!*) sets Homer in
the time of Gyges, whose reign began in the 18th Olympiad and
who Euphorion says was the first to be called by the name
tyrant.

We do not know what absolute date, if any, Theopompus
adduced for the Trojan war. Euphorion combined Theopompus'
synchronism between Homer and Archilochus with the common
synchronism of Archilochus with Gyges and thus stated that
Homer lived in the time of Gyges. How he arrived at an absolute
date in the 18th Olympiad, 708/5, we do not know. Clement
(*Strom.* 1.131) ascribes that date for the foundation of Thasos to
Xanthus of Lydia, but it is doubtful that Xanthus used absolute
dates and we do not know what Xanthus said that led Euphorion
to infer a date for Gyges, Archilochus, and the foundation of

Thasos in the 18th Olympiad. The date happens to be just 500 years after the date of the *Marmor Parium* (*FGrHist* 239 A 24) for the fall of Troy, but there is no basis for deciding whether or not that coincidence is significant. However that may be, the intermediate sources between Theopompus and Tatian did not combine the synchronism of Homer and Archilochus with any date for Gyges or any that could be considered Theopompus' date for the epoch of Troy. They combined both the synchronism and the interval with Eratosthenes' Olympiad system, since it was the chronographic standard. The 500-year interval correctly counted from Eratosthenes' epoch of Troy (1184) would yield a date for this Homer-Archilochus synchronism in 684, the first year of the 24th Olympiad. The Greeks did not have a numerical system as convenient as ours, and the time between the fall of Troy and the first Olympiad could be expressed only as an interval. In Eratosthenes' system the interval was 408 years. The remaining 92 years represent 23 Olympiads. Because of someone's poor arithmetic, the Homer-Archilochus synchronism came to be associated with Olympiad 23, and that date was also attached to the synchronism between Archilochus and Gyges.[3]

Eusebius knew this date for Archilochus through Tatian. He quotes Tatian's discussion of the date of Homer at *Praep. Euang.* 10.11.4. The same passage is the source of Eusebius' lengthy entry on Homer at AA 907 (1104/3, p. 66 Helm). Nevertheless, it is Hipponax, not Archilochus, whom Eusebius enters in the 23rd Olympiad. This error offers yet another illustration of how easily even foolish combinations could contaminate the tradition. Hipponax lived much later than Archilochus. According to the *Marmor Parium* (*FGrHist* 239 A 42) Hipponax flourished about 550 in the time of Cyrus. Pliny (*N.H.* 36.11) dates Hipponax to the 60th Olympiad (540/37). A comic invention, which Athenaeus (13, 599) attributes to Diphilus, portrayed Hipponax and Archilochus as lovers of Sappho. The anecdote led to a synchronism between Archilochus and Hipponax, which the sources of Eusebius' Olympiad chronicler combined with the Homer-Archilochus synchronism in Olympiad 23.[4]

The date for Archilochus in the 23rd Olympiad results from a complex set of false combinations. Combined again with a false synchronism between Archilochus and Hipponax, the date came to be associated with Hipponax alone. It is not uncharacteristic of Eusebius and his encyclopedic sources to transmit remnants of false combinations with the key element of a synchronism (here, Archilochus) missing. A similar situation occurs in Olympiad 42 (612/9), where Alcman and Stesichorus appear at a date originally associated with Sappho. More significantly, the chain of false combinations, compounded by sloppy arithmetic, that leads from a 500-year interval between Homer and an unknown date for the Trojan war through Gyges and Archilochus to the 23rd Olympiad and finally to Hipponax, is indicative of how unsystematic the Greek chronographic tradition can be. These dates for Archilochus and Hipponax should stand as a warning against any attempt to extract primitive tradition directly from chronographic dates by adducing formulas for genealogical and mathematical "systems."

The Date in the 29th Olympiad

Eusebius enters Hipponax in Olympiad 23 through false synchronism with Archilochus. Archilochus himself appears in Olympiad 29 (664/61) in synchronism with Simonides and Aristoxenus. This Simonides is the iambic poet of Amorgus who was regularly synchronized with Archilochus simply because both wrote early iambs.[5] The *Aristoxenus musicus* is, of course, not the Peripatetic philosopher from Tarentum, but the poet of Selinus whom Epicharmus (fr. 88, Kaibel *CGF*) called the first iambist. Eusebius dates him too early. The *floruit* of Aristoxenus could have been computed by reference to the foundation of Selinus. Thucydides (6.4) says that Selinus was colonized from Megara Hyblaea 145 years before Gelon (i.e., about 625). Eusebius (95f Helm) and Diodorus (13.59) date Selinus to 650. Aristoxenus appears in the *Canons* synchronized with his fellow practitioners of the archaic iamb at a date before the foundation of Selinus. Thus an unsystematic synchronism among the three most ancient iambic poets has come to be associated with the date of one of them. The fact that Archilochus appears first suggests that it is he to whom the date specifically refers.

Jerome enters the Archilochus-Simonides-Aristoxenus synchronism at Olympiad 29.1, 664/63, (so "O"—the manuscripts exhibit the usual variation). This year happens to be the last of Gyges' reign in the Lydian list of the *Canons*. Erwin Rohde once suggested, therefore, that the date derived from a desire on the part of the Christian chronographers to date the development of Greek culture as late as possible—in the case of Archilochus the latest possible date was the last year of Gyges. Eusebius does not indulge in invention of this sort. He transmits the Greek chronographic tradition as preserved, however imperfectly, in his sources. In fact, as Rohde himself tentatively hypothesized in a later article, Eusebius' entry for Archilochus preserves the date assigned to him by Apollodorus, the most influential of the Greek chronographers in matters of literary history.[6]

The evidence for the Apollodoran date of Archilochus appears in a fragment from the *Chronicle* of Nepos cited by Gellius. According to Gellius (17.21.8) Nepos' date for Archilochus fell within the reign of Tullus Hostilius: *Archilochum autem Nepos Cornelius tradit Tullo Hostilio Romae regnante iam tunc fuisse poematis clarum et nobilem.* Nepos also gave an absolute date expressed in the Olympiad system and as an interval from the foundation of Rome. That is how his work was organized. Gellius unfortunately did not report the precise date. The reign of Tullus Hostilius corresponds to 672–40 by Cato's reckoning of the founding of Rome. Both Nepos and Eusebius frequently transmit Apollodoran data. The fragment of Nepos is evidence that the Eusebian date is Apollodoran, and the Eusebian date supplies the precision missing in Gellius' citation.

The Apollodoran date for Archilochus within the interval afforded by the reign of Tullus Hostilius (672–40) cannot derive from synchronism with Gyges. Apollodorus dated the fall of Croesus to 547/46 and he followed Herodotus for Lydian chronology (*FGrHist* 244 F 28). The sum of Herodotus' regnal years for the Mermnads is 170 (1.14, 15, 25, 86) and he says (1.14) that Gyges ruled for 38 years. Thus for Apollodorus the reign of Gyges spanned the years corresponding to 716 through 679. Gyges died before the beginning of the interval within which, according to the fragment of Nepos, the Apollodoran acme of Archilochus must have fallen. Jacoby argued that Apollodorus rejected the synchronism between Archilochus and Gyges because he adopted the view of Glaucus of Rhegium (Plut. *de Mus.* 4) that Archilochus was younger than Terpander. According to Hellanicus (*FGrHist* 4 F 85) Terpander was victor at the first Carneian Festival. The establishment of the festival was dated to Olympiad 26, 676/73 (Olympic victor list, p. 95 Karst; cf. Sosibius *FGrHist* 595 F 3). Apollodorus accordingly dated Archilochus a few years later. But how he came to a precise absolute date in the 29th Olympiad Jacoby could not determine.[7]

Whatever opinion Apollodorus had about the relative chronology of Archilochus and Terpander, there is a better explanation for his having dated Archilochus after the end of Gyges' reign. Both Clement (*Strom.* 1.131.8) and Strabo (14, 647) maintain that Archilochus must have been active as a poet at the time of the destruction of Magnesia by a marauding band of Cimmerians. Strabo cites the line that proves the contention: Κλαίω τὰ Θασίων, οὐ τὰ Μαγνήτων κακά (fr. 19 Diehl). Apollodorus must also have taken note of this line and its implications. Archilochus mentioned Gyges and his riches. He also made reference to a disaster that Apollodorus had reason to believe should be dated after Gyges. According to Herodotus (1.15) it was during the reign of Gyges' son Ardys that the Cimmerians invaded Asia and captured Sardis. Apollodorus knew that Archilochus should be dated after the disaster that he mentioned. He inferred from Herodotus that the disaster had taken place during the reign of Ardys, that is, sometime after 679. The precise date he derived by applying his theorem of 40-year literary and philosophical successions to the date of Thales, 585/84. One such period (inclusively reckoned) before Thales would yield the date 624/23 (the birth date of Thales by the acme method) and a second interval brought him to 663/62, the second year of the 29th Olympiad.

Eusebius' date for Archilochus in the 29th Olympiad derives from Apollodorus. Apollodorus established an approximate date on the basis of the same evidence that modern historians use— the primary evidence of the poems suggesting that Archilochus lived at the time of the Cimmerian incursions into Asia Minor together with the evidence of Herodotus that such an invasion took place during the reign of Ardys. Computing a precise date is difficult. Modern historians adduce Assyrian annals to try to date Gyges, Ardys, and the Cimmerian invasions. Astronomical calculations can be called upon to date the solar eclipse that Archilochus mentions (fr. 74 Diehl).[8] Apollodorus had access neither to cuneiform documents nor to astronomical data. He called instead upon a chronographic theorem to compute a precise date within the required interval. Greek chronographers did indeed use artificial mathematical devices based on the theory of "successions." But wild distortions in the traditional chronology do not result, for the device was applied at the last stage in the process and in such a way as to introduce precision for a relative chronology based on the best available evidence.

10

Alcman and Stesichorus

a) OL 28.1 (668/67): Nudipedalia primum acta in Lacedaemone. (94^e)
AA 1351 (665/64): Der Knaben Nacktkampf ward
zuerst in Lakedemon veranstaltet. (184)
b) OL 30.3 (658/57): Alcmeon clarus habetur et Lesches
Lesbius qui paruam fecit Iliadem. (94^i)
AA 1358 (659/58): Lesches, der die Kleine Iliade schuf,
und Almeon ward gekannt. (185)
c) OL 42.2 (611/10): Stesichorus poeta clarus habetur.
(98^d)
AA 1408 (608/7): Stisechoros der Poet war gekannt.
(186)
d) OL 42.2 (609/8): Alcman ut quibusdam uidetur, agnoscitur. (98^e)
No corresponding Armenian entry.
e) OL 55.1 (560/59): Stesichorus moritur. (102^g)
AA 1458 (558/57): Stesichorus verstarb. (188)
f) OL 55.2 (559/58): Simonides clarus habetur. (102^h)
AA 1459 (557/56): Simonides war gekannt. (188)

Eusebius' entries for Alcman and Stesichorus show that his
sources and the sources of the *Suda* were collateral branches of
a vulgate chronology that derived from the *Chronicle* of Apollodorus, but transmitted a tradition contaminated by error, confusion, and false combination. Eusebius notes the *floruit* of
Alcman in the 30th Olympiad and again in the 42nd. The acme
of Alcman was a key date for Apollodorus, but the *Suda*'s
version suggests that the original Apollodoran date for Alcman
corresponded to one of the years of the 27th Olympiad, not
the 30th.

Analysis of the relevant entries must begin with a reconstruction of the Apollodoran chronology for Alcman and Stesichorus. Eusebius' pair of notices on the death of Stesichorus and the *floruit* of Simonides in the 55th Olympiad represents a corrupt version of an Apollodoran synchronism attested in a badly mutilated passage of Cicero's *de Re Publica* (2.10.20). Cicero's source for the Olympiad date in the passage was the *Chronicle* of Nepos, upon whom most Latin authors relied for dates in Greek history, and Nepos in turn had used Apollodorus.[1] The passage in question, as reconstructed by Mommsen and Rohde, reads as follows: *neque enim Stesichorus nepos eius* (sc. *Hesiodi*) *ut dixerunt quidam ex filia. quo enim ille mortuus eodem est anno natus Simonides olympiade sexta et quinquagesima.*[2] "Stesichorus was not the grandson of Hesiod on his mother's side, as some say. For Stesichorus died the same year that Simonides was born, in the fifty-sixth Olympiad."

The year of Simonides' birth, 556/55, when the 56th Olympiad was celebrated, is a historical date that Apollodorus derived from Simonides' own statement (fr. 77 Diehl) that he was in his 80th year when Adeimantus was archon (477/76). This same date for the death of Stesichorus is reported by the *Suda*: τοῖς δὲ χρόνοις ἦν νεώτερος ᾿Αλκμᾶνος τοῦ λυρικοῦ, ἐπὶ τῆς λζ΄ ὀλυμπιάδος (OL. 37, 632/29) γεγονώς. ἐτελεύτησε δ᾿ ἐπὶ τῆς νς΄ (OL. 56, 556/53). The *Suda's* date for the death of Stesichorus is that of Apollodorus, synchronized, as Cicero suggests, with the birth of Simonides. It is probable therefore that Apollodorus is also the source of the *Suda's* date for Stesichorus in Olympiad 37, 632/29. The *Suda* notes that Stesichorus flourished (ἦν) after Alcman and that he γέγονε in the 37th Olympiad. Under Alcman, the *Suda* says that he flourished in the 27th Olympiad, when Ardys was king of the Lydians: ἦν δ᾿ ἐπὶ τῆς κζ΄ ὀλυμπιάδος (OL. 27, 672/69)βασιλεύοντος Λυδῶν ῎Αρδυος. The *Suda's* notice for Stesichorus preserves an Apollodoran date and suggests a relationship between Stesichorus and Alcman. The two notices for Alcman and Stesichorus attest to an interval of forty years between the ἦν of Alcman (OL. 27) and the γέγονε of Stesichorus (OL. 37). The interval of forty years suggests that the acme method of Apollodorus is behind these dates.

Rohde argued that not all of the *Suda's* dates can be Apollodoran. An Apollodoran acme (40 years old) for Stesichorus in Olympiad 37 (632/29) would give Stesichorus 116 years at the time of his death in Olympiad 56 (556/53). The *Macrobioi* (26) assigns to Stesichorus a life span of 85 years, and Rohde interpreted this statement as Apollodoran. He accordingly computed Olympiad 35 (640) as the Apollodoran birth date, assigning the acme to Olympiad 45 (600).[3] The evidence of the *Macrobioi* is, however, irrelevant and inconclusive. The author is often in disagreement with Apollodorus. The life span of 85 years, in particular, has no significance, since the *Macrobioi* assigns the same 85 years to Anacreon, Carneades, Hellanicus, Lycurgus, and Pherecydes, and the figure therefore seems arbitrary. If Apollodorus dated the acme (ἦν) of Alcman to Olympiad 27 (672/69), as the notice of the *Suda* suggests, but possessed no evidence for the length of his life or the time of his death, he might simply have given the poet a τέλειος βίος of 80 years and dated his death to Olympiad 37 (632/29). This is the *Suda*'s date for the γέγονε of Stesichorus. As has been shown, Apollodorus synchronized the death of Stesichorus with the birth of Simonides. The notices of the *Suda* suggest that Apollodorus also synchronized the death of Alcman with the birth of Stesichorus.[4] The use of γέγονε in the sense of *natus est* is rare, but not without parallel in the *Suda*. There are a number of instances where the birth of a person is certainly indicated.[5] One such case occurs, significantly .enough, in the notice for Simonides: γέγονε δ᾽ ἐπὶ τῆς νϛ᾽ ὀλυμπιάδος (OL. 56. 556/53). The first year of the 56th Olympiad, 556/55, is the Apollodoran (and historical) date for the birth of Simonides.

Apollodorus synchronized the death of Stesichorus with the birth of Simonides, and the birth of Stesichorus with the death of Alcman. He set the acme of Alcman in one of the years of the 27th Olympiad. His scheme, as reconstructed thus far, was therefore as follows:

Olympiad 17	(712/9):	Birth of Alcman*
Olympiad 27	(672/69):	Acme of Alcman
Olympiad 37	632/29:	Death of Alcman
		Birth of Stesichorus
Olympiad 47	(592/89):	Acme of Stèsichorus*
Olympiad 56	(556/55):	Death of Stesichorus
		Birth of Simonides

* These inferences may require correction. If the acme of Alcman was in the last year of OL. 27 (as is suggested below), his birth by Apollodorus' inclusive count was in the first year

of OL 18. Similarly, if the birth of Stesichorus was in the first year of OL 37, his acme was in the last year of OL 46.

Elements of this system underlie Eusebius' entries for Alcman, Stesichorus, and Simonides. He preserves the Stesichorus-Simonides synchronism of Apollodorus. In both versions of the *Chronicle* the pair of notices is misaligned, and they appear in Olympiad 55 instead of in Olympiad 56. Furthermore, Eusebius or his source understood the γέγονε for Simonides as a *floruit* and accordingly entered his acme instead of his birth (cf. Syncellus 455: Σιμωνίδης ἤκμαζεν). The Alcman-Stesichorus synchronism appears in Olympiad 42 (612/9), instead of Olympiad 37. Eusebius enters the *floruit* of both Alcman and Stesichorus at Olympiad 42. For Apollodorus the year of the synchronism was not an acme date for either poet. It was the birth of Stesichorus that he synchronized with the death of Alcman. Eusebius' sources have again substituted a *floruit* for a birth date (Stesichorus) and compounded the error by making the synchronism with Alcman literal—both flourished in the same year. The reason for this confusion and for the change in the date from Olympiad 37 to Olympiad 42 emerges from the notice of the *Suda* for Sappho: γεγονυῖα κατὰ τὴν μβ΄ ὀλυμπιάδα (OL. 42, 612/9) ὅτε καὶ Ἀλκαῖος ἦν καὶ Στησίχορος καὶ Πιττακός. The *Suda* synchronizes Stesichorus with Sappho and Alcaeus at a date originally associated with the acme of Pittacus (below, chapter 13). Eusebius' sources combined the Alcman-Stesichorus synchronism of Apollodorus with the Stesichorus-Sappho synchronism of the literary vulgate. The result was combined with the Sappho-Alcaeus and Alcaeus-Pittacus synchronisms to bring the *floruit* of Alcman and Stesichorus to the 42nd Olympiad (612/9), the Apollodoran acme of Pittacus. Again, as in the case of Hipponax-Archilochus, the key element that made the combination possible and the date meaningful (here, Sappho) fails to appear.

The only certain date in the system of Apollodorus for Alcman, Stesichorus, and Simonides is the year of Simonides' birth in Olympiad 56.1, 556/55. The rest of the scheme derives through synchronism and combination from the placement of the acme of Alcman in Olympiad 27 (672/69). Rohde suggested that this date for Alcman was originally of the same reference as Eusebius' entry of the *floruit* of Alcman ("Alcmeon" is a standard variant) in Olympiad 30 (660/57). According to the notice of the *Suda*, Alcman flourished in Olympiad 27, when Ardys was king of the Lydians. The first year of the 27th Olympiad (672/71) marks the seventh year of Ardys for those who follow the Lydian chronology of Herodotus and date the fall of Croesus to 546. In the Lydian list of the *Canons* of Eusebius the seventh year of Adrys corresponds to the last year of the 30th Olympiad, 657/56 (OL. 31.1, Arm.). Rohde found the agreement of the *Suda* and Eusebius precisely at the seventh year of Ardys too striking to be coincidental. He did not, however, venture an explanation of the coincidence.[6]

The seventh year of Ardys has now acquired the status of chronographic epoch—a dubious honor for which there is, in this case, little warrant. Neither the *Suda* nor Eusebius actually connects Alcman with the seventh year of Ardys. The *Suda* cites an Olympiad number without specifying the year of the quadrennium. It is hazardous to assume, with Rohde, that the first year of the Olympiad is always meant whenever the year is not otherwise specified. The *Chronicle* of Eusebius is organized by Olympiads. His sources, like those of the *Suda*, dated the persons and events of Greek history by reference to Olympiads. Although synchronisms like the one between Alcman and Ardys in the *Suda* are common, precise regnal years have little significance for the placement of historical notices with respect to the *fila regnorum* of the *Canons*. In the case of Eumelus, for example (above, chapter 7), it could be said that he was a contemporary of Archias, the founder of Syracuse, and the *Marmor Parium* dates the foundation of Syracuse to the 21st year of Aeschylus. Neither this date for Syracuse nor the synchronism between Eumelus and Archias was known to Eusebius. He dates the foundation of Syracuse to the 10th Olympiad. But he found Eumelus dated to the fifth Olympiad, which happens to include the 21st year of Aeschylus in the Athenian list of the *Canons*. If the seventh year of Ardys is to have any significance for the *Suda*'s date for Alcman in Olympiad 27 or Eusebius' entry in Olympiad 30, the probable origin of such an expression for the date must be determined.

In the Bodleian manuscript of Jerome, the entry for Alcman appears at the third year of the 30th Olympiad, which corresponds to the sixth year of Ardys. The next entry, at Olympiad 30.4 = Ardys VII, is: *Histrus ciuitas in Ponto condita* (95[b] Helm). According to [Scymnus] 767, Istrus was founded by the Milesians when an army of Scythians crossed into Asia in pursuit of the Cimmerians. Herodotus (1.15) says the Cimmerians first entered Asia and ravaged Sardis during the reign of Ardys. Hence the conclusion has been drawn that the Cimmerian invasion took place during the seventh year of Ardys; this fact was remembered and eventually recorded, and for the Alexandrian chronographers the seventh year of Ardys marked an epoch to which different absolute dates might be assigned, depending on the different versions of Lydian chronology in use.[7] Thus, the *Suda*'s date for Alcman in Olympiad 27 and Eusebius' date in Olympiad 30 are different expressions of the same thing.

The seventh year of Ardys as a date for the Cimmerian invasion is a modern inference. There is no evidence that any ancient authority ever made precisely that association. It is unlikely that early Greek tradition, however great the impression left by the Cimmerian devastations, could date the Cimmerian attacks any more precisely than Herodotus does—during the reign of Ardys. There is a relationship of another kind between the variant dates of the *Suda* and Eusebius for Alcman and the Cimmerian invasions mentioned by Herodotus and the author of the *orbis descriptio*. Alcman was known as the poet Σαρδίων ἀπ' ἀκρᾶν (fr. 13 Diehl), but he was most famous as a practitioner of choral lyric at Sparta. The biographical tradition may have accounted for this double provenance by depicting Alcman as having fled to Sparta when Sardis was overwhelmed by the advancing Cimmerian hordes. Such a story, together with Herodotus' statement about the Cimmerian attack on Sardis, could produce a synchronism between Alcman and Ardys. At Sparta, Alcman was particularly associated with the Gymnopaedia. According to Athenaeus (15.20–22) the Gymnopaedia included choral dances of men and boys singing the ᾄσματα of Alcman. The institution of the festival of the Gymnopaedia would therefore provide an appropriate reference point for the dating of Alcman's acme, especially if the date could also be associated with the event that accounts for his having left Sardis.

Only Eusebius preserves a date for the institution of the Gymnopaedia. The placement of the entry varies in the manuscripts from the third year of the 27th Olympiad, 670/69 ("B"), to the fourth year of the 28th Olympiad, 665/64 (Arm.). According to the *Suda*, the festival was celebrated in honor of Spartiates, fallen at Thyrea. This connection of the festival with the Spartan-Argive dispute over territory in the Thyreatis is confirmed by Athenaeus (15.22) in a citation from Sosibius' περὶ θυσίων (*FGrHist* 595 F 5). Athenaeus says the celebration commemorated a victory at Thyrea. Eusebius' date for the institution of the festival does not accord with his own date for the Battle of Thyrea (720), the date of Solinus (7.9; 17th year of Romulus=735), or the implication of Herodotus (1.82) that the great Spartan victory at Thyrea took place about the time of the war between Croesus and Cyrus. As H. T. Wade-Gery demonstrated, Eusebius' date implies that the festival was originally instituted as an appeasement to the gods after the infamous Spartan defeat at Hysiae, which Pausanias dates (2.24.7) to the fourth year of the 27th Olympiad, 669/68.[8]

The weight of authority in the manuscripts of the *Chronicle* suggests that the Gymnopaedia was established in the first year of the 28th Olympiad, 668/67, the anniversary of the disaster. Deriving this date, perhaps, from Sosibius' *On Spartan Festivals*, Apollodorus had a *terminus ante quem* for Alcman of 668/67. The association with the Cimmerian invasions gave him a *terminus post quem* of 678, the first year of Ardys in Apollodorus' interpretation of Herodotus' Lydian chronology. It remained to establish a precise year within that interval. What follows is a hypothesis that provides an acceptable synthesis of the data without recourse to the theory that the seventh year of Ardys was remembered in primitive tradition and thus acquired the status of chronographic epoch. The association of Alcman with the first Gymnopaedia would have been most appropriate if the poet had been present in Sparta at the time of the disastrous battle the year before. Apollodorus therefore dated Alcman to 669/68 and united all the data. A man in flight does not waste time seeking a safe haven. Thus Apollodorus had Alcman flourish in Sardis in 669/68, flee in that year from the barbarian hordes, and arrive in Sparta just in time to learn of the disaster at Hysiae and be commissioned to compose hymnody to deprecate it.

Apollodorus synchronized Alcman with Ardys, but he expressed Alcman's date as an Athenian archon year. That the seventh year of Ardys can be associated both with the 27th and with the 30th Olympiads is a coincidence. Eusebius' date for Alcman in the 30th Olympiad derives from an unknown authority who shared with Apollodorus the belief that Alcman's relocation from Sardis to Sparta should be associated with the Cimmerian invasions. He did not, however, establish a date by reference to the Gymnopaedia. Instead, he used the tradition that associated the foundation of Istrus with the Cimmerian invasions, and he shared with the source of Eusebius a date for Istrus in the 30th Olympiad. Both dates for Alcman derive from a tradition that synchronized him with the Cimmerian invasions. But the seventh year of Ardys was never a "chronogrophic epoch" for the Cimmerians, much less an element of the oral tradition. Apollodorus established an absolute date by reference to the Gymnopaedia, while Eusebius' source used the foundation of Istrus. The Cimmerian invasion did not in itself offer an absolute date.

11

Lesches, Terpander, Arion

a) OL 30.3 (658/57): Alcmeon clarus habetur et Lesches
   Lesbius qui paruam fecit Iliadem. (94[1])
   AA 1358 (659/58): Lesches, der die Kleine Iliade schuf,
   und Alcmeon ward gekannt. (185)
b) OL 34.2 (642/41): Terpander musicus insignis habetur.
   (96[e])
   No corresponding Armenian notice.
c) OL 40.3 (619/18): Arion Methymnaeus clarus habetur.
   Qui a delfino in Taenarum dicitur transportatus. (97[k])
   AA 1406 (610/9): Arion der Methymnaer war gekannt;
   der durch einen Delphin nach Stenaron gerettet entkam.
   (186)

Eusebius' immediate source for much of his information
about early Greek chronology was an Olympiad chronicle in
which biographical notices were especially prominent. Most of
the dates for early Greek poets that Eusebius transmits from
this source derive from Apollodorus, although often by a tortuous route and in a corrupt or contaminated version. Eusebius'
entries for Lesches, Terpander, and Arion are of interest because they constitute an important exception to this general rule.
The dates are not Apollodoran, but they may very well derive
from an earlier authority whose methodology prefigures that of
Apollodorus. Analysis of these entries is difficult and the conclusions reached must be regarded as tentative, since the available evidence is even slimmer than usual. Such weak links as
there may be in the argument should accordingly serve as a
reminder that most hypotheses about the genesis of chronographic dates retain a conjectural status. Each must be considered

on its own merits, and there can be no general solution to problems that arise from a complex tradition.

There is no direct evidence for the Apollodoran date of Terpander. As Jacoby suggested, however, he probably agreed with Hellanicus (*FGrHist* 4 F 85a) in synchronizing him with the first Carnean festival at a date corresponding to the 26th Olympiad, 676/75 (Sosibius *FGrHist* 595 F 3).[1] Since Apollodorus dated Archilochus to 663/62 (above, chapter 9), he therefore also agreed with Glaucus of Rhegium (Plutarch, *de mus.* 4, 1132e) that Archilochus was younger than Terpander. There was disagreement on this question, however. Clement of Alexandria (*Strom.* 1.131) thought Hellanicus had dated Terpander much too early. In support of this contention he adduces a fourth-century authority, Phainias of Eresos, who believed Terpander to have been younger than Archilochus:

ναὶ μὴν καὶ Τέρπανδρον ἀρχαῖζουσί τινες. Ἑλλάνικος γοῦν τοῦτον ἱστορεῖ κατὰ Μίδαν γεγονέναι, Φανίας δὲ πρὸ Τερπάνδρου τιθεὶς Λέσχην τὸν Λέσβιον Ἀρχιλόχου νεώτερον φέρει τὸν Τέρπανορον, διημιλλῆσθαι δὲ τὸν Λέσχην Ἀρκτίνῳ καὶ νενικηκέναι.

There are some who make even Terpander ancient. Hellanicus claims he lived in the time of Midas. But Phainias sets Lesches of Lesbos before Terpander and maintains that Terpander was younger than Archilochus. Lesches won a contest with Arctinus.

Clement goes on to argue the date of Archilochus, associating him with the foundation of Thasos and concluding that Archilochus must have lived after the 20th Olympiad, 700/699. The conclusion seems hardly appropriate. Evidence that Archilochus was older than Terpander and lived after the 20th Olympiad does not prove that Hellanicus was wrong to date Terpander in the 26th Olympiad. Clement does not cite Hellanicus for that date, however, but for a synchronism with Midas. Eusebius preserves a date for Midas' death by bull's blood in the 21st Olympiad (92ᵃ Helm). If that was the date Clement knew, then his argument has some semblance of logic. Although it was not the date in 676 that Clement had in mind, he was right to think that Phainias' relative chronology could refute Hellanicus. By synchronizing Terpander with Midas, Hellanicus implied that he was older than Archilochus, who was regularly synchronized with Gyges, Midas' junior according to Herodotus (1.14).

Sosibius dated Terpander to 676/75. Eusebius dates him to the 34th Olympiad, 644/41, and this date agrees with that of the *Marmor Parium*, 644/43 (*FGrHist* 239 A 34). This is a date much later than any we know for Archilochus, and Clement says that Phainias in fact dated Terpander after Archilochus. The evidence is circumstantial, but the common source of Eusebius and the *Marmor Parium* for this later date for Terpander was probably Phainias.

Clement says that Phainias considered Lesches older than Terpander, and Eusebius—the only source of an absolute date for Lesches—sets him in the 30th Olympiad, about fifteen years older than Terpander.[2] Now, there is no way of determining from the fragment how much older than Terpander Phainias considered Lesches and Archilochus to have been or what his opinion was as to whether Lesches or Archilochus was the elder. Clement adds, however, still in indirect statement, that Lesches competed with Arctinus and won. If this comment is to be ascribed to Phainias, there are serious difficulties in the interpretation of the fragment and its relevance to Eusebius' dates. Eusebius enters Arctinus in the first Olympiad, and this date reflects the general opinion as reported by Dionysius of Halicarnassus (1.68.2) that Arctinus was the eldest of the poets within historical knowledge. According to Clement, Phainias synchronized Lesches with Arctinus. But Eusebius enters Lesches more than 100 years after Arctinus.[3]

Since, according to Eusebius, Arctinus flourished long before Lesches, Gelzer argued that their alleged contest is impossible and the entire fragment is chronologically worthless. Unger, on the other hand, emended the passage to bring Phainias into agreement with Glaucus of Rhegium on the relative chronology of Terpander and Archilochus. Thus, Terpander was older than Archilochus and Lesches was older than Terpander, so that the contest between Arctinus and Lesches becomes chronologically plausible.[4] The passage should not be emended. The problematic synchronism between Lesches and Arctinus ought not be interpreted in the light of the later chronographic date for Arctinus. The alleged contest is the counterpart in the cyclic epic of the legendary contest between Homer and Hesiod. Phainias may just as well have had a low date for Arctinus as a high date for Lesches. The fragment must be interpreted as it stands; and the structure of Clement's argument suggests that Phainias considered Lesches older than Terpander, but younger than Archilochus.[5]

Phainias' role in the development of Greek biography is debated. Even less is known about his contribution to the development of early Greek chronology.[6] Plutarch (*Solon* 32.3) cites him in a chronological context for an opinion about the date of Solon's death (fr. 21 Wehrli). Clement (*Strom.* 1.139) attributes to him a date for the return of the Heraclids corresponding to the year 1050 (fr. 19). Phainias wrote a "Prytanies" of his native Eresos. Analogy with Charon's "Prytanies" of the Lacedaemonians (*FGrHist* 262 T 1) and with the ἀρχόντων ἀναγραφή of Phainias' fellow Peripatetic Demetrius of Phalerum (*FGrHist* 228 F 1–3) suggests that the work was a chronicle. As a chronicler of a Lesbian city and a scholar known for his interest in the history of music (fr. 32), Phainias quite probably included in his chronicle dates for those poets of Lesbos who were noted for their contribution to the history of music.

Phainias apparently disagreed with his fellow islander Hellanicus about the date of their countryman Terpander. How he arrived at an absolute date for Terpander in the 640s we do not know. Jacoby accounted for the date of the *Marmor Parium* by pointing out that it is 200 years before the Panathenaic victory of Phrynis in 446 (*FGrHist* 239 A 34, Kom.). To use the victory of Phrynis as a starting point to compute the date of Terpander is plausible, for Phrynis too was from Lesbos (Mitylene); Terpander supposedly established a school of music that culminated with Phrynis, who in turn became the teacher of Timotheus (Schol. Aristoph. *Clouds* 967). Phainias perhaps established a relative chronology for Terpander within the history of music by placing him after the early iambists and before the dithyrambic innovations of Arion, yet another poet from Lesbos. The early iambists could be synchronized with Archilochus and through him with Gyges. As a poet of the cyclic epic, Lesches would have to be set before Terpander. Hence, Phainias would have the relative chronology in the order Archilochus, Lesches, Terpander, Arion. This is the order to which both Clement's citation and Eusebius' dates attest. Arion, according to Herodotus (1.12–24), was active at the court of Periander in the time of Alyattes. Following Herodotus for Mermnad chronology and setting the fall of Croesus in the 540s, Phainias could establish an interval between the early iambists (the end of Gyges' rule) and Arion (the beginning of Alyattes' rule) corresponding roughly to the years 670 to 620. This approximation he could then convert to an absolute date by applying a theory of musical successions similar to that subsequently used by Apollodorus. The fifth such succession, computed at 40 years each and starting from the Panathenaic victory of Phrynis in 446, yields a date within the required interval. The precise date was 645 if the five periods were counted as one (200 years with one terminus included), 641 if each of the five periods was counted separately with every terminus included. Thus Terpander's musical innovation and his *floruit* as a poet came to be dated to the 640s, as reported by Eusebius and the *Marmor Parium*. Which is the "correct" date, the *Marmor*'s 644 or Eusebius' 642, cannot be determined. There is a margin of error of one or two years in the interpretation of the *Marmor*'s epochal intervals, and the manuscripts of Jerome can attest only approximately to the original Eusebian date.[7]

While the *Marmor* is of some help in interpreting Eusebius' date for Terpander, there is no external control on the date for Lesches. We know only that Phainias considered him older than Terpander. Both Jerome and the Armenian version enter Lesches in synchronism with Alcman, and Rohde drew attention to the interval of ten Olympiads, that is, forty years, between Eusebius' dates for Alcman (OL. 30) and Arion (OL. 40). Now, according to the article of the *Suda* for Arion, some authorities considered him a student of Alcman. Hence Rohde concluded that the appearance of Arion in Olympiad 40 was based on this relationship with Alcman.[8] It seems more likely that the interval of forty years, if it is significant at all, expresses a relationship between Lesches and Arion, since both were poets of Lesbos. Some help in interpreting Eusebius' date for Lesches may therefore be sought by investigating the dates reported for Arion.

Any date for Arion's acme must of course preserve Herodotus' synchronism (1.23–24) of Arion with Periander. So the *Suda*, for example, dates Arion to Olympiad 38, for that Olympiad (628/25) was the Apollodoran date for the beginning of Periander's rule.[9] The *Suda*'s literal synchronism is not appropriate. For according to Herodotus' account of the story, several years elapsed between the beginning of Periander's reign and Arion's return to his court from Tarentum via the dolphin and Cape Taenarum. Herodotus says (1.24.1) that Arion had spent some time with Periander before he conceived the desire of going to Italy. We should therefore expect Apollodorus to have computed a date for the acme of Arion, synchronous with his

famous ride, a few years after his date for Periander. Evidence
that he did so is provided by Solinus (7.6), who reports Apollodoran dates through the medium of Nepos' *Chronicle*:

In Laconica spiraculum est Taenaron. est et Taenaron pro-
munturium aduersum Africae. in quo fanum Methymnaei
Arionis, quem delphine eo aduectum imago testis est aerea ad
effigiem casus et ueri operis expressa. praeterea tempus signa-
tum. olympiade enim undetricesima, qua in certamine Siculo
idem Arion uictor scribitur, id ipsum gestum probatur.

Solinus synchronizes a Sicilian victory of Arion with his return
to Greece on the dolphin in the 29th Olympiad. Either the text
is corrupt (*XXIX* instead of *XXXIX*) or Solinus made the
common error of confusing an Apollodoran birth date with the
acme. The 29th Olympiad, 664/61, is much too early. But a
date in the 39th Olympiad, 624/21, meets all the criteria and
can plausibly be attributed to Apollodorus, whose influence is
evident elsewhere in Solinus.[10] The date is several years after
the accession of Periander in Apollodorus' chronology, and
Herodotus' account requires such an interval. A further indication that this date for Arion derives from Apollodorus is the fact
that it happens to be forty years after Apollodorus' date for
Archilochus (663/62) and forty years before his date for
Thales (585/84). The precise date of the Apollodoran acme
for Arion was accordingly 624/23.

The forty-year interval in the *Canons* of Eusebius between
Alcman and Arion is coincidence. There may, however, be significance for this interval if it is considered as an expression of
a relationship between Lesches and Arion. The Eusebian date
for Arion is poorly attested in the extant versions. There is a
variation of almost ten years between the dates of Jerome and
the Armenian version. Since the Armenian entry appears so late
(610/9), it is not likely that either the Armenian or Jerome's
entry (619/18) can attest to a Eusebian date deriving from the
Apollodoran date in 624/23. Given the relative merits of the
manuscript traditions of the two versions, one must follow the
reading of the oldest manuscripts of Jerome as attesting to an
original Eusebian date in the 40th Olympiad (620/17). This
date is different from the vulgate synchronism of Arion with the
acme of Periander in Olympiad 38 (the *Suda*) and from the
Apollodoran date for Arion in Olympiad 39. Arion was from
Lesbos; there is a forty-year interval in the *Canons* between

Lesches of Lesbos and Arion; we know that Phainias considered Lesches older than Terpander; and Eusebius' date for Terpander about 15 years after Lesches is apparently the date established by Phainias. The evidential chain is weak, but there is sufficient ground for ascribing Eusebius' dates for Lesches and Arion, as well as the forty-year interval between them, to Phainias.

As has already been suggested, Phainias probably established a relative chronology for these poets of Lesbos because of their contributions to the history of music and poetry. Terpander was to be placed before Arion because Terpander introduced musical innovations that the poems of Arion presumably reflected. Arion, of course, had his own place in the history of music through his innovations in the dithyramb. Phainias perhaps considered Lesches the last representative of archaic epic, to be dated therefore shortly before Terpander began to write citharoedic poems in epic meter. The absolute date of Terpander depended on a theory of successions in the school of poetry established by Terpander and culminating with Phrynis. The absolute dates of Lesches and Arion as reported by Eusebius are separated by an interval of forty years inclusively counted. Lesches appears in Olympiad 30.3, 658/57, and Arion appears in Olympiad 40.2, 619/18. The fortieth year after this date for Arion is the first year of the 50th Olympiad, 580/79.

Some truly remarkable coincidences now emerge, which are of great interest for the development of early Greek chronology. The 50th Olympiad is the date of the naming of the Seven Sages, according to Eusebius' Olympic victor list (93 Karst), the *Canons* (101[e] Helm), Tatian (*ad Graec.* 41), and Clement (*Strom.* 1.129). There are grounds for believing that this date for the Seven Sages is in fact a very early estimate made long before Apollodorus.[11] Eusebius' date for Arion is the fortieth year before the naming of the Seven Sages in Olympiad 50. The Apollodoran date for Arion is the fortieth year before the acme of Thales, traditionally the first of the Seven to receive the title. Eusebius dates Lesches the fortieth year before Arion, while Apollodorus used that interval before his date for Arion to fix the acme of Archilochus (above, chapter 9). The evidence is slim and there are therefore some weak links in the argument. But if the attribution to Phainias of the Eusebian dates for Lesches, Terpander, and Arion is correct, it follows that Apollodorus' chronological methods were a development of Peripa-

tetic precedents. The use of a forty-year interval to represent a
literary or philosophical succession can be found as early as
Phainias. The use of base dates to start the computation of such
successions can also be found in Phainias' use of Phrynis' Panathenaic victory for the reckoning of Terpander's date and in his
use of a date for the Seven Sages as a starting point for Arion
and Lesches. The idea of the forty-year acme is attested for the
Peripatetic Aristoxenus, who assigned to Pythagoras the age of
forty when he left Samos to establish a philosophical school in
Italy (fr. 16 Wehrli). Apollodorus adopted these ideas. By
applying them in a systematic manner he developed structures
for early Greek chronology that soon became standard. He
sometimes found it necessary, for the sake of balance and consistency in the structure as a whole, to part company with the
Peripatetics in the matter of absolute dates. Apollodorus was
nevertheless deeply indebted to the Peripatetics for the fundamentals of chronographic theory.

In summary, then, Eusebius' dates for Lesches, Terpander,
and Arion all derive from the fourth-century scholar Phainias
of Eresos. Phainias included dates for the famous poets of his
native Lesbos in his local chronicle, "The Prytanies of Eresos."
He established a relative chronology for the poets on the basis
of his study of musical innovations. He then introduced absolute
dates by reckoning forty-year successions in such a way as to
systematize the relative chronology without introducing any
serious distortion.[12]

12

The Cypselids

a) OL 30.1 (660/59): Cypselus in Corintho tyrannidem exercuit ˙ann˙ XXVIII˙ (94^g)
   AA 1358 (658/57): Kepselos übte über die Korinther die Gewaltherrschaft 28 Jahre. (185)
b) OL 38.1 (628/27): Aput Corinthios tyrannidem exercuit Periander. (96^n)
   AA 1387 (629/28): Über die Korinther übte die Gewaltherrschaft Periander des Kipselos. (185)
c) OL 48.1 (588/87): Corinthiorum monarchia destructa est. (100^e)
   AA 1429 (587/86): Der Korinther Herrschaft endete. (187)
d) OL 49.4 (581/80): Isthmia post Melicerten et Pythia primum acta. (101^d)
   AA 1436 (580/79): Die Isthmien wurden nach Melikertes und die Pythien zuerst angeordnet. (187)

The reconstruction of a correct historical chronology for the Cypselid tyranny is a notorious crux. Eusebius' dates, together with fragments of the chronographic tradition preserved in other late authors, constitute the so-called high chronology. Beloch argued for a lower chronology on the basis of synchronisms he found implicit in Herodotus' Cypselid stories, and this view has won many adherents.[1] The absolute dates of the chronographic tradition are not, however, in disagreement with the synchronisms implied by Herodotus; and these dates, although they imply a precision inappropriate to so early a period, may well be as close an approximation as is possible.[2] An understanding of the tradition that underlies these dates is therefore imperative.

The chronographic texts are themselves difficult to interpret. They require close examination to determine exactly what dates the chronographic tradition as represented by our late sources assigned to the Cypselid tyranny. In this respect, Jacoby's reconstruction of Apollodorus' Cypselid chronology, although essentially correct, needs modification.

Jacoby's starting point was Eusebius' statement in the excerpt from Diodorus' history of the Corinthian kingdom (*Chron.* 1, 104 Karst) that the Bacchiad monarchy continued in one form or another until the tyranny of Cypselus, who seized power 447 years after the return of the Heraclids. Jacoby computed the interval from Eratosthenes' epoch for the return of the Heraclids in 1104/3 and derived a date of 657/56 for the first year of Cypselus' tyranny. Herodotus (5.92), Aristotle (*Pol.* 5, 1315b22), and Nicolaus of Damascus (*FGrHist* 90 F 57) all say that Cypselus ruled for thirty years. Apollodorus surely agreed. He must accordingly have dated the last year of Cypselus to 628/27 and the first year of his son and successor Periander to 627/26.[3]

That these inferences are approximately correct seems confirmed by two passages of Diogenes Laertius. Diogenes says (1.98) that Periander reached his acme in the 38th Olympiad (628/5) and that he held the tyranny for forty years. Diogenes also states (1.95) that Periander died at the age of eighty. Here he cites Sosicrates for the date of Periander's death. Sosicrates' chronology derives from his contemporary, Apollodorus.[4] This particular passage, however, is ambiguous and its interpretation highly controversial: Σωσικράτης δέ φησι πρότερον Κροίσου τελευτῆσαι αὐτον ἔτεσι τετταράκοντα καὶ ἑνὶ πρὸ τῆς τεσσαρακοστῆς ὀλυμπιάδος.

The passage is awkward Greek. It has been punctuated and interpreted in two ways. According to the first, a comma is placed after τετταράκοντα, so that the statement means "Sosicrates says that he died forty years before Croesus and one year before the forty-ninth Olympiad."[5] The precise date of Periander's death is thus 586/85, if we count inclusively the forty years before the epoch of Croesus in 547/46. One year before the 49th Olympiad, however, is Olympiad 48.4, 585/84. For Jacoby that discrepancy did not exist, since he thought the Apollodoran epoch of Croesus to be 546/45.[6] Nevertheless, the resultant date in 585/84 does not agree with Jacoby's interpretation of Eusebius' excerpt from Diodorus. Jacoby therefore punctuated after ἐνί, so that the passage means "Sosicrates says that Periander died forty-one years before Croesus, before the forty-ninth Olympiad." This interpretation yields a date for Periander's death in 587/86, and the result accords with Jacoby's interpretation of the chronographic excerpt. Still, the quotation from Sosicrates remains awkward, since there now seems no reason for him to have added the reference to the 49th Olympiad. Jacoby concluded that Diogenes must have made his excerpt too hastily and left out some phrase that would have made the mention of the 49th Olympiad meaningful. Following Schwartz, he added τρισί before πρό. Thus what Sosicrates (and Apollodorus) had originally said is that Periander died 41 years before Croesus (546 + 41 = 587) and three years before the 49th Olympiad (OL. 48.2, 587/86). Hence the first year of Periander was 627/26, his 40th year was 588/87, and he died in 587/86.[7]

Jacoby's interpretation accords reasonably well with Aristotle's statements (as emended) about the length of the Cypselid tyranny. According to the text (*Pol.* 5, 1315b22), Cypselus ruled for 30 years, Periander for 44 years, and Psamettichus (Periander's nephew) for three years. The dynastic total is 73 years and six months. The sum suggests that Periander's reign must have been 40 years and six months, rather than 44 years.[8] Thus Periander died a few months after the completion of his fortieth year, in 587/86, and the three years of Psammetichus end in the middle of the Olympic–archon year 584/83, the first year of the 49th Olympiad. Jacoby found confirmation in the statement of Solinus (7.14) that the Corinthians restored the Isthmian festival, after its interruption by the Cypselid tyranny, in the 49th Olympiad.[9]

The emendation of Aristotle's text must be accepted. Differences in methods of counting the years can reconcile a dynastic total of 73 years and six months with a sum of regnal years amounting to 74. But there is no way of reconciling the total with a sum of regnal years totaling 77, unless Periander and Psammetichus somehow shared the tyranny for three years. Such a situation can be imagined.[10] But it would have been sufficiently odd as to warrant a comment and an explanation from Aristotle. The emendation to the text of Diogenes-Sosicrates is less easily accepted, since it is pure conjecture, adduced to harmonize the evidence. We should therefore attempt to reconstruct the chronology without emending the text of Diogenes.

Diogenes says that Periander reached his acme in the 38th Olympiad (628/25), was tyrant for forty years, and died at the age of 80. The date of death is either 40 or 41 years before Croesus. The epoch of Croesus is the fall of Sardis, which Diogenes (1.38), following Apollodorus, dates to the 58th Olympiad (548/45). Periander died, then, in one of the years of the 48th Olympiad. Since he was tyrant for forty years and died at the age of 80, the acme in the 38th Olympiad must have been synchronized with Periander's first year as tyrant. If Periander was 40 in the first year of his tyranny, he was 80 years old and died in his 41st year as tyrant. Thus it is clear that Apollodorus agreed with Aristotle in assigning to Periander 40 years and six months of rule. Since he did not complete that 41st year, Apollodorus could say that he died at the age of 80 after 40 years as tyrant. Because Apollodorus agreed on this detail, it is reasonable to suppose that he also accepted Aristotle's 30 years for Cypselus and three years for Psammetichus.

To infer the exact dates we must begin where Apollodorus did, with a presumably historical date from which the regnal years could be counted. The starting point is suggested by the comment of Solinus that the Corinthians restored the Isthmian festival, after its interruption by the Cypselids, in the 49th Olympiad (584/81). Solinus is dependent upon Apollodorus for the information, through an epitome of the *Chronicle* of Nepos. Apollodorus did not, however, date the restoration of the festival by reference to his dates for the Cypselids. On the contrary, Apollodorus generated dates for the Cypselids by reference to a date for the first regular and historical celebration of the Isthmian festival.[11] The only evidence for that date, apart from Solinus, is the entry of the Eusebian *Canons*, which appears in the Oxford manuscript of St. Jerome at the fourth year of the 49th Olympiad, 581/80.

Eusebius states in a single notice that the Isthmian festival was reestablished and the Pythian games were first celebrated in 581. As always, an allowance of up to three or four years must be made in the date, since even the best of the extant manuscripts can attest only approximately to the original placement of an entry in the *Canons*. We know that the first regular Pythian festival was celebrated in the third year of the 40th Olympiad, 582/81.[12] Eusebius' concise notice implies that the Isthmian and Pythian festivals were first regularly celebrated in the same year. In terms of Olympic years, that cannot have been the case. The Isthmian games were celebrated biennially, as Pindar's reference to the festival shows.[13] According to Thucydides (8.9.1), it was in the spring of the year corresponding to 412 that the celebration of the Isthmian festival prevented the Corinthians from setting sail for Chios. The spring of 412, in the Olympiad system, falls toward the end of the fourth year of the 91st Olympiad. The biennial celebration must therefore have taken place in the spring of what would correspond to the second and fourth years of an Olympiad. The first celebration took place in the 49th Olympiad. Eusebius' notice implies that it was celebrated about the same time as the first Pythian games, celebrated in 582/81, but he mentions the Isthmian before the Pythian. Thus the first Isthmian festival must have been celebrated in the spring of 582, during the Olympic–archon year 583/82. That Eusebius' sources chose to synchronize the two festivals is not surprising. Either it was the date of the more famous Pythian celebration that was attached to the synchronism, or the sources reported only the Olympiad number.

For Apollodorus (or, perhaps, his source) the date of the first Isthmian celebration was the starting point for the Cypselid chronology. He knew and believed the tradition that this first of the regular, historical festivals was celebrated in thanksgiving for the liberation of the Corinthian state from the Cypselid tyranny. The fact that the celebration took place in the middle of a chronographic year enabled him to make intelligent use of the half-year included in Aristotle's account of the length of the tyranny. Psammetichus' three years ended with his expulsion shortly before the festival of thanksgiving in spring of 582. His first year therefore began in spring of 585. The half-year of Periander was the first six months of 586/85, and Periander died during that archon year. His 40th year was 587/86, and his tyranny began in 626/25. The 30 years of Cypselus began in 656/55 and ended in 627/26. The system, converted to the Olympiad years of our late sources is as follows:

OL 30.4 (657/56): Last year of Bacchiad rule
OL 31.1 (656/55): First year of Cypselus
OL 38.2 (627/26): 30th year of Cypselus
OL 38.3 (626/25): First year of Periander, his acme at age 40
OL 48.2 (587/86): 40th year of Periander
OL 48.3 (586/85): Death of Periander, at age 80, in mid-year

	First six months of Psammetichus
OL 49.1 (584/83):	Psammetichus completes 2½ years of rule
OL 49.2 (583/82):	Psammetichus rules six months and is assassinated
	The Corinthians proclaim the Isthmian celebration.

These Cypselid dates are all one year lower than those which Jacoby proposed. The difference is significant. For the reconstruction offered here both reveals the reasoning behind the traditional system and agrees with the fragmentary evidence, without recourse to textual emendation. The 447 years of the Diodorus excerpt for the interval between the return of the Heraclids and the tyranny of Cypselus is an expression of the length of Heraclid-Bacchiad rule. The kingship begins in 1103/2, immediately after their seizure of the territory when the Heraclids "returned." The 447th year of rule is 657/56, and Cypselus' tyranny begins the next year. Periander's first year is within the 38th Olympiad, when Diogenes dates his acme. Periander dies at the age of 80 after 40 full years of rule in the middle of what would have been his 41st year. The date is 586/85, 40 years by Apollodorus' inclusive count before the fall of Croesus in 547/46. More precisely, Periander died three years before the celebration of the first Isthmian festival, in the spring of 585. Thus he died one year before the celebration of the 49th Olympiad (summer, 584). The text of Diogenes, awkward as it is, can be read as it stands: "Sosicrates says he ried forty years before Croesus, and one before the 49th Olympiad." There is no descrepancy between the two expressions of the date. The 49th Olympiad was actually celebrated at the end of the chronographic year corresponding to OL 48.4, 585/84.[14] The previous year is therefore OL 48.3, 586/85, forty years before the fall of Croesus.[15]

The Apollodoran system is based on Aristotle's testimony for the duration of the Cypselid tyranny in combination with a date for the first Isthmian celebration. The Isthmian date may well be historical, but one must ask how Aristotle came by his figures for the duration of the individual tyrants' reign and what absolute dates he associated with them. Eusebius' Cypselid notices are fundamental to this question. It is essential to know if Apollodorus adopted exactly the same chronological scheme as Aristotle or if he (or anyone else) adapted Aristotle's Cypselid intervals to a different set of absolute dates. That is, we need to know whether the chronographic tradition that constitutes the so-called high chronology of the Cypselid tyranny was uniform.[16]

Apart from Diogenes Laertius and the report of the *Suda* that Periander flourished in the 38th Olympiad, only Eusebius gives absolute dates for the Corinthian tyranny. His entry on Periander, which appears at the first year of the 38th Olympiad, is clearly in agreement with the Apollodoran system. Like Diogenes and the *Suda*, Eusebius' sources reported only the Olympiad during which Periander reached his acme and became tyrant, without specifying the precise year within the quadrennium. Eusebius accordingly entered the notice at the first year of that Olympiad. His notices on Cypselus and on the end of the Cypselid *monarchia*, however, are more problematic. Eusebius' entry for the beginning of Cypselus' rule as tyrant in Corinth appears in the 30th Olympiad (660/57), with the manuscripts of Jerome and the Armenian version varying in the placement of the entry from the first to the third year of that Olympiad. The notice of the end of the *monarchia* appears at the first year of the 48th Olympiad (588/87), with the manuscripts showing a variation of only one year in the placement. The interval between Olympiad 30.1 (660/59) and Olympiad 48.1 (588/87) is, by inclusive counting, 73 years. This figure is the same as the dynastic total of Aristotle. The possibility therefore exists that Eusebius here preserves the fragments of a tradition that set the Aristotelian figures for the duration of the Corinthian tyranny in a different framework of absolute dates from that of Apollodorus. But there are many difficulties with the interpretation of a Eusebian date, with respect both to the manuscript tradition of the *Chronicle* and to the transmission of information through Eusebius' sources. It would therefore be wrong to conclude, without detailed analysis of text and tradition, that Eusebius reports a chronological system for the Cypselids independent of the Apollodoran vulgate.[17]

All versions of the entry—Latin, Armenian, and Greek (Syncel. 402)—assign to Cypselus 28 years as tyrant, rather than the 30 years of the other sources. This divergence from an otherwise uniform tradition cannot be accounted for in the manuscript variations for the dates of Cypselus and Periander. Much effort has been expended in unsuccessful attempts to account for these 28 years of Cypselus within the chronographic framework of the *Canons* or by appeals to the differences between inclusive and exclusive counting.[18] In fact, the wording of the notice can best be explained by reference to the characteristics of Eusebius' source material, since Apollodorus' date for Cypselus was 656/55, not 657/56. Eusebius depended for the majority of information included in the *spatium historicum* for persons and events of archaic Greek history on an Olympiad chronicler who transmitted an epitomized version of the Apollodoran vulgate. Apollodorus' dates had early been converted from Athenian archon years to the Olympiad system, and the epitomizers often included only the Olympiad number associated with a person or event and not the precise year. In the case of Cypselus and Periander, Apollodorus' dates corresponded to years within the 31st and 38th Olympiads. For an authority who knew only the Olympiad numbers, Cypselus ruled for seven Olympiads or 28 years. Eusebius' notice on Cypselus thus derives from the same kind of material as Diogenes' statement (1.98) that Periander flourished in the 38th Olympiad and was tyrant for forty years. Such versions of the Apollodoran system, reporting only Olympiad numbers, were later and less precise than that of Sosicrates, who reported the exact dates.

Eusebius' entry on Cypselus, then, derives from Apollodorus. The appearance of the notice at a date from two to four years earlier than that established by Apollodorus is but one of many examples of such shifts in the relative placement of text and numerals in the *Canons*. The entry should therefore not be regarded as evidence that there ever existed a chronographic system for the Cypselids different from that of Apollodorus. Frequently the translators and scribes can be blamed for displacements in the relative position of historical notices in the chronological framework. In this case, the manuscript evidence suggests that the error was Eusebius' own. A parallel instance can be found in Eusebius' entries of Stesichorus and Simonides in the 55th Olympiad. The synchronism is Apollodoran, but it originally belonged to the 56th Olympiad (above, chapter 10). Exactly what compositional difficulties are the original cause of these errors only the discovery of the original *Chronicle* itself would reveal. Perhaps we would find a correspondence between page-endings and compositional error.

The notice on the destruction of the Corinthian *monarchia* in the 48th Olympiad also owes its origin to the late, epitomized version of the Apollodoran system. For Apollodorus the Cyp-

selid tyranny ended with the assassination of Psammetichus in
583/82, the second year of the 49th Olympiad. The encyclopedic
epitomizers of knowledge were not interested in obscure persons
like Psammetichus. On the other hand, Periander was one of
the Seven Sages and among the most famous of the ancient
tyrants. His dates were therefore duly recorded in the epitomes,
but in the shorthand manner of Diogenes (1.98): "Periander
flourished in the 38th Olympiad and was tyrant for forty years."
The inference that he died and his tyranny came to an end in
the 48th Olympiad is obvious. Since the memory of Psammetichus did not penetrate to these late sources, the death of Periander was interpreted as the end of the period of the tyrants
in Corinth. Again, as in the case of Cypselus and the acme of
Periander, the epitomized version did not specify a precise year
within the Olympiad. Eusebius is thus true to his sources (and
the manuscript tradition of the *Chronicle* true to the original)
in entering the notice at the first year of the Olympiad, although
for Apollodorus the death of Periander was dated to the year
corresponding to the third of the 48th Olympiad (586/85).[19]

There is no indication in the *Canons* of Eusebius or elsewhere that there ever existed absolute dates for the Cypselid
tyranny in Corinth different from those of Apollodorus. The
Apollodoran chronology is in agreement with the regnal intervals reported by Aristotle, and Aristotle's figures are of such
precision as to indicate that they belong within the framework
of an absolute chronology. The traditional dates had therefore
already been established by the time of Aristotle and were incorporated without modification into the universal chronologies
of Eratosthenes and Apollodorus. The synchronism between the
celebration of the first Isthmian festival and the assassination
of Psammetichus, the starting point for the generation of absolute dates, should also be ascribed to Aristotle (or his chronological source). This synchronism results in the inclusion of a
half-year within the figures for the duration of the tyranny,
because the Isthmian games were celebrated in the spring, a few
months before the beginning of chronographic archons' or Olympiad years. It remains to ask how the figures for the length of
rule assigned to each of the tyrants were determined and why
the half-year was given to Periander rather than to Psammetichus.

The thirty years of Cypselus belong to Corinthian tradition, as Herodotus (5.92) reports it, and this figure is not to be regarded as derived from chronographic computation on the part of Herodotus or his sources.[20] Herodotus does not report an estimate of the length of Periander's reign nor does he say how the problem of the succession to Periander, discussed at 3.53, was resolved. The tradition may have been vague on the first point and divided on the second. It was clear at least that Periander's rule had been long and that of his successor, if any, quite short. The forty years of Periander may constitute a theoretical expression of the length of a long reign. The appearance of this figure for Periander is yet another indication that Peripatetic scholarship anticipated Apollodorus in using theoretical forty-year intervals for chronological construction.

The assignment of the half-year to Periander and three years to Psammetichus, as well as the generation of the entire system, must be closely associated with the work of Aristotle and Callisthenes in establishing an official, dated list of Pythian victors. Very little of this important work survives. The dedicatory inscription (*Syll*[3] 275 = Callisthenes *FGrHist* 124 T 23) names Aristotle and Callisthenes as the redactors of the list. If the restoration of the inscription is correct, the catalogue began with the archonship at Delphi of Gylidas. According to the *scholia* on Pindar (*hyp. Pyth.* b, d), it was during the archonship of Gylidas at Delphi and of Simonides at Athens that the ἀγὼν χρηματίτης was held in celebration of an Amphictyonic victory over Cirrha in the First Sacred War. The redaction of the catalogue of victors thus must have required Aristotle to deal with the events of the First Sacred War, and Plutarch (*Solon* 11.2) specifically affirms that he did. The *Marmor Parium* (*FGrHist* 239 A 37) dates the fall of Cirrha and the celebration of the *agon chrematites* to 591/90, while Pausanias (10.7.4) says the contest was celebrated in Olympiad 48.3, 586/85, and constituted the first Pythiad. The date of the *Marmor* is the correct one, insofar as the official list is concerned, while Pausanias has apparently confused the fall of Cirrha and the *agon chrematites* with the date for the end of the war. According to the scholiasts, the Cirrhans continued to fight from the hills after the fall of their city and were finally defeated in the sixth year. At that time, that is, 586/85, the Amphictyonic commander proclaimed an ἀγὼν στεφανίτης. That festival was celebrated in 582/81, according to both the *Marmor* (A 38) and Pausanias

(10.7.5, "second Pythiad"), and in the *scholia* to Pindar this celebration was counted as the first of the regular quadrennial Pythiads.[21]

Aristotle and Callisthenes dated the fall of Cirrha to 591/90 and the end of the First Sacred War to 586/85. As modern commentators have noted, the absence of Corinthian participation on one side or the other in this war is so conspicuous as to require an explanation. The most obvious is that it was at this time that Periander was quarreling with the Corcyreans and with his rebellious son, being himself aged and unequal to the management of public affairs (Herodotus 3.53).[22] Aristotle perhaps offered such an explanation, and he also accepted the tradition that the restored Isthmian festival had first been celebrated in thanksgiving for the end of tyrannical rule. He therefore synchronized the death of Periander and the accession of Psammetichus with the end of the Sacred War. The synchronism results in a half-year for Periander during 586/85 and three years for Psammetichus, ending shortly before the celebration of the Isthmian games in the spring of 583/82 and several months before the celebration of the first Pythiad and the beginning of the chronographic year corresponding to 582/81.

In summary, then, the traditional or "high" chronology of the Cypselid tyranny, represented for us in the fragments of Apollodorus and in the *Chronicle* of Eusebius, results from a set of combinations in which chronographic computation as such plays but a small role. The dates of the Pythian celebrations in 591/90 and 582/81 derive from the Delphic records which Aristotle and Callisthenes codified. The date of the first Isthmian celebration probably rests on Corinthian records, although it might derive simply from approximate synchronization with the first Pythiad, on the basis of the cycle of repetition for the two festivals as observed in classical times. The dates for the Sacred War derive partly from the official date of the *agon chrematites*, partly from the position of Solon in the Athenian archon list (594/93) and the tradition (Plutarch, *Solon* 11) that his prestige was based on Amphictyonic connections, partly from Callisthenes' chronological doublet with the ten-years-long Third Sacred War.[23] The generation of Cypselid dates thus depends on the tradition surrounding the Isthmian celebration, the significance of Corinth's failure to participate in the Sacred War, the reliability of Herodotus' report about the length of Cypselus' rule, and finally the application of the theoretical forty-year interval to Periander's tyranny. Each member of this multifarious set may be regarded as suspect on one ground or another, and the details are open to endless debate. The structure as a whole, however, is sound. We should therefore call the chronographic dates "traditional" not "high." No other system ever existed.

13

Pittacus, Sappho, and Alcaeus

a) OL 43.2 (607/6) : Pittacus Mitylenaeus, qui de septem sapientibus fuit, cum Frynone Atheniensi Olympionice congressus eum interfecit. (98^g)

AA 1409 (607/6) : Pittak der Mitylenäer, einer von dem Sieben Weisen, kämpfte mit Phrion dem Athener den olympischen Einzelkampf und tötete jenen. (186)

b) OL 45.1 (600/599) : Sappho et Alchaeus poetae clari habentur. (99^d)

AA 1421 (595/94) : Sappho und Alkeos als Poeten gekannt. (187)

As is the case with the Cypselids, the dates of Eusebius and cognate sources in the chronographic tradition are the basis for reconstructing the chronology for the careers of Pittacus, Sappho, and Alcaeus. Attempts to lower these traditional dates have not won general favor. Indeed, it is quite possible that the date of Pittacus' *aesymneteia* could be found in some Mitylenean equivalent of the Athenian archon list. It is not, however, likely that such a date derived from archival records contemporary with Pittacus himself. Nevertheless, even if one takes an extremely negative view about the existence of such records and concludes that Lesbian annals were the product of construction in the late fifth or early fourth century, it can be shown that the dates that our late authorities preserve rest on solid tradition.

Eusebius does not transmit a date for Pittacus' acme or for his *aesymneteia*. His dates for Pittacus' victory over Phrynon, however, and for Pittacus' contemporaries the poets Sappo and Alcaeus are fragments of a tradition that sought to establish a systematic chronology for the events surrounding the whole career of Pittacus. The most nearly complete report of that tradition appears in Diogenes Laertius' *Life of Pittacus* (1.74–81), a compilation of dates and facts culled from a variety of sources. Two passages in particular are crucial for the reconstruction of the chronographic tradition on Pittacus. In the first (1.74–5) Diogenes specifically cites the *Chronicle* of Apollodorus, but he gives no dates. The second is a chronological summary (1.79) that reports exact dates, but Diogenes does not name his source. The first passage provides the following relative chronology:

1) Pittacus, together with the brothers of Alcaeus, overthrew the tyrant Melanchrus.
2) In the war between Mitylene and Athens for possession of territory in the Troad, Pittacus engaged in single combat with the Athenian commander Phrynon, an Olympic victor, and killed him.
3) Later on, according to Apollodorus' *Chronicle*, the dispute was submitted to the arbitration of Periander, who decided in favor of Athens.
4) Meanwhile, the Mityleneans entrusted their government to Pittacus, who set affairs in order, laid down his office after ten years of rule, and lived for ten years more.

Only the third statement can be attributed directly to Apollodorus, but his influence on the biographical tradition was such as to suggest that the entire series of statements derives from Apollodorus' *Chronicle*.

In the second passage, his chronological summary (1.79), Diogenes says that Pittacus flourished in the 42nd Olympiad (612/9) and died in the archonship of Aristomenes, the third year of the 52nd Olympiad (570/69), at an age of more than 70. The form of the latter statement, including the name of the archon, a precise Olympic year, and the approximate age at the time of death, is of the type that Diogenes elsewhere transmits under the name of Sosicrates.[1] Sosicrates was Diogenes' usual authority for precise Apollodoran dates. His work was one of Diogenes' sources for the *Life of Pittacus*, as the citation at 1.75 (for an apothegm, not a date) shows. The date of Pittacus' death, at an age of more than 70, should therefore be ascribed to Sosicrates and Apollodorus. His *floruit* in Olympiad 42 also derives from Apollodorus, as comparison with the article of the *Suda* suggests.[2] The *Suda* dates the birth (γέγονε) of Pittacus

to the 32nd Olympiad (652/49) and states that it was in the 42nd
Olympiad that he ousted the tyrant Melanchrus. Thus Pittacus
was 40 years old when he overthrew Melanchrus, and the date
is the same as that to which Diogenes assigns his acme. The
method of Apollodorus is operative.

Since it is clear that Apollodorus is the ultimate authority
for both passages of Diogenes and for the article of the *Suda*
on Pittacus, the Apollodoran chronology can be partially reconstructed by inserting into the narrative of 1.74–75 the dates
reported at 1.79 and in the *Suda*. But there is a serious difficulty
in the text of 1.79. If Pittacus was 40 years old at the time of
his acme in the 42nd Olympiad (612/9), his age when he died
in 570/69 was more than 80 years, not merely more than 70, as
Diogenes asserts. Rohde accordingly emended the passage to
have Pittacus die at an age of "more than 80." Such an emendation is, however, not justified paleographically. Jacoby in *Apollodors Chronik* therefore argued for leaving the passage as it
stands, imputing to Diogenes an erroneous compression of material drawn from several sources. This hypothesis is inadequate.
For the statement about the time of Pittacus' death is a unified
whole taken from Sosicrates, who gave the age as well as the
date. Jacoby's alternative hypothesis, subsequently offered for
FGrHist 244 F 27, is more plausible, although it involves emendation of the text. Jacoby suggested that there is a dittography
in the text. The "two" of the acme date (OL 42, μβ´) was
accidentally repeated at some stage in the transmission and
wrongly inserted into the Olympiad number associated with
Pittacus' death (νβ´ instead of ν´). Sosicrates originally had
said that the date of Pittacus' death in the archonship of Aristomenes was the third year of the 50th Olympiad, 578/77.[3]

With this emendation, unfortunately necessary, reconstruction can proceed. It must be conceded, of course, that the argument is rendered more hypothetical than one would like, since
it rests on an emended text. Apollodorus synchronized the acme
of Pittacus with the overthrow of Melanchrus, and he dated
the synchronism to one of the years corresponding to the 42nd
Olympiad. Eusebius preserves this date indirectly. He enters
Stesichorus in Olympiad 42, because he was sometimes synchronized with Sappho and Alcaeus, who were in turn commonly
synchronized with Pittacus in the year of his acme.[4] Of greater
interest are Eusebius' dates for Pittacus himself and for Sappho
and Alcaeus. He enters Pittacus in Olympiad 43, several years

after the Apollodoran acme, and the notice refers specifically to the contest with Phrynon. Sappho and Alcaeus appear at yet a third date, synchronized in the 45th Olympiad (600/599). These notices and the dates they carry aid in our interpretation of the Apollodoran tradition that Diogenes reports.

Pittacus died in 578/77, according to Apollodorus, at an age of more than 70. Diogenes says that he held office in Mitylene for ten years and lived for another ten years after his abdication. In Apollodorus' system, then, the last ten years of Pittacus' life were the years from 587/86 to 578/77 and his ten-year term as *aesymnetes* lasted from 597/96 to 588/87. Apollodorus dated the acme of Pittacus at the age of 40 to the 42nd Olympiad (612/9); and he said it was then that Pittacus, in concert with the brothers of Alcaeus, ousted the tyrant Melanchrus. Sometime during the interval between the end of the tyranny of Melanchrus in 612 and the beginning of Pittacus' administration of government in 597, three events occurred for which Apollodorus is likely to have given a date. Diogenes mentions the first two events, and he expressly cites the *Chronicle* of Apollodorus for the relative chronology. After the ouster of Melanchrus, Pittacus fought and killed the Athenian Phrynon in a dispute subsequently submitted to the arbitration of Periander. Apollodorus' date for the war with Athens and for Periander's arbitration is not attested. But Eusebius preserves a date for the battle with Phrynon, and the best manuscripts agree in placing the entry at the second year of the 43rd Olympiad, 607/6. This date is within the interval required for Apollodorus by Diogenes' account, and it is also ten years before Apollodorus' date for the beginning of Pittacus' term as *aesymnetes*. This ten-year interval is significant, because the *aesymneteia* lasted for ten years and Apollodorus allowed an interval of ten years more for Pittacus' retirement and old age. The third event that Apollodorus must have dated between the acme of Pittacus and his election as *aesymnetes* is the exile of the disaffected aristocrats, including Alcaeus, from Mitylene. According to Aristotle (*Pol.* 1285a35), who quotes a poem of Alcaeus in support of his statement, the Mityleneans elected Pittacus *aesymnetes* to lead them against the exiles, at whose head stood Antimenides and his brother the poet Alcaeus. Alcaeus participated with his countrymen in the war against Athens. It was on the occasion of an Athenian victory during this war that Alcaeus supposedly threw away his shield, an

incident that he memorialized in his poetry (Herodotus 5.94–
5, Strabo 13.1.38, fr. 428 LP). Apollodorus must therefore
have dated an exile of Alcaeus during the ten years between
Pittacus' battle with Phrynon and his election to the leadership
of Mitylene against the party of Alcaeus.

It is within this interval from 607 to 597 that Eusebius dates
the *floruit* (*clari habentur*) of Sappho and Alcaeus. At approximately the same date the *Marmor Parium* (*FGrHist* 239 A 36)
records the flight from Mitylene of Sappho during the archonship of Critias I. The epochal interval is lost beyond restoration,
and the date of Critias' archonship is not otherwise known. The
intervals recorded on the stone in A 35 and A 37 show that the
date must have been between 604 and 592, and the last three
years can be excluded as already associated with other archons'
names. This notice of the *Marmor* has long been connected with
Eusebius' entry of Sappho and Alcaeus in Olympiad 45.1, 600/
599, as deriving from the same tradition.[5] That tradition can
therefore be restored by combining the evidence of Eusebius
with that of the *Marmor*. Eusebius preserves the date lost on
the stone, while the notice of the *Marmor* reports the fact underlying Eusebius' *floruit*—it was at this time that Sappho and
Alcaeus chose exile in preference to the tyranny of Pittacus.[6]
If, as seems probable, Eusebius' entry is Apollodoran, then
Apollodorus dated the acme of Alcaeus to the time of his
supposed leadership of the exiled aristocrats and synchronized
Sappho with him. Hence, Eusebius' sources reported a *floruit*
rather than the exile.

Apollodorus' chronology for the career of Pittacus can now
be summarized as follows:[7]

OL 42 (612/9): Pittacus and Alcaeus' brothers join in over-
throwing the tyrant Melanchrus. Pittacus reaches his acme at
the age of forty. (Diogenes, the *Suda*)

OL 43.2 (607/6): Pittacus kills Phrynon during the war
against Athens. (Eusebius, Diogenes)

607–597: At some time during this interval Periander served
as arbitrator and decided in favor of Athens. (Diogenes)

OL 45.1 (600/599): Sappho and Alcaeus go into exile, together with other disaffected aristocrats. Alcaeus assumes the
leadership and reaches his acme at the age of 40. (Eusebius)

OL 45.4 (597/96) : Pittacus is elected to a ten-year term as *aesymnetes* of Mitylene and leads the fight against the exiled aristocrats, including Alcaeus. (Diogenes)

OL 48.2 (587/86) : Pittacus resumes private life after ten years of rule. (Diogenes)

OL 50.3 (577/76) : Death of Pittacus at an age of more than seventy. (Diogenes)

The value of this tradition as evidence for historical chronology depends on the means by which Apollodorus or his Lesbian authorities inferred these dates. Jacoby's belief that the dates of Pittacus' *aesymneteia*, at least, and possibly also of Melanchrus' expulsion were known to the Alexandrian chronographers through the medium of the local chronicles of Lesbos begs the question.[8] Dates for Pittacus could be read in a local history, but one still wants to know how the author came by them. These events are too early to have been contemporaneously recorded by reference to established chronological convention. The dates must result, at least partially, from reconstruction.[9] There may have existed both in documents and in memorized tradition evidence from which Hellanicus and other Lesbian chroniclers could reconstruct an annalistic list of magistrates so as to infer a date for Pittacus' *aesymneteia*. If so, the chronology is sound indeed, since the date of the *aesymneteia* was no doubt the starting point for the rest of the chronology. But even if the date could not so easily be extrapolated from an annual list, the tradition was sufficiently full to permit an ancient scholar to generate a system of absolute dates worthy of confidence.

The poems of Alcaeus no doubt provided sufficient evidence for the establishment of a relative chronology. Alcaeus may have also stated that Pittacus' *aesymneteia* (for Alcaeus, "tyranny") lasted for ten years and he probably gave some indication of Pittacus' age at that time, perhaps suggesting that he was "past his prime." To construct an absolute chronology one could use, among other things, the synchronism between Periander and the war of Mitylene with Athens. That Periander had served as arbitrator may have been stated by Alcaeus when he commented on his own experiences in the war (fr. 428 LP). In any case, the tradition was well established by the time of Herodotus, who reports it at 5.94–95.

Dates for Periander had been established that fixed his forty-year reign as tyrant of Corinth as spanning the years 626 to 586 (above, chapter 12). Pittacus' heroic victory in single combat with Phrynon would have to be dated within this interval. The analogy of Pittacus' position as *aesymnetes* of Mitylene with Solon's selection as *diallaktes* of Athens might suggest an approximate synchronism between the two, and Plutarch (*Solon* 14) makes such a connection. The synchronism gains force from the inclusion of both Pittacus and Solon, along with Periander, among the Seven Sages. The position of Solon in the archon list had been established at the year corresponding to 594/93. This date could be taken as the approximate midpoint of Pittacus' *aesymneteia* and used for more precise computations. If Pittacus was exercising his office about 594, he retired about 590. On the assumption that he was an elder statesman when he retired, an appropriate age could be assigned to Pittacus at the time of his abdication. For Apollodorus that age would be 64, an age that emerges from Apollodoran calculations in other instances that require the dating of a person in his old age.[10]

Aged 64 about 590, Pittacus would have been 40 and at his acme about 614. The choice of a precise year is facilitated by the presence of a chronographically epochal date about that time that could be worked into the traditions surrounding Pittacus. That date is the year 612/11, when the war between Alyattes of Lydia and Thrasybulus, the tyrant of Miletus, had been brought to an end by negotiations.[11] Periander rendered valuable advice to Thrasybulus whereby he was enabled to bring the Lydians to terms (Herodotus 1.20), and this service could be considered the beginning of that prestige in international affairs which made Periander a good choice as arbiter for the war between Athens and Mitylene. With the acme at age 40 thus dated to 612/11, the precise year of Pittacus' abdication at the age of 64 is 588/87. The tradition included ten years of retirement to match the ten years of magistracy, so that Pittacus' death falls in the year 578/77 at an age of more than 70.

The use of the ten-year interval from the end of the *aesymneteia* suggested its application from the beginning also. The year 607/6 thus became an appropriate date for some event in Pittacus' career. The relative chronology provided by Alcaeus suggests the association of the ouster of Melanchrus with the acme in 612/11 and the victory over Phrynon with this later date in 607/6. Apollodorus perhaps dated Periander's arbitration to the same year. The ὕστερον of Diogenes' citation thus means that Periander was called in to arbitrate immediately after the battle of the champions when Pittacus' victory restored the balance of power. The possibility is enhanced by the fact that 607/6 is Periander's 20th year in the traditional Cypselid chronology.[12] Having dated the beginning of Pittacus' *aesymneteia* to 597/96 and knowing the tradition reported by Aristotle that he owed his election to the threat posed by the exiled aristocrats under the leadership of Antimenides and Alcaeus, Apollodorus would be led to a synchronism between the acme of Alcaeus and the beginning of the *aesymneteia*. Since there already existed a date for the exile of Sappho, as attested for us by the *Marmor Parium*, that did not contradict the dates he had established for Pittacus, Apollodorus accepted it and incorporated the date into his system. With the exile dated to 600/599, the system allows three years for the exiles to gain sufficient strength to pose a threat serious enough for the appointment of an *aesymnetes*.

The *Marmor Parium* records only a fragment of the tradition that dated Sappho's exile to 600/599. Alcaeus was no doubt also included as having been in exile at that time. The date may have been established by a procedure similar to that suggested for Apollodorus. Since the persons and events involved belong to the history of Lesbos, a likely authority for the date is Phainias of Eresos, whose date for Terpander was transmitted to the author of the *Marmor* (above, chapter 11). As has been suggested (chapter 11), Phainias followed the tradition that dated the Seven Sages to 580, and he used that date as a starting point for the generation of other dates. Synchronizing Pittacus with the Seven Sages in 580 and assuming that Pittacus had gained his reputation for wisdom as *aesymnetes*, Phainias could arrive at a date of 590 for his abdication and 600 for the beginning of his rule. It follows at once that the exile of Alcaeus, Sappho, and their company of fellow aristocrats belongs to that time. Apollodorus accepted Phainias' date for the exile, but preferred other computations for the precise dates of Pittacus. Among the reasons for his departing slightly from Phainias in this matter, Apollodorus disagreed with him on the date for the acme of Thales (below, chapter 14). He also desired to compute dates that produced synchronisms at certain epochal years (e.g., 612/11) and thus allowed interconnections among the various elements of his chronological system (e.g., between Lydia, Miletus, Corinth, and Mitylene at 612/11) to be easily made.

How many of the dates in Apollodorus' system and how much of the complex methodology underlying them he inherited from such Lesbian chroniclers as Phainias and Hellanicus, we do not know. What is important enough to warrant so tortuous an argument as that presented here is the conclusion that, even if the traditional chronology results entirely from chronographic construction, it was a construction based on careful synthesis of the available evidence—not simply a mathematical invention. The dates that result are only approximate, since they do not derive from annalistic, contemporary archival record. They are far from arbitrary, however, and we have no evidence for any better approximation.

14

Thales

a) OL 35.1 (640/39): Thales Milesius, Examyis filius, primus physicus philosophus agnoscitur, quem aiunt uixisse usque ad ˙LVIII˙ olympiadem. (96ᵇ)
AA 1376 (640/39): Thalles von Amilos, der Milesier, war als erster Physiker gekannt; und es wird berichtet, er habe sein Leben bis zur 48ᵗᵉⁿ Olympiade ausgedehnt. (185)

b) OL 48.3 (586/85): Solis facta defectio, cum futuram eam Thales antedixisset. (100ᶠ)
OL 49.3 (582/81): Alyattes et Astyages dimicauerunt. (101ᵉ)
AA 1433 (583/82): Die Sonne ward verfinstert nach Thales des Weisen Vorausverkündigung. Aliates und Azdahak lieferten eine Schlacht. (187)

c) OL 50.2 (579/8): Septem sapientes appellati. (101ᵉ)
OL 50.4 (577/6): Astyages contra Lydos pugnat. (101ᶠ)
AA 1439 (577/6): Die Sieben Weisen wurden genannt. (187)
AA 1441 (575/4): Azdahak lieferte gegen die Lyder einen heftigen Kampf. (187)

d) OL 58.1 (548/47): Thales moritur. (103ʰ) Cyrus Sardis capit. (103ⁱ)
AA 1468 (548/47): Thales stirbt. (189)
No corresponding Armenian notice.[1]

Eusebius' entries relevant to Thales are of great interest for several reasons. He transmits (including an error deriving from an early textual corruption) the traditional, Apollodoran dates for the birth of Thales; for the solar eclipse at the time of the Lydo-Median war, which Thales was supposed to have foretold;

and for Thales' death at the time of the fall of Sardis. The
dates for the eclipse and for the fall of Sardis are within a few
months of the dates that modern scholars have established for
these events on the basis of evidence independent of the Greek
chronographic tradition. They are, however, dates of the first
half of the sixth century and are therefore too early to have
been contemporaneously recorded in annalistic Greek records.
It is not sufficient to note that the traditional dates are nearly
correct. One wants to know how Hellenistic scholars were able
to infer these dates. Eusebius' notices, since they transmit the
Apollodoran chronology on Thales in its entirety, provide an
entrée to this question. Eusebius also has entries that show how
complex the tradition was that reached his sources, and the
extant texts exhibit those notices in such a way as to provide an
excellent example of how important it is always to approach
Eusebian evidence in the role of textual critic as well as historian.
The entry on the naming of the Seven Sages derives from a
tradition independent of Apollodorus. Of the two notices on
the war between the Lydians and the Medes, one derives from
Apollodorus but is wrongly positioned in the extant texts, while
the other represents a contamination between the Apollodoran
system for Thales and an independent tradition on the naming
of the Seven Sages.

The Traditional Chronology

Eusebius enters the *floruit* of Thales in the 35th Olympiad,
the eclipse in the 48th, and Thales' death in the 58th Olympiad.
According to Diogenes (1.37–8), Apollodorus dated the birth
(γέγονε) of Thales to the first year of the 35th Olympiad (640/
39). Diogenes states that he died at the age of 78, but he adds
that according to Sosicrates Thales died at the age of 90 in the
58th Olympiad (548/45), after having advised Croesus on
how to make the crossing of the Halys without benefit of a
bridge. The 90-year life span reckoned from the 58th Olympiad
produces a birth date in near agreement with that given by
Diogenes on the authority of Apollodorus, while the 78 years
reckoned from the same terminus suggest a birth date in the
620s. According to Pliny (*N.H.* 2.53), whose information derives from Apollodorus through the *Chronicle* of Nepos, Thales
predicted a solar eclipse that occurred in the fourth year of the

48th Olympiad, 585/84. If this year marked the Apollodoran acme of Thales, then his birth was in the fortieth year before the eclipse, 624/23, and his death at the age of 78 was dated (on inclusive reckoning) to 547/46. The year 624/23 corresponds to the first year of the 39th Olympiad. In an early epitome of Apollodorus, the Olympiad number was miscopied as 35 instead of 39, an error easily understood on paleographical grounds (ΛΕ instead of ΛΘ).² This error had corrupted the Apollodoran tradition even before it reached Sosicrates. Sosicrates commented on the discrepancy between the birth date and the 78-year life span ending in 547/46, and he accordingly stated that Thales must have been in his nineties at the time of his death.³

By the time the Apollodoran dates reached the sources of Eusebius, the error in the birth date had been further compounded by the not uncommon mistake of designating a birth date as a *floruit*. Both the corruption and the confusion are present also in the article of the *Suda* for Thales, where his γέγονε is assigned to the 35th Olympiad. Only Porphyry seems to have known the correct Apollodoran birth date, but the evidence is difficult to interpret. Arabic sources cite Porphyry (*FGrHist* 260 F 1) as having stated that Thales was the first of the Seven Sages and flourished 123 years after Nebuchadnezzar. If the Babylonian era of Nabonassar (747) is the terminus, then the interval of 123 years yields the correct Apollodoran birth date of Thales in 624, and one may suppose that Porphyry's translator mistakenly expressed the date as a *floruit*. How Porphyry knew the correct date despite the early textual corruption that affected all versions of the Apollodoran chronology can be explained: Porphyry understood the acme method, so instead of changing the reported life span, as Sosicrates did, he made the necessary correction in the transmitted birthdate. If so, one must then explain why Eusebius and the *Suda,* whose sources included the *Historia Philosophica* of Porphyry, transmitted the uncorrected corruption. Eusebius must have excerpted the date from his Olympiad chronicler, rather than from Porphyry, and the *Suda*'s date derives from a cognate source. Another interpretation is, however, equally viable. The Arabic citations have specific reference to Thales as the first of the Seven Sages. Demetrius of Phalerum (*FGrHist* 228 F 1) said that Thales was the first of the Seven Sages, and he dated the naming of the Seven Sages to 582/81. Apollodorus accepted this date for the epoch of the Seven Sages, and that is perhaps the date that Porphyry transmitted. In that case, it was Nebuchadnezzar the Great to whom the Arabic source refers. His 23rd year in the astronomical canon was 582/81, and the source's interval of 123 may be a textual corruption.[4]

The Arabic evidence is moot. Jacoby's interpretation of the other evidence, however, is sound and it has deservedly won almost universal acceptance.[5] It needs correction only in that Apollodorus' date for the fall of Sardis was 547/46, not 546/45 as Jacoby consistently maintained; and this correction requires less manipulation of Diogenes' text, thus making Jacoby's argument both tighter and smoother.[6] In synchronizing Thales' acme with the eclipse and his death with the fall of Sardis, Apollodorus was following Herodotus. His account is fundamental to the dating of Thales, no less for ancient scholars than for modern. Herodotus (1.74–5) associates Thales with two events of Lydian history. The first is the solar eclipse, supposedly predicted by Thales, which happened during the heat of battle in the sixth year of the war between Alyattes of Lydia and Cyaxares, king of the Medes. The phenomenon was sufficiently startling to bring an end to the war, through the arbitration of Labynetus of Babylon, and with the marriage of Alyattes' daughter to Astyages, the son of Cyaxares. The second event occurred when Croesus declared war against Cyrus and brought his armies to the river Halys. Thales helped to effect a crossing by causing the river to flow in two channels instead of one. Although Herodotus expresses some incredulity, he does not deny that Thales was present on that campaign. Apollodorus therefore used these stories to date Thales. He synchronized his acme with the famous eclipse. Since the last that was definitely known of him was his alleged participation in the war of Croesus against Cyrus, Apollodorus synchronized his death with the end of that war and the fall of Sardis. Because he gave his age at the time of death as 78 and dated the acme of Thales at the age of 40 to 585/84, Apollodorus' date for the fall of Sardis must have been 547/46.[7]

These synchronisms are typically Apollodoran. The computations are straightforward, despite the necessary assumption of an early corruption in the text of the birth date. One must carry the argument further, however, and ask how Apollodorus derived the dates 585/84 for the eclipse and 547/6 for the fall of Sardis. The latter date was Apollodorus' starting point for the construction of an absolute chronology for the Lydian kings, whose dates when imposed upon Herodotus' narrative were central to Apollodorus' dates of persons and events in early Greek history. The former date, the acme of Thales, Apollodorus used as a fixed point from which to count literary and philosophical successions at intervals of the fortieth year. On the old assumption that Apollodorus used a date corresponding to 546/45 for the fall of Sardis, one might suspect that the Apollodoran date for the acme of Thales synchronous with the famous eclipse was simply computed as one chronographic interval at the fortieth year before the fall of Sardis. But in all the fragments of Apollodorus that mention the fall of Sardis and permit the inference of an exact date, it is the year 547/46 that emerges. The two fundamental dates in 585/84 and 547/46 are therefore not directly related to one another chronographically, since they are not at the fortieth year apart. The two dates are independent of each other and demand separate investigation.

The Date of the Fall of Sardis

HERODOTUS' ACCOUNT

One cannot infer from Herodotus an exact date for the fall of Sardis. A fixed chronological framework can be imposed only upon Herodotus' figures for the number of years in the reigns of each of the Persian kings. Cyrus overthrew Astyages and ended a 35-year rule (1.130). He died after 29 years of rule (1.214). Cambyses and the false Smerdis together ruled 8 years (3.66–67), and Darius had a reign of 36 years (7.4). Herodotus gives a number of such "lists," including one for the Lydians, but the Persian list is the only one that can be associated with an absolute date. Xerxes was in his sixth year of rule when he invaded Europe (7.7, 20) and he entered Attica when Calliades was archon (8.51). Herodotus may not have intended these statements as fixed points of absolute chronology, but they could certainly be so used by Hellenistic scholars. The year of Calliades' archonship corresponds to 480 and the reign of Cyrus could thus be computed as beginning in 558 and ending in 530. Herodotus does not state in what year of his reign Cyrus defeated Croesus and captured Sardis. He can be interpreted as implying, however, that Croesus made preparations for war very shortly after Cyrus' overthrow of Astyages, in order to make a surprise attack (1.46, 75). The war ended rather sooner than Croesus had expected and the three years of grace supposedly awarded him by Apollo (1.91) might suggest that his fall should be dated about three years after that of Astyages. It is clear (1.130) that Herodotus, in recounting the story of Cyrus' successful revolution against Astyages, neither understands nor implies that there was any overlap between the 35 years of Astyages and the 29 years of Cyrus. Using the account of Herodotus, Hellenistic scholars could infer a *terminus post quem* for the fall of Sardis at the year 555. Since Croesus was already on the throne at the time Astyages was overthrown (1.46) and ruled for fourteen years (1.86), the latest possible date for his fall is the 15th year of Cyrus, 544.

Hermann Strasburger argued that this interval (555–44) can be reduced within two years in either direction from 546 without appeal to sources outside of Herodotus, and he suggested that the chronographers, in particular Apollodorus, derived their date by the same procedures of cross-reference within the text of Herodotus. What Strasburger's study really shows, however, is that these methods will not pin down Herodotus to an exact date for the fall of Sardis. It is furthermore quite unlikely that a chronographer could or would have followed exactly the same procedure as that used by Strasburger or have derived the same result.[8]

The Pre-Alexandrian Tradition

Apollodorus' date for the fall of Sardis in 547/46 cannot have been derived directly from Herodotus' account. What little evidence there is from the earlier chronographic tradition does not suggest that this date for the fall of Sardis was ever in circulation before the time of Eratosthenes and Apollodorus.

The debris of Ctesias' Persian history (*FGrHist* 688) permits no inference about what date, if any, he used for the fall of Sardis. Ctesias gave the regnal years for the kings of Assyria, Media, and Persia; unfortunately, the fragments do not allow a definitive reconstruction.[9] Since the Lydian kingdom does not, strictly speaking, have a place in the succession of empires in upper Asia, Ctesias need not have included a list of their kings or a date for the fall of Sardis. The excerpt from Ctesias' account of Cyrus' campaigns that appears in Photius (*Bibl.* cod.

72) states that Cyrus ruled for 30 years and it mentions the war with Croesus, but it does not date any of Cyrus' exploits.

Clement of Alexandria (*Strom.* 1.117, 131) attributes to Xanthus and Euphorion a date for the beginning of Gyges' reign corresponding to the 18th Olympiad (708/5). The date is eight years later than that which would follow from Herodotus' account using 547/46 for the end of the Lydian kingdom. Either Xanthus and Euphorion used a date for the fall of Sardis some eight years later than that of Apollodorus or they used a version of the Lydian list different from that of Herodotus and Apollodorus. Therefore, neither Xanthus nor Euphorion can be considered the source of Apollodorus' date. Clement also (1.131) attributes a date for Gyges in the 15th Olympiad (720/17) to Dionysius. Such an Olympiad date can be made to fit Herodotus' account using the Apollodoran date for the fall of Sardis. But Clement's authority is Dionysius of Halicarnassus, himself an Apollodoran excerptor, and not the *Persica* of the earlier Dionysius of Miletus (*FGrHist* 687).[10]

Lydian dates specifically attested by an author earlier than Eratosthenes and Apollodorus are those of the *Marmor Parium* (*FGrHist* 239). Alyattes was king in 605 (A 35), Croesus sent embassies to Greece during the archonship of Euthydemus, 556/55 (A 41), and his kingdom fell to Cyrus sometime before 536 (A 42). This last date is provided by restoration of the epochal interval in A 43. Both the epochal interval and the name of the archon in A 42 are lost. The date was probably in the 540s. If the archonship of Euthydemus was supposed to have been Croesus' first year, then the date of his fall must have been fourteen years later in 542. The date of the embassies is probably Atthidographic, deriving from false synchronism with the beginning of Pisistratus' second exile.[11] In other words, Greek tradition concocted Lydian dates by reversing Herodotus' synchronism of the Pisistratid tyranny with the war of Croesus and Cyrus. Thus the *Marmor*'s dates for Lydian kings derive from false reasoning and suggest that a precise date for the fall of Sardis was not yet current.

BEROSSUS

The date of Apollodorus for the fall of Sardis in 547/46—a date that he no doubt shared with Eratosthenes—agrees with the date that modern historians have established in autumn of

547. This agreement could, of course, be coincidental. But the date of Eratosthenes and Apollodorus cannot be derived from earlier Greek sources. Furthermore, it establishes a chronology for the war between Croesus and Cyrus that disagrees with the Greek tradition represented by Xanthus, Euphorion, and the notices of the *Marmor Parium*. Since the date is both correct and independent of the earlier Greek tradition, it may very well derive from the same ultimate sources as those upon which modern historians rely—Babylonian records. The modern date is based on a controversial entry in the Babylonian document known as the *Nabonidus Chronicle*. This document, composed in Babylon during the Seleucid period, is a copy of a fifth-century literary chronicle whose sources were archival records.[12] Whatever the correct interpretation of the entry in the *Nabonidus Chronicle*, we need not doubt that Cyrus' conquest of Lydia was included in the Babylonian literature.

About the time that the extant *Nabonidus Chronicle* was composed, these Babylonian literary histories were studied by the polymath Berossus of Babylon. He wrote (in Greek) three books of Babylonian history, of which the third dealt with the period from Nabonassar to the death of Alexander (747–323). The work was dedicated to Antiochus Soter and was thus composed about 270. Such fragments as exist of the third book show Berossus to have fulfilled his claim that he carefully examined and faithfully preserved the Babylonian sources. Berossus was an elder contemporary of Eratosthenes, and there is no reason to doubt that Eratosthenes read his book and acquired a copy of it for the Alexandrian library. Berossus must have translated the regnal dates of the Babylonian sources into some system intelligible to Greeks, perhaps by reference to the Seleucid era. Eratosthenes established Olympiad dates for those events he considered epochal for Greek history and included them in his *Chronographia*. It was no doubt he who dated the beginning of Cyrus' reign in Persia to the first year of the 55th Olympiad (560/59), a date that Eusebius (*Praep. Euang.* 10.10.5, citing Africanus) says all authorities accepted. That is, he added the 29 years assigned Cyrus by Herodotus to the Babylonian date of his death and found that his reign began before the completion of Olympiad 55.1 (i.e., before midsummer of 559). The date of the fall of Sardis he equated with the second year of the 58th Olympiad, 547/46.[13]

The Date of Thales' Eclipse

Apollodorus' date for the fall of Sardis, then, derives ultimately from archival evidence. How he obtained a date for the
now-famous eclipse with which he synchronized the acme of
Thales is a more difficult question. Herodotus' account of the
circumstances that attended this phenomenon has made it among
the most discussed of historical eclipses. The debate has concentrated on determining the astronomical date of this eclipse
and on whether Thales could in fact have predicted it. Little
consideration has been given to the question of how Apollodorus
could have known the date.

Herodotus reports the eclipse as having occurred during the
sixth and last year of the war between Alyattes and Cyaxares
(1.74–75). With the fall of Sardis dated to 547/46 and synchronized with the fourteenth regnal year of Croesus (1.86),
the 57 years of Alyattes (1.25) cover the period from 617 to
561. Herodotus reports the 35 years of Astyages (1.130) as
being separate and distinct from the 29 years (1.214) of Cyrus.[14]
The 40 years of Cyaxares (1.106) thus run from 633 to 594.
Apollodorus nevertheless dated the eclipse to 585/84, well
within the reign of Astyages by any reasonable interpretation
of Herodotus.

After long debate, modern scholars, with the aid of sophisticated eclipse tables permitting the magnitude and path of totality
to be computed, now agree that 28 May 585 was the date of
this eclipse. It is the only eclipse within acceptable chronological
limits that was total in the presumed vicinity of the battle (Halys
river) during the normal campaigning season.[15] It is generally
assumed in discussions of the problem that the Apollodoran
acme of Thales in the year to which Pliny and Eusebius date
the eclipse supports this identification.[16] The tools for making
such computations were not available to Hellenistic scholars.
It is in fact surprising that Apollodorus came within a few
months of the correct date, especially since it leads to a contradiction with Herodotus on the name of the Median king.

DOCUMENTS

The eclipse took place before there were any regular archival
procedures or chronological conventions in Ionian Greece. Fur-

thermore, the fact that Herodotus has Lydian chronology wrong seems to rule out the possibility that there existed in Sardis documentary records that would have permitted the precise dating of the war. The problems of Herodotus' Median chronology are notorious, and we cannot presume the existence of archival sources in Ecbatana that might eventually have brought the date to Apollodorus. The only possible documentary sources are Babylonian. Herodotus says (1.74) that Labynetus of Babylon served as arbitrator when the parties decided, because of the eclipse, to cease hostilities. This Labynetus has been identified with Nebuchadnezzar II (604–562).[17] It is therefore distinctly possible that a record of this arbitration found its way into the annals of his reign. This possibility cannot be entirely excluded. It seems unlikely, however, that this particular event, if it was ever recorded in the first place, would have been selected for inclusion in the literary chronicles of Babylon. The case cannot be proved one way or another. Since the possibility is remote, we should look elsewhere.

There was a record of ancient astronomical observations that Ptolemy (*Almagest* 3.7) says was preserved nearly complete from the epoch of Nabonassar (747). Ptolemy (4.6) uses this record for descriptions of lunar eclipses observed at Babylon as early as the first year of Mardokempad (721). Ptolemy's Babylonian record is either a copy of that used by Hipparchus in the middle of the second century B.C. or an excerpt from Hipparchus' writings. It is a reasonable assumption that this record was among the astronomical texts that Berossus made available to Greek scholarship in the early third century.[18] Eratosthenes and Apollodorus would then, at least theoretically, have had access to the Babylonian astronomical record. Whether the eclipse associated with Thales could have been included in this document is another matter. What little we know of Babylonian astronomy in the sixth and seventh centuries B.C. has to do with lunar theory. There is not one ancient solar eclipse report that derives from the document to which Ptolemy refers. This fact alone renders it unlikely that a date for Thales' eclipse found its way to Alexandrian scholarship through Babylonian records.

The question whether the eclipse of 28 May 585 could, even theoretically, have been included in the Babylonian astronomical record is directly related to the problem of whether Thales could have predicted the phenomenon. J. K. Fotheringham consistently maintained that Thales could and did predict the eclipse by applying to the eclipse of 17 May 603, the Babylonian theory of an 18-year *saros* cycle, after which both lunar and solar eclipses can be expected to repeat themselves at roughly the same observational point. If it is true that the *saros* was being used at that time for this purpose, Babylonian astronomers may well have looked for and recorded confirmation of the theory by carefully observing anticipated eclipses throughout the Near East. Otto Neugebauer, however, has demonstrated that such a theory is wrong. There existed in 600 B.C. no method in Babylonian astronomy for the prediction of solar eclipses.[19]

The eclipse of 28 May 585 was one of particularly large magnitude. But even in the vicinity of the battlefield (presumably somewhere along the Halys river), totality was achieved only 45 minutes before sundown. Although the phenomenon may have been sufficiently striking to cause the combatants to cease hostilities (a somewhat dubious tradition), it was not even visible in Babylon. Without the means to predict the occurrence of an eclipse elsewhere, and unable to observe this particular one in progress, the Babylonians cannot be expected to have preserved and transmitted a record of Thales' eclipse.

It is therefore vain to adduce the astronomical data and the Apollodoran date in support of each other. Apollodorus' date for the acme of Thales in the year of the eclipse must be accounted for chronographically. That is, we must ask what kinds of considerations enabled Apollodorus to establish the precise date in 585/84 and why, since astronomical evidence was unavailable, he dated the eclipse to the reign of Astyages instead of following Herodotus and choosing a date within the reign of Cyaxares. A brief review of the evidence is in order.

Testimonia

The fundamental evidence for the Apollodoran date is Pliny, *N.H.* 2.53: *apud Graecos autem inuestigauit primus omnium Thales Milesius olympiadis XLVIII anno quarto praedicto solis defectu, qui Alyatte rege factus est urbis conditae CLXX.* Pliny names only the Lydian monarch of the time. That Apollodorus understood the year 585/84 as being within the reign of the Median Astyages, and not Cyaxares, is clear from a statement of Cicero (*de diuin.* 1.49.112), who like Pliny depended, through Nepos, on Apollodorus: *et quidem idem* (Thales) *defectionem solis, quae Astyage regnante facta est, praedixisse fertur.*

A variant of the Apollodoran date is to be found in Laurentius Lydus (*de ostentibus* 9), whose immediate source is not known: προγνωσθῆναι δὲ τοῦτο παρὰ μὲν Ἕλλησι πρὸς Θαλοῦ τοῦ Μιλησίου ἐπὶ τῆς ἐνάτης καὶ τεσσαρακοστῆς ὀλυμπιάδος, ἔτει ἑβδομηκοστῷ καὶ ἑκατοστῷ τῆς κτίσεως Ῥώμης ὕστερον. Laurentius wrote in Greek, but he was a renowned scholar of *Latinitas* and may well have used Latin sources for this statement. Laurentius dates the eclipse to the 49th Olympiad (584/81) and the 170th year after the foundation of Rome. Pliny also gives the date as *a.u.c.* 170, and this was the dating system that Nepos used to translate Apollodorus' Athenian archon years into a Roman chronographic system. Pliny used the Varronian date corresponding to 753 for the foundation of Rome, according to which the year 1 was synchronized with Olympiad 6.3. Others believed (e.g., Censorinus, *de die nat.* 21.4–6) that the Varronian date corresponded to Olympiad 6.4, while Dionysius of Halicarnassus (1.74.2) equated a foundation date supposedly deriving from Cato with Olympiad 7.1. By either of these latter equations Laurentius would have expressed Nepos' *a.u.c.* 170 as corresponding to the 49th Olympiad.[20]

The same Olympiad date appears in Solinus (15.16), with specific reference to the Lydo-Median war: *bello denique, quod gestum est olympiade nona et quadragesima, anno post Ilium captum sescentesimo quarto, inter Alyattem Lydum et Astyagem Mediae regem, haustu mutui sanguinis firmata sunt iura pacis.* Solinus (40.4, 16–17) occasionally preserves Apollodoran information through an epitomized version of Nepos. Like Cicero, Solinus states that the war was waged by Alyattes and Astyages. This statement therefore derives from Nepos, and the date in Olympiad 49 should be considered an expression of Nepos' *a.u.c.* 170. Solinus confused the matter by also expressing the date as an interval of 604 years from the fall of Troy. This interval would yield a date in Olympiad 50, a date that is otherwise attested for Thales. But it seems more likely that Solinus (or his source) made an arithmetical error in the conversion of the Olympiad number to an interval from Troy. He made the mistake of multiplying the Olympiad number by 4 (49x4=196) and adding the result to the Eratosthenic interval of 408 years from the fall of Troy to the first Olympiad; thus he obtained the sum 604, having failed to make the necessary subtraction of four years.[21]

The dates in Olympiad 49 reported by Laurentius and Solinus are variant expressions of the Apollodoran acme of Thales in the year corresponding to Olympiad 48.4. But there did exist a date in the 49th Olympiad that can be associated with Thales and that was established before the time of Apollodorus. Diogenes Laertius (1.22) says that Thales was the first of the Seven Sages to receive the title σοφός, the honor being conferred in the archonship of Damasias (582/81), according to Demetrius of Phalerum (*FGrHist* 228 F 1), when the whole college of seven was also recognized as wise. This date has nothing to do with the eclipse or the Lydo-Median war. It derives from the date for the establishment of the Pythian games in the second archonship of Damasias (*Marmor Parium*, *FGrHist* 239 A 38) on the basis of a tradition similar to Plato's (*Protagoras* 343 A), that the Seven Sages met at Delphi and there dedicated the firstfruits of their wisdom.[22]

The Epoch of the Seven Sages

The prevailing view among scholars is that all dates for Thales, the naming of the Seven Sages, and the Lydo-Median war derive either from Herodotus and Apollodorus or from Demetrius of Phalerum. There are difficulties with this hypothesis, however, and the evidence of Eusebius is crucial. Eusebius follows the Apollodoran chronology in the dates for Thales' birth (including the early corruption in the Olympiad number and with *floruit* expressed instead of birth), the eclipse he was believed to have predicted, and his death at the time of the war between Croesus and Cyrus. The manuscript variants for the placement of these entries cannot be adduced in support of an argument otherwise. But Eusebius also has a notice on the naming of the Seven Sages, entered in the 50th Olympiad (580/77) in both versions of the *Chronicle*. Furthermore, there are two separate entries on the Lydo-Median war. The first appears in the 49th Olympiad in both versions, and in the Armenian it is coupled with the notice on Thales' eclipse. Alyattes and Astyages are specifically named as the combatants. The second entry states that Astyages attacked the Lydians and it appears in the 50th Olympiad in Jerome, the 51st in the Armenian version.

Eusebius' entry on the naming of the Seven Sages appears in

both versions of the *Chronicle* immediately after the notice on the establishment of the Isthmian and Pythian festivals. An error by one Olympiad is not uncommon in the *Canons* of Eusebius and Busolt therefore suggested that Eusebius had received and intended to write Demetrius' date for the naming of the Seven Sages in synchronism with the establishment of the first regular Pythian games in the third year of the 49th Olympiad, 582/81. But the notice appears at the 50th Olympiad in both versions of the *Chronicle* and that this was the original placement of the entry is attested by the excerpt of Cyril (*con. Iul.* 1.13), an early user of the *Chronicle*, who also dates the Seven Sages to the 50th Olympiad. Jacoby, adopting a suggestion of Erwin Rohde, argued that this date for the Seven Sages is a variant of the Apollodoran acme of Thales, with which he believed Apollodorus had synchronized the epoch of the Seven Sages. The Apollodoran acme of Thales in the year of the eclipse, 585/84, is the 33rd year of Alyattes if the fourteenth and last year of Croesus is dated to 547/46 (for Jacoby the fall of Sardis is 546/45, but he dates the last year of Croesus to 547/46). In the Lydian list of the *Canons* as reproduced by Jerome, the 33rd year of Alyattes falls in the second year of the 50th Olympiad, precisely where the notice on the naming of the Seven Sages appears in the best manuscripts. In the Armenian version, the 33rd year of Alyattes corresponds to the last year of the 50th Olympiad, where the Armenian enters the Seven Sages. Jacoby concluded that Apollodorus had specifically associated Thales and the Seven Sages with the 33rd year of Alyattes. This synchronism was translated into a date in the 50th Olympiad by those who used the version of the Lydian king lists that Eusebius included in the *Canons*. Hans Kaletsch carried the argument to its extreme. The association of Thales, the eclipse, and the Lydo-Median war with the 33rd year of Alyattes does not begin with Apollodorus or his epitomators. That synchronism was a part of the primitive tradition. Herodotus himself, Kaletsch suggested, although he did not mention the precise regnal year in the narrative, had the 33rd year of Alyattes "tatsächlich vor Augen" when he wrote of these events.[23]

If Rohde, Jacoby, and Kaletsch are right, then the answer to our question is immediately apparent. Apollodorus received the ancient tradition that the eclipse had occurred in the 33rd year of Alyattes. He derived the absolute date by counting off the regnal years of Croesus and Alyattes from his date for the fall of Sardis in 547/46. The resulting date in 585/84 fell within the reign of Astyages by Apollodorus' interpretation of Herodotus, so he concluded that Herodotus must have been wrong in naming Cyaxares as the Median king of the time. The eclipse-battle occurred during a war between Alyattes and Astyages.

The hypothesis is not convincing for several reasons. First, Apollodorus organized his chronicle by Athenian archon years, not the regnal years of the Lydian kings. Even if he had, in this case, mentioned the precise regnal year of Alyattes, it is not likely that his epitomators would have excerpted it. Their first concern was to convert Apollodorus' eponymous dates to the numbered Olympiad system. The conversion was more easily made directly from Athenian years to Olympic years than through a list of Lydian kings. Second, Greek tradition could seldom associate an event with a precise year like the 33rd of Alyattes before the chronographers had worked out systematic chronologies. If Thales' eclipse was an exception, then Herodotus would surely have included the regnal year in the text as he did in the case of the war between Alyattes and Thrasybulus (1.19). Finally, the entire theory is based on the appearance of the 33rd year of Alyattes in the 50th Olympiad of the Eusebian *Canons*, where notices on the Seven Sages and the Lydo-Median war also appear. This juxtaposition is coincidental.

The date for Thales and the Seven Sages in the 50th Olympiad is well attested. In addition to the entries of the *Canons*, the date appears in Eusebius' list of Olympic victors (93 Karst), in Clement (*Strom.* 1.65, 129), and in Tatian (*ad Graecos* 41). This date is not a variant of the Apollodoran acme of Thales. On the contrary, it derives from a relative chronology that can be traced as far as the fourth century B.C., according to which Thales and the Seven Sages had lived about one hundred years before the Persian Wars. Demetrius of Phalerum refined the estimate by synchronizing the Seven Sages with the first Pythiad in 582/81. No evidence suggests that Apollodorus changed the date, synchronizing the Seven Sages with the acme of Thales. In fact, he seems to have adopted Demetrius' synchronism, preferring a date for the naming of the Seven Sages that coincided with the acme of none of them. Demetrius' date for the naming of the Seven Sages was the chronographic standard. The earlier estimate continued to circulate, however, and it was eventually converted to an absolute date corresponding to the first year of the 50th Olympiad, 580/79, transmitted to Clement, Tatian, and Eusebius in the popular Olympiad chronicles. Since Thales was the most prominent of the Seven Sages, the date was particularly associated with him, and it therefore came to be combined with the tradition about the Lydo-Median war. Consequently, a notice on the war appears in the *Canons* of Eusebius in synchronism with the Seven Sages at the 50th Olympiad.[24]

A SOLUTION

There is no evidence that there existed a date for Thales' eclipse corresponding to 585/84 before the time of Apollodorus. How he derived that date without astronomical evidence remains to be explained, as does his disagreement with Herodotus about the name of the Median king. Apollodorus' influence on the tradition was such that once he had stated that Astyages was king at the time of the eclipse-battle, all later authors (including Cicero, Eusebius, and Solinus) followed suit.

There can be only one explanation for Apollodorus' statement, subsequently so influential, that Astyages had been king in the year of the eclipse-battle. Herodotus had stated unequivocally (1.74, 103) that Cyaxares was king and personally fought in the battle. An equally authoritative source must have made a statement from which Apollodorus concluded that Astyages' name should be closely associated with the battle. It now appears from a papyrus fragment (*P. Ox.* 2506 fr. 98) that this authority was a contemporary of the events in question, none other than the poet Alcaeus. The papyrus is a fragment of a commentary on Alcaeus. We do not have the poem, and the papyrus is badly damaged. Nevertheless, the commentator refers to the poet's return a third time from exile because of something to do with a war between Astyages and Alyattes. Unfortunately, it is not certain whether the reference to the war between Astyages and Alyattes actually derives from a poem of Alcaeus, or is explanatory material adduced independently by the scholiast. There is, however, a fragment of a poem (Z 27, L-P) referring to the exploits of Alcaeus' brother Antimenidas on mercenary service in the Babylonian empire. Another fragment (B 16) suggests that he fought in the Palestinian campaigns of Nebuchadnezzar, sometime between 601 and 585. Whether Alcaeus served in the armies of the Near East when in exile, we do not know, and it is vain to speculate whether he or his brother actually fought in the Lydo-Median war. Still, the stakes in the war were large even for the Greeks of the coast and nearby islands. The *modus uiuendi* established between the Greeks and the Lydians would be disrupted by a Median victory over the armies of Lydia. Because Antimenidas is known to have been in the Near East about this time and since the war had serious consequences anyway for persons like Alcaeus, we need not doubt that the commentator's statement about a war between Alyattes and Astyages derives from a poem of Alcaeus.[25]

Now, Herodotus stated that the eclipse-battle had been fought in the time of Cyaxares, resulting in a settlement and a marriage alliance that ended all hostilities. Alcaeus, on the other hand, made some kind of reference to a war between Astyages and Alyattes. Apollodorus had but one way out of the difficulty. He must have concluded that Astyages served as commander-in-chief of the armies, although his father was still king. This means that Cyaxares was quite old at the time and near the end of his reign. Herodotus states that he actually fought (1.103) in the eclipse-battle before coming to terms and arranging for his son to marry the Median princess. Apollodorus understood these events as the last that was known of Cyaxares. He accordingly dated the eclipse-battle to the year of Cyaxares' death. Following the usual chronographic practice, which assigns partial years to the successor, Apollodorus designated the year of Cyaxares' death as the first regnal year of Astyages. Hence his epitomators could state that Astyages was king in the year of the eclipse.

Apollodorus accounted for the apparent contradiction between Herodotus and Alcaeus and for Herodotus' failure to assign Astyages his due role in the war by "correcting" the historian's chronological implications. The narrative implies that the war was fought more than 35 years (the length of Astyages' reign) before the accession of Cyrus as king of Persia and thus sometime before 594. Apollodorus believed that the 35 years should be counted from the time of Cyrus' accession as king of the combined empire of the Persians and the Medes. That the correct date for this event was after Cyrus' first regnal year in Persia Apollodorus knew from the same source that yielded a date for the fall of Sardis—Berossus' version of what we know as the *Nabonidus Chronicle*. Cyrus conquered Ecbatana in the 6th year of Nabonidus, Sardis fell in the 9th year, and Cyrus liberated Bayblon in the 17th year of Nabonidus. He died in the year corresponding to 530 after 9 years as king of Bablyon. According to Herodotus, he had ruled 29 years in all. Hence the fall of Astyages should be dated to 550, and his first regnal year, the year of the eclipse-battle, to 585/84.

Thus Apollodorus (perhaps following Eratosthenes for this Median chronology) computed, without reference to astronomical data, the date 585/84 for the eclipse associated with Thales, and it was he who said that the eclipse occurred during a war between Astyages and Alyattes at a date that could be considered within the reign of Astyages rather than Cyaxares.[26]

Summary

Eusebius' dates for Thales derive from Apollodorus' computations of his birthdate, his acme at the time of eclipse, and his death when Cyrus captured Sardis. He also preserves an independent tradition that dated Thales and the Seven Sages one hundred years before the Persian Wars. Combined with the statement of Demetrius and Apollodorus that there had been an official Delphic proclamation of the Seven as Wise, this tradition led to an epoch for the naming of the Seven Sages in the 50th Olympiad. The two notices on the Lydo-Median war reflect these two traditions. The first (101[e] Helm) is an Apollodoran statement about the war between Alyattes and Astyages at (or near) the Apollodoran date. The second (101[f]) derives from the same Apollodoran statement, but it is associated with the date of another tradition. Textual difficulties complicate the matter.

Jerome enters the eclipse in the 48th Olympiad, but the war in the 49th. The Armenian version combines the two notices in a single entry at the 49th Olympiad. Both translators are in a sense correct, and these entries must, as always, be considered variant testimonies to the same original Eusebian text. The Armenian version is right in preserving a combined notice about the eclipse and the war, while Jerome is a better witness to the position that the notice occupied in the original *Canons*. Eusebius did not have two different dates for the eclipse and the war. He entered both in the latter years of the 48th Olympiad, perhaps side by side. Jerome and his bookman introduced a downward shift in the latter portion of the notice. In this case, it can be explained exactly how the error happened. Eusebius had entered the eclipse and the Lydo-Median war side by side in the *spatium historicum* of the 48th Olympiad. That was the last Olympiad on Jerome's 26-line page. Jerome was dictating the notices associated with Olympiad 48.4. His bookman entered the first part of the notice (the eclipse) at that year but, having used the last line, he was forced to turn the page and write the second part (the war) at the top of the next page and hence in the next Olympiad. The Armenian version shifted the combined notice down by two or three years, a displacement evident in every entry in the right margin of this page of the Armenian *Canons* (e.g., Solon in 591, compared to Jerome's 594).

Eusebius' second notice about the Lydo-Median war immediately follows the entry on the naming of the Seven Sages in both versions of the *Canons*. In Jerome, the entries stand at the 50th Olympiad. That this was the original placement is shown by the frequent citation of that date for the Seven Sages in other authorities. In the Armenian version the two notices appear slightly lower—the Seven Sages at the last year of the 50th Olympiad, the Lydo-Median war immediately thereafter but standing at a year of Olympiad 51. This pair of notices exemplifies contamination of the Apollodoran system with the dates of an independent tradition. The date in the 50th Olympiad for Thales and the Seven Sages was combined with the Apollodoran statement that Thales flourished at the time of the Lydo-Median war. Eusebius' notices cannot be taken as evidence that there was such a war after 585 nor do they attest to a war different from that which Herodotus mentions.[27]

15

Anaximander and Anaximenes,
Pythagoras and Pherecydes

a) OL 51.1 (576/75): Anaximander Milesius physicus agnoscitur. (101ᵍ)
AA 1444 (572/71): Anaximandros der Milesier war als
Physiker gekannt. (187)
b) OL 55 (560/57): Anaximenes physicus agnoscitur. (102ʳ)
No corresponding Armenian notice.
c) OL 59.4 (541/40): Ferecydes historicus clarus habetur.
(103ⁿ)
AA 1475 (541/40): Pherikides der Geschichtschreiber,
der Lehrmeister des Pithagoras, war gekannt. (189)
d) OL 62.3 (530/29): Pythagoras physicus philosophus
clarus habetur. (104ⁱ)
AA 1484 (532/31): Pithagoras war als physiker Philosoph gekannt. (189)
e) OL 70.4 (497/96): Pythagoras philosophus moritur.
(107ʳ)
AA 1517 (499/98): Pithagoras der Philosoph starb.
(191)

The dates transmitted in our sources for persons and events
of the period between 550 and 450 are of especial interest, because hard evidence begins to merge with chronographic reconstruction. The fall of Sardis is the first of a series of events that
serve for ancients and moderns alike as secure chronological
references. Even so, the traditional chronology remains difficult,
for there still did not exist contemporary narratives or archival
sources from which precise dates for everything could be inferred

directly. Absolute chronology for this period continues to depend on tradition and reconstruction. The counting of generations is clearly inappropriate for establishing the chronology of the recent past. Furthermore, one wonders how devices such as the 40-year acme and the 40-year intellectual "succession" could be applied without distorting the tradition. Analysis of the dates for the sixth-century philosophers Anaximander, Anaximenes, Pythagoras, and Pherecydes shows how this transitional period was handled, vindicating the traditional chronology. But the difficulties in the extant texts also show how meticulous one must be with criticism of source and tradition before adducing the chronographic texts as historical evidence.

The Apollodoran Dates

Reconstruction of the chronographic system within which these philosophers' dates were originally embedded proceeds, as usual, from combination of the Eusebian texts with Diogenes Laertius, the articles of the *Suda*, and other cognate texts dependent on the biographical vulgate of Apollodorus. Diogenes cites Apollodorus by name for the chronology of Anaximander and Anaximenes, but he does so in a confusing pair of statements (2.2–3) that remain problematical. The Greek, at least, is straightforward, so that the passages can be cited in translation:

1) D.L. 2.2. (Anaximander): "A summary exposition of his doctrines was made that Apollodorus of Athens somehow happened upon. For indeed he says in his *Chronicle* that in the second year of the fifty-eighth Olympiad (547/46) Anaximander was sixty-four years old and died a little later, having reached his acme at just about the time of Polycrates the tyrant of Samos.

2) D.L. 2.3. (Anaximenes): He flourished, as Apollodorus says, in the sixty-third Olympiad (528/25), and he died at the time of the fall of Sardis.

ANAXIMANDER

According to the first statement, Anaximander, if he was 64 years old in 547/46, reached his Apollodoran acme at the age of 40 in 571/70, the second year of the 52nd Olympiad. Diogenes also synchronizes his acme with Polycrates, the tyrant of Samos. The date of Polycrates, however, was about 530, for he was a contemporary of Cambyses, as both Herodotus (3.39, 125) and Thucydides (1.13.6) attest. A synchronism between Anaximander and Polycrates would therefore have been absurd for Apollodorus, and Jacoby accordingly bracketed this last phrase in Diogenes' statement, arguing that the synchronism properly belongs to the biography of Pythagoras, whose acme Apollodorus did synchronize with Polycrates. Diogenes' statement results from inaccurate epitomizing of the Apollodoran material, omitting the information necessary for the transition from Anaximander to Polycrates, namely, that Anaximander was the teacher of Pythagoras.[1] There are, of course, other interpretations. M. E. White adduced the unchanged text of Diogenes as evidence that a tyranny existed at Samos in 570, the tyrant being the more famous Polycrates' father.[2] Jules Labarbe, on the other hand, argued that Polycrates, with an acme about 530, would have been assigned a birthdate about 570. If the date was expressed by the epitomators as a γέγονε, it could easily have been misinterpreted as a *floruit*, entered as such in the Olympiad chronicles and synchronistic handbooks, finally resulting in the appearance of a synchronism between Anaximander and Polycrates as well as other false combinations.[3] The problem requires separate treatment, however, and is accordingly deferred to the next chapter. The appearance of Polycrates' name in Anaximander's biography does not, in any case, affect the Apollodoran dates of Anaximander himself. Aged 64 in 547/46, he reached his acme at the age of 40 in 571/70, as is confirmed by the statement of Hippolytus (*ref. haer.* 1.6.7) that he was born in the third year of the 42nd Olympiad, 610/9, the fortieth year earlier.

ANAXIMENES

Diogenes' statement about Anaximenes is chronological nonsense. In the Apollodoran system the fall of Sardis always refers to the defeat of Croesus in 547/46. Diogenes thus seems to report for Anaximenes a *floruit* (Olympiad 63, 528/25) twenty years after his death. Jacoby and most editors of the text therefore reverse the position of the two chronological references. Hence Anaximenes flourished at the time of the fall of Sardis in 547/46 and died about twenty years later in the 63rd Olympiad.[4] This is not a case of radical emendation of the text. Diogenes no doubt wrote what the manuscripts attest. The confusion can be attributed to the excerptors whom Diogenes read. The error fortunately did not affect all the texts descended from Apollodorus. That Anaximenes' *floruit* was associated with the fall of Sardis is confirmed, at least obliquely, by the article of the *Suda* on him. The *Suda* says that he flourished in the 55th Olympiad (560/57), at the time of the fall of Sardis, when Cyrus of Persia defeated Croesus. The sources of the *Suda* correctly transmitted the synchronism between the acme of Anaximenes and the fall of Sardis, making it clear that the reference is to Cyrus' defeat of Croesus. The sources assigned the wrong date to the synchronism, however, associating Anaximenes with the 55th Olympiad. Olympiad 55 was the universal chronographic date for the accession of Cyrus.[5] The compiler of the *Suda*'s report introduced the date for Cyrus instead of that for Croesus' fall. It would be wrong, therefore, to treat Diogenes' statement in isolation from the cognate testimonia, interpreting it as it stands in the text so as to date Anaximenes later. One such suggestion is that the fall of Sardis is here a reference to the sack of the city during the Ionian Revolt about 496.[6] Thus Diogenes can be understood as saying that Anaximenes flourished about 525 and died about 496. But in texts deriving from Apollodorus, as Diogenes specifically says his does, the fall of Sardis is always a reference to the defeat of Croesus. The *Suda* associates Anaximenes with that event, Hippolytus (*ref. haer.* 1.7.8) dates him to Olympiad 58, the usual and correct date for the fall of Sardis, and Eusebius confirms the synchronism indirectly by agreeing with the sources of the *Suda* in dating the *floruit* of Anaximenes to Olympiad 55, the epoch of Cyrus.

PHERECYDES AND PYTHAGORAS

Diogenes (1.121) reports the *floruit* (γέγονε) of Pherecydes of Syros, the teacher of Pythagoras, as having been in the 59th Olympiad (544/41). Jacoby ascribed the date to Apollodorus since the vast majority of Diogenes' dates in the first book are Apollodoran. There is confirmation in other sources that often preserve Apollodoran data. Eusebius enters Pherecydes in the 59th Olympiad. Cicero (*Tusc. disp.* 1.38) dates Pherecydes to the reign of Servius Tullius, that is, about 550; and Pliny (*N.H.* 7.205) synchronizes him with Cyrus. The *Suda* reports a birthdate in Olympiad 45 (600/597), synchronized with the Seven Sages. The numeral is a corruption of the Apollodoran birthdate in Olympiad 49 ($\overline{\text{ME}}$ instead of $\overline{\text{MΘ}}$), forty years before Diogenes' date for his *floruit*.[7]

Of the several dates reported for Pherecydes' famous student Pythagoras, his acme in the 62nd Olympiad (532/29) synchronized with the tyranny of Polycrates is the Apollodoran date. The Peripatetic scholar Aristoxenus of Tarentum, who was acquainted with fourth-century Pythagoreans of South Italy, and an authority whom Apollodorus respected, said (fr. 16 Wehrli) that Pythagoras was forty years old when he saw the tyranny of Polycrates taking root and therefore left Samos for Italy. Such a statement fit Apollodorus' method exactly, so he synchronized the acme of Pythagoras with Polycrates.[8]

Aristoxenus was an influential authority. This particular fragment is especially noteworthy, since it so clearly anticipates Apollodorus' method. In fact, it was in Aristoxenus' writings on Pythagoreanism that Apollodorus found the philosophical model upon which he based much of his chronological method. Apollodorus' chronology for Pythagoras and for persons and events associated with him reveals the logical basis of his method for systematizing the tradition. Aristoxenus' influence on Apollodorus has long been recognized, but the intricacies of the system have not fully been perceived. How Apollodorus derived precise dates for the acmes of Anaximander, Anaximenes, Pherecydes, and Pythagoras has not been satisfactorily explained. Analysis will show that there is a tight relationship among these dates. The relationships lead to a fuller understanding of Apollodorus' method, demonstrating how he dealt with sixth-century chronology. A combination of historical evidence with theoretical intervals permitted him to systematize a complex tradition in such a way as to yield a sound absolute chronology. His system employed other intervals in addition to the forty years of the acme, providing the flexibility necessary to prevent the model of intellectual successions from distorting the chronology.

The Evidence of the Extant Texts

The extant evidence is fraught with difficulties and open to multiple interpretations. Before analysis of the Apollodoran dates can proceed, it must be shown that these texts—especially Eusebius and the *Suda*—do in fact attest to the Apollodoran chronology as being the vulgate, rather than to some other tradition. Much can be learned in the process about the nature of the texts themselves and of the late tradition, often corrupt and contaminated, that they represent.

ANAXIMANDER

Diogenes' statement (2.2) that Apollodorus dated the 64th year of Anaximander to Olympiad 48.2, 547/46, and Hippolytus' date (1.6.7) for his birth in Olympiad 42.3, 610/9, corroborate each other to prove that the Apollodoran acme of Anaximander was Olympiad 52.2, 571/70. Whether this was the Eusebian date, however, is unclear. In the most authoritative manuscripts of St. Jerome (the "O" and "S" families), the entry on the *floruit* of Anaximander appears between the first and third years of the 51st Olympiad, 576–74. "F" has the notice at the third year of the 50th Olympiad, 578/77, while in "B" the entry is at Olympiad 52.2, 571/70. In the Armenian version, the notice is entered at the first year of Olympiad 52, 572/71. One cannot simply conclude, however, that "B" has the right reading or argue that the Armenian version supports "B" in attesting to Olympiad 52 as the original Eusebian date. Both "B" and the Armenian manuscript consistently set the notices of this portion of the *Chronicle* several years lower than do the "O–S" manuscripts of Jerome. It is therefore accidental that "B" exhibits the Apollodoran date. The reading of "F" at the other extreme, in the 50th Olympiad, is also plausible, and also wrong. Cyril, whose excerpts constitute the earliest Greek witness, dates Anaximander and the Seven Sages to the 50th Olympiad (*con. Iul.* 1.13). Such a synchronism with the Seven Sages is not unreasonable. In this case, however, Cyril combined two excerpts. All the manuscripts of Jerome (including "F" and "B") and the Armenian version show an interval of three or four years between the entry on the Seven Sages and that on Anaximander.

The manuscript evidence therefore suggests that Olympiad 51, not Olympiad 50 or 52, was the original placement in the *Canons* for the *floruit* of Anaximander. We are presented with another instance where Eusebius entered a notice one Olympiad earlier than the Apollodoran date.[9] The appearance of Stesichorus and Simonides in Olympiad 55 instead of Olympiad 56 is a parallel case, and so is the entry of Cypselus in Olympiad 30 instead of Olympiad 31. In Jerome such departures from the reading of his source (the Eusebian text) sometimes correspond with the beginning or the end of one of his 26-line pages (above, chapter 14). The same may be the case with Eusebius' departures from his sources. If so, then one page of the Eusebian *Canons* contained the entries from Olympiad 52—the Apollodoran date of Anaximander—through Olympiad 56—the Apollodoran date for a synchronism between Stesichorus and Simonides. These years would have occupied 38 lines of text, a number appropriate for Greek manuscripts of the period.[10] Whatever the exact cause, the entry of Anaximander in Olympiad 51 instead of Olympiad 52 arises from textual difficulties, and it must not be used as evidence for a variant date in the chronographic tradition.[11]

ANAXIMENES

Diogenes (2.3) attests to an Apollodoran acme for Anaximenes at the time of the fall of Sardis, 547/46. The *Suda* dates him to Olympiad 55, stating also that he flourished at the time of the fall of Sardis, when Cyrus defeated Croesus. The sources of the *Suda* combined Apollodorus' synchronism of Anaximenes with the war of Cyrus and Croesus, with the vulgate date for the accession of Cyrus in Olympiad 55.1, 560/59. Eusebius also dates Anaximenes to Olympiad 55, his notice of the philosopher's *floruit* appearing in that Olympiad in all but one of the manuscripts of Jerome. "B" as usual has the notice too low, while the entry does not appear at all in the Armenian version. The Floriacensis fragments ("S") happen to be extant for this leaf of Jerome, showing the notice in a broad space of the right (secular) page between the Olympiad number and the numeral that marks the first year of the Olympiad. The corresponding lines of the left page contain text announcing the beginning of the Persian *filum*. For several lines this text interrupts the vertical run of numerals to describe the destruction of the Median empire and the accession of Cyrus. The position of the notice therefore suggests that Eusebius found Anaximenes dated in his source to the time of Cyrus, the date expressed as Olympiad 55 without specification of a precise year within the quadrennium. Eusebius' source was accordingly similar to those used by the compilers of the *Suda*. Eusebius' Olympiad chronicler excerpted only the Olympiad number and the synchronism with Cyrus, omitting the additional synchronism with the fall of Sardis.

The point is worth belaboring. Eusebius and the *Suda* share a common tradition for many of their dates. A fuller under-standing of that tradition can therefore sometimes be obtained by combining the two witnesses. In this case, the *floruit* for Anaximenes in Olympiad 55 to which Eusebius attests is com-prehensible only as the result of a mistaken date for the fall of Sardis. A statement such as that which the *Suda* preserves must have existed at some stage in the transmission of the Apollodoran material to Eusebius to explain how Anaximenes' date came to be associated with the 55th Olympiad, instead of the 58th. The entry exemplifies a general *caveat*—Eusebius' dates can be under-stood and adduced as evidence only in the context of all relevant data in the cognate texts. In the case of Anaximenes, Eusebius and the *Suda* received a version of the Apollodoran tradition less true than that which reached Hippolytus. Hippolytus, as we have seen (*ref. haer.* 1.7.8), dated Anaximenes to Olympiad 58.1. In his version of the tradition the synchronism between Anaximenes and the fall of Sardis was correctly associated with the 58th Olympiad, although specification of the exact year (OL 58.2, 547/46) had disappeared and Hippolytus therefore designated it as the first.

PHERECYDES

Diogenes (1.121) dates Pherecydes of Syros, the teacher of Pythagoras, to Olympiad 59 (544/41). Eusebius enters Phere-cydes in that Olympiad, the Armenian version agreeing with the oldest manuscripts of Jerome in setting the notice at the fourth year (541/40). The entry is problematic, however, because the sources confuse homonyms. Eusebius preserves dates for two persons named Pherecydes, and he characterizes them both as historians. Besides the notice in question, there is at Olympiad 81 (456/53): *Ferecydes secundus historiarum scriptor agno-scitur* (111[k] Helm). Five applications of the name Pherecydes are attested. The problem is to determine which two Eusebius notes. Andron of Ephesus (cited at *D.L.* 1.119) knew of two from Syros—one an astronomer, the other a philosopher, the teacher of Pythagoras and son of Babys. Eratosthenes (*FGrHist* 241 F 10) acknowledged the existence of only one Syrian—the son of Babys—and one younger Pherecydes, the Athenian genealogist. The *Suda* reports three—one from Syros, an "elder" Pherecydes of Athens, and a "younger" Pherecydes from Leros. Apollodorus, however, agreed with Eratosthenes that there were only two persons of this name, of whom the Athenian was the younger. His opinion is reflected in the *Suda*'s excerpt from Porphyry (*FGrHist* 260 F 21), denying the existence of any Pherecydes older than the Syrian.[12]

Now, Eusebius characterizes his first Pherecydes as a historian, but he also calls him the teacher of Pythagoras. This qualification, omitted in the "O"–"S" manuscript tradition of Jerome, is attested as Eusebian by Syncellus (451) and the Armenian version.[13] The Pherecydes in question is therefore the Syrian son of Babys whom Eratosthenes, Apollodorus, and Porphyry considered the elder of two persons by that name. Eusebius' younger Pherecydes is either the Lerian, whom the *Suda* designates as younger than the son of Babys, or the Athenian genealogist who Eratosthenes said was the younger. Eusebius refers to his younger Pherecydes as "Pherecydes the Second."[14] This Pherecydes cannot be the *Suda*'s Lerian, for he was the third person of that name. Eusebius' second Pherecydes is therefore the Athenian.

Eusebius' two Pherecydes are identical with those of Eratosthenes, Apollodorus, and Porphyry. His first entry transmits a date for the Syrian son of Babys who was the teacher of Pythagoras. Because Eusebius and Diogenes agree in the date at Olympiad 59, 544/41, and since both authors preserve Apollodoran material, the date can reasonably be ascribed to Apollodorus. Eusebius' sources added an extra dimension of confusion to the problem of the homonym Pherecydes by designating both persons as historians, instead of calling the elder a philosopher. The error derives from ambiguity in the meaning of συγγραφεύς. The word generally means "writer of prose," but it was most frequently applied to historians. Pherecydes of Syros was considered the first prose writer, while the younger Pherecydes was supposed to have been the first Athenian prose writer. In both cases Eusebius' sources interpreted the word in the narrow sense of "historiographer."[15]

Pythagoras

Eusebius' entry of the *floruit* of Pythagoras presents no textual difficulty. Both the Oxford manuscript of Jerome and the Armenian version enter Pythagoras in the 62nd Olympiad,

532/29. This was the vulgate date, deriving from Apollodorus' computation of his acme.

Apollodorus' Method

The Eusebian texts attest, with some corruption and confusion, to the Apollodoran dates for the acmes of Anaximander (Olympiad 52), Anaximenes (Olympiad 58), Pherecydes (Olympiad 59), and Pythagoras (Olympiad 62). The next question is how Apollodorus arrived at these dates, none of which can be presumed to have been derived directly from contemporary record.

In the first place, Apollodorus disagreed with Eratosthenes on the date of Pythagoras. Such a name appeared in the Olympic victor lists (e.g., Eusebius' list, 93 Karst), and Eratosthenes held (*FGrHist* 241 F 11) that it was the philosopher who competed in the games of the 48th Olympiad (588/87), was adjudged too old to compete among the boys, and won a victory in boxing among the men.[16] Apollodorus, as has been noted, followed Aristoxenus in dating the philosopher's 40th year to the time of his emigration from Samos to Italy when Polycrates' power took hold. Jacoby thought that Apollodorus simply combined this statement of Aristoxenus with the fixed epochal date of Polycrates to yield an acme for Pythagoras in 532/31. The acme of Anaximander falls in the 40th year earlier, 571/70. Apollodorus knew and accepted a tradition that made Anaximander the teacher of Pythagoras (attested by Porphyry *V.P.* 2) and, by setting his 64th year in 547/46, produced a date for his acme to support that tradition. In Jacoby's view, Apollodorus dated the acme of Anaximenes to 546/45 because it was the 40th year after the acme of Thales (585/84) and coincidentally also the epoch of the fall of Sardis. For the date of Pherecydes, Jacoby found no plausible explanation, rightly rejecting the hypothesis of Rohde that the *floruit* in 544/43 derived from synchronizing the acme of Pherecydes with the midpoint of Cyrus' reign.[17]

This set of explanations is inadequate. Although Polycrates could be synchronized with Cambyses (530–522), a fixed epochal date in 532/31 does not result. Nor did the alleged book of Anaximander provide a starting point for the chronology. The 40-year interval between the acme of Anaximander and Pythagoras is too obviously contrived to make credible the widely held view that the age of 64 in the year 547/46 is a primary written tradition deriving from Anaximander himself.[18] Furthermore, Apollodorus' date for the fall of Sardis was in fact not 546/45, as Jacoby asserted, but 547/46. The best evidence for this date is that Apollodorus computed the ages of both Thales (78) and Anaximander for that year. The acme of Anaximenes at the time of the fall of Sardis should therefore be associated with 547/46 and not with 546/45, the 40th year after the acme of Thales.

What emerges is that Apollodorus expressed the ages for these philosophers as a group at the year 547/46, the epoch of the fall of Sardis (above, chapter 14). The case is analogous to that of the historians Hellanicus, Herodotus, and Thucydides. Apollodorus stated their ages for the year of the epoch of the Peloponnesian War, 432/31 (*FGrHist* 244 F 7). A closer parallel appears with Apollodorus' dates for the three tragedians, Aeschylus, Sophocles, and Euripides. He expressed their ages for the year 456/55 as 64, 40, and 25, respectively (below, chapter 17), the epochal date being that of Aeschylus' death. In the case of the philosophers, Thales died at age 78 in 547/46, Anaximander published his book in that year at the age of 64 and died shortly thereafter, and Anaximenes in 547/46 reached his acme at the age of 40. Particularly remarkable is that Pythagoras, since he flourished in 532/31, 40 years after Anaximander, was 25 years old in 547/46. Thus in the epochal year of the fall of Sardis, Anaximander, Anaximenes, and Pythagoras were of the same age relative to each other as Aeschylus, Sophocles, and Euripides in the year 456/55.

These relative ages are most interesting. With the acmes of master and pupil set 40 years apart, it is natural to ask the age of a student when he began to receive his tutelage. Apollodorus chose the age of 25 as the appropriate point. It follows immediately, of course, that the elder of the pair was the 40th year older, 64. Furthermore, the age of 64 is useful to date something allegedly associated with a person's mature years—for Anaximander the publication of his doctrines—while the age of 25 serves as the date of a youthful first entry to fame. Euripides was at that age when he made his first dramatic presentation.

These ages—25, 40, and 64—are appropriate enough for biographical chronology in themselves, and they are especially useful in the application of the acme method. Moreover, the numerology itself forms an arithmetical pattern. The acme at age forty is, of course, one half the perfect life of eighty years. The number 40 has the factors 8 and 5. It stands in a ratio of 8 :5 to the number 25 and 5 :8 to the number 64. Five is the square root of 25, 8 is the square root of 64, and 8 times 5 equals 40. In other words, the numbers 25, 40, and 64 form a geometrical proportion of the type $a^2/ab = ab/b^2$, where $a = 5$ and $b = 8$. Neither the numbers nor their ratios are the invention of Apollodorus. They derive from Pythagoreanism. Apollodorus adopted these theoretical ages and the intervals between them from Aristoxenus. It is from this philosophical model, rather than from genealogical chronology, that Apollodorus' method of the acme derives. Whether Apollodorus was the first to use the theory for chronology we do not know. There were probably precedents in the antiquarian work of Aristoxenus and his fellow Peripatetics, so that we should attribute to Apollodorus the final synthesis rather than the invention.[19]

Apollodorus' method was capable of elaborate combinations and great flexibility through the use of theoretical ages at 25 and 64 years, as well as at 40 and 80 years. The shorter intervals of 15 and 25 years enabled him to deal with traditions to which the 40-year interval of the acme was inappropriate. Naturally, Apollodorus did not apply the theory arbitrarily. He used it in the absence of precise data to systematize the received tradition, but only if its application produced no inconsistency or distortion. Apollodorus did not always demand of his chronography that it display this kind of mathematical harmony, as his dates for the three historians show. Hellanicus, Herodotus, and Thucydides were considered contemporaries of somewhat different ages. The theoretical chronography would suggest that some epoch be found at which the three were 64, 40, and 25 years old or, in a variation of the system, 64, 55, and 40 years old. But Apollodorus had synchronisms that he thought appropriate for the separate computation of their acmes. At the beginning of the Peloponnesian War, he said, the three historians were 65, 53, and 40 years of age.[20]

It is therefore not enough simply to observe that the Apollodoran dates of Anaximander, Anaximenes, and Pythagoras are in mathematical symmetry, this being a significant feature of his method. It is also necessary to ask why Apollodorus thought it appropriate to apply the ratios as he did. The answer is most interesting, showing how chronographic theory blends with doxographic tradition and historiographic record to produce an acceptable absolute chronology.

Thales' association with Croesus' war against Cyrus had been reported by Herodotus (1.75). Apollodorus synchronized his death with the fall of Sardis, computing his age at the time as 78 by reference to the acme at 585/84 (above, chapter 14). In the doxographic tradition deriving from Theophrastus, Anaximander was the companion, pupil, and successor of Thales (DK 12 A 9–11). That is, he was a younger contemporary of Thales and would have flourished a few years after Thales did. In the same tradition, Anaximenes was the companion, pupil, and successor of Anaximander (DK 13 A 5, 10). These relationships are not such as to permit the application of 40-year intervals between successions, since companionship implies a closer contemporaneity. With Thales' age fixed as 78 in 547/46, the assignment to Anaximander and Anaximenes of the theoretical ages of 64 and 40 at that epoch provides a precision consistent with the tradition.

For Pythagoras, Apollodorus had Aristoxenus' statement that he was 40 years old and left Samos for Italy at the time of Polycrates' tyranny. Knowing the synchronism between Polycrates and Cambyses attested by Herodotus and Thucydides, and using Herodotus' Persian chronology, Apollodorus could infer a date corresponding to about 530 for Polycrates and the acme of Pythagoras. The difficulty is to obtain a precise date. Relationships between Pythagoras and the Milesians are not well attested for authors before Apollodorus. Later sources are specific in stating that Pythagoras had been a student of Anaximander.[21] Perhaps Apollodorus himself invented the relationship to provide a chronographic connection between philosophical and literary successions based on Thales and those of the Western schools. In any case, the establishment of a 40-year interval between Anaximander and Pythagoras permitted Apollodorus to compute a precise date for the acme of Pythagoras that would accord with the tradition that he had been 40 years old at the time of Polycrates. Anaximander had been assigned the age of 64 at the time of the fall of Sardis, so Pythagoras, being 40 years younger, was 25 years old at the epoch of 547/46, and he accordingly reached his acme in 532/31, the time of Polycrates.

A firmer connection between Pythagoras and the learning of Asia Minor could be made through Pherecydes of Syros. The tradition that Pherecydes was the teacher of Pythagoras may be as old as the fifth century.[22] The association was certainly made in Peripatetic biography, for both Dicaearchus and Aristoxenus stated that Pythagoras had seen to his master's needs when he lay sick and dying on Delos.[23] One dating for Pherecydes was that which synchronized him with the Seven Sages in the early sixth century.[24] By Eratosthenes' dating of Pythagoras' 18th year to the supposed Olympic victory in 588, Pythagoras properly appears as a younger contemporary of Pherecydes. But for Aristoxenus and Apollodorus, who synchronized Pythagoras with Polycrates, Pherecydes by that dating would have been some fifty years older than his pupil. Aristoxenus and Dicaearchus tried to resolve the difficulty by supposing that Pythagoras' service to his dying master had taken place before the emigration to Italy.[25] Apollodorus, however, reinterpreted the synchronism between Pherecydes and the Seven Sages, so as to maintain a close chronological relationship between Pherecydes and Pythagoras. This he achieved by dating the birth, not the *floruit*, of Pherecydes to the epoch of the Seven Sages, that is, to 582/81. Hence his acme was 543/42, the second year of the 59th Olympiad.[26] With the acme fixed at that time, Pherecydes was some eleven years older than Pythagoras and Apollodorus was enabled to follow that tradition according to which Pythagoras had been absent from Croton at the time of the Cylonian revolution because he was tending to Pherecydes.[27] The system also incorporated the doxographic tradition that Pherecydes was a student of Thales by dating his acme 40 years after the epoch of the Seven Sages.[28]

These relationships among the acmes of Anaximander, Anaximenes, Pherecydes, and Pythagoras established, it remained for Apollodorus to adduce plausible synchronisms to determine the dates of their deaths. According to Diogenes, Apollodorus dated Anaximander's death shortly after his 64th year in 547/46. Both Anaximander and Pherecydes were considered to have been teachers of Pythagoras. Some sort of synchronism between the two would therefore be appropriate. At the time of Pherecydes' acme in 543/42, Anaximander was 68 years old. The four years correspond well to the μετ' ὀλίγον of Diogenes' citation, and Apollodorus perhaps synchronized the death of the one teacher with the acme of the other.

The death of Anaximenes in Olympiad 63 might reflect a synchronism through Pythagoras with Polycrates' tyranny. The exchange of letters between Anaximenes and Pythagoras that

Diogenes reproduces (2.5, 8.49) is certainly false, but the tradition on which the letters are based may be quite old. Anaximenes was supposed to have congratulated Pythagoras for his decision to flee from the tyranny of Polycrates and settle in the West. He complains in the letter that the unsettled conditions of the eastern Aegean, with the double threat of tyranny and the Persian king, made study impossible. The dramatic date of such an exchange would be shortly after 532, clear evidence of unsettled conditions being Polycrates' murder by the satrap of Sardis (Herodotus 3.125). Pliny (*N.H.* 33.27) dates the death of Polycrates to Olympiad 63.4, 525/24. If the date is Apollodoran, it would serve also as the date of Anaximenes' death.[29]

Eusebius dates the death of Pythagoras to 497/96, according to the best manuscripts of Jerome. The date is probably Apollodoran, as so many Eusebian dates are, resulting in a life span for Pythagoras of 75 years. Such an age for Pythagoras at the time of his death is among those reported.[30] The tradition about Pythagoras' later years and the circumstances of his death is notoriously problematic. Apollodorus seems to have adopted something like that version which Diogenes (8.40) reports on the authority of Heraclides' *Epitome of the Lives of Satyrus*. Pythagoras was absent from Croton at the time of the Cylonian disorder because he was attending to Pherecydes on his death bed at Delos. When Pythagoras returned to find the philosophical aristocracy in trouble, he betook himself to Metapontum and invited by starvation the metamorphosis of death. How the date in the 490s was derived is unclear. Perhaps Apollodorus had evidence for the dating of the Crotoniate *stasis* that would permit an inference as to the time of Pythagoras' death. Or perhaps the date of Pythagoras' death was remembered by his followers through an annual memorial ceremony at which it was regularly announced how many years had elapsed since the master's departure. In that case Aristoxenus, since he was personally acquainted with what Diogenes (8.46) calls the last generation of Pythagoreans, could have converted the interval to an absolute date and made it available to later chroniclers like Apollodorus. We lack the evidence, but somehow Apollodorus believed that he had a historical date for Pythagoras' death in 497/96, resulting in a life span of 75 years instead of the theoretical 80. The political disorder had broken out when the master was absent on an unhappy, but necessary mission. No source reports one, but this version of matters would also provide an approximate date for the death of Pherecydes, two or three years before that of Pythagoras. A synchronism was at hand to fiix the date more precisely. Anaxagoras was born in 499/98, and Apollodorus could synchronize the death of Pherecydes with the birth of Anaxagoras.[31]

Summary

Apollodorus' dates for Anaximander, Anaximenes, Pythagoras, and Pherecydes show how Greek chronology could use theoretical mathematical devices in conjunction with traditional synchronisms and a few dates properly judged historical (e.g., fall of Sardis, accession of Cambyses) to produce an elaborate set of mutually related combinations. The result introduces the desired chronological precision into the tradition and represents in final form a careful judgment on controversial issues contained within the tradition. The approximate date of Pythagoras' acme was known on the basis of acceptable traditions synchronizing him with Polycrates and Polycrates with Cambyses. The exact date depends upon the introduction of Pythagoras into a mathematical expression of doxographic relationships applied to an epochal date—the fall of Sardis. Thus, while the approximate date of Pythagoras is dependent on that of Polycrates, a precise date for Polycrates depends on the date for Pythagoras' acme, not vice versa. The chain of reasoning that leads from the dates of Thales and the fall of Sardis through the doxographic tradition on Anaximander and Anaximenes to the acme of Pythagoras establishes a new chronological reference in 532/31. This date, once computed for Pythagoras, was the starting point for the dates of Polycrates and persons associated with him. These dates are discussed in the next chapter.

16

Polycrates, Ibycus, and Anacreon

a) OL 60.1 (540/39) : Ibycus carminum scriptor agnoscitur. (103°)

No corresponding Armenian notice.

b) OL 61.1 (536/35) : Anacreon lyricus poeta cognoscitur. (104^f)

AA 1481 (535/34) : Anakreon war als Liederdichter gekannt. (189)

c) OL 61.4 (533/32) : Aput Samum tyrannidem exercent tres fratres Polycrates Sylus et Pantagnostus. (104^g)

AA 1482 (534/33) : Samos' Gewalthaber sind Krates und Silos, zu denen auch Pandokostos, die Brüder, gewesen. (189)

The chronographic tradition about Polycrates, Anacreon, and Ibycus provides an excellent example of how difficult it can be to extract solid information from the extant sources even for dates of the late sixth century and even for a person as renowned as Polycrates. Eusebius dates the insurrection of Polycrates and his brothers to the 530s. He enters the *floruit* of Anacreon and of Ibycus, both of whom were associated with the court of Polycrates, about the same time. Eusebius accordingly reports a tradition fully consistent with the evidence of Herodotus (3.39, 120) and Thucydides (1.13.6) that Polycrates lived at the time of Cambyses, whose accession can be dated to 530. Other authorities, however, with sources cognate with those of Eusebius, transmit information about persons associated with Polycrates—especially Anacreon and Ibycus—that seems to contradict this tradition. Consequently, a debate has arisen over the true historical dates of the Samian tyranny and the names and number of the persons who were tyrant there. Analysis of the chronographic evidence is more arachnean than one would like, because so many different interpretations have been made in the context of this debate.

The Problem

Herodotus (3.39) states that Polycrates made himself master of Samos by insurrection, at first ruling jointly with his brothers Syloson and Pantagnotus, then exercising a sole tyranny after having murdered Pantagnotus and banished Syloson. Herodotus' narrative implies (3.40–44) that these events had taken place shortly before Cambyses' war against Polycrates' erstwhile ally, Amasis of Egypt.[1] Aristoxenus (fr. 14 Wehrli) synchronized the 40th year of Pythagoras with the tyranny of Polycrates, and Apollodorus (above, chapter 15) dated the acme of Pythagoras to 532/31. Only Eusebius transmits an exact date for the revolution of the three brothers. The notice appears at 533/32 in the best manuscript authority, with minor variations in the rest.

The direct evidence attests to a uniform tradition according to which the famous Samian tyranny of Polycrates began in the 530s B.C. Some scholars have argued, however, that tyranny at Samos in fact was established long before the 530s.[2] The argument is based on archaeological evidence, an inference from Herodotus' narrative (3.48) that the Samians had been the scourge of the seas for a generation before Polycrates, and from scattered references to Samian dynasts other than Polycrates. Proof of this hypothesis has been sought in the late texts that transmit the chronographic tradition on persons associated with Polycrates. Eratosthenes' identification of Pythagoras with the Olympic victor of 588, combined with Aristoxenus' synchronism between Polycrates and Pythagoras, might suggest that Eratosthenes believed that Polycrates had been tyrant as early as the 560s. Strabo says that Pythagoras twice left behind him the tyranny at Samos—at first when it was just springing up and a second time when he returned to find the tyranny still in existence. Meanwhile he had visited Egypt and Babylon. This report, together with the statement of Iamblichus that Pythagoras spent 22 years in Egypt and 12 in Babylon, could imply that the tyranny had endured at Samos for more than 40 years before Pythagoras finally departed for Italy about 530.[3]

Pythagorean biography is notoriously too inconsistent to permit the statements of several sources to be so combined. Attention therefore focuses on fragments of the chronographic tradition relating to Polycrates, Anaximander, Ibycus, and Anacreon. At issue are the following three passages:

1) Diogenes Laertius (2.2) on Anaximander: . . .

Ἀπολλόδωρος ὁ Ἀθηναῖος ὅς καί φησιν αὐτὸν ἐν τοῖς Χρονικοῖς τῷ δευτέρῳ ἔτει τῆς πεντηκοστῆς ὀγδόης Ὀλυμπιάδος ἐτῶν εἶναι ἑξήκοντα τεττάρων καὶ μετ' ὀλίγον τελευτῆσαι, ἀκμάσαντά πη μάλιστα κατὰ Πολυκράτην τὸν Σάμου τύραννον.

Apollodorus of Athens says in the *Chronicle* that he was sixty-four years in the second year of the fifty-eighth Olympiad (547/46) and died shortly thereafter, flourishing about the time of Polycrates the tyrant of Samos.

2) The *Suda* on Ibycus: ἐνθένδε εἰς Σάμον ἦλθεν ὅτε αὐτῆς ἦρχεν ὁ Πολυκράτης ὁ τοῦ τυράννου πατήρ. χρόνος δ' ἦν οὗτος ἐπὶ Κροίσου ὀλυμπιὰς νδ'.

From there (Rhegium) he came to Samos when its ruler was Polycrates the father of the tyrant. That was the time of Croesus, Olympiad 54 (564/61).

3) The *Suda* on Anacreon: γέγονε κατὰ Πολυκράτην τὸν Σάμου τύραννον ὀλυμπιάδι νβ'· οἱ δ' ἐπὶ Κύρου καὶ Καμβύσου τάττουσιν αὐτὸν κατὰ τὴν νε' ὀλυμπιάδα.

He flourished at the time of Polycrates the tyrant of Samos in Olympiad 52 (572/69); some place him in the time of Cyrus and Cambyses at the 55th Olympiad (560/57).

All three of these passages can lead to the conclusion that a tyrant named Polycrates ruled Samos from about 570, for the acme of Anaximander, if he was 64 years old in 547/46, falls in the year 571/70, and Diogenes synchronizes the acme with Polycrates. The same date appears in the *Suda*'s note on Anacreon, according to which Anacreon is synchronized with Polycrates in Olympiad 52, one of the years 572 to 569. The article on Ibycus introduces an additional complication. A Polycrates was indeed ruler of Samos by the time that Ibycus arrived in the 560s, and he was the father of the tyrant. According to Herodotus (3.39) Polycrates' father was named Aeaces. The evidence of these passages has generally been rejected for chronological impossibility and confused nomenclature. Some scholars have emended the texts to bring them into agreement with the standard tradition that Polycrates, the son of Aeaces, became tyrant at Samos in the 530s.[4] M. E. White, however, used these statements in support of the hypothesis that Samian tyranny was well established by the time of Polycrates. The sources misnamed the earlier tyrant, who was in fact Aeaces, the father of Polycrates. J. P. Barron took a more radical approach. The Polycrates named in these texts was the son of Aeaces and ruled Samos as tyrant beginning about 570. He was succeeded by his son Polycrates II, who at first ruled jointly with his brothers Pantagnotus and Syloson, then assumed the sole tyranny.[5] Jules Labarbe resolved the difficulties without doing violence to the texts. The orthodox date for Polycrates in 532 is a date for his *floruit*. By the usual formula according to which one flourished at the age of 40, Polycrates was born in 572. The birth date was expressed as a γέγονε and came to be misinterpreted as a *floruit*. Hence the acme of Polycrates was reported in chronographic texts 40 years too early. The result is a synchronism with Anaximander in 571, the shift of the Polycrates-Anacreon synchronism from 532 to 572, the apparent interval of about 40 years between Pythagoras' two departures from a tyrannized Samos, and a confusion on the part of some authors who believed that there must have been two tyrants named Polycrates in order to account for a tyranny's spanning so long a time.[6]

Labarbe's discussion of these problems correctly addresses itself to the nature of the texts involved. Confusion arising from the ambiguous γέγονε, false synchronisms, and transferred dates are characteristic of the late texts that preserve the fragmentary debris of Greek chronographic tradition. The evidence of these texts cannot be introduced into historical arguments like that relating to the duration of the Samian tyranny in the absence of a reasonable hypothesis about the genesis of the tradition reported and the quality of its transmission to the late sources. Labarbe's hypothesis is plausible, but his fundamental premise bears further examination. Was 532/31 in fact the Apollodoran acme of Polycrates at the age of 40? The date for Polycrates in Olympiad 62, 532/29, is also the Apollodoran date for the acme of Pythagoras. Most reports of this date mention both Polycrates and Pythagoras.[7] It does not necessarily follow, however, that the year 532/31 was the Apollodoran acme of both.

The prior question must be addressed: exactly how did Apollodorus deal with the tradition on Polycrates, Anacreon, and
Ibycus?

Polycrates

The notices of the *Suda* often help elucidate the evidence of
Eusebius. Conversely, the entries of Eusebius serve as a control
on the statements of the *Suda*. Eusebius and the authors of the
Suda often report information in such a way as to show that their
sources were cognate. The *Suda* sometimes reveals the rationale
of a Eusebian date, and Eusebius often reports dates more accurately than the *Suda*. The combination of the two can result in
a fuller picture of the tradition common to them both. Diogenes
too derives chronological information from a cognate source;
and he cites Apollodorus often enough to indicate that this material, known in various forms to our late authors, descended
from epitomes based on his *Chronicle*. Hence, the evidence of
Diogenes, Eusebius, the *Suda*, and other authorities dependent
on the Apollodoran vulgate should be examined together, in the
light of what is known about Apollodorus' chronological method,
so as to set the individual fragments in as nearly complete a
chronographic context as possible.

The Apollodoran date for the acme of Pythagoras derives
from combining the Pythagoras-Polycrates synchronism of Aristoxenus, the Polycrates-Cambyses synchronism of Herodotus,
and a chronographic theorem that set Pythagoras in a special
relationship to Anaximander and Anaximenes at the epochal
year of the fall of Sardis, 547/46 (above, chapter 15). This
understanding of the genesis of the tradition explains why a
connection appears in the text of Diogenes between the acme of
Anaximander and the tyranny of Polycrates. Apollodorus treated
Anaximander, Anaximenes, and Pythagoras together at the year
547/46, stating their respective ages at the time of the fall of
Sardis. He added that Pythagoras, who was still young at the
epoch of 547/46, flourished in the time of Polycrates. In an
epitomized version Pythagoras disappeared and this last synchronism came to be transferred to the person whose name appeared first in the set, Anaximander. It does not follow that
Polycrates was ever traditionally dated to the year of Anaximander's acme, 571/70. A similar case can be seen in Eusebius'

entry of Stesichorus in Olympiad 42, 612/9 (above, chapter 10). In the *Suda*'s version of the tradition, Stesichorus was synchronized with Sappho, Sappho was synchronized with Alcaeus and Pittacus, and the entire set was dated to Olympiad 42, the Apollodoran acme of Pittacus. The chain of relationships led in an epitomized version to a date for Stesichorus in Olympiad 42. Only the presence of Sappho makes the reasoning possible. She was herself assigned an acme not in Olympiad 42, when Pittacus flourished, but in Olympiad 45 (600/599), when Pittacus became aesymnetes (above, chapter 13). In the version that reached the source of Eusebius, Sappho had disappeared entirely, just as Pythagoras had vanished from the report on Anaximander that Diogenes read.

One result of the special relationship between Anaximander and Pythagoras in the year 547/46 is the computation of Pythagoras' acme in the year 532/31. The date agrees closely with the original synchronisms among Pythagoras, Polycrates, and Cambyses. Inserted into Aristoxenus' statement about Pythagoras, this year is a date for Pythagoras' emigration from Samos to Italy. The date for the acme of Pythagoras could therefore be used as a starting point for the more precise dating of Polycrates. Aristoxenus had said (fr. 16 Wehrli) that at the age of forty Pythagoras left Samos for Italy because of the tyranny of Polycrates. We do not know the whole context of Aristoxenus' statement. Probably he agreed with the well-attested tradition (usually attributed to Timaeus) that Pythagoras twice left Samos—the first time for extended travel and study, the second, after a brief period of residence, when he left Samos to settle in Italy and establish his philosophical order there.[8] For Apollodorus, the earlier journey would have been the time that Pythagoras became associated with the philosophers of mainland Asia Minor. This earlier departure need not be connected with an earlier manifestation of tyranny. The fact that Strabo (16, 635) and Iamblichus (*V.P.* 11) make precisely that association proves nothing. The Pythagorean hatred of tyranny was proverbial, and it is easy to understand how this particular doublet came into being.

Aristoxenus' version of the story was probably that Pythagoras returned from his travels on the mainland to find Samos in *stasis* and the government in the hands of the three sons of Aeaces. He worked to restore order. When Polycrates had killed the one brother and banished the other, Pythagoras concluded that the situation was hopeless and departed for Italy. In the later version common to the sources of Strabo and Iamblichus, the original report had become condensed and was known in a form similar to that in which Porphyry (*V.P.* 9) preserves the fragment of Aristoxenus: "seeing the tyranny of Polycrates become so much more intense (συντονωτέραν) that it behooved a free man not to endure the despotism of his administration, Pythagoras made his departure for Italy." The comparative in the statement combined with the proverbial Pythagorean hatred of tyranny led to the belief that Pythagoras' earlier voyage too had been a free man's protest against tyranny.

For Aristoxenus and Apollodorus, however, the increase in the degree of oppression was to be identified with Polycrates' usurpation of the sole tyranny on the basis of Herodotus' report that he ruled at first jointly with his brothers, then alone. Pythagoras' 40th year, computed through his relationship to Anaximander at 532/31, was synchronized with the harsher phase. The insurrection of the three brothers Apollodorus therefore dated to the preceding year, 533/32. This is the year at which the Oxford manuscript of Jerome enters Eusebius' notice on the tyranny of the *tres fratres*, with less than the usual variation among the manuscripts (534/33 Arm., 530/29 "B"). In the absence of corroborative testimony, the position of the notice even in the best manuscripts would prove nothing. As it happens, there is other evidence to suggest that the year 533/32 was associated in the chronographic tradition with the Samian tyranny.

Diodorus (10, fr. 3.1) dates the *floruit* (ἐγνωρίζετο) of Pythagoras to the archonship of Thericles in the 61st Olympiad. The precise date of Thericles' archonship is known from Dionysius of Halicarnassus (4.41.1) as corresponding to Olympiad 61.4, 533/32. Jacoby saw this date for Pythagoras as being so close to the Apollodoran acme that it must somehow be related to Apollodorus' system.[9] Jacoby was right, but it remains to explain how the variant arose. Since Pythagoras' *floruit* was synchronized with the Samian tyranny, Diodorus' slightly divergent date for Pythagoras must preserve an element of Apollodorus' chronology for Polycrates. The confusion in Diodorus derives from synchronizing Pythagoras with the beginning of the Samian tyranny of the three brothers, dated to 533/32, instead of from the original Apollodoran synchronism of Pythagoras with the more intense phase when Polycrates, beginning in 532/31, ruled

alone. That is, the epitomator from whom Diodorus' information descends excerpted the date for the beginning of the Samian
tyranny and synchronized Pythagoras with Polycrates in the last
year of the 61st Olympiad. In the version known to Clement, on
the other hand, the epitomator had excerpted the date for Pythagoras' *floruit* and synchronized Polycrates with him in the
62nd Olympiad.[10] Eusebius' source had both dates—the insurrection of the three brothers in Olympiad 61 and the acme of
Pythagoras in Olympiad 62.

Anacreon

Eusebius' date for Polycrates, Pantagnotus, and Syloson in
the 61st Olympiad derives from Apollodorus and the intricate
chronological system from which Apollodorus inferred the date
of Pythagoras' acme. In the same Olympiad Eusebius enters
the *floruit* of Anacreon. All the manuscripts of Jerome and the
Armenian version agree in entering Anacreon immediately before
the notice on the three brothers. The entry on Polycrates, Pantagnotus, and Syloson properly belongs where it appears in the
best witnesses, the 61st Olympiad. Eusebius' date for Anacreon,
therefore, was also Olympiad 61. The date derives from synchronism with Polycrates. Herodotus (3.121) reported that
Anacreon was prominent at the court of Polycrates, and Apollodorus could find evidence to confirm the association in the poetry
of Anacreon himself, for Strabo (16, 638) says that the poetry
of Anacreon made frequent mention of Polycrates. The problem
is whether the synchronism between Anacreon and Polycrates in
Olympiad 61 represents the acme, in the Apollodoran sense, of
both of them.

The article of the *Suda* for Anacreon synchronizes him with
Polycrates at a date expressed as a γέγονε in Olympiad 52,
572/69. It is wrong to emend the numeral to 62 in order to
bring the expression into agreement with what is assumed to be
the orthodox date of Polycrates. Olympiad 62 is a date specifically for Pythagoras, and the evidence of Eusebius with the
support of Diodorus suggests that the Polycrates-Anacreon synchronism belongs in Olympiad 61. If Anacreon flourished in his
40th year in the archonship of Thericles, 533/32, when Polycrates and his brothers seized control of the Samian government,
then his birth would be dated to Olympiad 52.1, 572/71. Thus

the *Suda*'s γέγονε in this instance represents a birth date. In that case, the article seems to imply that Anacreon was born in the time of Polycrates, who must therefore be assumed tyrant as early as 572. Barron accordingly took the statement, along with Diogenes' (2.2) report that Anaximander flourished at the time of Polycrates, as evidence that "the father of the tyrant" mentioned in the *Suda*'s article for Ibycus was also named Polycrates and was also tyrant of Samos.[11] Labarbe argued that the expression should be interpreted as a birth date for both Anacreon and Polycrates. Subsequently misunderstood as a *floruit* for Polycrates, the expression led to all manner of confusion and invention.[12]

Barron's argument contradicts the evidence of Herodotus that the famous Polycrates was son of Aeaces. Such a contradiction can be allowed only on the assumption that the chronographers possessed evidence that could be considered of higher authority than Herodotus. Barron believed that such evidence was to be found in a poem of Anacreon, paraphrased in Himerius' 29th Oration, that the famous thalassocrat fulfilled the Homeric prayer τῷ πατρὶ Πολυκράτει to become greater than his father. The text of Himerius is not secure for this crucial phrase. Another witness uses the nominative, so that the Polycrates mentioned is the young man himself.[13] The assumption that there existed a tradition contradicting Herodotus on Polycrates' patronymic as well as his date should not be based on an author like Himerius, especially when the text is corrupt. Labarbe's hypothesis is accordingly attractive. His argument is based on the premise that the chronographic tradition reported an acme for Polycrates at the age of 40 when he became tyrant in the 530s. Thus Anacreon and Polycrates both flourished about 533, both were born in 572, and that is what the sources of the *Suda* said, in one form or another. An exact synchronism between Anacreon and Polycrates, however, is not appropriate. All the textual difficulties notwithstanding, Himerius does paraphrase a poem of Anacreon that suggests that the poet, already famous, had been brought to Samos as tutor of the young Polycrates. That is, Anacreon flourished while Polycrates was still young.

The evidence of that poem was available to Apollodorus, who had specific ways of dealing with master-pupil relationships. He could set the two persons an entire intellectual generation of forty years apart, if that was what the evidence seemed to require, resulting in a synchronism between the pupil's birth and the master's acme. If the forty-year interval seemed too large to fit the tradition, Apollodorus could suppose that the teacher reached his acme when the pupil was an ἔφηβος, that is, about 16. This expression of the relationship would result in the master's being at the theoretical age of 64 when the pupil had reached his acme at 40. A closer contemporaneity could be accommodated by dating the master's acme to the time that the pupil reached the theoretical age of first fame at 25. This last possibility affords the most plausible hypothesis for Anacreon and Polycrates, since it yields a satisfactory explanation for all the evidence.

Eusebius enters Anacreon's *floruit* in the 61st Olympiad when Polycrates in concert with his brothers first came to power, and this juxtaposition can attest to a synchronism between acme and first fame. That Apollodorus in fact dated the acme of Anacreon at the 40th year of life to 533/32 is supported by the *Suda*'s date for his γέγονε in Olympiad 52, 572/69. For Polycrates, the only indication of his age that the extant tradition preserves is Herodotus' (3.124) story that at the time of his death Polycrates' daughter was as yet unmarried. This story together with the fact that Polycrates' thalassocratic ambitions were cut short by his untimely demise suggests that Polycrates was not yet 40 years old when he died. Apollodorus could thus best systematize the tradition by assigning to Polycrates the age of 25 when he first seized power in 533/32, dating the acme of his friend and teacher, Anacreon of Teos, to the same year.

The *Suda* synchronizes the birth of Anacreon in Olympiad 52, 572/69, with Polycrates. Labarbe's hypothesis that Olympiad 52 was also the traditional birthdate for Polycrates may not be correct. One must not conclude, however, that tradition reported an earlier tyrant of Samos, whether named Polycrates or Aeaces, who could be dated to 572. The transfer of a synchronism correct at one point in the careers of two individuals to a date appropriate only to one of them is an error characteristic of sources that epitomized late synchronistic annals. An interesting parallel is Eusebius' entry at Olympiad 70.1, 500/499 (107ᵉ Helm) : *Hellanicus historiografus et Democritus philosophus et Heraclitus cognomento tenebrosus et Anaxagoras physicus clari habentur.* Of the four persons included in the synchronism, all of whom are assigned a *floruit* about 500, only Heraclitus was traditionally dated to an acme at that time (OL 69.4, 501/0). Hellanicus was born in the first year of the next

Olympiad, 496/95. Apollodorus dated the 20th year of Anaxagoras to 480/79, his birth therefore to 499/98, and his acme at the age of 40 to 460/59. Thus it is the birth date that is the rationale for his inclusion in the synchronism at Olympiad 70. Democritus is supposed to have said that he was a young man when Anaxagoras was old. Apollodorus therefore dated his birth to the year of Anaxagoras' acme, 460/59.[14] A synchronism between Democritus and Anaxagoras is appropriate at 460/59, when Democritus was born and Anaxagoras flourished. But the late sources transferred the synchronism to the year of Anaxagoras' birth and designated the date as a *floruit* for both. Similarly, for Anacreon an excerpt like Ἀνακρέων ἦν (*floruit*) ὅτε ἐγένετο ὁ Πολυκράτης τύραννος τῆς Σάμου was contracted to Ἀνακρέων γέγονε κατὰ Πολυκράτην τὸν Σάμου τύραννον and combined with Ἀνακρέων γεγενῆται (*natus est*) κατὰ τὴν νβ′ ὀλυμπιάδα to produce the statement that now appears in the *Suda*: γέγονε κατὰ Πολυκράτην τὸν Σάμου τύραννον ὀλυμπιάδι νβ′.

With this birthdate the *Suda* combines a report of Anacreon's *floruit* in the time of Cyrus and Cambyses, the 55th Olympiad. Now, Anacreon was at Samos in the time of Polycrates, who was in turn synchronized with Cambyses. Since he was a poet of Teos, one might suppose that he left his homeland when the Teians abondoned the city to Cyrus and moved to Abdera (Herodotus 1.168). Hence it could be said that Anacreon flourished in the time of Cyrus as well as of Cambyses. The date assigned to the synchronism was Olympiad 55, 560/57, the usual chronographic date for the accession of Cyrus.[15]

Ibycus

Apollodorus dated the acme of Anacreon to 533/32, in synchronism with young Polycrates' coup, and Eusebius preserves that date. For the date of Ibycus we are on less secure ground. Eusebius entered him in either the 59th or the 60th Olympiad, and the manuscript variants do not allow us to make a clear choice. The date may well derive from Apollodorus, however, and represent an expression of Ibycus' relationship to Polycrates as a teacher somewhat older than Anacreon. Again the case is complicated by difficulties in the *Suda*'s notice, and again those difficulties have been used in support of an early date for tyranny at Samos.

A lyric fragment (*P. Oxy.* 1790) generally attributed to
Ibycus (fr. 3 Diehl) concludes with an address to Polycrates
promising him a fame no less immortal than the poet's own
verses: καὶ σύ, Πολύκρατες, κλέος ἄφθιτον ἑξεῖς/ ὡς
κατ' ἀοιδὰν καὶ ἐμὸν κλέος. . The identity of this Polycrates has been debated. The comparison in the preceding lines
with the youthful beauty of Priam's son Troilus suggests, as
Lesky puts it, that this is "a piece of courtly flattery addressed
to a handsome and well-born youth." Lesky and Bowra identified the young man with the Polycrates of Rhodes who appears
in the difficult text of Himerius' references to Anacreon. Barron
denied the existence of Polycrates of Rhodes, and he identified
the young man of Himerius' account with the Herodotean tyrant. He believed, however, that the tyrant's father was also
named Polycrates and he suggested that Ibycus' poem was addressed to the elder Polycrates at the height of his power. This
interpretation, in Barron's view, is supported by the *Suda*'s date
for the visit of Ibycus to Samos in the time of Polycrates' father,
Olympiad 54, 564/61.[16]

As in the case of Anacreon, so with Ibycus these radical departures from Herodotus' tradition about the Samian tyranny
are not justified by late chronographic texts whose sources were
very often corrupt and contaminated. The fragment of Ibycus,
in context, makes necessary the conclusion of Lesky that it is
addressed to a handsome youth named Polycrates. There is no
reason to deny that the young Polycrates was the same who became the fabled tyrant of Samos. The obvious inference is surely
the right one—both Anacreon and Ibycus served as tutors to
Polycrates while he was still a very young man, and both left
evidence of the fact in their poems. This evidence was available
to Hellenistic scholars. Apollodorus used the tutor-pupil relationships implied in these poems to compute the dates of the poets
relative to Polycrates. The acme of Anacreon he synchronized
with Polycrates' usurpation in 533/32, perhaps the tyrant's 25th
year of age. Eusebius preserves this synchronism in the 61st
Olympiad (536/33), and it is therefore a reasonable hypothesis
that his date for Ibycus bears some relationship to the Apollodoran tradition.

The contention that Eusebius enters Ibycus in the 61st Olympiad and therefore attests to a general synchronism among
Anacreon, Ibycus, and Polycrates is based on Schoene's edition,
which prominently exhibits the readings of the Berne manuscript.[17] The discovery of better manuscript authorities has

shown that the placement of the entries in the Berne manuscript is generally too low. For the Ibycus entry there is no control in the Armenian version, which omits the notice entirely. For this page of Jerome, the Floriacensis fragments are extant, but the leaf is torn and the entry on Ibycus cannot be read. "M" has the notice at Olympiad 59.3, 542/41, "O" and "L" at Olympiad 60.1, 540/39, and "A" at Olympiad 60.3, 538/37. Ibycus originally appeared, then, either in Olympiad 59 or in Olympiad 60, but not in Olympiad 61. If the hypothesis is correct that Apollodorus dated Polycrates' 25th year to 533/32, he was in his middle teens at an age appropriate to receive Ibycus' praise of his youthful beauty about ten years earlier. If Apollodorus fixed the precise year as his sixteenth, the date for Ibycus' poem would have been 542/41, the third year of the 59th Olympiad. The assignment of Ibycus' *floruit* to that year would result in the poet's being twenty-four years older than the youth. This relationship is one of those made possible by Apollodorus' use of theoretical ages at 25, 40, and 64 years. The relative chronology was suggested by the fact that Ibycus had praised Polycrates' youthful beauty, while Anacreon was a companion of Polycrates (Herodotus 3.121) as well as his teacher. Apollodorus dated the insurrection of Polycrates to 533/32, the year before Pythagoras' departure, then applied his theoretical ages to systematize the relative chronology, resulting in an acme for Ibycus in 542/41 and for Anacreon in 533/32.

The apparently contradictory notice of the *Suda* for Ibycus is a less pure and less precise version of this tradition. Apollodorus assigned the *floruit* of Ibycus to the time of Polycrates' youth. It follows that Ibycus, like Anacreon, came to Samos when Polycrates was still under his father's guidance. This is the essence of the *Suda*'s report. The statement that Polycrates' father "ruled" on Samos is the kind of vague expression that might be expected of a Byzantine encyclopedist, and it should not be taken seriously as evidence for the archaic period. The authors of the *Suda* guessed wrong about the name of Polycrates' father, which should be Aeaces. The date in Olympiad 54, 564/61, does not support the hypothesis that there did rule on Samos an earlier tyrant who was the father of the Herodotean Polycrates. This is a separate piece of information added from a different source to gloss the earlier statement. The 54th is the Olympiad of Croesus' accession in Sardis, as the *Suda* says, not a date for Ibycus' arrival in Samos or for the "reign" of Polycrates' father.

The information about Ibycus that came to the sources of the *Suda* was that he flourished on Samos when Polycrates was very young. The information was not dated, but an approximate date could be inferred. Polycrates was very young and the time at issue was therefore to be associated with the *floruit* of his father. Since Polycrates' tyranny was synchronized with Cambyses, the generation earlier was the time of Cyrus and Croesus. The *Suda*'s authority therefore identified the date of Ibycus' fame in Samos as "the time of Croesus" and added the chronographic date for Croesus' accession, Olympiad 54. Comparison with the date of Aesop, however, suggests another possibility. Deposed in 547/46 after 14 years of rule, Croesus came to the throne in 561/60, Olympiad 54.4. This date for Croesus underlies the date given by Eusebius (OL 54), the *Suda* (OL 54), and the *Chronicon Romanum*, *FGrHist* 252 B 4, (563/62), for the death of Aesop. Aesop had served as an ambassador for Croesus to Delphi. It is likely, therefore, that Apollodorus dated his death to the time of Croesus' fall in 547/46. The phrase *time of Croesus* was misinterpreted as a reference to his accession. An alternate interpretation for the date of Ibycus is therefore possible: Apollodorus did not have recourse to his theoretical ages to date Ibycus, Anacreon, and Polycrates. He synchronized the acme of Anacreon with Polycrates' insurrection in 533/32, making no guess as to Polycrates' age at the time. He did believe Ibycus older than Anacreon, however, so he synchronized his acme with the epoch of Croesus in 547/46. The sources of the *Suda* misinterpreted the epoch of Croesus and reported the date of his accession. The sources of Eusebius transmitted the correct date in Olympiad 58. Either Eusebius himself or Jerome entered the notice too low, perhaps because of overcrowding in the *spatium historicum* at the epoch of the fall of Sardis.

Summary

No firm conclusion about the exact date of Ibycus' *floruit* can be reached, although some plausible hypotheses may be hazarded. One important conclusion can, however, be stated without the least hesitation: the evidence of the late chronographic and biographical texts, although difficult, does not attest to the existence of a tradition about the Samian tyranny different from that reported by Herodotus. Diogenes, Eusebius, and the

Suda report elements of Apollodorus' synthesis of what was always an essentially uniform tradition. The idiosyncracies of their respective intermediary sources inevitably introduced some errors and confusion into the report. These anomalies attest to the book tradition of an age that produced epitomators and encyclopedists, not to the preservation of a tradition deriving from higher authority than Herodotus.

There may be problems for some historians in reconciling the tradition of a short, late tyranny in Samos with what can be surmised about the history of the island in the first half of the sixth century. Before an appeal is made to late fragmentary texts in an attempt to lengthen the period of tyranny, some fundamental assumptions about archaic Greece should be called into question. In particular, the idea that acceleration in the rate of cultural change during the archaic period must have been catalyzed by a tyranny demands serious reconsideration. The harbor project and the fleet, the tunnel and the aqueduct, the great temple in honor of the national deity all bear witness to a powerful Samos. But is it really necessary to assume, as Aristotle did (*Pol.* 1313b24), that such projects are the work of a tyrant? Herodotus made no such assumption. He attributed the work to the Samians in general (3.60). Polycrates in all his glory may well have presided over the collapse of a flourishing maritime republic whose power had been established in the early sixth century by a stable aristocracy. When Cyrus gained possession of the Phoenician fleet in 539, the situation in the eastern seas was significantly altered. That *stasis* broke out in Samos over the policy now to be adopted is not surprising. A young aristocrat named Polycrates, well born and well educated, led his faction to power, pursuing an ambitious and aggressive policy aimed at naval supremacy. His magnificent attempt succeeded only in delaying for ten years the inevitable presence of Persian power on Samos.

17

The Tragedians

a) OL 71.1 (496/95): Aeschylus tragoediarum scriptor agnoscitur. (107[h])
AA 1519 (497/96): Eschilos, der Gesangdichter, war gekannt. (191)

b) OL 75.4 (477/76): Aeschylus tragoediarum scriptor agnoscitur. (109[g])
AA 1541 (475/74): Eschilos der Gesangdichter war gekannt. (192)

c) OL 77.2 (471/70): Sofocles tragoediarum scriptor primum ingenii sui opera publicauit. (109[m])
AA 1545 (471/70): Sophokles der Gesangdichter erschien zuerst. (192)

d) OL 77.4 (469/68): Sofocles et Euripides clari habentur. (109[p])
AA 1548 (468/67): Sophekles und Euripides waren gekannt. (192)

e) OL 81.3 (454/53): Aristarchus tragoediografus agnoscitur. (112[a])
AA 1563 (453/52): Aristarchus der Gesangdichter lebte. (193)

f) OL 84.2 (443/42): Euripides tragoediarum scriptor clarus habetur et Protagoras sophista, cuius libros decreto publico Athenienses combusserunt. (113[e])
AA 1573 (443/42): Euripides der Gesangdichter; und Protagoras der Sophist, dessen Bücher die Athener zu verbrennen beschlossen. (193)

g) OL 85.3 (438/37): Theaetetus mathematicus agnoscitur Aristofanes clarus habetur et Sofocles poeta tragicus. (114[b])

AA 1577 (439/38): Theethetios der Mathematikos, war gekannt. (193)

AA 1579 (437/36): Sophekles war als Gesangdichter gekannt. (193)

h) OL 93.1 (408/7): Euripides aput Archelaum et Sofocles Athenis moritur. (116[d])

AA 1606 (410/9): Euripides stirbt bei Archelaos, und Sophekles zu Athen. (194)

The first study in this collection, that on Lycurgus, deals with chronographic tradition for the transitional period between what the chronographers regarded as mythical and historical times. An appropriate conclusion is reached with the fifth century, the transitional period when the basis for traditional chronology passes from chronographic reconstruction to contemporary record. Eusebius' entries on the three great tragedians Aeschylus, Sophocles, and Euripides span the entire fifth century. This set of notices therefore illustrates the characteristics of the chronographic tradition for the period during which both official and historiographical systems of chronology began. Tradition, record, and mathematical construction combine to produce chronological systems within which it is often difficult to distinguish the contemporary record from the scholarly inference. The problem is, as always, complicated by the fragmentary nature of the evidence. The systems are not preserved intact nor in a historiographical context that reveals the evidence on which they are based. Furthermore, the fragments themselves are transmitted in difficult texts like the *Chronicle* of Eusebius, beset with their own problems of source and tradition.[1]

For the tragedians, Eusebius transmits what looks superficially like a haphazard collection of synchronisms, *floruits*, and isolated facts deriving from several different reports of their careers. He enters the *floruit* (*agnoscitur, clarus habetur*) of each of the three tragedians twice, with yet a third notice for Sophocles, attesting to his first presentation. In each case one might argue that Eusebius' source had dated some particular play and speculate as to which play it was. Some fragments survive of the records that were kept of the dramatic presentations at Athens. These records could have supplied the primary basis for Eusebius' notices. When the entries are considered as a set, however, an entirely different perspective on fifth-century chronology emerges. Eusebius' notices are fragments of an elaborate chronographic system based on theoretical construction as well as historical fact. As usual, Eusebius' notices about the tragedians represent the biographical vulgate of Apollodorus.

The Apollodoran Chronology

Apollodorus' dates for Aeschylus are not attested, but his chronology for Sophocles and Euripides can be inferred from a passage of Diodorus together with a statement included in Diogenes Laertius' *Life of Socrates*. Diodorus (13.103.4) specifically cites the *Chronicle* of Apollodorus for synchronizing the deaths of Euripides and Sophocles, and he states (13.103.3) that Sophocles died at the age of 90 in 406/5. Diogenes (2.44) cites Apollodorus for the date of Socrates' birth in 469/68, then adds (2.45) that Euripides (like Socrates, supposedly a student of Anaxagoras) was born in 480/79. As Jacoby pointed out, Sophocles' age at the time of his death derives from the synchronism of his acme with the death of Aeschylus. According to the *Marmor Parium* (*FGrHist* 239 A 59) and the scholiast to Aristophanes (*Acharn.* 10), Aeschylus died in the archonship of Callias I, 456/55. Assigned an acme at the age of 40 in that year, Sophocles was 90 years old when he died in 406/5, the archonship of Callias III. This date for Sophocles' death is also attested by the *Marmor Parium* (*FGrHist* 239 A 64) and by the *hypothesis* to *Oedipus at Colonus*.

For Euripides, Apollodorus adopted Timaeus' synchronism (*FGrHist* 566 F 105) of his death with the beginning of Dionysius' tyranny in Syracuse, 406/5 (Diodorus 13.95.1, Dion. Hal. *A.R.* 7.1.5). According to the *Marmor Parium* (*FGrHist* 239 A 63), Euripides died the year before Sophocles, in 407/6. But Apollodorus preferred to synchronize his death with that of Sophocles in the next archon year. Euripides' birth is dated to the year of Salamis, 480/79. The result is curious. Euripides was born in the archonship of Calliades, and he died in the archonship of Callias III. Jacoby believed that Apollodorus was moved to adopt these dates for the birth and death of Euripides by the similarity in the archons' names, for Euripides' first dramatic presentation was dated to the archonship of Callias I, 456/55 (*vit. Eur.*, 134 West.), a date that Jacoby believed documentary. Hence Apollodorus produced a system based on a mnemonic device, focusing on the epochal date 456/55, the archonship of Callias.[2]

Jacoby's attribution to Apollodorus of the date 456/55 for Sophocles' acme and 480/79 for the birth of Euripides is correct. His understanding of the reasoning behind the system, however, is incomplete. The similarity in the eponymous dates is an accidental result, not the genesis of the system. If one computes the ages of the three tragedians for the epochal year 456/55, the same mathematical model emerges as that which Apollodorus used for the philosophers at 547/46. Apollodorus' dates for Aeschylus are not attested, but it is likely, as Jacoby suggested, that he synchronized the acme of Aeschylus with the birth of Euripides in 480/79. Thus Aeschylus was 64 years old when he died in 456/55. In that year Euripides reached the age of 25, by inclusive count, and Sophocles achieved his acme at the age of 40. These are the theoretical ages that Apollodorus used for Anaximander, Anaximenes, and Pythagoras at the epoch of the fall of Sardis, 547/46 (above, chapter 15). An examination of how this chronographic theorem was applied to the tragedians sheds new light both on the Apollodoran system and on the nature of our evidence for fifth-century chronology. A more nearly complete reconstruction of the Apollodoran system becomes possible, as well as a fuller explanation of its genesis. Furthermore, there may well be even less documentary basis for these dates than Jacoby thought.

There was neither record nor uniform tradition for the birth dates of the three tragedians, as the variation among our sources attests.[3] This fact is not surprising, since all three were born before attention to such detail developed. On the other hand, the dates of their death were likely a matter of record. The *Marmor Parium* (*FGrHist* 239) transmits a date for the death of each of the three—Aeschylus in the archonship of Callias I, 456/55 (A 59); Euripides in the archonship of Antigenes, 407/6 (A 64); Sophocles in the archonship of Callias III, 406/5 (A 65). All authorities agreed on these dates, except that Apollodorus, following the lead of Timaeus and Eratosthenes, preferred to lower the date of Euripides' death by a few months in order to report it under the same archon year as that of Sophocles.[4] There is no reason to doubt the historicity of the *Marmor*'s dates in these cases or to question that they derive from contemporary record. Whether the author of the *Marmor* had the dates directly from the Atthidographers or through such intermediaries as Aristoxenus' περὶ τραγῳδοποιῶν is immaterial.

The extent to which there existed documentary record for every stage of their careers is, however, less easily judged. Jacoby's reconstruction proceeds from the premise that the date of Euripides' first presentation in 456/55 derived from documentary evidence. Records were certainly kept of the victories in the dramatic festivals from early in the fifth century. The later biographical tradition was interested in the total number of victories, while chronography noted the date of the first. The *Marmor Parium* records the first victory of Aeschylus in 485/84, that of Sophocles in 469/68, and Euripides' in 442/41 (*FGrHist* 239 A 50, 56, 60). That there existed complete, official records of the unsuccessful competition before the middle of the fifth century is, however, not so certain. The extant fragments, at least, do not permit such a conclusion. It cannot therefore be presumed that a record of the first entry into competition of any of the three tragedians was extant, and we should be hesitant about accepting as historical the date of a first presentation that was not also a victory. Chronological evidence about the poets' early literary careers may not have existed. There did, however, exist records of their victories; and since the name of the archon who had granted the poet a chorus was included, those records provided dates. In addition, some documentary evidence existed for the careers of Aeschylus and Sophocles, quite apart from their literary activity. Aeschylus' participation in the battle of Marathon was memorialized in his epitaph. Sophocles served as *Hellenotamias* (Delian League Treasurer) in 443, his name was included in the college of generals for the year 441/40, and he was a *Proboulos* in 413.[5]

There was good evidence, then, for the dates of the poets' deaths, their victories, and a few events in the civic life of Aeschylus and Sophocles. Their birth dates and the dates of their first presentation, however, had to be inferred, and a system had to be imposed on the relative chronology that the available evidence suggested. One knew, of course, that Aeschylus was considerably older than Sophocles and that Euripides was younger than his more popular contemporary. An informal expression of these relationships could be made by reference to the Persian Wars. Aeschylus was firmly associated, both as citizen and poet, with the wars for freedom. According to one tradition, Aeschylus was a mature man at the time of the Persian Wars, having fought in the battles of Marathon, Salamis, and Plataea (*vit. Aesch.*, 118 West.), Sophocles was among a chorus of boys who celebrated the great naval victory off Salamis (*vit. Soph.*, 127 West.), while Euripides was born on the very day of the battle (*vit., Eur.*, 134 West. et passim). The details may be doubted. In particular, the statement that Euripides was born on the day of the battle is clearly a synchronistic invention.[6] The general tradition, however, is reliable and may be quite old: At the time of the wars for freedom, Aeschylus was a grown man, Sophocles a young boy, and Euripides no more than an infant.

This statement of the relative chronology underlay early efforts to compute the precise ages of the poets at various stages in their careers. The chronology of the *Marmor* is a good example. Aeschylus' first victory was 485/84, midway between the battles of Marathon and Salamis, and Euripides was supposed to have been an infant at the time of the wars. Thus the *Marmor* (A 50) synchronizes the birth of Euripides with the first victory of Aeschylus. Hence Euripides was 44 years old at the time of his own first victory in 442/41 (A 60) and 79 years old when he died in 407/6 (A 63).[7] The *Marmor* states that Aeschylus was 35 years old when he fought in the battle of Marathon (A 48) and 69 years old when he died in 456/55 (A 59). The computation derives from assigning to Aeschylus the age of 40 at the time of his first victory in 485/84, a statement that represents a formal expression of the tradition that he was a mature man during the Persian Wars. The *Marmor* says Sophocles was 28 at the time of his first victory in 469/68 (A 56) and 92 when he died in 406/5 (A 64). This computation derives, as Jacoby suggested, from assuming that Sophocles was an ἔφηβος at the age of 17 when he allegedly led the chorus of boys in celebration of the victory off Salamis.[8]

Variations on this kind of methodology, an unsystematic combination of the victory dates with the relative chronology implied by the synchronisms with the Persian Wars, can be detected in other pre-Apollodoran sources. Philochorus, for example (*FGrHist* 328 F 220), stated that Euripides was over 70 at the time of his death. Jacoby argued that Philochorus based the estimate on the date of Euripides' first presentation in 456/55, assuming that the poet must have been at least 20 years old at the time and thus over 70 when he died 50 years later.[9] But the presumption that the date of the first presentation is documentary may be false. Philochorus could proceed instead from the date of the first victory in 442/41, avoiding more precision than the tradition allowed. If Euripides was born "about the time of the Persian Wars," he was about 40 when he won the prize, and his age when he died in 407/6 could be estimated at "more than 70 years." Timaeus (*FGrHist* 566 F 105 and Komm.) synchronized the birth of Euripides directly with the year of Salamis, leading to Eratosthenes' opinion, subsequently the vulgate, that Euripides was 75 when he died (*FGrHist* 241 F 12), as well as to all manner of romantic fables about his mother's pregnancy (e.g., the *Suda* s.v. Euripides). The *Suda*'s date for Sophocles' birth in Olympiad 73, 488/85, if it is not a textual error, may reflect a synchronism like the *Marmor*'s between the birth of Sophocles and the first victory of Aeschylus. The *Macrobioi* (24) assigns to Sophocles an age of 95 at the time of his death. The figure suggests a synchronism according to which Aeschylus flourished at an age of about 40 at the time of the Persian Wars, while Sophocles was a youth of 20 years.[10]

Such was the tradition as it existed before Apollodorus—a mass of unsystematic and conflicting data. Without making significant changes in the received tradition, Apollodorus introduced both system and mathematical symmetry by applying his theory of ideal ages to the year of Aeschylus' death. The available evidence could be accommodated by theorizing that in the archonship of Callias I, 456/55, Aeschylus was 64 years old, Sophocles was 40, and Euripides was 25.[11] Thus Euripides was one full intellectual generation younger than Aeschylus and was born in the year that Aeschylus reached the age of 40, the archonship of Calliades, 480/79, when Sophocles would have been 16 years old. Apollodorus accepted the slight downward shift in the date of Euripides' death introduced by Timaeus and formalized by Eratosthenes, so that Sophocles died at the age of 90 in the archonship of Callias III, 406/5, and Euripides died in the same year at the age of 75. The computation also produced the remarkable coincidence that in the year of Sophocles' generalship, 441/40, Euripides reached his acme at the age of 40.[12]

For Apollodorus' system of biographical chronology the theoretical age of 25 marked a first entrance to fame. In the case of the three tragedians, Apollodorus used this age to determine the year when the poet had been granted his first chorus. That the age was appropriate was suggested by the fact that Sophocles' first victory was always associated with his first

presentation. The date was 469/68 when Sophocles, by Apollodorus' count, was 27 years old.[13] Euripides' 25th year was 456/
55, Apollodorus' epochal year, and Apollodorus stated that he
made his first presentation at that time. Thus the statement of
the *vita* (134 West.) according to which Euripides first produced in the archonship of Callias, the first year of the 81st
Olympiad (456/5), is based on Apollodorus' theoretical model
rather than on documentary evidence.[14] That the same device
was used to date Aeschylus' first presentation is suggested by the
statement of the *Suda* that he entered the dramatic contests at
the age of 25.[15] Since Apollodorus assigned to Sophocles the age
of 40 when Aeschylus was 64, the year of Aeschylus' first presentation at the age of 25 also marks the year of Sophocles'
birth. These synchronisms—*floruit* of Sophocles, first presentation of Euripides; birth of Sophocles, first presentation of
Aeschylus—are sufficiently striking as to undermine confidence
in the documentary nature of first-presentation dates.

The full chronology of Apollodorus for the three tragedians,
derived from combining the 64-40-25 theorem with the date of
Aeschylus' death, can be summarized as follows. Those entries
marked with an asterisk (*) derive from chronographic theory.

OL 65.2 (519/18): Aeschylus' birth*
OL 71.2 (495/94): Aeschylus' first presentation,
                aged 25*
                Sophocles' birth*
OL 73.4 (485/84): Aeschylus' first victory
OL 75.1 (480/79): Aeschylus' acme, aged 40*
   (Calliades)   Sophocles' ἐφηβεία, aged 16*
                Euripides, birth*
OL 77.4 (469/68): Sophocles' first victory
OL 81.1 (456/55): Aeschylus' death at age of 64
   (Callias I)   Sophocles' acme, aged 40*
                Euripides' first presentation, aged
                25*
OL 84.3 (442/41): Euripides' first victory
OL 84.4 (441/40): Sophocles' generalship
                Euripides' acme, aged 40*
OL 93.3 (406/5): Euripides' death (slightly down-
                dated*)
   (Callias III) Sophocles' death
                Dionysius' accession as tyrant in
                Syracuse

Few of these dates are, strictly speaking, historical, but none of them can be far from the truth. Apollodorus systematized what was known and made plausible inferences about what was not known. Unfortunately, Apollodorus exists for us only in fragments and in theoretically based reconstructions like that offered above. We do not possess the original *Chronicle* of Apollodorus. Nor was it available to the synchronistic sources of the authors who, like Eusebius' Olympiad chronicler, transmitted the fragments. The epitomators condensed for convenient perusal what they thought were the essential chronological "facts" of Apollodorus, not including chronographic method or other distracting detail.

The Eusebian Entries

Eusebius' collection of notices on the tragedians illustrates how the Apollodoran information was transmitted. The two notices, *Aeschylus agnoscitur*, in Olympiads 71 and 75 preserve Apollodorus' dates for Aeschylus' first presentation in the year corresponding to Olympiad 71.1 (495/94) and his acme in Olympiad 75.1 (480/79). In both cases, Aeschylus' name and the date were excerpted and transmitted to Eusebius' source with the specific reference—first presentation or acme—omitted. The second notice is one of a series—Xerxes' invasion, the battles of Thermopylae, Salamis, Plataea, and Mycale, the walling of the Piraeus—all of which belong to the epoch of the Persian Wars. The fact that the notice on Aeschylus appears a few years after 480 is therefore not significant. All of these notices were entered in Eusebius' source under Olympiad 75, perhaps without specification of the year within the quadrennium. Eusebius should perhaps have made a clear division in chronographic format for the epoch of the Persian Wars, similar to the epochal divisions that mark the fall of Troy and the first Olympiad. Since he did not, there was insufficient space to make it plain that all of these notices were to be associated with the year 480/79.

Both Jerome and the Armenian translator have two entries on tragedians in Olympiads 77–78 (472/68)—*Sofocles tragoediarum scriptor primum ingenii sui opera publicauit* and *Sofocles et Euripides clari habentur*. The Oxford manuscript of Jerome has the first notice at Olympiad 77.2, 471/70, and it appears in the same Olympiad year (AA 1545) in the Armenian version. The second notice appears at Olympiad 77.4, 469/68, in the Oxford and Berne manuscripts. "A" and the Armenian version differ slightly in entering the notice one line lower, Olympiad 78.1 (468/67). The first entry notes Sophocles' first presentation. The second entry notes his *floruit* in synchronism with Euripides. The second notice appears, at least in some manuscripts, at the date traditionally and correctly associated with Sophocles' first victory in the archonship of Apsephion, 469/68. According to Plutarch (*Cimon* 8.8), Sophocles was making his first presentation when Cimon and his fellow generals accorded him that victory.[16] The Eusebian texts have a separate entry for the first presentation, which does not mention a victory and which appears two or three years earlier than the *floruit* entered at the date of the first victory. In both Jerome and the Armenian version this notice on Sophocles' first presentation appears at the date that marked Sophocles' 25th year in Apollodorus' system, Olympiad 77.2, 471/70. Apollodorus dated the first presentations of Aeschylus and Euripides to their respective 25th years. Apollodorus certainly knew and reported the first victory of Sophocles in the archonship of Apsephion. The Eusebian evidence raises the possibility that Apollodorus disagreed with the tradition represented by Plutarch and considered Sophocles' first presentation and first victory to have been separate occasions.

This kind of evidence is very difficult to interpret, given the nature of the texts involved. That the second notice derives ultimately from the date of Sophocles' first victory need not be doubted. The fact that a *floruit*, rather than a first victory, is noted means only that we are dealing with an abbreviated excerpt. The case is analogous to the entry of Aeschylus' *floruit* in Olympiad 71, the Apollodoran date of his first presentation. The inclusion of Euripides is not surprising, although he was only twelve years old at the time of Sophocles' first victory. This kind of vague synchronism is typical of the sources. In this case the origin of the synchronistic excerpt can be identified in a context that also attests to the Apollodoran derivation of the entry. Diogenes (2.44) cites Apollodorus (*FGrHist* 244 F 34) for the date of Socrates' birth in the archonship of Apsephion. After concluding his remarks on the chronology of Socrates, Diogenes adds that both he and Euripides were students of Anaxagoras and that Euripides was born in the archonsip of Calliades, 480/

79. The comments on Euripides derive, like the date for Socrates, from Diogenes' Apollodoran source. Apollodorus mentioned Euripides in a discussion on Socrates because both were believed to have been influenced by Anaxagoras and they were near contemporaries, Euripides having been born in the twelfth year before Socrates. Apollodorus certainly also mentioned Sophocles, because, coincidentally enough, the year that Apollodorus computed (70th year before death in 400/399) as that of Socrates' birth was also the year of Sophocles' first victory. That is, under the archonship of Apsephion, Apollodorus commented on Socrates' birth and Sophocles' first victory, and he reminded the reader that Euripides was a close contemporary of Socrates. As the information passed through the epitomizing process, the names of Sophocles and Euripides were excerpted together with the date and associated only with the vague γέγονε or ἐγνωρίζετο

The more interesting question is why the Eusebian texts have a separate entry for Sophocles' first presentation at the year that marked his 25th. The possibility that Eusebius or his sources recognized the significance of the 25th year in Apollodorus' system and its association, in the case of the tragedians, with first presentation is remote indeed. Neither methodological sophistication nor chronographic invention had a role in the composition of these texts. It is noteworthy that the first entry does not mention a victory. If a separation between first presentation and first victory can be attributed to Apollodorus, the notice becomes very significant indeed. If the tradition represented by Plutarch is sound, then Apollodorus rejected solid tradition simply to flesh out a theoretical system. On the other hand, if Apollodorus used the theoretical model partly as an indication of the inferential nature of his conclusions, then we must ourselves abandon Plutarch's tradition. A telescoping of two very similar events separated by only a few years' time into a single story is common in Plutarch. A parallel can be found in his confusion between Cimon's two Eastern campaigns—the battle of the Eurymedon and the Cyprus campaign (*Cimon* 13.4–5, 18.6–7).[17] The conclusion, then, is that for Sophocles, as well as for Euripides and Aeschylus, it was not known when the poet had produced his first play, and biographers were obliged to guess.

Too much stands in the way of so bold a conclusion, based on nothing but the evidence of Eusebius. The notices can be otherwise explained, on a hypothesis of multiple sources. Many different epitomes were made of Apollodorus for a variety of purposes, and excerpts from more than one version of the Apollodoran system could eventually be brought together by a single author—in this case either Eusebius himself or his Olympiad chronicler. The two notices are thus different epitomes of the same Apollodoran data. The inclusion of Euripides in the second notice has already been explained. The combined note was firmly associated with Olympiad 77.4 (469/68), Sophocles' first victory, and thus transmitted through one channel to Eusebius or his source. The wording of the first notice is clear, first presentation, but in the process of transmission the fact that a victory had ensued was omitted—perhaps on the assumption that for Sophocles, at least, everyone knew that first presentation implied first victory. The notice was transmitted through another tradition to Eusebius or his source, and in this tradition specific Olympiad years were not cited. Only the Olympiad number was given, and the entry hence came to be set at the first year of Olympiad 77 instead of the fourth. Perhaps both notices were associated only with the Olympiad number and distributed through the space allowed for that Olympiad along with the other entries to be noted there. The conclusion is essentially the same in either case. Eusebius received the date of Sophocles' first presentation in Olympiad 77 from two sources. In one case it was expressed as a *floruit* and a synchronism with Euripides was added. In the other, Sophocles' first presentation was specifically noted, but the victory was not.

In Olympiad 81, 456/53, Eusebius enters *Aristarchus tragoediografus agnoscitur*, with the manuscript authorities varying in the placement of the entry from the line corresponding to the Olympiad number to the fourth year of the Olympiad. Olympiad 81.1, 456/55, the archonship of Callias I, is the year of the great synchronism in Apollodorus' system: death of Aeschylus at age 64, acme of Sophocles at age 40, first presentation of Euripides at age 25. Of Aristarchus the *Suda* says he was σύγχρονος Εὐριπίδη Apollodorus perhaps included the lesser tragedians in his system and synchronized Aristarchus with Euripides in the year of the epochal synchronism. On the other hand, the sources common to Eusebius and the *Suda*, unable to find a date for Aristarchus, may have associated him with the epochal year themselves. As often happens, the key persons in the synchronism at that date are missing. In any case, it is clear that this notice of Eusebius derives from Apollodoran influence.

The entry on the *floruit* of Euripides, in synchronism with that of Protagoras, appears in Olympiad 84, with the usual slight variations among the manuscript authorities in the exact placement. Olympiad 84.4, 441/40, was the acme of Euripides in Apollodorus' sustem. The appearance of Protagoras in synchronism with Euripides at that date is also Apollodoran. Diogenes (9.56) specifically cites Apollodorus (*FGrHist* 244 F 71) for a life span of 70 years for Protagoras and an acme in Olympiad 84. Diogenes does not specify a year within the quadrennium. Jacoby argued for Olympiad 84.1, 444/43, the year of the colonization of Thurii, as Apollodorus' formalization of the tradition (D.L. 9.50 = Heraclides Ponticus fr. 150 Wehrli) that Protagoras wrote laws for Thurii.[18] Eusebius, however, mentions a public decree of the Athenians condemning Protagoras and ordering his books to be burnt. The story appears in Diogenes (9.52–54), and it is possible that Apollodorus accepted the tradition. Diogenes names as author of the decree Pythodorus, one of the 400. If Apollodorus dated the condemnation of Protagoras to the time of the 400 in 412/11 and his death at the age of 70 (the figure derives from Plato, *Meno* 91[e]) immediately thereafter to the year 411/10, the birth of the sophist would fall in 480/79 and his acme in 441/40. The computation results in Protagoras' having the same dates as Euripides, and their friendship was proverbial (e.g., D.L. 9.54). It is therefore possible that Apollodorus did not date Protagoras by reference to the foundation of Thurii, but synchronized his birth with that of Euripides. The synchronism was suggested both by their traditional friendship and by Apollodorus' belief that Protagoras had been condemned by the 400 shortly before his death at the age of 70. The computation also results, interestingly enough, in Protagoras' having been born in the archonship of Calliades and dying in the archonship of Callias II (411/10), while his almost-exact contemporary Euripides died five years later in the archonship of Callias III.

In Olympiad 85, the manuscripts enter Theaetetus, Sophocles, and Aristophanes. The Armenian omits Aristophanes and has a separate entry for Theaetetus.[19] The notice is Apollodoran only if its original reference was Olympiad 84, a shift in the *Canons* that will surprise no one. Olympiad 84.4, 441/40, was the year of Sophocles' generalship. For Aristophanes it is possible that Olympiad 84 marked his birth in the Apollodoran system. The *Suda* dates his *floruit* (γεγονὼς ἐν τοῖς ἀγῶσι) to Olympiad 114 (324/21), an impossible reading that has been plausibly corrected to Olympiad 94, 404/1.[20] If Aristophanes flourished in Olympiad 94 for Apollodorus, he was born in Olympiad 84. Eusebius' sources have in that case again confused a birthdate with a *floruit*.

Such an argument is on shaky ground, for Eusebius' notice on Sophocles and Aristophanes does appear in Olympiad 85 (440/37), and there is no evidence for the Apollodoran date of Aristophanes other than the corrupt text of the *Suda*. Another understanding of the notice is possible, one that may well be correct. Both in Jerome and in the Armenian version the notice appears immediately after the entry on Phidias and the chryselaphantine Athena. Phidias properly belongs to this Olympiad, since Olympiad 85.2, 439/38, was the Atthidographic date for the dedication of the statue.[21] Persons associated with the so-called Periclean Age may well have been assigned to that date in the synchronistic sources. The inclusion of Aristophanes and perhaps Theaetetus, as well as Sophocles, in such a synchronism is wrong, but understandable.

Eusebius' last notice on the fifth-century tragedians appears at Olympiad 93, 408/5, where he synchronizes the death of Euripides at the court of Archelaus with that of Sophocles in Athens. The synchronism is false, at least as far as chronographic Olympiad and archon years are concerned, but it was popularized by Apollodorus, a further testimony to the Apollodoran origin of Eusebius' entries on the tragedians. The accession of Dionysius as tyrant in Syracuse, which Apollodorus, following Timaeus, synchronized with the death of Euripides, appears immediately after the entry on Sophocles and Euripides in both versions. The notice on the death of Euripides and Sophocles appears either at the first year of the Olympiad or in the space corresponding to the Olympiad number in all the manuscripts of Jerome. It is just above the Olympiad number (technically, therefore, in Olympiad 92) in the Armenian version. Again Eusebius' sources transmitted only the Olympiad number, not the precise year within the quadrennium (OL 93.3).

Conclusion

Even for the fifth century, much of the traditional chronology rests on inference rather than evidence. As with the earlier period, however, the inferences were good ones designed to synthesize a larger body of evidence and tradition than is now extant. The traditional chronology must stand, but one must not be too insistent about the absolute historicity of every detail. It is plausible to suppose, for example, that the date of Euripides' first presentation derives from the official records of the Attic festivals. There are, however, so many synchronistic coincidences in the traditional chronology, when considered as a whole, that one must concede the possibility that even a date so late and so important as that of Euripides' first presentation may be a chronographic inference, not a documentary fact. Furthermore, the traditional chronology itself must be reconstructed from texts like the *Chronicle* of Eusebius. The tortuous path from the extant texts through source criticism to the Hellenistic tradition and from there to the original sources of information must be traversed before the evidence can meaningfully be judged. Each problem is separate, each analysis is intricate, each hypothesis is tentative. Case studies such as those presented here can be multiplied, but there is no general solution. These conclusions are not negative. Every detail is suspect, but the traditional chronology is structurally sound. The discovery of mathematical symmetry sometimes leads to a better understanding of the chronographic tradition, but it does not undermine it and it does not allow us to manipulate the tradition by substituting our own numerology for that of the Greeks.

Notes

Notes to Chapter I

1. An example of how easily errors can be made, even by the best of modern scholars, is found on p. 130 of Felix Jacoby, *Apollodors Chronik*, Philologische Untersuchungen 16 (Berlin 1902). In commenting on Eusebius' entry of the First Messenian War, which appears at Olympiad 9.1 (744/43) in Schoene's edition (81ᵍ), Olympiad 8.3 (746/45) in Helm's edition (89ᶜ), AA 1274 (742/41) in both Petermann's (82ᵃ) and Karst's (182) editions of the Armenian, Jacoby asserts that the Armenian version enters the notice at Olympiad 10.1 (740/39). Apparently his eye caught the numeral 10 standing to the left of AA 1274 in Petermann's edition. The number does not refer to Olympiads, but to years *ab urbe condita*.

2. The panegyric on Eusebius' life written by Acacius, his successor as bishop of Caesarea, is mentioned by Socrates (*H.E.* 2.4) but otherwise lost without a trace. For modern treatment see especially E. Schwartz, "Eusebios," *RE* 6 (1907) 1370-1439 (*Griechische Geschichtschreiber* [Leipzig 1959] 495-598), whose account is followed here, and D. S. Wallace–Hadrill, *Eusebius of Caesarea* (London 1960).

3. Jerome *de vir. ill.* 81.

4. On the career of Pamphilus see E. Schwartz, *RE* 6 (1907) 1370-72, and Eva Hoffman-Aleith, "Pamphilos," *RE* 18 (1949) 349-50.

5. For the work of Eusebius and Pamphilus on the text of the Bible see Wallace-Hadrill, *Eusebius* 59-71; A. Harnack, *Geschichte der altchristliche Literatur bis Eusebius* I² (reprinted. Leipzig 1958) 543-50; *The Cambridge History of the Bible*, ed. P. R. Ackroyd and C. F. Evans, 3 vols. (Cambridge 1970), vol. 1: *From the Beginnings to Jerome*, esp. 314–16, 357–63; and Bruce M. Metzger, *The Text of the New Testament*, 2d ed., (Oxford 1968) 7, 214–15.

6. E. Schwartz, *RE* 6 (1907) 1376, 1387, 1390.

7. There are some differences between the intervals cited here and those actually exhibited in the *Canons*. Here Eusebius cites Eratosthenes' (*FGrHist* 241 F 1) interval of 408 years between the fall of Troy and the first Olympiad, but in the *Canons* and in Eusebius' preface (11 Helm) the interval is reduced to 406 years. Here Eusebius sets an interval of 400 years between the fall of Troy and the Moses-Cecrops synchronism, while in the preface to the *Canons* the interval is given (correctly) as 329. Perhaps Eusebius was citing from memory and did not actually have the *Chronicle* before him when he wrote this passage of the *Praep. Euang.*

8. The preface and the first few pages of the *Canons* are missing in the Armenian version. A Greek version of the preface appears in Syncellus 121-24.

9. Eusebius cites more intervals in the preface than in the *Praep. Euang.* and the computations are more precise.

10. For examples of this usage see Felix Jacoby, *Apollodors Chronik* 20.

11. This description of the "epitome" follows from Eusebius' reference to the *Chronicle* (*Ecl. Proph.* 1), χρονικοὺς συντάξαντες κανόνας ἐπιτομήν τε τούτοις παντοδαπῆς ἱστορίας Ἑλλήνων τε καὶ βαρβάρων ἀντιπαραθέντες and from the conclusion to the preface (18-19 Helm), *quae uniuersa in suis locis cum summa breuitate ponemus.*

12. Photius, *Bibl.* cod. 34. Modern treatment is found in Heinrich Gelzer, *Sextus Julius Africanus und die byzantinische Chronographie*, 2 vols. in 1 (Leipzig 1880 and 1898), reprinted by B. Franklin (New York 1967).

13. That Eusebius invented such chronological tables has of course been doubted. Curt Wachsmuth, *Einleitung in der Studium der alten Geschichte* (Leipzig 1895) 127-202 ("Weltchroniken"), attributes the tabular form to Castor (p. 139). Against Wachsmuth, Rudolf Helm has convincingly argued the case for Eusebian invention in his *Eusebius' Chronik und ihre Tabellenform*, Abh. Berl. phil.-hist. Kl. 1923, nr. 4 (Berlin 1924) 9-13.

14. On these additions see Rudolf Helm, *Hieronymus' Zusätze in Eusebius' Chronik und ihr Wert für die Literaturgeschichte*, Philologus Supplement 21, no. 2, 1929.

15. Compare the note that Jerome enters at Constantine XX (231ᶠ Helm): *Huc usque historiam scribit Eusebius Pamphili martyris contubernalis.*

16. The details must be left to the discussion of these hypotheses below. Briefly, (1) is the opinion of the most recent editors, J. K. Fotheringham and R. Helm; (2) is the suggestion of D. S. Wallace-Hadrill, *JThS*, n.s. 6 (1955) 248-53; (3) is the hypothesis suggested by Alfred Schoene (*Weltchronik*) and developed by Josef Karst in his edition of the Armenian version; (4) is the extreme position of Eduard Schwartz.

17. See Theodor Mommsen, ed., *Chronica Minora*, 2 vols., Monumenta Germaniae Historica, auct. ant. 9 and 11 (Berlin 1892, 1894).

18. Scaliger's discussion of the manuscripts appears at 5ff. of the *animadversiones* (*Thesaurus Temporum*, ed. alt. Amsterdam 1658), reproduced in part by Schoene in the introduction to his edition of Jerome (xxix). According to Mommsen (*Hermes* 24 [1889] 398) Scaliger's *Priores* all descend from the Codex Londinensis, Mus. Brit. 16974. For Scaliger himself the group was best represented by the Codex Leidensis, Lat. Bibl. Publ. 30. The three *Posteriores* are the Codex Bernensis 219 (Scaliger's Bongarsianus), Codex Leidensis, Scal. 14, and Codex Leidensis, Voss. C. 110.

19. A brief summary of the life and work of Scaliger can be found in J. E. Sandys, *A History of Classical Scholarship* II, 199-204 (Cambridge 1908; reprint ed. New York: Hafner, 1958). A more recent discussion is Anthony T. Grafton, "Joseph Scaliger and Historical Chronology: The Rise and Fall of a Discipline," *History and Theory* 14 (1975) 156-85. The misuse of Scaliger's Greek Olympiad chronicle is discussed by Henry Clinton in the preface (xxvi) to vol. 2 of *Fasti Hellenici*, 3d ed. (Oxford 1841).

20. L. T. Spittler, "Historia Critica Chronici Eusebiani," *Commentationes societatis regiae scientiarum Gottingensis*, Phil.-Hist. Class. 8 (1785-86) 39-67.

21. This account of the vicissitudes of the Armenian version is based on the

comments of H. Petermann in the introduction to his edition (Berlin 1866).

22. Aucher and his edition were excoriated in particular by Niebuhr, "Historischer Gewinn aus der armenischen Uebersetzung der Chronik des Eusebius," *AbhBerl* 1820–21 (*Kl. Schr.* I, 179–304) and by St. Martin in the *Journal des Savants* (February 1820) 97–112, the latter underscoring his comments by pointedly referring to Zohrab as Dr. and to Aucher as Mr.

23. Of greater importance than the epitome translated into Latin for Schoene's edition by E. Roediger is the Syriac epitome commonly attributed to Dionysius of Tell-Mahre, Patriarch of Antioch (818–45). This epitome is preserved in Cod. Vat. Syr. 162. It was first published by H. Tulberg (Upsala 1850) and is available with Latin translation in the edition of C. Siegfried and H. Gelzer, *Eusebii Canonum Epitome ex Dionysii Telmaharensis Chronico petita* (Leipzig 1884). The latter epitome has dates; the former does not. The Siegfried-Gelzer edition must be used with caution, because the editors allowed themselves to be influenced by other Eusebian derivatives both in preparing the translation and in athetizing certain passages as being not of Eusebian origin. Compare the comments of E. Schwartz, *RE* 6 (1907) 1381, who characterizes the edition as "zu ungenau gearbeitet." Unfortunately, even if one can read Syriac he is not likely to find Tulberg's edition in the library. Siegfried-Gelzer is difficult enough to obtain.

24. *Eusebi Chronicorum Libri Duo.* Vol. I: *Eusebi Chronicorum Liber Prior. Armeniam uersionem latine ad libros manuscriptos recensuit* H. Petermann, *Graeca fragmenta collegit et recognouit, appendices chronographias sex adiecit* A. Schoene (Berlin 1875). Vol. II: *Eusebi Chronicorum Canonum Quae Supersunt. Armeniam uersionem latine factam e libris manuscriptis recensuit* H. Petermann, *Hieronymi uersionem e libris manuscriptis recensuit* Alfred Schoene, *Syriam epitomen latine factam e libro Londinensi* E. Roediger (Berlin 1866). Both volumes have been reprinted by Weidmann Verlag (Dublin/Zurich 1967).

25. A. Schoene, *Praef.* xxxii. The suspicious section of Jerome's preface is printed in italics on p. 2 of Schoene's edition, relegated to the critical apparatus on p. 5 of Helm's edition.

26. Schoene reports the identification of the Paris fragments as belonging with "S" in *Weltchronik des Eusebius* (Berlin 1900) 26. See also L. Traube, *Codices Graeci et Latini photographice depicti*, Suppl. I, 1902. For detailed description of the manuscripts, see the editions of Schoene, Fotheringham, and Helm, as well as Schoene's *Weltchronik*. Only those essentials which bear directly on the problem of the original format of the *Canons* and the relative merits of the Armenian and Latin versions can be included here.

27. A. Schoene, *Praef.* xxxiv–xxxvii.

28. Curt Wachsmuth, *Einleitung in der Studium der alten Geschichte* (Leipzig 1895) 163–76. Cf. Alfred von Gutschmid, "De Temporum notis quibus Eusebius utitur in Chronicis Canonibus," *Schriften Kiel* 15 (1868) 3–28 (*Kleine Schriften I* [Leipzig 1889] 448–82).

29. Th. Mcmmsen, "Die älteste Handschrift der Chronik des Hieronymus," *Hermes* 24 (1889) 383–401 (*Gesam. Schr.* VII, 597–605); J. K. Fotheringham, *The Bodleian Manuscript of Jerome's Version of the Chronicle of Eusebius* (Oxford 1905). Schoene reported the Middlehillensis as Appendix V in the 1875 volume of his edition, the Paris fragments in *Weltchronik* (above, n. 26).

30. Th. Mommsen, "Die armenischen Handschriften der Chronik des Eusebius," *Hermes* 30 (1895) 321–38 (*Gesam. Schr.* VII, 580–96).

31. C. Siegfried and H. Gelzer, *Eusebii Canonum Epitome ex Dionysii Telma-*

harensis Chronico petita (Leipzig 1884); H. Petermann, *praef. ed.* (Berlin 1866) LIII–LV; A. von Gutschmid, "Über Schoenes Ausgabe der Chronik des Eusebius" and "Untersuchungen über die syrische Epitome der Eusebischen Canones," *Kl. Schr.* I (Leipzig 1889) 417–47, 483–529; Curt Wachsmuth, *Einleitung in der Studium der alten Geschichte* (Leipzig 1895) 163–76. Note that the years of Abraham included in Roediger's translation of Cod. Mus. Brit. Syr. Add. 14643 for the Schoene-Petermann edition are an editorial addition provided to facilitate cross-reference. Cf. above, n. 23.

32. Alfred Schoene, *Die Weltchronik des Eusebius in ihrer Bearbeitung durch Hieronymus* (Berlin 1900).

33. Eduard Schwartz, "Die Königslisten des Eratosthenes und Kastor," *AbhGott.* phil.-hist. Kl. 40.2 (1894–95) 1–96; "Eusebios," *RE* 6 (1907) 1370–1439 (*Griechische Geschichtschreiber* 495–598); cf. the remarks published in vol. 3 (Einleitungen, Übersichten, Register) of Schwartz' *GCS* edition of the *Historia Ecclesiastica* (*Eusebius Werke* II, Leipzig 1903, 1908, 1909). The quotation is from *RE* 1383.

34. According to Jacoby (*Apollodors Chronik* 402), the computation is falsely attributed to Apollodorus, who did not deal with the mythical period.

35. Josef Karst, *Die Chronik des Eusebius aus dem armenischen übersetzt, Eusebius Werke* V (*GCS* 20) (Leipzig 1911). This edition is extremely scarce and cannot be found in most American university libraries, which were established after 1911 and therefore not among the subscribers of the *GCS* when the edition was published. Many scholars are therefore using the unsatisfactory Schoene-Petermann edition reprinted in 1967 by Weidmann Verlag. The *GCS* should reissue the volume with correction of the occasional printing errors (the number 138 on p. 125, l. 16, for example, is wrong; Aucher has 128, Petermann 228) after new collation with the manuscript.

36. J. Karst, Einl. XIX–XXIII.

37. H. Petermann, *Praef. Ed.* LIII–LV; J. Karst, Einl. XXXIV–LIV.

38. J. K. Fotheringham, *The Bodleian Manuscript of Jerome's Version of the Chronicle of Eusebius Reproduced in Collotype* (Oxford 1905); "On the List of Thalassocracies in Eusebius," *JHS* 27 (1907) 75–89; *Eusebii Pamphili Chronici Canones: Latine uertit adauxit, ad sua tempora produxit S. Eusebius Hieronymus* (London 1923).

39. Rudolf Helm, *Die Chronik des Hieronymus, Eusebius Werke* VII, i and ii (*GCS* 24 and 34) (Leipzig, 1913, 1926); 2d ed. in 1 vol. (*GCS* 47) Berlin 1956. The second edition was revised under Helm's supervision with a printed 26-line text and the critical apparatus both to the date and text of the entries appearing at the bottom of the page.

40. Rudolf Helm, *Eusebius' Chronik und ihre Tabellenform, AbhBerl.* phil.-hist. Kl. 1923 Nr. 4 (Berlin 1924) 1–56; "Die Liste der Thalassokratien in der Chronik des Eusebius," *Hermes* 61 (1926) 241–63. Wachsmuth's attribution of synchronistic tables to Castor appears in *Einleitung in der Studium der alten Geschichte* (Leipzig 1895) 139; Schoene categorically denied that Eusebius invented the format, but he adduced no arguments (*Weltchronik* 275). On Africanus, see H. Gelzer, *Sextus Julius Africanus und die byzantinische Chronographie* (Leipzig 1880, 1898). It is a common failing (e.g., in the case of Herodotus) to attribute to lost authors the achievements of those whose work remains to be read. It may seem strange that no one before Eusebius composed such a work, but the fact remains that there is no evidence that anyone did.

41. Erich Caspar, *Die älteste römische Bischofsliste: kritische Studien zum Formproblem des eusebianischen Kanons*, Schriften der Konigsberger Gelehrte Gesellschaft, Geisteswiss. Kl. II Nr. 4 (Berlin 1926) ; "Helm, *Eusebius Werke* VII," *GGA* 189 (1927) 161–84.

42. Rudolf Helm, "Die neuesten Hypothesen zu Eusebius' (Hieronymus') Chronik," *SBBerl* phil.-hist. Kl. 21 (1929) 371–408 ; cf. Einl. XXXIII ff. in the 1956 edition.

43. Karl Mras, "Nachwort zu den beiden letzen Ausgaben der Chronik des Hieronymus," *Wiener Studien* 46 (1928) 200–215.

44. *Theodosio VIIII et Constantio III* (Consuls in 420) : *Hieronymus presbyter moritur anno aetatis suae XCI prid. Kal. Octobris* (Mommsen, *Chron. Min.* I, 469). According to Mommsen, the earliest redaction of the *chronicon consulare* closed with the year 433, so that we are dealing with the evidence of a person who was a younger contemporary of Jerome.

45. Fotheringham (*praef. ed.* XXIV) suggested that Olympiad numbers are special because the Olympic year beginning in summer did not match the Syro-Macedonian imperial year beginning in the fall which, according to C. H. Turner (*JThS* 1 [1900] 187–92), was Eusebius' standard. But Eusebius had no qualms about equating Olympiad years with Macedonian years or even Roman years. See the comments on Polybius, Porphyry, and Eusebius of A. E. Samuel, *Greek and Roman Chronology* (Munich 1972) 194. Olympiad numbers are special for Eusebius because his synchronistic tables represented an innovative combination of king-list chronography with the popular genre of the Olympiad chronicle.

46. *Hic finis Chronicorum Eusebii Librorum* (Latin translation included in the Zohrab-Mai edition of Eusebius, reprinted for vol. 19 of Migne's *Patrologiae Cursus Completus* [*Series Graeco-Latina*]).

47. R. Helm, *Eusebius' Chronik und ihre Tabellenform* 41, suggests Olympiad 264.3 as the terminus of the edition that Eusebius cites in his early works. D. S. Wallace-Hadrill, "The Eusebian Chronicle: the Extent and Date of Composition of its Early Editions," *JThS*, n.s. 6 (1955) 248–53, accepted Karst's argument that the Armenian version represents a first edition and believed on the basis of the note about the persecution that the earlier edition ended in 303 and was subsequently revised in the light of new information.

48. On Panodorus and Annianus as sources of Syncellus, see H. Gelzer, *Sextus Julius Africanus und die byzantinische Chronographie* II (Leipzig 1898) 191; R. Laqueur, "Synkellos," *RE* 55 (1932) 1387–1410; and Otto Seel, "Panodorus," *RE* 36 (1958) 631–35. The dates of Theophilus can be derived from Nicephorus' (Patriarch of Constantinople 858–67, 877–86) list of the Alexandrian bishops (p. 779 Dindorf) in conjunction with Jerome's date for the accession of Peter as bishop in 373 (247c Helm). According to Nicephorus, Theophilus was ordained to the office fifteen years later and served for 28 years. Pandorus and Annianus thus flourished between 388 and 416. The additional synchronism of Panodorus with Arcadius suggests that Panodorus published his work before 408, while Annianus published between 408 and 416.

49. Certain of the manuscripts of St. Jerome, notably the Lucca manuscript (Bibl. Cap. 490), contain notices that are surely Eusebian but do not appear in the O-S tradition. Whether this is evidence of collation with a Greek version, perhaps that of Panodorus, or of omission in the O-S manuscripts is a problem for separate consideration. See A.A. Mosshammer, "Lucca Bibl. Capit. 490 and the Manuscript Tradition of Hieronymus' (Eusebius') Chronicle," *California*

Studies in Classical Antiquity 8 (1975) 203–40, where I argue for the latter hypothesis.

50. Cf. above, n. 45.

51. This decision was dictated at least in part by the fact that the larger Latin characters made it difficult to accommodate the side-by-side format. The Latin version does, however, apparently preserve at least one instance of the side-by-side format in the notices of Olympiads 59 and 60 (103 Helm).

52. Somewhat more reliable control on the dates is occasionally provided in the excerpts from the *Chronicle* included in the *Contra Iulianum* of Cyril of Alexandria. He was a younger contemporary of Eusebius who cited the *Chronological Canons* by Olympiads—not years of Abraham or years since Adam. On Cyril as an early witness, see E. Hiller, *RhM* 25 (1870) 253–62, and H. Gelzer, *Sextus Julius Africanus und die byzantinische Chronographie* II (Leipzig 1898) 97.

53. The reconstruction is based on the arguments and illustrations of Helm in the works cited (above, nn. 39 and 40). I disagree with some of Helm's reconstructions, a fact that shows how tentative such attempts remain. The effort has nevertheless to be made in dealing with individual notices.

Notes to Chapter 2

1. An example of an error of the first type is W. Aly's attempt "Theognis," *RE* 57 (1934) 1973, to show that the date of Eusebius and the *Suda* for Theognis in Olympiad 59 (544/41) was intended to be a date in Olympiad 58 (548/45), a major epoch for Apollodorus. An example of the more serious pitfall can be found in the table of 9 and 13 year intervals drawn up on the basis of the extant Eusebian texts by M. Miller, "Archaic Literary Chronography," *JHS* 75 (1955) 54–58.

2. For a discussion of the synchronisms and computations see Jean Sirinelli, *Les Vues historiques d'Eusèbe de Césarée* (Paris 1961) 31–99.

3. For the computation of the Olympic era at 776/75 see E. J. Bickerman, *Chronology of the Ancient World* (London 1968) 76, and A. E. Samuel, *Greek and Roman Chronology* (Munich 1972) 190. On the historicity of the early list see K. J. Beloch, *Gr. G.* I.2 (1926) 148–54 (negative), A. Brinkmann, "Die Olympische Chronik," *RhM* 70 (1915) 622–37 (affirmative); and, for a general account of the problem, see F. Jacoby in the introduction to *FGrHist* 407–16 ("Elis und Olympia"). A good discussion of Hippias as redactor appears in W. den Boer, *Laconian Studies* (Amsterdam 1954) 42–54. For the list itself as reconstructed from all sources see L. Moretti, "Olympionikai, i vincitori negli antichi agoni olimpici," *Atti della Accademia Nazionale dei Lincei*, ser. 8, vol. 8 *Memorie* (1959) 59–198. Eusebius' list (89–103 Karst) contains only the stadion victors, who were considered eponymous after Hippias' redaction had gained currency. Thucydides, for example (3.8; 5.49.1), identifies Olympiads (not for chronological purposes) by reference to the pancratiast.

4. See R. Meiggs and D. Lewis, *A Selection of Greek Historical Inscriptions* (Oxford 1969) 9–12 (no. 6), and the references cited there. B. D. Merritt published the first fragment, *Hesperia* 8 (1939) 59–65.

5. The publication of Herodotus' work in final form has generally been dated about 425. But see Charles W. Fornara, "Evidence for the Date of Herodotus'

Publication," *JHS* 91 (1971) 25–34, who argues for a date between 420 and 415.

6. The opinion of Eduard Meyer (*Geschichte des Altertums* 3², 210) that Herodotus had no interest whatsoever in chronology no longer holds sway. The reaction, however, has been too extreme in trying to impose "system" on the narrative: N. G. L. Hammond, "Studies in Greek Chronology of the sixth and fifth centuries B.C.," *Historia* 4 (1955) esp. 381–85; H. Strasburger, "Herodots Zeitrechnung," *Historia* 5 (1956) 129–61; H. Kaletsch, "Zur lydischen Chronologie," *Historia* 7 (1958) 1–47. Hammond argues that Herodotus reckoned by Athenian archon years, at least in books 7 through 9. Strasburger and Kaletsch reject this view, but believe that Herodotus used the archonship of Calliades as a fixed epoch for chronological calculation. Most extreme are the studies of M. Miller, "The Earlier Persian Dates in Herodotus," *Klio* 37 (1959) 29–52, "The Herodotean Croesus," *Klio* 41 (1963) 58–94, "Herodotus as Chronographer," *Klio* 46 (1965) 109–28. More moderate views, attributing to Herodotus a sense of time but avoiding too much systematization, may be found in W. den Boer, "Herodot und die Systeme der Chronologie," *Mnemosyne* 20 (1967) 30–60, and K. von Fritz, "Herodot: Chronologische Methoden und Probleme," *Die Griechische Geschichtsschreibung* (Berlin 1967) 364–406.

7. See F. Jacoby, *Apollodors Chronik,* Philologische Untersuchungen 16 (Berlin 1902) 138–42.

8. On the problem of the ephorate see the recent general works on Sparta, where the extensive bibliography on this subjct can also be found: K.M.T. Chrimes, *Ancient Sparta* (Manchester 1949); W. den Boer, *Laconian Studies* (Amsterdam 1954); G. L. Huxley, *Early Sparta* (London 1962); F. Kiechle, *Lakonien und Sparta* (Munich 1963); H. Michell, *Sparta* (Cambridge 1964); A.H.M. Jones, *Sparta* (Oxford 1967); W. G. Forrest, *A History of Sparta 950–192* B.C. (London 1968). Jacoby, *Apollodors Chronik* 142, maintained that the date was based on a complete list the authenticity of which could not be doubted. He was much more skeptical in *Atthis* (282.55, 305.24) suggesting that it was only in the time of Chilon (556/55) that the office became important enough to be used for dating and wondering if Charon of Lampsacus might not have extended the list back to 754/53. den Boer follows this latter view in placing the beginning of ephor dating about the time of Chilon (80–82). He suggests that this system of dating stood in conflict with the older generational chronology based on the succession of the kings and that Charon played a role in an unsuccessful attempt to make the annalistic system victorious (33–35). Forrest (20) considers the early list an invention, possibly concocted by Timaeus. Kiechle (220–42) suggests that the list was officially reconstructed up to Elatus at some time in the fourth century on the basis of newly discovered documentary evidence that contradicted the Lycurgus legend. In the midst of all this controversy and speculation, only Jones (30) seems to have taken note of the fact that, whatever may be the origin of the eighth-century date, there is no evidence for a list.

9. Whether Charon's πρυτάνεις were the kings, the ephors, or both has been debated. The title is glossed twice in the *Suda*, the prytanies being called archons and the whole work characterized as a chronicle· πρυτάνεις (ἢ ἄρχοντας) τοὺς τῶν Λακεδαιμονίων (ἔστι δὲ χρονικά) One of the Spartan kings was named Prytanis, but the title is often applied to elected magistrates. Both πρύτανις and ἄρχων have a wide variety of meanings, and the issue cannot be settled on linguistic grounds. Since the work was a

chronicle it probably included both the kings and the ephors, for as far back as eponyms were used as official dates.

10. The view of den Boer, *Laconian Studies* 82 ff. that the list of ephors was a factor in the "struggle for a chronological pattern" is based on his belief that an *anagraphe* of the list was accomplished in Chilon's time. General considerations suggest that there was no chronographic incentive for an attempt to replace king lists with an ephor list, and if a politically motivated struggle to do so had ever taken place, some trace of it would be left in our sources. On the date of Charon, which cannot be fixed more precisely than late fifth or early fourth century, see F. Jacoby, "Charon von Lampsacus," *Abhandlungen zur griechischen Geschichtschreibung* (Leiden 1956) 178–206.

11. See F. Jacoby, introduction to *FGrHist* 402–7 ("Delphi").

12. F. Jacoby, *Atthis* (Oxford 1949) 180.

13. The theory of Ulrich von Wilamowitz, *Aristoteles und Athen* (1893), and T. J. Cadoux, "The Athenian Archons from Kreon to Hypsichides," *JHS* (1948) 70–123, that an official list complete with historical annotations was continuously kept from the time that the annual archonship was established, was demolished by Félix Jacoby in *Atthis* (Oxford 1949). Jacoby was too optimistic, however, about the possible archival base of the early list itself. He accepted the assumption that an *anagraphe* was drawn up in the first half of the seventh century and continuously kept with little disturbance (pp. 173 and 349 n. 36). Jacoby's comment on p. 88 strikes to the heart of the issue: "But we had better expressly state that in every Greek chronicle the list of eponymous officials is to a greater or lesser degree constructed: no list of officials of the mother country (and for that matter no list of victors) began to be kept before the seventh century." The evidence in fact suggests that for *seventh* we should read *fifth*.

14. Attempts to introduce fundamental alterations in the structure of early Greek chronology are best known in the work of Karl Julius Beloch. See especially the second of the two volumes in Band I of his *Griechische Geschichte,* 2d ed. (Leipzig 1926).

15. τοὺς μὲν οὖν χρόνους εξακριβῶσαι χαλεπόν ἐστι, καὶ μάλιστα τοὺς ἐκ τῶν Ὀλυμπιονικῶν ἀναγομένους, ὧν τὴν ἀναγραφὴν ὀψέ φασιν Ἱππίαν ἐκδοῦναι τὸν Ἠλεῖον, ἀπ᾽ οὐδενὸς ὁρμώμενον ἀναγκαίου πρὸς πίστιν. Cf. den Boer's discussion of the passage, *Laconian Studies* 45–47.

16. K. J. Beloch, *Gr. G.* I.2 (1926) 148–54.

17. The most important studies include E. Schwartz, "Die Königslisten des Eratosthenes und Kastor," *AbhGött.,* phil.-hist. Klasse 40.2 (1894–95) 1–96; F. Jacoby, *Apollodors Chronik* (Berlin 1902); T. Lenschau, "Agiaden und Eurypontiden," *RhM* 88 (1939) 123–46; K.M.T. Chrimes, *Ancient Sparta* (Manchester 1949); W. den Boer, *Laconian Studies* (Amsterdam 1954). Although the details are debatable, den Boer's concept of a "struggle for the chronological pattern" is the only kind of approach that can do justice to the complexity of the problem. On the difficulties involved in even reconstructing the ancient versions of the lists from the extant testimonia, see W. G. Forrest, "Two Chronographic Notes," *CQ,* n.s. 19 (1969) 95–110.

18. F. Jacoby, "Die Attische Königslisten," *Klio* 2 (1902) 406–39, *Apollodors Chronik* (Berlin 1902), esp. 403–13; K. J. Beloch, *Gr. G.* I.2 (1926) 155–70; T. J. Cadoux, "The Athenian Archons from Creon to Hypsichides," *JHS* 68 (1948) 70–123; A. E. Samuel, "The Athenian Archon List," in *Greek and Roman Chron-*

ology (Munich 1972) 195–206.

19. M. Miller, "The Accepted Date for Solon," *Arethusa* 2 (1969) 62–86.

20. A. E. Samuel, *Greek and Roman Chronology* (Munich 1972) 243.

21. Chronographic work is attributed to Antiochus by R. von Compernolle, *Étude de chronologie et d'historiographie siciliotes* (Brussels 1959) 409 ff., and M. Miller, *The Sicilian Colony Dates* (Albany, N.Y. 1970) 68 ff. But see F. Jacoby, *FGrHist* 555 Komm., and K. von Fritz, *Die Griechische Geschichtsschreibung* I (Berlin 1967) 507–16.

22. Plutarch (*Solon* 11.1) cites Aristotle (fr. 572) for the list of Pythian victors. A Delphic inscription (*Syll.*³ 275) bestows praises on Aristotle and Callistenes (*FGrHist* 124 T 23) for drawing up the list. On Callisthenes and the chronology of the Sacred Wars see *FGrHist* 124 F 1 and Komm.

23. The testimonia are collected with commentary in F. R. Wehrli, *Die Schule des Aristoteles*, 2 vols. (Basel 1944, 1953). Cf. A. Momigliano, *The Development of Greek Biography* (Cambridge, Mass. 1971).

24. Ephorus' chronological pattern, at least for the very early portions of the work, proceeded on the basis of estimates expressed relatively in generations and synchronisms, not absolute dates or arithmetical expressions of the generational intervals. The number 735 represents the computation of Clement or his source on a base date of 335/34. It is therefore fruitless to speculate on how many generations the 735 years represented for Ephorus, since neither the interval nor the base date is necessarily his. Cf. Jacoby on F 223. We really know very little about Ephorus' chronology. The comments of G. L. Barber, *The Historian Ephorus* (Cambridge 1935) are inadequate, and the whole question demands fresh investigation.

25. In addition to the literature cited in n. 6, see the following: V. Costanzi, "L'Opera di Ellanico di Mitilene," *Riv. Stor. Ant.* 8 (1904) 343–53; C. F. Lehman-Haupt, "Chronologiches zur griechische Quellenkunde," *Klio* 6 (1906) 127–39; A. R. Burn, "Dates in Early Greek History," *JHS* 55 (1935) 130–46; K. von Fritz, "Herodotus and the Growth of Greek Historiography," *TAPA* 67 (1936) 315–40; T. Lenschau, "Agiaden und Eurypontiden," *RhM* 88 (1939) 123–46; L. Pearson, *Early Ionian Historians* (Oxford 1939); D. W. Prakken, "Herodotus and the Spartan kinglists," *TAPA* 71 (1940) 460–72, "The Boeotian Migration," *AJP* 64 (1943) 417–23, *Studies in Greek Genealogical Chronology* (Lancaster, Pa. 1943); A. R. Burn, "Early Greek Chronology," *JHS* 69 (1949) 70–73; F. Mitchel, "Herodotus' Use of Genealogical Chronology," *Phoenix* 10 (1956) 48–69; Robert Drews, "The Fall of Astyages and Herodotus' Chronology of the Eastern Kingdoms," *Historia* 18 (1969) 1–11; M. Miller, *The Sicilian Colony Dates* (Albany, N.Y. 1970), *The Thalassocracies* (Albany, N.Y. 1971); A. E. Samuel, *Greek and Roman Chronology* (Munich 1972): 241–45. The fundamental study is that of Eduard Meyer, "Herodots Chronologie der griechischen Sagengeschichte, mit Excursen zur Geschichte der griechischen Chronographie und Historiographie," *Forschungen zur alten Geschichte* I (Halle 1892) 151–88. Jacoby discusses genealogical chronology in *Apollodors Chronik* (Berlin 1902) 38–51.

26. The 40-year hypothesis is that of Meyer, "Herodots Chronologie." The calculation based on a 39-year period is that of M. Miller, "Herodotus as Chronographer," *Klio* 46 (1965) 109–28, who speculates that the equation 39 times 23 equals 897 used for the Heraclid genealogy here suggested to Herodotus the use of the 23-year period elsewhere—e.g., for the 22 Lydian Heraclids who ruled for 505 years.

27. M. Miller, *Klio* 46.

28. Ibid., p. 109.

29. Cf. W. den Boer, "Political Propaganda in Greek Chronology," *Historia* 5 (1956): 162–77.

30. See F. Mitchel, *Phoenix* 10 and M. Miller, *Klio* 46

31. Cf. K. von Fritz, *Gr. Geschichtsschr.*, 364 ff.

32. H. Kaletsch, "Zur lydischen Chronologie," *Historia* 7 (1958) 1–47, with bibliography.

33. The comments of C. G. Starr, "The Credibility of Early Spartan History," *Historia* 14 (1965) 263–64, bear repeating: "Herodotus shows us what sorts of inherited chronological indications the classic Greeks could really use. . . . Herodotus refused to be a guide back into the seventh century. This failure is really a mark of his good judgment that men's memories would not extend so far."

Notes to Chapter 3

1. R. van Compernolle, *Étude de chronologie et d'historiographie siciliotes* (Brussels 1959) 409 ff.; M. Miller, *The Sicilian Colony Dates* (Albany, N.Y. 1970) 68–116.

2. M. Miller, *The Thalassocracies* (Albany, N.Y. 1971), adduced many such constructions. Eusebius has a date for Hesiod in 767/66 (87^f Helm) which differs from all others attested. It results from contamination and combination in the tradition (below, chapter 6), but Miller's arithmetical constructions (p. 108) provide another kind of answer: Jerome dates the thalassocracy of Minos to 1250/49 and that of the Carians to 721/20. Thalassocracy dates "should" be based either on the fall of Eretria in 491/90 or on that of Chalcis in 506/5. The year 721/20 is not a "chronographic" number of years from either date. But the interval between Minos and the Carians is 529 = 23x23 years, while the date for Hesiod is 46 = 23x2 years before the Carian thalassocracy and therefore falls in the chronographic series. The required link to the fall of Chalcis is provided by adducing chronographic equations that show that the date for Hesiod in 767/6 is 261 = 27x9⅔ = 36x7¼ years before 506/5.

3. This is the hypothesis of Eduard Meyer, *Forschungen zur Alten Geschichte* I (Halle 1892–9) 160 ff. Cf. D. W. Prakken, *Studies in Greek Genealogical Chronology* (Lancaster, Pa. 1943) 22–24. For criticism of the thesis, characterized as a series of conjectures, see L. Pearson, *The Early Ionian Historians* (Oxford 1939) 106, and F. Mitchel, "Herodotus' Use of Genealogical Chronology," *Phoenix* 10 (1956) 64–66.

4. See Prakken, *Studies* 58 ff., and Mitchell, *Phoenix* 10, 52 f.

5. Hermann Diels, "Chronologische Untersuchungen über Apollodors Chronika," *RhM* 31 (1876) 1–60.

6. Felix Jacoby, *Apollodors Chronik*, Philologische Untersuchungen 16 (Berlin 1902). Long unobtainable in many American university libraries, the book has now been reprinted by Arno Press (New York 1973). Apollodorus' method is discussed pp. 39–59. Summary treatment appears in the commentary to *FGrHist* 244. In the following pages the fragments of Apollodorus are cited by reference to *FGrHist* 244. See also Eduard Schwartz, "Die Königslisten des Eratosthenes und Kastor," *AbhGött*, phil.-hist. Kl. 40.2 (1894–95) 1–96; Erwin Rohde, "Studien zur

Chronologie der griechisches Litteraturgeschichte," *RhM* 36 (1881) 380–434, 524–75, "Γέγονε in den Biographica des Suidas," *RhM* 33 (1878) 161–220, 620–22, 638, both studies reprinted in *Kleine Schriften* I (Leipzig 1901) 1–184.

7. For Apollodorus' secondary sources see F. Jacoby, *Apollodors Chronik* 51–57.

8. See chapter 14. Jacoby dated the epoch to 546/45.

9. See Hermann Strasburger, "Herodots Zeitrechnung," *Historia* 5 (1956) 129–61 and Hans Kaletsch, "Zur lydischen Chronologie," *Historia* 7 (1958) 1–47.

10. F. Jacoby, *Apollodors Chronik* 39–47. Although Apollodorus himself may not have used the word, *akmê* and its verbal derivatives are common in the extant texts. Since the publication of Diels' fundamental article, *acme* has become a technical term for the Apollodoran *floruit* at age 40.

11. See chapter 11 on the possible attribution to Phainias of Eresos of methodology similar to that of Apollodorus.

12. The Apollodoran acme is reported (although in a corrupt text) by the *Suda* on Socrates, citing Porphyry's *Historia Philosophica*.

13. See chapters 9 and 11.

14. See chapter 15.

15. On the date of Themistocles' death see *FGrHist* 244 F 342. Nepos, *Aristides* 3.3, dates Aristides' death to the fourth year after Themistocles' flight which, on the Apollodoran chronology, would be 468/67. That this was the year of Eurymedon for Apollodorus is a reasonable hypothesis (Jacoby, *Apollodors Chronik* 241). A date for Cimon's acme in that year would accord well with the tradition that he was a μειράκιον (Plutarch, *Cimon* 4.4) at the time of his father's death shortly after Marathon and the ill-fated Parian campaign. Simonides' death in Olympiad 78 (468/65) at the age of 89 is reported by the *Suda* s.v. That the same year marked the acme of his nephew Bacchylides is suggested by the notice of Eusebius entering the *floruit* of Bacchylides and Diagoras in that year (110ᵇ Helm). For Diagoras the date was originally that of his birth in the Apollodoran system. See F. Jacoby, *Diagoras ὁ Ἄθεος*, *AbhBerl*, Sprach, Lit., u. Kunst, 1959, no. 3, and L. Woodbury, "The Date and Atheism of Diagoras of Melos," *Phoenix* 19 (1965) 178–211. The date is also associated with Herodotus (Eusebius 110ᵃ Helm) and Panyassis (the *Suda* s.v.), but these are not Apollodoran.

16. On the tragedians see chapter 17. On the historians see *FGrHist* 244 F 7 Komm. and, for a somewhat different argument about the genesis of Apollodorus' computations, A. A. Mosshammer, "The Apollodoran Akmai of Hellanicus and Herodotus," *GRBS* 14 (1973) 5–13.

17. Jacoby comments on the "half-acme" in general, *Apollodors Chronik* 48. He finds evidence for its use in the chronology of Aristophanes (p. 301) and of Menander (p. 361). In both instances the argument rests on highly corrupt texts, and in Menander's case Jacoby's reconstruction actually implies an age for "ersten auftreten" of 21, inclusively counted.

18. The case is presented in "Geometrical Proportion and the Chronological Method of Apollodorus," *TAPA* 106 (1976) 291–306. What follows is a summary of the most salient points. See also chapters 15, 16, and 17.

19. The *Suda*'s date in Olympiad 70 is not Apollodoran, but a combination of the age for first presentation with the date for Aeschylus' birth attested by the *Marmor Parium*. Cf. chapter 17.

20. The theory of proportionals underlies not only Pythagorean geometry, but also harmonics and cosmology, leading to the mystical equation of numbers with the essences of reality. See Thomas Heath, *A History of Greek Mathematics* I

(Oxford 1921) 84–90, and Paul-Henri Michel, *De Pythagore à Euclide* (Paris 1950) 365–411.

21. See fr. 1–9 Wehrli and Komm.

22. Iamblichus, *vit. Pyth.* 11; Theophrastus *apud* Simplicium DK 12 A 9, 13 A 5.

23. See chapters 9 and 11.

24. Even Jacoby sometimes "nods." The Apollodoran intervals reported for Herodotus (*FGrHist* 244 F 7b) lead to an acme in 445/44, not to the "epoch of Thurii" in 444/43. See *GRBS* 14 (1973) 5–13.

25. The 39-year generation as a component of chronographic equations based on 23, 27, 36, and 39 is the hypothesis of M. Miller, first reported by A. R. Burn, "Early Greek Chronology," *JHS* 69 (1949) 70–73. Miller's work has since been published. See especially "Herodotus as Chronographer," *Klio* 46 (1965) 109–28; "The Herodotean Croesus," *Klio* 41 (1963) 58–94; *The Sicilian Colony Dates* (Albany, N.Y. 1970); and *The Thalassocracies* (Albany, N.Y. 1971).

Notes to Chapter 4

1. A. A. Mosshammer, "The Archonship of Themistocles in the Chronographic Tradition," *Hermes* 103 (1975) 222–34.

2. See chapter 5.

3. Atthidography is cited by the late authors as οἱ τὰ ᾿Αττικὰ συγγραψάμενοι (Clement, *Strom.* I. 104.2); ῾Ελλάνικός τε καὶ Φιλόχορος οἱ τὰς ᾿Ατθίδας ἱστοροῦντες (Eusebius *P.E.* 10.10.8); and ἡ ᾿Αττικὴ χρονογραφία (Eusebius, *P.E.* 10.10.7). Eusebius' Pisistratid entries are not included in this collection of studies, because they have little to contribute to our understanding of Greek chronographic method or to the solution of the historical problem. They are of interest, however, as a testament to the some-times very poor health of the late tradition. The first notice appears at a year (562/61, p. 102ᵉ Helm), which suggests that the original reference of the entry was the archonship of Comeas (561/60), when Pisistratus first seized power. But the notice says that Pisistratus in that year made a crossing into Italy! No such voyage is known, and the only reasonable (but unprovable) hypothesis is that the entry is somehow a reference to the flight to Eretria, perhaps having been confused in transmission with *Etruria* and then broadened to *Italia*. The second notice appears at a date (542/41, p. 103ᵐ Helm) whose original reference must have been Pisistratus' return from second exile and hence his third and final seizure of the tyranny. But the entry says he became tyrant for the second time. Hippias and Hipparchus are entered as joint tyrants at the year of Pisistratus' death (528/27, p. 104ᵏ Helm), showing that Thucydides' insistence that Hippias was the tyrant could not win the allegiance of the tradition over the vulgate. Like-wise, Hipparchus is named as tyrant in the entry on Harmodius and Aristogiton (106ᵃ Helm). The notice appears at 520/19, much too early, artificially synchro-nized with the epochal year of Israel's liberation. It is a violation of the tradition underlying Eusebius' notices to suggest, as Beloch does (*Gr. G.* I.2 [1926] 289ff), that Eusebius alone, by stating that Pisistratus ruled for the second time in the 540s, preserves a remnant both of the genuine Atthidographic tradition and of the truth.

4. See chapter 9.

5. Castor dealt with the mythical period, and the Sicyonian, Argive, and Athenian lists were therefore appropriate references. The Athenian list overlaps with the beginning of the Olympiads, and Castor could switch to Olympiads without having to deal with the early kings of Sparta, Corinth, or Macedonia. The old hypothesis that Castor was Diodorus' chronological source has been abandoned (Jacoby, *FGrHist* 250 Komm.). On the problems associated with Eusebius' version of the Diodoran lists see chapter 5.

6. Eusebii Praefatio (8 Helm): *in priori libello quasi quandam materiam futuro operi omnium mihi regum tempora praenotaui.* Cf. Syncellus 122: ἔνθεν ὁρμηθεὶς ἐν μὲν τῇ πρὸ ταύτης συντάξει ὕλας ἐκπορίζων ἐμαυτῷ χρόνων ἀναγραφὰς συνελεξάμην παντοίας.

7. Eusebius, *Eclogae Propheticae* 1.27: χρονικοὺς συντάξαντες κανόνας ἐπιτομήν τε τούτοις παντοδαπῆς ἱστορίας Ἑλλήνων τε καὶ βαρβάρων ἀντιπαραθέντες.

8. Cf. Rudolf Helm, "De Eusebii in Chronicorum libro Auctoribus," *Eranos* 22 (1924) 1–40.

9. Photius, *Bibliotheca* cod. 34. Compare Syncellus 614, where it is stated that the Resurrection took place in the year 5531 and that there are 192 years from the Resurrection to Olympiad 250 (A.D. 221).

10. Fragments from the third book deal with events before Olympiad 1, and Syncellus (197) cites the third book for the synchronism of the first Olympiad with the first year of Ahaz. Syncellus then cites the fourth book for the same synchronism, but the passage suggests that Africanus was making a cross-reference to his own earlier statement (ᾧ συντρέχειν ἀπεδείξαμεν τὴν πρώτην Ὀλυμπιάδα). There are no other citations of the fourth book. Fragments of the fifth book deal with the interpretation of Daniel's hebdomads, with the career of Herod the Great, and with the crucifixion. H. Gelzer, *Sextus Julius Africanus* (Leipzig 1880) 26–29, considers the first Olympiad the beginning of the fourth book and Alexander's conquest of Persia the end. An event more closely connected with sacred history is a likelier beginning; and the First Captivity, which Eusebius dates to 747, is a good candidate. Alexander's conquest of Persia is the first event mentioned in *Maccabees* and would therefore have been an appropriate division of books for Africanus.

11. In the Armenian version there is a column of years *ab Vrbe condita* entered by decades in the extreme left margin. Jerome does not enter this *filum*, and there is no way of knowing whether it was in the original.

12. The book number is cited only for the Assyrian list and nowhere else in the fragments of Castor. Since the Athenian, Argive, and Sicyonian lists overlap considerably with the Assyrian list (the Argive and Sicyonian are entirely included within the time span of the Assyrian), they must all have been in the same book. Eusebius also cites Castor for the list of Latin kings from Aeneas to Amulius Silvius (142 Karst). The pages that actually included the Roman lists are missing from the Armenian manuscript.

13. The *Suda* cites the *Historia Philosophica* for the date of Homer (*FGrHist* 260 F 19). Cyril cites the first book for information about the Seven Sages and Pythagoras, the third book for Socrates, and the fourth for Plato (*FGrHist* 260 F 5, 6, 8, 14). The *Suda* cites the work for information about Empedocles and Gorgias (*FGrHist* 260 F 22–23). This material can only have come from the

second book, which was therefore devoted to the history of philosophy between Pythagoras and Socrates.

14. On the side-by-side organization of the *spatium historicum* see chapter 1. The hypothesis that there was some correspondence between columns on the page and source books on the writer's table cannot be tested, since the original cannot be reconstructed.

15. Joseph Scaliger, *Thesaurus Temporum* (Leyden 1606, Amsterdam 1658) p. v: *Nihil enim luculentum, uetustum, excellens in eo est, quod non ex Africano deprompserit, cuiusmodi praestantissimum illud et numquam satis laudatum Dynastiarum Aegyptiarum monumentum, reges Assyriae, Stadionicae, reges Sicyonii, Argiuorum, Atheniensium, et alia multa, quae in priorem librum Chronologiae suae contulit.*

16. E.g., E. J. Bickerman, *Chronology of the Ancient World* (London 1968) 91.

17. Heinrich Gelzer, *Sextus Julius Africanus und die byzantinische Chronographie* 2 vols. (Leipzig 1880, 1898) I 161–62. Syncellus (614) says Africanus' work went to the 250th Olympiad. The chronographic Roman year would have been identified as Olympiad 250 even before the celebration of the festival.

18. H. Gelzer, *Sextus Julius Africanus,* suggested (II, 80) that because Eusebius wrote for Christians who were thoroughly familiar with the work of Africanus "hat er nicht nöthig, dieses *expressis verbis* als Quelle zu nennen."

19. E. Schwartz, "Eusebius," *RE* 6 (1907) 1378; *Griechische Geschichtschreiber* (Leipzig 1959) 507.

20. Editorial titles, some deriving from the eighteenth-century copies and some from the modern editor, significantly alter the appearance of the note in the Schoene-Petermann edition. On the manuscript evidence see Karst, p. 262 n. 216.

21. E. Schwartz, *RE* 6, 507. Schwartz therefore was forced to deny the usual identification of Minucius' Cassius with Cassius Hemina.

22. F. Jacoby, *FGrHist* 259 Komm., made this identification and suggested that the chronicle of Porphyry was a continuation of his master's unfinished work. Jacoby did not, however, consider the possible implications for the authorship of Eusebius' Olympic victor list. He shared the general opinion in assigning it to Africanus (*FGrHist* 3b Komm., p. 223, in the introduction to the section "Elis und Olympia"). Gelzer, *Sextus Julius Africanus* II, 24, considered the possibility that Eusebius used Longinus or Phlegon as a control on the list excerpted from Africanus.

23. See Aulitzky, "Longinus," *RE* 26 (1927) 1401–15, and Heinrich Dörrie, "Longinus," *Kleine Pauly* 3 (1969) 731–32.

24. Syncellus 197: Ὁ δὲ Ἀφρικανὸς ἐν τῷ τρίτῳ λόγῳ τῶν Ἱστορικῶν γράφει. Ἀναγραφῆναι δὲ πρώτην τὴν τεσσαρεσκαιδεκάτην (Ὀλυμπιάδα), ἡνίκα καὶ Κόροιβος στάδιον ἐνίκα τότε ἐβασίλευσεν Ἄχαζ ἐπὶ Ἱερουσαλὴμ ἔτος πρῶτον.

25. See H. Gelzer, *Sextus Julius Africanus* I, 162.

26. Cf. A. E. Samuel, *Greek and Roman Chronology* (Munich 1972) 194 n. 2. Samuel points out that Eusebius, for example, dates the murder of Caesar to the Ides of March in Olympiad 184. Olympiad 184 began in 44 B.C., but the actual celebration of the 184th Olympiad did not take place until after the murder of Caesar.

27. Cf. Eusebius, 174d Helm, and Jacoby on *FGrHist* 256 F 1. For the eclipse, see Theodor Oppolzer, *Canon of Eclipses* (Dover ed. 1962) #2957.

28. F. Jacoby in the ap. crit. to *FGrHist* 259 (Cassius Longinus) cites a letter from Karst to this effect.

29. An Arabic source cites the *Chronicle* in a Syriac exemplar for the fact that Thales was the first of the Seven Sages (*FGrHist* 260 F 1). Another Arabic source cites a Syriac exemplar of the *Historia Philosophica* for the same fact (F 1c).

30. Cf. F. Jacoby, *FGrHist* 260 Komm.

31. Eusebius extracts material from Abydenus, Castor, Diodorus, and Cephalion, then presents a list that he says comes from "the most reliable books." The entire list cannot come from Porphyry, who began with the fall of Troy. Eusebius apparently tried to strike a compromise between his two main authorities—Castor and a slightly different version of the later portion of the list that Porphyry said he got from Castor. The synchronism between Teutamus and the fall of Troy derives from Ctesias (Diodorus 2.21.8, 2.22.2).

32. Eusebius says (143 Karst) that he will present a list of emperors together with the eponym (consul) and Olympiad dates of their accession. The Armenian manuscript ends at this point, and the list is not preserved.

33. Cf. Syncellus 616, where he says that Africanus was true to the apostolic tradition in dating the Incarnation to 5500, but that he erred by two years in dating the Passion and Resurrection to 5531.

34. H. Gelzer, *Sextus Julius Africanus.*

35. On this hypothesis, see chapter 1.

36. The fragments are collected in Migne, *Patrologiae Cursus Completus, Series Graeco-Latin,* vol. 10, 63 ff., and Routh, *Reliquiae Sacrae,* II^2 230 ff.

37. See n. 15.

38. R. Helm, "De Eusebii in Chronicorum libro auctoribus," *Eranos* 22 (1924) 39–40.

39. For example, the notice on Prometheus (35^e Helm): *Secundum quorundam opinionem his temporibus fuit Prometheus, a quo homines factos esse commemorant.* At *P.E.* 1.10.23 Eusebius quotes Africanus as having dated Prometheus 94 years later than Ogyges, whom Eusebius in the *Canons* enters 94 years before Prometheus (30^k Helm).

40. For the evidence, see Helm, *Eranos* 22 (1924) 1–40. Either Eusebius used Africanus for this period or he and Africanus both used the same epitome of Josephus.

41. The text is that of Alfred Schoene, *Eusebi Chronicorum* (Berlin 1875, Zurich 1967) I, App. vi. 207–8.

42. H. Gelzer, *Sextus Julius Africanus* 177.

43. These comments do not, of course, dispose of the *Excerpta Barbara* as a witness to Africanus once and for all. We must, however, reject the facile notion that the *Excerpta,* wherever Africanus name appears, is for that entire folio wholly independent of Eusebius. Much of the argument presented here is necessarily negative. Fresh examination of what Africanus' work *did* look like is badly needed.

44. H. Gelzer, *Sextus Julius Africanus,* 180.

45. It is noteworthy that the one notice in this collection that can without hesitation be attributed to Africanus contains peculiar material. The causes of the Peloponnesian War, according to Africanus, were Aspasia's whores and the Megarian Decree. Africanus transmitted the popular gossip, but his sources do

not belong to the mainstream of the historiographic tradition. Eusebius simply notes *Initium belli Peloponnesiaci* (114ᵍ Helm).

46. Eratosthenes, *FGrHist* 241 F 1 (Clement, *Strom.* 1.138.1–3).

47. Africanus, *Chronographiae*, bk. 5, quoted by Eusebius, *Demonstratio Euangelica* 8.2.50. The argument, briefly, is as follows: From the 20th year of Artaxerxes, the fourth year of the 83rd Olympiad (445/44), when Nehemiah began to refortify Jerusalem, to the second year of the 202nd Olympiad (30/31) when in the 16th year of Tiberius the Resurrection of Christ brought salvation to mankind is a period of 475 Julian years. These 475 years of 365¼ days each are approximately the equivalent of 490 Hebrew (lunar) years of 354 days each (365¼ times 475 is 173,483.75 days, while 490 times 354 is 173,460 days). Thus the 70 year-weeks (hebdomads) of Daniel are to be interpreted as 70 times 7 lunar years.

48. Africanus as cited by Eusebius, *Dem. Evang.* 8.2

49. Cf. Eusebius (St. Jerome 114ᶠ Helm) at Olympiad 86.4 (433/32): *Neemiam, qui muros Hierusalem construxit, consummasse opus XXXII anno Artaxerxis regis Persarum Ezras memorat. Si quis autem ab hoc tempore LXX hebdomadas a Danihelo scriptas numeret, quae faciunt annos CCCCXC, repperiet eas in regno Neronis expletas, sub quo obsideri Hierusalem coepta secundo postea Vespasiani anno capitur.* Eusebius disagreed with Africanus in the interpretation of the seventy hebdomads. For Eusebius the period of 490 Julian years began with the completion of Nehemiah's walls in 433/32, and not with the beginning of the work in 445/44. Thus, even for sacred history Africanus was not Eusebius' principal source.

50. The synchronism is preserved by the grammarian Leo (Cramer II, 261.23) and by Cedrenus 91d, 97b. The fragments are discussed by Gelzer, *Sextus Julius Africanus* 173.

51. For an example of this first source see Diogenes 2.2, for the second 1.101, and for the third 1.98. On the relationship between Apollodorus and Sosicrates, see R. Laqueur, "Sosikrates," *RE* 52 (1927) 1160–65.

52. On Nepos' chronicle as the intermediary between Apollodorus and the Latin sources see Erwin Rohde, "Studien zur Chronologie der griechischen Litteraturgeschichte," *RhM* 36 (1881) 535; *Kleine Schriften* I (Leipzig 1901) 70; and Felix Jacoby, *Apollodors Chronik* (Berlin 1902) 31–38, where he discusses the Apollodoran influence on the later tradition in general.

53. See chapter 9. Additional examples are discussed in detail throughout Part 2.

54. On this famous case, see chapter 14.

55. See Erwin Rohde, "Γέγονε in dem Biographica des Suidas," *RhM* 33 [1878] 161–220; *Kleine Schriften* I (Leipzig 1901) 114–79. Rohde counts 6 certain and 4 probable uses of γέγονε in the sense of *natus est* (e.g., in the notices of the *Suda* for Homer, Pittacus, Simonides, Pindar, Democritus). He notes 88 sure and 17 probable uses in the sense of *floruit*. He also suggests that in the cases of Solon and Sosiphanes there is a possibility that a date which originally referred to the time of death has been expressed with a γέγονε. Apollodorus did not use γέγονε, ἤκμαζεν, or any of their synonyms. He gave archon year, event, and age. Expressions like ἤκμαζεν and γέγονε came into use when the chronicle was excerpted and circulated in the form of synchronistic epitomes with the dates converted to the Olympiad system.

56. See chapter 5.

57. On the dates of the Messenian War see chapter 8; on Archilochus and Hipponax, chapter 9.

58. See chapter 10.

Notes to Chapter 5

1. See especially Censorinus, *de die natali* 21. 1–2, where he distinguishes three chronological periods: the *tempus adelon* from the beginnings of man to the cataclysm, the *tempus mythicon* from the cataclysm to the first Olympiad, and the *tempus historicon*, beginning with the first Olympiad. The *tempus mythicon* closes, he says, with the slightly more than 400 years between the fall of Troy and the first Olympiad, years *quos solos, quamuis mythici temporis postremos, tamen quia a memoria scriptorum proximos, quidam certius definire uoluerunt.* Cf. the comment of Eusebius at the epoch of the first Olympiad (86ᵈ Helm): *Ab hoc tempore Graeca de temporibus historia uera creditur. Nam ante hoc, ut cuique uisum est, diuersas sententias protulerunt.*

2. Clement's excerpt cites an interval of 297 years between the προηγούμενον ἔτος τῶν πρώτων Ὀλυμπιάδων and the diabasis of Xerxes. The interval of 48 years between the diabasis of Xerxes (480/79) and the beginning of the Peloponnesian War (432/31) shows that the intervals are reckoned exclusively. The 297 years thus imply the date 777/76 and Clement's phrase is a reference to the year preceding the beginning of the Olympiad system. This distinction between the first Olympiad and a chronographic epoch in the year preceding is often misunderstood. (e.g., by Porphyry in the passage cited in the text). Eratosthenes made the distinction for two reasons. The first Olympiad marked the beginning of the historical period and the preceding year therefore marked the end of the mythical period. That an epoch should be chosen for the end of a period seems odd. But the chronographers had to reconstruct the mythical period, working backwards. Thus the year before the first Olympiad is the beginning of the mythical period for purposes of counting backwards from Olympiad One. The second reason for the distinction is that the chronographic Olympic year began after the actual celebration of the games and often had to be equated with calendar years beginning in the fall. Thus all the heraldry leading to the festival celebration takes place in the chronographic year before the one to which the Olympiad gives its number.

3. See chapter 4.

4. The reasons for this two-year shift, as well as other discrepancies in Eusebius' Lacedaemonian list, are discussed later in chapter 5 in connection with the third entry on Lycurgus.

5. F. Jacoby, *Apollodors Chronik* 80–91.

6. The reasons for this divergence from an otherwise uniform tradition are discussed by W. den Boer, "Political Propaganda in Greek Chronology," *Historia* 5 (1956) 162–77.

7. F. Jacoby, *Apollodors Chronik* 108–18. The 18-year regency is specifically attested by the *Suda*'s article on Lycurgus.

8. The *Macrobioi* reports an 85-year life span for Anacreon, Carneades, Hellanicus, Pherecydes, and Stesichorus, as well as for Lycurgus.

9. See chapter 2.

10. An interesting discussion of such problems appears as Part 1 of W. den Boer's *Laconian Studies* (Amsterdam 1954): "The Struggle for the Chronological Pattern," pp. 3–150.

11. F. Jacoby, *Apollodors Chronik* 114–15, 123–24.

12. See also W. den Boer, *Laconian Studies* 120–21.

13. H. Gelzer, *Sextus Julius Africanus* I, 176.

14. See chapter 4.

15. In Jacoby's reconstruction of the Assyrian list of Castor (*FGrHist* 250 F 1) the reign of Sardanapallus begins in 882 and Jacoby accordingly comments on the synchronism with Lycurgus that it derives from the Eratosthenic date. In commenting on the Athenian list, however (*FGrHist* 250 F 4), Jacoby says that the synchronism with Thespieus is an interpolation from Africanus.

16. Dindorf (p. 349) interpreted the text as meaning that the synchronism between Lycurgus and Alcamenes was to be found in Apollodorus' eighth book. Angelo Mai suggested the correct emendation in his edition of the *Chronicle* of Eusebius (II, 317). Cf. F. Jacoby, *Apollodors Chronik* 127 n. 13.

17. F. Jacoby, *Apollodors Chronik* 80–91.

18. E. Schwartz, "Die Königslisten des Eratosthenes und Kastor," *AbhGött.* phil.-hist. Kl. 40.2 (1894–95) 1–96.

19. Clement, *Strom.* 1.139 = Ephorus *FGrHist* 70 F 223: 735 years before the diabasis of Alexander in the archonship of Euaenetus (335/34).

20. For a different approach to the problem see W. G. Forrest, "Two Chronographic Notes," *CQ*, n.s. 19 (1969) 95–110. Forrest suggests that the Diodoran lists and the synchronism between the first Olympiad and the tenth year of Alcamenes and Theopompus are Ephoran, while the lists of the *Canons* are Apollodoran. For Jacoby's reconstruction see *Apollodors Chronik* 80–97.

21. Eusebius (87ᵏ Helm): 350 years from the beginning of the kingship (1103) to the establishment of the ephorate. cf. Jacoby, *Apollodors Chronik* 138–42.

22. E. Schwartz, "Königslisten" 67.

23. F. Jacoby, *Apollodors Chronik* 138–42.

24. See chapter 2 for the argument that there never existed a list of ephors reaching back to the eighth century.

25. F. Jacoby, *Apollodors Chronik* 122–27.

26. F. Kiechle, *Lakonien und Sparta, Vestigia* 5 (Munich 1963) 227–32.

27. See above, n. 24.

28. The arguments for a Greek redaction underlying Syncellus and the Armenian version are presented in chapter 1.

29. This conclusion is similar to Jacoby's (confusion between two Lycurgi, together with textual corruption), but it is based on entirely different arguments. F. Jacoby, *Apollodors Chronik* 126–27, attempted to account for a date expressed as the 18th year of Alcamenes, while the hypothesis offered here accounts for a date expressed as an interval and converted by Eusbius to an absolute date corresponding to 796 B.C.

Notes to Chapter 6

1. E.g., Jerome (77ᶜ Helm) at the year 914: *In Latina historica haec ad verbum scripta repperimus: Agrippa aput Latinos regnante Homerus poeta in Graecia*

claruit, ut testantur Apollodorus grammaticus et Euforbus historicus ante urbem Romam conditam •ann• CXXIIII• et, ut ait Cornelius Nepos, ante olympiadem primam •ann• C. Jacoby discusses the problematic notice (one of Jerome's Roman addenda), *Apollodors Chronik* 105–6, and *FGrHist* 244 F 63 Komm.

2. See chapter 5 for the argument interpreting 885/84 as the Apollodoran acme of Lycurgus rather than, with Jacoby, dating the acme to 914/13.

3. Solinus derives from Apollodorus through Nepos. On the date for Hesiod see Jacoby, *Apollodors Chronik* 118–21.

4. See Jacoby's discussion of Ephorus' fragments, especially *FGrHist* 70 F 1, 102 and of the *Marmor, FGrHist* 239 A 24, 28, 29.

5. This interpretation of Porphyry's date is similar to that of Erwin Rohde, "Studien zur Chronologie der griechischen Litteraturgeschichte," *RhM* 36 (1881) 380–434, 524–75 (*Kleine Schriften* I, 1–113, esp. 89–91). Rohde computed the intervals differently, however, attributing to Apollodorus a date for Hesiod in 806 and to Porphyry a date in 807. Eusebius' 809 (the correct date) he considered a "geringe verschiebung."

6. For Sosibian chronology in the sources of Eusebius see chapter 8. Rohde discusses Sosibius' version of the Homer-Lycurgus synchronism in *Kleine Schriften* I, 59–61.

7. Such an argument is presented by Molly Miller, *The Thalassocracies* 108–9. Miller believes that chronographic dates are mathematical expressions of generations and fractions of generations computed at 23, 27, or 39 years from appropriate base dates. The date for Hesiod in 767/66, on this theory, is "261 = 27 x 9⅔ = 36 x 7¼ years before 506/5, the year of the fall of Chalkis to Athens and of the beginning of the Eretrian thalassocracy." The year also falls on Miller's 23-year periodization of thalassocracies from that of Minos in 1250/49 to the Carian in 721/20.

Notes to Chapter 7

1. In Jerome's version the notice on Eumelus in the ninth Olympiad is combined with that on the Erythrean Sibyl, but there is no evidence that such a synchronism ever existed in the tradition. The Armenian version enters the notices separately. There must have been two separate notices in Eusebius' original, entered side by side in the *spatium historicum*.

2. See E. Rohde, *Kleine Schriften* I, 127, with reference to other suggestions.

3. See above, n. 1 of chapter 5.

4. On the synchronism between Eumelus and the First Messenian War, cf. T. J. Dunbabin, "The Early History of Corinth," *JHS* 68 (1948) 59–69, especially p. 67.

5. Eusebius also has a date for the epic poet Cinaethon in the 4th Olympiad (764/63): *Cinaethon Lacedaemonius poeta, qui Telegoniam scripsit, agnoscitur* (87ᵍ Helm). Very little is known of Cinaethon, except that his name was associated with cyclic epic and some authorities (e.g., Pausanias 2.3.7) considered him Lacedaemonian. Only Eusebius preserves a date for him, and it happens to be forty years (one "literary generation") before Sosibius' date for the end of the First Messenian War. The interval may be significant, but there is no evi-

dence to prove it. On the Sosibian chronology for the Messenian Wars see chapter 8.

6. Apollodorus' dates for the Messenian Wars are discussed in chapter 8.

Notes to Chapter 8

1. On the hopelessly complex problem surrounding the chronology of the Messenian wars, necessarily oversimplified here, see in addition to Jacoby's discussion in *Apollodors Chronik* 128–37, E. Schwartz, *Hermes* 34 (1899) 429 ff. and *Philologus* 92 (1937) 19 ff.; J. Kroymann, *Sparta und Messenien*, *NPhU* 11 (1937) and *Pausanias und Rhianos* (Berlin 1943); F. Jacoby, *FGrHist* 265 Komm. (Rhianos); F. Kiechle, *Messenische Studien* (Diss. Erlangen 1957); H. T. Wade-Gery, "The 'Rhianos-Hypothesis,'" in *Ancient Society and Institutions: Studies presented to V. Ehrenberg* (Oxford 1966) 289 ff.

2. The attribution of these dates to Sosibius is discussed by Jacoby, *Apollodors Chronik* 128–32.

3. F. Jacoby, *Apollodors Chronik* 129.

4. Ibid., n. 7.

5. Ibid., p. 131.

6. We do not know the exact dates of Sosibius, but he seems to have been an older contemporary of Apollodorus. See F. Jacoby, *FGrHist* 595 Komm.

Notes to Chapter 9

1. A third date in 682/81 was known to the author of the *Marmor Parium*, if it is correct that some reference to Archilochus appeared in ep. 33. See Felix Jacoby, *Das Marmor Parium* (Berlin 1904) 50, and *FGrHist* 239 A 33 Komm. The date is not related to either of those under discussion in this chapter and it does not seem appropriate to argue the authority or rationale of a date whose very existence is in doubt. On the problem of the date of Archilochus in general, see especially A. Blakeway, "The Date of Archilochus," *Greek Poetry and Life: Essays to G. Murray* (Oxford 1936) 33–58; F. Jacoby, "The Date of Archilochus," *CQ* 35 (1941) 97–109; G. Tarditi, "In margine alla cronologia di Archiloco," *RFIC* 87 (1959) 113–18; M. Treu, *RE* Suppl. XI (1968) 136–49; Peter Green, *The Shadow of the Parthenon* (Berkeley 1972) 268–75.

2. The synchronism between Gyges and Archilochus at Herodotus 1.12 has been rejected by some editors (e.g., Wesseling, Stein) on linguistic grounds. Jacoby (*Apollodors Chronik* 143 n. 2) defends the passage. Both sides seem to be right. Herodotus mentioned Archilochus in the passage but the phrase ἐν ἰάμβῳ τριμέτρῳ and perhaps even the synchronism per se, κατὰ τὸν αὐτὸν χρόνον γενόμενος are a later interpolation. Oenamaus (*ap.* Eusebius, *Praep. Euang.* 6.7–8) associates Archilochus with the colonization of Thasos, but the Delphic injunction to the Parians that he quotes there is addressed to Archilochus' father, Telesicles. The date of the foundation of Thasos was not known on independent evidence, but was synchronized with Archilochus and through him with Gyges. Hence, as von Gutschmid pointed out (cited by

Rohde, *Kl. Schr.* I, 151), the dates vary in accordance with the different versions of Lydian chronology. Dionysius' 15th Olympiad (720/17) is an inference from Herodotus' 170 Mermnad years if the year corresponding to 547/46 was used as a starting point for exclusive count. On Lydian chronology, both literary (chrono-graphic) and historical, see Hans Kaletsch, "Zur lydischen Chronologie," *Historia* 7 (1958) 1–47, and the bibliography cited there.

3. E. Rohde (*Kl. Schr.* I, 95, 154) suggested that the 500 years is a rounded approximation for an original 496. He maintained that Olympiad 23 is a date chosen for Archilochus because it fell approximately in the middle of Gyges' reign. Clearly, it is the 500-year interval that was original, deriving from Theopompus, not the Olympiad date. That the 23rd Olympiad is approximately the middle of Gyges' reign in the Lydian *filum* of Eusebius is coincidence.

4. On the false synchronism see F. Jacoby, *Apollodors Chronik* 146–47.

5. Cf. Clement, *Strom.* 1.131. The article of the *Suda* for Simonides of Amorgus dates him ϰαὶ αὐτός 490 years after the Trojan war. The phrase suggests a synchronism and, as Rohde points out (*Kl. Schr.* I, 96), the synchronism must be with Archilochus. Unfortunately, the *Suda* does not have an article on Archilochus. The date of the sources both for Simonides and Archilochus was probably Olympiad 23, as the following considerations show. The *Suda* (s.v. Simmias of Rhodes) dates the foundation of Amorgos 406 years after the Trojan war. The foundation date of Amorgos was derived through synchronism with Simonides, as was the date of Thasos through synchronism with Archilochus and Gyges. The 490 years for Simonides and the 406 years for Amorgos suggest that 496 was the original reading in the sources for both notices. The 496 years reckoned correctly from Eratosthenes' epoch produce the date in the 23rd Olympiad. That is, the authors of this material recognized the discrepancy between the 500-year interval and the Olympiad date for Archilochus. They "corrected" the interval instead of the Olympiad number. Rohde argued that 496 was the original interval, but see n. 3 above.

6. E. Rohde, *Kl. Schr.* I, 154 (*RhM* 33 [1878] and 96 (*RhM* 36 [1881]).

7. F. Jacoby, *Apollodors Chronik* 142–50; "The Date of Archilochus," *CQ* 35 (1941) 97–109. Cf. *FGrHist* 244 F 336, Komm: "wie er gerade auf 664 kam weiss ich nicht."

8. On the historical date for the Cimmerian attack, Archilochus, and Gyges see Kaletsch, *Historia* 7 (1958) 25–30. Kaletsch argues for 645 as the true date of the attack on Sardis. The synchronism between Gyges and Archilochus is correct, because Gyges too fell victim to the Cimmerians. Kaletsch fixes the date of his fall at 652. Since the eclipse mentioned by Archilochus (fr. 74 Diehl) is that of the year 648, all is in order. But it must be noted that Kaletsch, in fixing the death of Gyges seven years before the Cimmerian attack on Sardis, is using the "7th year of Ardys," which he supposes to have been a chronographic epoch. The 7th year of Adrys as a date for the Cimmerian invasion is a modern inference from the chronographic evidence and we cannot be sure that the chronographers themselves made precisely that association. Even if they did, it should not be taken as primary historical evidence. On this "epoch" see chapter 10.

Notes to Chapter 10

1. On the importance of the lost *Chronicle* of Nepos as the intermediary be-

tween Apollodorus and the Latin authors, see Jacoby, *Apollodors Chronik* 34.

2. For the reconstruction of the passage see Mommsen, *RhM* 15 (1860) 167 (*Ges. Schr.* VII, 41); Rohde, *RhM* 36 (1881) 569 (*Kl. Schr.* I, 106); Jacoby, *Apollodors Chronik* 196, *FGrHist* 244 F 337.

3. *Kleine Schriften* I, 155–58.

4. Cf. F. Jacoby, *Apollodors Chronik* 196–200.

5. E. Rohde, *Kl. Schr.* I, 114–84, found six certain and four possible uses of γέγονε in the sense of *natus est* (e.g., in the notices of the *Suda* for Homer, Pittacus, Simonides, Pindar, Democritus), as opposed to eighty-eight certain and seventeen probable uses in the sense of *floruit*. He also noted that in the case of Solon and Sosiphanes there is a possibility that a date originally referring to the death of a person was transmitted as a γέγονε. In all of these cases the authors of the *Suda*, like Eusebius' Olympiad chronicler, understood the γέγονε as a *floruit*. The fault lies with the excerptors and not with Eusebius or the authors of the *Suda*.

6. E. Rohde, *Kl. Schr.* I, 157. Eusebius' notice mentions both Alcman and Lesches. In Jerome, Alcman is named first. In the Armenian version the order is reversed. This difference suggests that in the original separate notices for Alcman and Lesches were entered side by side at approximately the same date. Ἀλκμαίων, the reading attested by all versions, is simply another form of the name (cf. Clinton, *Fasti Hellenici* I, 216).

7. E. Meyer, *GdA* I, 545, accepted by Hogarth, *CAH* III, 507. Cf. Kaletsch, "Zur lydischen Chronologie," *Historia* 7 (1958) 27. Kaletsch has reservations about the "chronographic epoch," but takes the seventh year of Ardys as correct for the Cimmerian attack on Sardis.

8. H. T. Wade-Gery, "A Note on the Origin of the Spartan Gymnopaidiai," *CQ* 43 (1949) 79–81. Cf. G. L. Huxley, *Early Sparta* (London 1962) 54.

Notes to Chapter 11

1. F. Jacoby, *Apollodors Chronik* 148.

2. In the versions of both Jerome and the Armenian translator, Alcman and Lesches are entered together in a single notice. But Alcman appears first in the Latin version, while Lesches appears first in the Armenian version and in the excerpts of Syncellus (p. 402). This difference in the order suggests that Eusebius had originally entered two separate notices, side by side at approximately the same year without intending any more purposeful synchronism to be read. The treatment offered here is accordingly predicated on the conclusion that in Eusebius' source there were discrete notices for the two poets.

3. On the dates for Arctinus, see chapter 7.

4. H. Gelzer, "Das Zeitalter des Gyges," *RhM* 30 (1875) 253–54. Unger, *Abh.bayr.* 17 (1885) 530. See the apparatus to the *GCS* edition of Clement (Berlin, 1960).

5. For more detailed argument on this puzzling passage, see "Phainias of Eresos and Chronology," *California Studies in Classical Antiquity* 10 (1977) 105–132.

6. R. Laqueur, *RE* 19 (1938) 1565–91 ("Phainias") emphasizes Phainias' role

in the development of Greek biography through a detailed study of comments attributed to him in Plutarch's lives of Themistocles and Solon. A. Momigliano, *The Development of Greek Biography* (Cambridge, Mass., 1971) 77–78, expresses skepticism and is willing to attribute biography, properly so called, only to Aristoxenus among the Peripatetics.

7. M. Miller, *The Thalassocracies* (Albany, N.Y. 1971) 109–10, in discussing the dates of Terpander associates them with the tradition (Plutarch, *de mus.* 1132e) that Terpander won four Pythian victories. Miller takes the entries of Jerome and Syncellus (402 and 403) as attesting to different Eusebian dates for Terpander and associates them with Pythian victories in 650, 642, and 634. The musical revolution dated by the *Marmor* to 644 thus falls between the first two victories. Such argumentation is based on a wrong understanding of the Eusebian texts. Jerome, the Armenian version, and Syncellus attest in different ways to the same original *Chronicle*.

8. E. Rohde, *Kl. Schr.* I, 156–57.

9. See chapter 12.

10. That we should read Olympiad 39, instead of 29, in the text of Solinus was suggested long ago by Henry Clinton, *Fasti Hellenici* I (Oxford 1834) 193. For Apollodoran influence (through Nepos) on Solinus, see Jacoby, *Apollodors Chronik* 34. Jacoby does not discuss the date for Arion.

11. On the dates for Thales and the naming of the Seven Sages, see chapter 11. The date in Olympiad 50 (580/79) derives from an early, rough estimate to the effect that the era of the Seven Sages was about 100 years before the Persian Wars.

12. The temptation to attribute Eusebius' date for Alcman in the 30th Olympiad to Phainias and hence to validate Rohde's suggestion that the interval of forty years between the dates for Alcman and Arion is significant must be resisted. Although Phainias may well have generated dates for the famous poets of his homeland in the context of his "Prytanies" and even perhaps adduced a date for Archilochus as a *terminus post quem*, there is no evidence for attributing to him a systematic chronology of early Greek poetry more generally. The date of the Marmor, ep. 33, is not quite forty years before Phainias' date for Terpander. We must therefore also resist the temptation to supply Archilochus here and attribute the date to Phainias. It seems superfluous, in any case, to try to explain a date we do not know even to have existed. Cf. chapter 9, n. 1.

Notes to Chapter 12

1. K. J. Beloch, *Gr. G.* I², 2, pp. 274–84, E. Will, *Corinthiaka* (Paris 1955), 363–440, and most recently M. Miller, *Sicilian Colony Dates* (Albany, N.Y. 1970), 198–237.

2. See J. Ducat, "L'Archaïsme à la recherche de points de repère chronologiques," *BCH* 86 (1962) 165–84; M. Cataudella, "Erodoto e la cronologia dei Cipselidi," *Maia* 16 (1964) 219–25, J. Servais, "Hérodote et la chronologie des cypsélides," *AntCl.* 38 (1969) 28–81; and H. Berve, *Die Tyrannis bei den Griechen*, 2 vols. (Munich 1967) 13, 520. That the chronographers should be found in agreement with Herodotus is what one would expect, since Herodotus was for them, as for us, the most important source. On the difficulties of dating Corinthian pottery without reference to the chronographic dates see T. J. Dunbabin, *The*

Western Greeks (Oxford 1948) 435–71.

3. F. Jacoby, *Apollodors Chronik* 150–55.

4. See ibid., p. 32, and R. Laqueur, "Sosikrates, *RE* 52 (1927) 1160–65.

5. The list of scholars who support this punctuation is long and includes Petavius, Westermann, Clinton, Meyer, and Busolt. See especially H. Diels, "Chronologische Untersuchungen über Apollodors Chronika," *RhM* 31 (1876) 19–20. For the full list see F. Jacoby, *Apollodors Chronik* 151 n. 2.

6. On 547/46 as the correct date of Apollodorus' epoch of Croesus see chapter 14.

7. F. Jacoby, *Apollodors Chronik* 150–55; E. Schwartz, "Die Königslisten des Eratosthenes und Kastor," *AbhGött.*, phil.-hist. Kl. 40.2 (1894–95) 73 n. 1.

8. Th. Hirsch, Th. Roeper, *Philologus* 20 (1863) 722. Cf. Jacoby, *Apollodors Chronik* 152 n. 4, and Alois Dreizehnter, *Aristoteles' Politik* (Munich 1970). Servais (n. 2) 29–32 attempts to account for Periander's 44 years and Cypselus' 28 years (Eusebius) against the orthodox 40 and 30 by appealing to the differences between manners of counting regnal years. But the 44 and the 28 are not reported in conjunction with one another, so that this kind of explanation is inappropriate.

9. Solinus 7.14: *hoc spectaculum per Cypselum tyrannum intermissum Corinthii olympiade quadragesima nona solemnitati pristinae reddiderunt.*

10. M. Miller, *Sicilian Colony Dates* (Albany, N.Y. 1970) 209 hypothesizes that Periander and Psammetichus switched places and ruled simultaneously for three years—Periander in Corcyra, Psammetichus in Corinth. But in that case Periander, since he had a total of 44 years, would have survived the end of tyranny by six months—an odd way of counting regnal years.

11. Cf. F. Jacoby, *Apollodors Chronik* 155 n. 9. Jacoby seems to have reversed the situation. He implies that the chronographers dated the festival by reference to an already established date for the end of the tyranny.

12. *Marmor Parium*, *FGrHist* 239 A 38. On the date, see T. J. Cadoux, "The Athenian Archons from Creon to Hypsichides," *JHS* 68 (1948) 100.

13. Pindar, *Nem.* 6, 39–41; cf. *schol.* Pindar *Isthm.* 1, inscr. a.

14. Cf. above, nn. 1 and 2 for chapter 5.

15. As has already been indicated (above, n. 5), there is ample precedent for punctuating and interpreting the passage in this way. The argument does not depend entirely on this minute point, however. Alternatively one might hypothesize that the date that Diogenes excerpted from Sosicrates was in fact that to which Apollodorus dated the end of Periander's tyranny 41 years before Croesus. Diogenes or his immediate source understandably misinterpreted it as a date for his death. What is missing from the excerpt, then, to make the reference to the 49th Olympiad appropriate is a comment like that of Solinus to the effect that the Isthmian games were celebrated in the 49th Olympiad as a festival of liberation.

16. K. Beloch, *Gr. G.* I², 2, p. 275, refuses "dem Kopf zu verbrechen" over the origin of chronographic dates, but he takes the date of the first Isthmian celebration as historical (p. 279) and uses it in support of a low chronology for the Cypselids on the assumption that it was they who raised the festival to Panhellenic significance. Even if it were true (there is no evidence for it) that the Cypselids enhanced the Isthmian festival, which had supposedly been in existence since mythical times, the Corinthians, when they sought to erase the memory of the Cypselids, would have counted the first celebration of the modern free state as the first official festival. Cf. Berve (above, n. 2) 19, 25, 530.

17. M. Miller, *Sicilian Colony Dates* (Albany, N.Y. 1970) 217, suggests that the dates of Eusebius, 660–588, are those established by Callisthenes. Cypselus rules for 28 years, the reign of Periander begins in 632, and the end of his reign and beginning of Psammetichus' are synchronized with the fall of Cirrha in 591/90. But this theory leaves unexplained how the three years of Psammetichus were derived, and Miller is forced to admit that Callisthenes must have agreed with the 30 years of the other sources for Cypselus.

18. E. Schwartz (n. 7) 47, argued that "Eusebius" (for Schwartz it was an interpolator who is responsible for the existence of the chronological tables in their present form) reckoned the 447-year interval of the Diodorus excerpt from 1102, the date of the *Canons* for the return of the Heraclids, instead of from the Apollodoran 1104. Such a computation yields a date of 655/54 for the beginning of the tyranny of Cypselus, 28 years before the traditional date for Periander. Helm (p. 339^g) has a cryptic note on the entry: "(1238 [s. S. 85] + 90 + 28 = 1356)." He seems to be suggesting that the 28 years of Cypselus represent the gap in the shortened Corinthian list of the *Canons,* which ends at AA 1238, between the end of 90 one-year prytanies and the beginning of the tyranny of Cypselus. But the 90 years of prytanies are not included in the *Canons* and, in any case, the notice specifically assigns the 28 years to Cypselus, not to an arithmetic gap. On the reasons for the discrepancy between the Corinthian list and the 447 year interval see chapter 5.

19. That this notice derives from a confusion between the death of Periander and the end of the tyranny was recognized by Scaliger (p. 89 nn. of *Thes. Temp.*) and this explanation has been accepted by most authorities (e.g., Jacoby *Apollodors Chronik* 154, where references to divergent opinions may be found).

20. How "tradition" remembered such numbers and what their value is as historical evidence is a problem that demands special investigation. Although 30 years could represent one generation on the estimate of three generations to a century, it does not follow that this figure is derived from the conscious application of generational chronology.

21. That these are the dates underlying our ambivalent sources is now generally agreed. See the discussion of T. Cadoux, *art. cit.* (n. 10) 98–101.

22. W. G. Forrest, "The First Sacred War," *BCH* 80 (1956) 47.

23. Callisthenes (*FGrHist* 124 F 1) said that the first Sacred War had also lasted ten years. The *agon chrematites* of 591/90 provides an approximate midpoint for the dating of the fall of Cirrha. If Solon owed his election as archon and mediator in 594/93 to influence gained by his advocacy of Athenian participation in the war, the year 595/94 becomes a starting point for the computation. Thus the war ended in 586/85, the tenth year after its declaration, the sixth from the fall of Cirrha.

Notes to Chapter 13

1. Diogenes cites Sosicrates for a precise Olympiad year in the *Life* of Solon (1.62), for the archon's name in the *Life* of Solon and that of Anarcharsis (1.62, 101), for the age at death in the *Life* of Thales (1.38). In this last case, where there was already corruption in an Apollodoran text when Sosicrates used it, Sosicrates took it upon himself to "correct" the length of the life span. On Sosic-

rates, see Jacoby, *Apollodors Chronik* 31–32, who suggests that even where he is not specifically cited Sosicrates is most often the immediate source for Diogenes' dates, and R. Laqueur, "Sosikrates," *RE* 52 (1927) 1160–65.

2. Cf. E. Rohde, "Die Zeit des Pittacus," *RhM* 42 (1887) 475–78 = *Kl. Schr.* I, 185–88.

3. E. Rohde, *RhM* 42; F. Jacoby, *Apollodors Chronik* 156–65, *FGrHist* 244 F 27 Komm. Cf. H. Berve, *Die Tyrannis bei den Griechen*, 2 vols. (Munich 1967) 574–75, who also accepts this emendation.

4. The *Suda* s. v. Sappho: "Flourishing in the 42nd Olympiad, when Alcaeus, Stesichorus, and Pittacus also existed." This is a case where an Apollodoran synchronism (Sappho-Alcaeus-Pittacus) belonging to one date (OL. 45, 600/597) has become associated with another Apollodoran date for one of its members (the acme of Pittacus). On the synchronism between Stesichorus and Sappho see also chapter 10. For the synchronism between Sappho, Alcaeus, and Pittacus cf. Strabo 13.2.3: συνήκμασε δὲ τούτοις (Pittacus and Alcaeus) καὶ ἡ Σαπφώ

5. E. Rohde, *Kl. Schr.* I, 176; F. Jacoby, *Apollodors Chronik* 160, *FGrHist* 239 A 36 Komm.; D. L. Page, *Sappho and Alcaeus* (Oxford 1959) 225; A. Lesky, *A History of Greek Literature*, trans. Willis and de Heer (New York 1966) 138.

6. The φυγοῦσα of the *Marmor* is a restoration, but it is the only reading that will fit epigraphically, and some papyrus fragments (98 LP), although badly damaged, contain references to exile. See D. L. Page *Sappho and Alcaeus* 97.

7. This reconstruction is of course tentative, since it rests on an emended text of Diogenes and on Eusebian entries whose dates are always subject to transcriptional error. Other explanations are possible. The date of Pittacus-Phrynon, for example, may have originally been in Olympiad 42, the acme of Pittacus, in which case we are dealing with another instance of error by approximately one Olympiad. The date of Sappho and Alcaeus may have originally been synchronized precisely with the beginning of Pittacus' *aesymneteia* in the fourth year of the 45th Olympiad, in which case we have another example of transmission to Eusebius of only the Olympiad number. These difficulties must be admitted. The reconstruction will nevertheless supply the best explanation as to how Apollodorus generated the dates.

8. F. Jacoby, *Apollodors Chronik* 163; *FGrHist* 244 F 27 Komm.

9. Jacoby's general argument in the *Atthis* (Oxford 1949) tells against too simple a view. His comment there on local chronicles (p. 88) is noteworthy: "But we had better expressly state that in every Greek chronicle the list of eponymous officials is to a greater or lesser degree constructed: no list of officials of the mother country (and for that matter no list of victors) began to be kept before the seventh century."

10. See chapters 15, 16, and 17, and A. A. Mosshammer, "Geometrical Proportion and the Chronological Method of Apollodorus," *TAPA* 106 (1976) 291–306.

11. With the last (14th) year of Croesus dated to 547/46 (chapter 14) the first of Alyattes' 57 years is 617/16, and his 6th year, which was the 12th and last of the war between Lydia and Miletus (Herodotus 1.19–22), is 612/11.

12. Busolt, *Gr. G.* II² 252, notes that 607/6 is the midpoint of Periander's reign and suggests that the war was traditionally dated to that time. Jacoby, however, (*Apollodors Chronik* 164), believes that the entry of Periander into the dispute must have been dated some years later than the battle with Phrynon.

The attempt of Beloch, *Gr. G.* I² 2, p. 358, to redate the whole affair to the time of Pisistratus' son Hegesistratus (ca. 550) is not supported by Herodotus (5.94–95). Cf. Page, *Sappho* 155.

Notes to Chapter 14

1. The Armenian version does not have a notice corresponding to the *Cyrus Sardis capit* of Jerome's *spatium historicum*. The Armenian does have "Krysos ward von Kyros gefangen, und das Lyderreich erlosch" (spanning p. 189 between Olympiads 58 and 59) at the end of the Lydian *filum*.

2. Cf. H. Diels, "Chronologische Untersuchungen über Apollodors Chronika," *RhM* 31 (1876) 15–19; E. Rohde, "Γέγονε in dem Biographica des Suidas," *RhM* 33 (1878) 211–12 = *Kl. Schr.* I, 169; F. Jacoby, *Apollodors Chronik* 174–83, *FGrHist* 244 F. 28.

3. This is the crucial passage for the question of the relationship between Sosicrates and Apollodorus. Diogenes frequently cites Sosicrates for dates that agree with the Apollodoran system. Sosicrates' 90 years for Thales are best explained as a computation based on a corrupt version of Apollodorus. Sosicrates' general agreement with Apollodorus is therefore to be attributed to the fact that Sosicrates used the *Chronicle* of Apollodorus. The two were contemporaries, and Apollodorus seems to have used Sosicrates' *Kretika*, while Sosicrates used Apollodorus' *Chronika*. Cf. Jacoby, *Apollodors Chronik* 32, and R. Laqueur, "Sosikrates," *RE* 52 (1927) 1160–65.

4. Cf. F. Jacoby, *Apollodors Chronik* 180 n. 11, where he emends the number to 23 and *FGrHist* 260 F 1 (Porphyry), where he suggests that Porphyry had the correct Apollodoran date. For the argument that Apollodorus accepted Demetrius' date, see A. A. Mosshammer, "The Epoch of the Seven Sages," *California Studies in Classical Antiquity* 9 (1976) 165–80.

5. The argument is summarized and accepted, for example, by Kirk and Raven, *The Presocratic Philosophers* (Cambridge 1960) 74. The sole dissenter is Beloch, who calls the reconstruction (*Gr. G.* I² 2, p. 352) "eine Reihe willkürlicher Korrekturen."

6. Jacoby used 546/45 as Apollodorus' date for the fall of Sardis. He never argued the case. Jacoby seems to have chosen this date not from the fragments of Apollodorus but from the conclusion that this was the date to be inferred from the *Nabonidus Chronicle*. Jacoby was therefore forced to say that there is something wrong with the 78 years in Diogenes' text and to conclude that they were, contrary to Apollodorus' wont, reckoned exclusively. He also raised Sosicrates' 90 years to 94 in order to reach OL. 35 from OL 58. Both expedients are unnecessary. The 78-year life span is correct. Sosicrates need only be supposed to have said that Thales, if he was born in OL. 35, must have been in his 90s at his death.

7. On 547/46 as the correct interpretation of the Apollodoran evidence, see also the discussion (chapter 15) on Anaximander, and H. Kaletsch, "Zur lydischen Chronologie," *Historia* 7 (1958) 39.

8. H. Strasburger, "Herodots Zeitrechnung," *Historia* 5 (1956) 129–51. See especially W. den Boer's criticism, "Herodot und die 'Systeme' der Chronologie," *Mnemosyne* 20 (1967) 30–60.

9. For an attempt, see John Forsdyke, *Greece Before Homer*, Norton ed. (New York 1964) 68–76.

10. The specific reference of Clement's dates is the foundation of Thasos, synchronized with Archilochus and through him with Gyges. On these dates and for the identification of Clement's Dionysius with the Halicarnassian, see Rohde, *Kleine Schriften* I, 151. Dionysius of Miletus no doubt included the conquest of Sardis among the *res gestae* of Cyrus, but it does not follow that he gave a date.

11. The controversy about the Atthidographic dates of the Pisistratid tyranny is notorious, and the literature enormous. For the date 556/55 (second exile) see F. Jacoby, *Atthis* (Oxford 1949) 194 and Franz Heidbüchel, "Die Chronologie der Peisistratiden in der Atthis," *Philologus* 101 (1957) 70–89. For the bibliography on variant opinions see H. Berve, *Die Tyrannis bei den Griechen* 2 vols. (Munich 1967) 544–45.

12. S. Smith, *Babylonian Historical Texts* (London 1924) 98. Cf. Kaletsch, *Historia* 7 (1958) 39.

13. See E. Schwartz, "Berossos," *RE* 5 (1897) 309–16 = *Griechische Geschichtschreiber* (Leipzig 1959) 189–99; C. F. Lehmann-Haupt, "Berossos," *RlA* 2 (1938) 1–17; and Robert Drews, "The Babylonian Chronicles and Berossus," *Iraq* 37 (1975) 39–55. For the testimonia see *FGrHist* 680.

14. Herodotus uses his usual formula: so-and-so died (was overthrown) after x years of rule. Attempts to show that Herodotus knew the correct date of the fall and supposed an overlap between Atsyages and Cyrus fail. On this point, see Kaletsch, *Historia* 7, Strasburger, *Historia* 5 and den Boer, *Mnemosyne* 20.

15. F. K. Ginzel, *Spez. Kanon der Finsternisse* (Berlin 1899) 169 and Oppolzer, *Canon of Eclipses* (Dover ed., 1962) no. 1489.

16. So, for example, F. Boll, "Finsternisse," *RE* 6 (1909) 2353.

17. Weidner, "Labynetos," *RE* 23 (1924) 311–12; F. H. Weissbach, "Kyaxares," *RE* 22 (1922) 2246–50, and "Nabonadios," *RE* 32 (1935) 1483–89; cf. Strasburger, *Historia* 5, 144, and den Boer, *Mnemosyne* 20.

18. *FGrHist* 680 (Berossos) T 3–6, esp. T 3 (Josephus *c. Ap.* 1.129):

μάρτυς δὲ τούτων Βηρῶσος, ἀνὴρ Χαλδαῖος μὲν τὸ γένος, γνώριμος δὲ τοῖς περὶ παιδείαν ἀναστρεφομένοις, ἐπειδὴ περί τε ἀστρονομίας καὶ περὶ τῶν παρὰ Χαλδαίοις φιλοσοφουμένων αὐτὸς εἰς τοὺς Ἕλληνας ἐξήνεγκε τὰς συγγραφάς.

It is not certain whether these astronomical writings were a separate entity or part of the Babylonian history. See Drews, *Iraq* 37.

19. J. K. Fotheringham, "Cleostratus," *JHS* 39 (1919) 164–85, "A Solution of Ancient Eclipses of the Sun," *Royal Astronomical Society Monthly* 81 (1920) 104–26, "Historical Eclipses," *Oxford Lectures in History* (Oxford 1921), "Eclipse—Ancient Eclipses," *Encyclopedia Britannica* VII (1970) 909. But see Otto Neugebauer's discussion of the Saros, in *Exact Sciences in Antiquity* (Providence, 1957) 141–42.

20. On the identity of the dates reported by Pliny and Laurentius Lydus, see Jacoby, *Apollodors Chronik* 179.

21. This is the same kind of computational error that results in the date for Homer and Archilochus as 500 years after Troy being set in the 23rd Olympiad (chapter 9).

22. Cf. F. Jacoby, *Apollodors Chronik* 182, and Wehrli's comment on Demetrius fr. 149.

23. Busolt, *Gr. G.* I² 697; E. Rohde, *Kl. Schr.* I, 159; F. Jacoby, *Apollodors Chronik* 182. H. Kaletsch, *Historia* 7, 16–19.

24. The case is presented in A. A. Mosshammer, "The Epoch of the Seven Sages," *California Studies in Classical Antiquity* 9 (1976) 165–80, and the details of the argument are therefore omitted here.

25. The *Oxyrhynchus Papyri* XXIX (London 1963) with comment by D. L. Page. See George Huxley, "A War Between Astyages and Alyattes," *GRBS* 6 (1965) 201–6. On Antimenidas in the Babylonian armies, see D. L. Page, *Sappho and Alcaeus* (Oxford 1955) 224.

26. Alcaeus mentioned the war, but it cannot be assumed that he referred to the eclipse.

27. Whether Apollodorus' date for the war is absolutely correct is another matter. There are difficulties with the tradition about the eclipse-battle that are not dispelled by the fact that Apollodorus' date is nearly in agreement with an astronomical date. But that is a question beyond the scope of this book, and it must therefore be reserved for separate investigation.

Notes to Chapter 15

1. F. Jacoby, *Apollodors Chronik* 189, 215; *FGrHist* 244 F 29, 339; cf. H. Diels, "Chronologische Untersuchungen über Apollodors Chronika," *RhM* 31 (1876) 25.

2. M. White, "The Duration of the Samian Tyranny," *JHS* 74 (1954) 36–43; J. P. Barron, "The Sixth Century Tyranny at Samos," *CQ*, n.s. 14 (1964) 210–29. Earlier attempts to date a Samian tyranny to 570 are discussed by Jacoby, *Apollodors Chronik* 191 n. 4.

3. J. Labarbe, "Un Décalage de 40 ans dans la chronologie de Polycrate," *AntCl.* 31 (1952) 153–88.

4. F. Jacoby, *Apollodors Chronik* 193, *FGrHist* 244 F 66; cf H. Diels, *RhM* 31, 27 and E. Rohde, *Kl. Schr.* I, 163.

5. Eusebius, *Praep. Euang.* 10.10.5; cf. Olympic victor list, p. 94 Karst.

6. Most recently, G. B. Kerferd, "The Date of Anaximenes," *MH* 11 (1954) 117–21, who argues that Diogenes unemended carries Apollodorus' date, while the notices of Eusebius, the *Suda*, and Hippolytus have nothing to do with Apollodorus. Jacoby refuted the entirely similar arguments of Unger (*Philologus* Suppl. IV) in *Apollodors Chronik* 193–96.

7. E. Rohde, *Kl. Schr.* I, 201; F. Jacoby, *Apollodors Chronik* 210, *FGrHist* 244 F 338. The corruption of 49 to 45 is the same as that in Thales' birthdate, of 39 to 35.

8. Cf. H. Diels, *RhM* 31, 25, and F. Jacoby, *Apollodors Chronik* 189. The date in the 62nd Olympiad and the synchronism with Polycrates are well attested. See Clement, *Strom.* 1.65; Tatian, *ad Graec.* 41; Iamblichus, *vit. Pyth.* 35; and Cicero, *de Rep.* 2.28.

9. F. Jacoby, *Apollodors Chronik* 190 n. 2a, calls the reading of "B" for Anaximander "richtig." Elsewhere (p. 132), however, he notes that the shift by one Olympiad is so frequent in the *Canons* "dass man eine besondere ursache dafür suchen möchte."

10. Alfred Schoene, *Die Weltchronik des Eusebius* (Berlin 1900) 131–32, argued that Eusebius' page had about 35 lines. See also Helm's comments in the introduction to his 1956 edition, XXVII.

11. M. Miller, "Archaic Literary Chronography," *JHS* 75 (1955) 54–58, suggested that the numbers 9 and 13 were variant fractional generation lengths. The Apollodoran date for Anaximander in 572 is 13 years after the *floruit* of Thales, while the Eusebian date for Anaximander in 576 is 9 years after Thales. The texts cannot support such manipulations.

12. On the problem of the homonym Pherecydes, see F. Jacoby, "The First Athenian Prose Writer," *Mnemosyne* 13 (1947) 13–64, *Abhandlungen zur Griechischen Geschichtschreibung von Felix Jacoby* (Leiden 956) 100–143.

13. For Jerome the phrase is attested in cod. Ox. Mert. 315 (*Pythagorae magister*) and, in corrupted form, in the Lucca manuscript (*pothami magister*). See A. A. Mosshammer, "Lucca Bibl. Capit. 490 and the Manuscript Tradition of Hieronymus' (Eusebius') Chronicle," *California Studies in Classical Antiquity* 8 (1975) 203–40.

14. Jerome: *Pherecydes secundus historiarum scriptor agnoscitur* (111[k] Helm); Armenian: Phereklides der Zweite, Geschichtschreiber, war gekannt (192 Karst); *Chron. Pasch.*: Φερεκύδης ὁ δεύτερος ἱστοριογράφος ἐγνωρίζετο (306 Dindorf). The possibility that Eusebius meant to call the Pherecydes of Olympiad 59 the first historian and the Pherecydes of Olympiad 81 the second historian is excluded by the appearance at Olympiad 72 of *Hellanicus historiografus* (107[e]) and at Olympiad 78 of *Herodotus historiarum scriptor* (110[a]).

15. Cf. F. Jacoby, *Apollodors Chronik* 213 n. 10.

16. No pretense is made here to deal comprehensively with the problems of Pythagorean biography. For Eratosthenes' dating and the detail associated with it, see Jacoby, *Apollodors Chronik* 222–24, and Kurt von Fritz, "Pythagoras," *RE* 47 (1963) 172–209.

17. F. Jacoby, *Apollodors Chronik,* 189–92 (Anaximander), 193–96 (Anaximenes), 215–27 (Pythagoras); E. Rohde, *Kl. Schr. I,* 158–62.

18. Despite the skepticism of Jacoby and the obvious artificiality of the dates, the belief persists (e.g., Kirk and Raven, *Presocratic Philosophers,* 100 n. 1) that definite evidence about Anaximander's age could be found in his book. That Anaximander was even the author of the book in question is dubious. The "summary exposition of his doctrines" was probably written by Theophrastus.

19. Cf. chapter 3 and A. A. Mosshammer, "Geometrical Proportion and the Chronological Method of Apollodorus," *TAPA* 106 (1976) 291–306.

20. Thucydides' acme was synchronized with the beginning of the war, which he witnessed and interpreted. Jacoby believed (*Apollodors Chronik* 277–84) that the acme of Herodotus was synchronized with the foundation of Thurii in 444/43 and that the acme of Hellanicus was set in the year 456/55 because it constituted a literary epoch in connection with the biography of the three tragedians. But Apollodorus' numbers actually lead to an acme for Herodotus in 445/44 and for Hellanicus in 457/56. For a hypothesis on the origin of these computations see A. A. Mosshammer, "The Apollodoran *Akmai* of Hellanicus and Herodotus," *GRBS* 14 (1973) 5–13.

21. Porphyry, *vit. Pyth.* 2; Iamblichus, *vit. Pyth.* 11; Apuleius, *Florida* 15.20.

22. The tradition perhaps derives from the remark of Ion of Chios (D.L. 1.120) that Pherecydes' soul was at pleasure if it obeyed Pythagoras' teachings. Cf. Kirk and Raven, *Presocratic Philosophers,* 51.

23. Dicaearchus fr. 34 Wehrli; Aristoxenus fr. 14 Wehrli.

24. Diogenes (1.42) says Pherecydes was sometimes included among the Sages and he quotes (1.43) a letter supposedly written to Pherecydes by Thales.

25. See Wehrli's commentary to Aristoxenus fr. 18.

26. This conclusion is supported by the article of the *Suda*, according to which Pherecydes γέγονε at the time of the Seven Sages and was born (τετέχθαι) in the 45th Olympiad. The first statement attests either to the old synchronism with the Seven Sages or to Apollodorus' adaptation according to which Pherecydes' birth was to be synchronized with the Seven. The ambiguous γέγονε can be interpreted either way. The second statement, however, is a clear reference to a birthdate, but the numeral has been corrupted from 49th Olympiad to 45th. It follows also that Apollodorus adopted Demetrius' date for the Seven Sages in 582/81 and did not, as Jacoby maintained (*Apollodors Chronik* 182), change it to 585/84. See A. A. Mosshammer, "The Epoch of the Seven Sages," *California Studies in Classical Antiquity* 9 (1976) 165–80.

27. This is the first of two alternatives offered by Iamblichus, *vit. Pyth.* 248 ff.

28. Jacoby's difficulty (*Apollodors Chronik* 212) is therefore resolved. Jacoby maintained that the date of Pherecydes in Olympiad 59 was connected somehow with a 40-year interval after Thales. But he could not make the computation work, since he had assumed that Apollodorus synchronized the epoch of the Seven Sages with the acme of Thales, slightly more than 40 years before Pherecydes' acme.

29. Cf. F. Jacoby, *Apollodors Chronik* 195. Kerferd, *MH* 11, prefers to associate the unsettled conditions with the Ionian Revolt.

30. Syncellus (469) reports two variants for Pythagoras' age at death—99 and 75. Age 99 appears also in Tzetzes, *Chil.* 11. 92, and Iamblichus, *vit. Pyth.* 265. Jacoby (*Apollodors Chronik* 224) connects the 99 years with Eratosthenes' statement that Pythagoras was the boxer of Olympiad 48 (588/87) and with a hypothesis attributed to Apollonius that Pythagoras died shortly after the destruction of Sybaris in 511. Aged 18 in 588, Pythagoras would have been 99 in 507.

31. Jacoby (*Apollodors Chronik* 213) ascribes to Apollodorus the 85-year life span reported for Pherecydes by the *Macrobioi*, resulting in a date for his death of 499. But 85 years is a life span assigned arbitrarily to a number of persons in the *Macrobioi* and it has no significance for the reconstruction of the Apollodoran system. The date for Anaxagoras' birth derives from Demetrius of Phalerum (*FGrHist* 228 F 2), who stated that he was twenty years old in the archonship of Calliades (480/79).

Notes to Chapter 16

1. The accession of Cambyses provides a *terminus ante*, while Pisistratus' victory at Pallene supplies a *terminus post*, for Polyaenus (1.23.2) states that the brothers had assistance from Pisistratus' ally, Lygdamis of Naxos. See Th. Lenschau, "Polykrates," *RE* 42 (1952) 1726–35.

2. M. E. White, "The Duration of the Samian Tyranny," *JHS* 74 (1954) 36–43; J. P. Barron, "The Sixth Century Tyranny at Samos," *CQ* 14 (1964) 210–29. H. Berve, *Die Tyrannis bei den Griechen*, 2 vols. (Munich 1967) 581–82, defends the traditional chronology.

3. Eratosthenes *FGrHist* 241 F 11; Strabo 14, 636; Iamblichus, *Vit. Pyth.* 19.

4. See H. S. Long's edition of Diogenes (Oxford 1964) and A. Adler's edition of the *Suda* (Stuttgart 1928–38) for the many suggestions.

5. See n. 2 above.

6. J. Labarbe, "Un Décalage de 40 ans dans la chronologie de Polycrate," *AntClass* 31 (1962) 153–88.

7 The *locus classicus* is Clement of Alexandria, *Strom.* 1.65: Πυθαγόρας δὲ κατὰ Πολυκράτη τὸν τύραννον περὶ τὴν ἑξηκοστὴν δευτέραν ὀλυμπιάδα εὑρίσκεται.

8. A. Delatte, "La Chronologie pythagoricienne de Timée," *MusB.* 19 (1920) 1 ff. K. von Fritz, "Pythagoras," *RE* 47 (1963) 179–87, points out that the chronological details cannot be attributed to Timaeus. All that can with certainty be traced to him is the two departures from Samos.

9. F. Jacoby, *Apollodors Chronik* 220.

10. For the text, see n. 7.

11. J. P. Barron, *CQ* 14, 221.

12. J. Labarbe, *AntClass* 31, 155.

13. J. P. Barron, *CQ* 14, 219–21. The text of Himerius is difficult in two crucial places. Himerius speaks of a young Polycrates who was king not only of Samos but of all the Greek sea. This is clearly a reference to the Herodotean Polycrates. But the text then reads ὁ δὴ γοῦν τῆς Ῥόδου Πολυκράτης ἦρα μουσικῆς καὶ μελῶν. . . . C. M. Bowra, "Polycrates of Rhodes," *CJ* 29 (1934) 375–80, and D. L. Page, "Ibycus' Poem in Honor of Polycrates," *Aegyptus* 31 (1951) 170, argued for the existence of a Polycrates of Rhodes, son of the thalassocrat. The second difficulty occurs with ὁ παῖς διὰ τῆς λύρας πονῶν τὴν Ὁμηρικὴν ἔμελλε πληρώσειν εὐχὴν τῷ πατρὶ Πολυκράτει. Since the young man is the future thalassocrat, we should expect the father's name to be Aeaces. Another manuscript reads Πολυκράτης thus identifying the boy as Polycrates and leaving the father unnamed. That makes sense.

14. Apollodorus *FGrHist* 244 F 7, 31, 36, 340.

15. Cf. Strabo, 644: the Teans went to Abdera in the time of Anacreon.

16. Albin Lesky, *A History of Greek Literature*, trans. Willis and de Heer (New York 1966) 183; C. M. Bowra, *CJ* 29; J. P. Barron *CQ* 14, and "Ibycus to Polycrates," *BICS* 16 (1969) 118–49.

17. M. E. White, *JHS* 74, 42; J. P. Barron, *CQ* 14, 223.

Notes to Chapter 17

1. For treatment of other fifth-century entries in the *Canons* see A. A. Mosshammer, "The Apollodoran Akmai of Hellanicus and Herodotus," *GRBS* 14 (1973) 5–13, and "The Archonship of Themistocles in the Chronographic Tradition," *Hermes* 103 (1975) 222–34.

2. Felix Jacoby, *Apollodors Chronik* 250–60, and *FGrHist* 244 F 34–35.

3. Aeschylus: *MP* A 48 (35 years old in 490) and A 59 (died at age 69 in 456/55, thus born 525/24 or 524/23), the *Suda* s.v. (died at age 58), *vit. Aesch.* 121 West (died at age 63), Apollodorus (born 519/18).

Sophocles: *MP* A 56 (28 years old in 469/68) and A 64 (died at age 92 in 406/5, thus born 498/97 or 497/96), *Macrobioi* 24 (died at age 95); the *Suda* s.v. (born OL 73, 488/85); *vit. Soph.* 127 West (born OL 71.2, 495/94), the last being the Apollodoran date.

Euripides: *MP* A 50 (born 485/84), the *Suda* s.v. (born 480/79, died at age 75), *vit. Eur.* 135 West. (born 480/79, died at age 75 according to Eratosthenes, over 70 according to Philochorus); the *Suda*'s is the Apollodoran chronology.

4. Timaeus (*FGrHist* 566 F 105), cited by Plutarch (*Mor.* 717C), synchronized the death of Euripides with the accession of Dionysius, dated to 406/5 on the evidence of Philistus (*FGrHist* 556 F 3). That Eratosthenes adopted the synchronism is suggested by the fact that he gave Euripides' age at death as 75, a figure possible on the vulgate birthdate of 480/79 only if Eratosthenes dated his death to 406/5 and counted inclusively.

5. The list of generals is transmitted in a fragment of Androtion (*FGrHist* 324 F 38). The identification of the poet with the Hellanotamias of 443 and the Proboulos of 413 is debated, but this is not the place to argue that case. See Harry C. Avery, "Sophocles' Political Career," Historia 22 (1973) 509–14. Aeschylus' epitaph is preserved by the *vita*, p. 120 West.; and Pausanias (1.14.5) found it remarkable that it mentioned his participation in the Persian Wars but not his literary career. For the evidence pertaining to documentary record of the dramatic festivals see G. Kaibel and A. Wilhelm, *Urkunden dramatischer Aufführungen in Athen* (Vienna 1906) and A. W. Pickard-Cambridge, *The Dramatic Festivals of Athens,* 2d ed., revised by Gould and Lewis (Oxford 1968).

6. The synchronism appears in Plutarch's citation of Timaeus (*FGrHist* 566 F 105). As is often the case with fragmentary citations, it is impossible to be sure whether Plutarch knew the synchronism from Timaeus or added it from elsewhere. It was the vulgate by Plutarch's time, and only the synchronism between Euripides' death and Dionysius can definitely be attributed to Timaeus.

7. The numerals giving the age cannot be completely read, but it is clear that the author is computing from the birth date that he elsewhere cites.

8. F. Jacoby, *FGrHist* 239 A 56 Komm.

9. *FGrHist* 328 F 220 Komm. Cf. *Apollodors Chronik* 259, where Jacoby characterizes the *vita*'s date for first presentation as "dem ersten sicheren datum in leben des dichters."

10. A brief survey of the most relevant evidence is given here. It would be pointless to attempt to account for every easily corruptible numeral in every text. One could, for example, debate endlessly about the origin and purport of the *vita*'s statement on Sophocles (127 West.) that he was 17 years younger than Aeschylus and 24 years older than Euripides.

11. The *vita*'s 63 years for Aeschylus (121 West.) may represent the Apollodoran dates computed exclusively. For Euripides, the Apollodoran computation is preserved in the statement of one of his biographers (139 West) that he was 25 when he made his first presentation. The biographer who gives the date (134–35 West.) elsewhere (134 West.) states that Euripides was 26 at the time, although he dates the birth (133 West.) to 480/79. For Sophocles, Apollodorus' computation is represented in the statement of Plutarch (*Mor.* 785B) that Sophocles was 55 years old at the time of the alleged poem to Herodotus. The poem was dated to the year of the generalship. The age is an inference from the Apollodoran system.

12. This is an excellent example of how difficult it is to decide exactly what mixture of documentary evidence and chronographic theory underlies fifth-century dates. A synchronism between the acme of Euripides and the generalship

of Sophocles may have been one of Apollodorus' starting points. If so, that helps explain why he accepted the synchronism between Euripides' birth and the year of Salamis and why he deemed it appropriate to apply the theoretical ages at the epoch of 456/55.

13. The association of first presentation with first victory appears in Plutarch, *Cimon* 8.8.

14. One biographer gives the age as 25, another as 26. But the latter is inconsistent with himself. See above, n. 11.

15. The text dates this contest to Olympiad 9 (ϑ´), 744/1. It is usually emended to Olympiad 70 (ο´) through comparison with the statement of the *Suda* on Pratinas that he competed with Aeschylus and Choerilus in the 70th Olympiad (500/497). This statement is frequently taken as documentary fact (e.g., Lesky, *History of Greek Literature*, 230, and 242). On the contrary, the date in Olympiad 70 derives from combining the Apollodoran age of 25 with the birthdate attested by the *Marmor*'s source (above, n. 3). The Apollodoran date is attested by Eusebius, as is argued below.

16. The text is specific that this was first presentation: πρώτην γὰρ οιδασκαλίαν τοῦ Σοφοκλέους ἔτι νέου καθέντος 'Αφεψίων ὁ ἄρχων κτλ.

17. The confusion is common. Eusebius, for example, enters a notice that, by its mention of the end of the war with Persia, ought to be associated with the Cyprus campaign in 450 but at a date that can be associated only with the Eurymedon campaign. OL 79.4 (461/60): *Cimon iuxta Eurymedontem Persas nauali pedestrique certamine superat. Et Medicum bellum conquiescit.* The date is clearly too late for Eurymedon and too early for Salamis. It does not represent a compromise, however, between the two dates. The association with the end of conflict resulted in the battle's being dated to the Olympiad of Artaxerxes' accession, since it was he who entered into the agreement of peace. Perhaps the confusion in the notice was compounded by combining it with the date of Cimon's ostracism.

18. F. Jacoby, *FGrHist* 244 F 71–72. Jacoby recognized the difficulty in his thesis. For if Protagoras flourished in 444/43 and died at age 70, he was dead by the time of the decree if it was indeed passed by the 400. Jacoby chose 444/43 on the assumption that the epoch of Thurii was one of Apollodorus' synchronistic years including the acmes of Herodotus, Protagoras, and Melissus. The "epoch of Thurii" is a myth. Herodotus flourished the year before the foundation of Thurii (*GRBS* 14, above, n. 1). For Melissus as for Protagoras the sources cite only the Olympiad, not the precise year. Melissus was probably dated to the year of his Samian admiralship, when Sophocles was an Athenian general (the *Suda* on Meletos, Diodorus 12.27), OL 84.4, 441/40.

19. The date is too early even for the birth of the Platonic Theaetetus, who was still quite young when he met Socrates shortly before the latter's death. Rohde (*Kl. Schr.* I, 123) suggested that an older mathematician of the same name is meant.

20. See F. Jacoby, *Apollodors Chronik* 301.

21. Philochorus *FGrHist* 328 F 121. Philochorus' reference is specifically to dedication. The date is not also to be associated with condemnation, since Eusebius notes Phidias' *floruit* in connection with the statue. On the interpretation of the scholion that preserves the fragment, see Otto Lendle, "Philochoros über den Prozess des Phidias," *Hermes* 83 (1955) 284–303.

Selected Bibliography

Ackroyd, P. R., and Evans, C. F., eds. *The Cambridge History of the Bible.* 3 vols. Cambridge 1970.

Avery, Harry C. "Sophocles' Political Career." *Historia* 22 (1973) 509–14.

Barber, G. L. *The Historian Ephorus.* Cambridge 1935.

Barron, John P. "Ibycus to Polycrates." *Bulletin of the London Institute for Classical Studies* 16 (1969) 118–49.

———. "The Sixth Century Tyranny at Samos." *Classical Quarterly,* n.s. 14 (1964) 210–29.

Beloch, Karl Julius. *Griechische Geschichte.* 8 vols. 2d ed. Berlin 1912–26.

Berve, Helmut. *Die Tyrannis bei den Griechen.* 2 vols. Munich 1967.

Bickerman, E. J. *Chronology of the Ancient World.* London 1968.

Blakeway, Alan J. "The Date of Archilochus." *Greek Poetry and Life: Essays Presented to Gilbert Murray on his 70th Birthday.* Oxford 1936. Pp. 33–58.

Bowra, C. M. "Polycrates of Rhodes." *Classical Journal* 29 (1934) 375–80.

Brinkmann, A. "Die Olympische Chronik." *Rheinisches Museum für Philologie* 70 (1915) 622–37.

Burn, A. R. "Dates in Early Greek History." *Journal of Hellenic Studies* 55 (1935) 130–46.

———. "Early Greek Chronology." *Journal of Hellenic Studies* 69 (1949) 70–73.

Cadoux, T. J. "The Athenian Archons from Kreon to Hypsichides." *Journal of Hellenic Studies* 68 (1948) 70–123.

Caspar, Erich. *Die älteste römische Bischofsliste: kritische Studien zum Formproblem des eusebianischen Kanons.* Schriften der Konigsberger Gelehrte Gesellschaft, Geisteswiss. Kl. 2, no. 4. Berlin 1926.

———. "Helm, *Eusebius Werke* VII." *Göttingische gelehrte Anzeigen* 189 (1927) 161–84.

Cataudella, M. R. "Erodoto e la cronologia dei Cipselidi." *Maia* 16 (1964) 204–24.

Chrimes, K. M. T. *Ancient Sparta. A Reexamination of the Evidence.* Manchester 1949.

Clinton, Henry. *Fasti Hellenici.* 3 vols. 3d ed. Oxford 1834–51. Reprint ed. New York: Burt Franklin, n.d.

Costanzi, V. "L'Opera di Ellanico di Mitilene." *Rivista Storia Antica* 8 (1904) 343–53.

Delatte, A. "La chronologie pythogoricienne de Timee." *Musée belge* 19 (1920) 5–13.

den Boer, W. "Herodot und die 'Systeme' der Chronologie." *Mnemosyne* 20 (1967) 30–60.

———. *Laconian Studies.* Amsterdam 1954.

———. "Political Propaganda in Greek Chronology." *Historia* 5 (1956) 162–77.

Diels, Hermann. "Chronologisches Untersuchungen über Apollodors Chronika." *Rheinisches Museum für Philologie* 31 (1876) 1–60.

Drews, Robert. "The Babylonian Chronicles and Berossus." *Iraq* 37 (1975) 39–55.

———. "The Fall of Astyages and Herodotus' Chronology of the Eastern Kingdoms." *Historia* 18 (1969) 1–11.

Ducat, J. "L'Archäisme à la recherche de points de repère chronologiques." *Bulletin de correspondance hellénique* 86 (1962) 165–84.

———. "Note sur la chronologie des Kypsélides." *Bulletin de correspondance hellénique* 85 (1961) 418–25.

Dunbabin, T. J. "The Early History of Corinth." *Journal of Hellenic Studies* 68 (1948) 59–69.

———. *The Western Greeks.* Oxford 1948.

Fornara, Charles W. "Evidence for the Date of Herodotus' Publication," *Journal of Hellenic Studies* 91 (1971) 25–34.

Forrest, W. G. "The First Sacred War." *Bulletin de correspondance hellénique* 80 (1956) 33–51.

———. *A History of Sparta 950–192* B.C. London 1968.

———. "Two Chronographic Notes," *Classical Quarterly,* n.s. 19 (1969) 95–110.

Forsdyke, John. *Greece Before Homer.* Norton ed. New York 1964.

Fotheringham, John Knight. "Historical Eclipses." *Oxford Lectures in History.* Oxford 1921.

———. *The Bodleian Manuscript of Jerome's Version of the Chronicle of Eusebius Reproduced in Collotype.* Oxford 1905.

———. *Eusebii Pamphili Chronici Canones: Latine vertit adauxit, ad sua tempora produxit S. Eusebius Hieronymus.* London 1923.

———. "On the List of Thalassocracies in Eusebius." *Journal of Hellenic Studies* 27 (1907) 75–89.

Gelzer, Heinrich. *Sextus Julius Africanus und die byzantinische Chron-*

ographie. 2 vols. in 1. Leipzig 1880, 1898. Reprint ed. New York: Burt Franklin, 1967.

————. "Das Zeitalter des Gyges." *Rheinisches Museum für Philologie* 30 (1875) 230–68.

Ginzel, F. K. *Spezieller Kanon der Finsternisse.* Berlin 1899.

Gomme, A. W. *A Historical Commentary on Thucydides.* Oxford 1945.

Grafton, Anthony T. "Joseph Scaliger and Historical Chronology: The Rise and Fall of a Discipline." *History and Theory* 14 (1975) 156–85.

Hammond, N. G. L. "Studies in Greek Chronology of the Sixth and Fifth Centuries B.C." *Historia* 4 (1955) 371–411.

Harnack, A. *Geschichte der ältchristliche Literatur bis Eusebius.* 2 vols. 2d ed. Reprint ed., Leipzig 1958.

Heidbüchel, Franz. "Die Chronologie der Peisistratiden in der Atthis." *Philologus* 101 (1957) 70–89.

Helm, Rudolf. *Die Chronik des Hieronymus, Eusebius Werke* VII, i and ii. Die griechischen christlichen Schriftsteller der ersten Jahrhunderte 24, 34. Leipzig 1913, 1926. 2d ed. *GCS* 47. Berlin 1956.

————. "De Eusebii in Chronicorum libro Auctoribus." *Eranos* 22 (1924) 1–40.

————. *Eusebius' Chronik und ihre Tabellenform.* Abhandlungen der Berliner Akademie, phil.-hist. Kl. 1923, no. 4. Berlin 1924.

————. "Die Liste der Thalassokratien in der Chronik des Eusebius." *Hermes* 61 (1926) 241–63.

————. *Hieronymus' Zusätze in Eusebius' Chronik und ihr Wert für die Literaturgeschichte.* Philologus Supplement 21, no. 2. Berlin 1929.

————. "Die neuesten Hypothesen zu Eusebius' (Hieronymus') Chronik." *Sitzungsberichte der preussische Akademie,* phil.-hist. Kl. 21 (1929) 371–408.

Hiller, E. "Eusebius und Kyrillus." *Rheinisches Museum für Philologie* 25 (1870) 253–62.

Hoffman-Aleith, Eva. "Pamphilos." *Real-Encyclopädie der klassischen Altertumswissenschaft* 18 (1949) 340–50.

Huxley, George. *Early Sparta.* London 1962.

————. "A War Between Astyages and Alyattes." *Greek, Roman, and Byzantine Studies* 6 (1965) 201–6.

Jacoby, Felix. *Apollodors Chronik, Eine Sammlung Der Fragmente.* Philologische Untersuchungen 16. Berlin 1902. Reprint ed., New York: Arno Press, 1973.

————. *Atthis, the Local Chronicles of Ancient Athens.* Oxford 1949.

————. "Die Attische Königslisten." *Klio* 2 (1902) 406–39.

————. "The Date of Archilochus." *Classical Quarterly* 35 (1941) 97–109.

————. "The First Athenian Prose Writer." *Mnemosyne* 13 (1947) 13–

63. Reprinted *Abhandlungen zur griechischen Geschichtschreibung.* Leiden 1956. Pp. 100–143.

———. *Die Fragmente der griechischen Historiker.* 15 vols. Berlin and Leiden 1923–58.

———. *Das Marmor Parium.* Berlin 1904.

Jones, A. H. M. *Sparta.* Oxford 1967.

Kaibel, Georg and Wilhelm, Adolf. *Urkunden dramatischer Auffürhungen in Athen.* Vienna 1906.

Kaletsch, Hans. "zur lydischen Chronologie." *Historia* 7 (1958) 1–47.

Karst, Josef. *Die Chronik des Eusebius aus dem armenischen übersetzt, Eusebius Werke* V. Die griechischen christlichen Schriftsteller der ersten Jahrhunderte 20. Leipzig 1911.

Kerferd, G. B. "The Date of Anaximenes." *Museum Helveticum* 11 (1954) 117–21.

Kiechle, Franz. *Lakonien und Sparta, Untersuchungen zur ethnischen Struktur und zur politischen Entwicklungen Lakoniens und Spartas bis zum Ende der archaischen Zeit.* Munich 1963.

———. *Messenische Studien.* Erlangen 1957.

Kirk, G. S., and Raven, J. E. *The Presocratic Philosophers.* Cambridge 1960.

Kroymann, J. *Pausanias und Rhianos.* Berlin 1943.

———. *Sparta und Messenien, Untersuchungen zur Ueberlieferung der messenichen Kriege.* Neue philologische Untersuchungen 11. Berlin 1937.

Labarbe, Jules. "Un Décalage de 40 ans dans la chronologie de Polycrate." *L'Antiquité classique* 31 (1962) 153–88.

Laqueur, R. "Phainias." *Real-Encyclopädie der klassischen Altertumswissenschaft* 19 (1938) 1565–91.

———. "Sosikrates." *Real-Encyclopädie der klassischen Altertumswissenschaft* 52 (1927) 1160–65.

Lehmann-Haupt, C. F. "Berossos." *Reallexicon der Assyriologie* 2 (1938) 1–17.

———. "Chronologisches zur griechische Quellenkunde," *Klio* 6 (1906) 127–39.

Lenschau, Th. "Agiaden und Eurypontiden." *Rheinisches Museum für Philologie* 88 (1939) 123–46.

———. "Polykrates." *Real-Encyclopädie der klassischen Altertumswissenschaft* 42 (1952) 1726–35.

Lesky, Albin. *A History of Greek Literature.* Translated by Willis and de Heer. New York 1966.

Meiggs, R., and Lewis, D., eds. *A Selection of Greek Historical Inscriptions.* Oxford 1969.

Metzger, Bruce M. *The Text of the New Testament.* 2d. ed. Oxford

1968.

Meyer, Eduard. *Forschungen zur alten Geschichte.* 2 vols. Halle 1892, 1899.

Michell, H. *Sparta.* Cambridge 1964.

Miller, Molly. *The Sicilian Colony Dates.* Albany, N.Y. 1970.

————. *The Thalassocracies.* Albany, N.Y. 1971.

————. "The Accepted Date for Solon. Precise but Wrong?" *Arethusa* 2 (1969) 62–86.

————. "Archaic Literary Chronography." *Journal of Hellenic Studies* 75 (1955) 54–58.

————. "The Earlier Persian Dates in Herodotus." *Klio* 37 (1959) 29–52.

————. "The Herodotean Croesus." *Klio* 41 (1963) 58–94.

————. "Herodotus as Chronographer." *Klio* 46 (1965) 109–28.

Mitchel, Fordyce. "Herodotus' Use of Genealogical Chronology." *Phoenix* 10 (1965) 48–69.

Momigliano, Arnaldo. *The Development of Greek Biography.* Cambridge, Mass. 1971.

Mommsen, Theodor. "Die älteste Handschrift der Chronik des Hieronymus." *Hermes* 24 (1889) 383–401.

————. "Die armenischen Handschriften der Chronik des Eusebius." *Hermes* 30 (1895) 321–38.

————, ed. *Chronica Minora.* 2 vols. Monumenta Germaniae Historica, auct. ant. 9, 11. Berlin 1892, 1894.

Moretti, L. *Olympionikai, i vincitori negli antichi agoni olimpici.* Atti della Accademia Nazionale dei Lincei Series 8, volume 8. Rome, 1959.

Mosshammer, Alden A. "The Apollodoran Akmai of Hellanicus and Herodotus." *Greek, Roman, and Byzantine Studies* 14 (1973) 5–13.

————. "The Archonship of Themistocles in the Chronographic Tradition." *Hermes* 103 (1975) 222–34.

————. "The Epoch of the Seven Sages." *California Studies in Classical Antiquity* 9 (1976) 165–80.

————. "Geometrical Proportion and the Chronological Method of Apollodorus." *Transactions of the American Philological Association* 106 (1976) 291–306.

————. "Lucca Bibl. Capit. 490 and the Manuscript Tradition of Hieronymus' (Eusebius') Chronicle." *California Studies in Classical Antiquity* 8 (1975) 203–40.

————. "Phainias of Eresos and Chronology," *California Studies in Classical Antiquity* 10 (1977) 105-132.

Mras, Karl. "Nachwort zu den beiden letzen Ausgaben der Chronik des Hieronymus." *Wiener Studien* 46 (1928) 200–215.

Niebuhr, Barthold G. "Historischer Gewinn aus der armenischen Uebersetzung der Chronik des Eusebius." Abhandlungen der Berliner

Akademie (1820–21). Reprinted *Kleine Schriften* I, 179–304.

Oppolzer, Theodor. *Canon of Eclipses.* Dover ed. New York 1962.

Page, D. L. *Sappho and Alcaeus.* Oxford 1959.

———. "Ibycus' Poem in Honour of Polycrates." *Aegyptus* 31 (1951) 158–72.

Pearson, Lionel. *Early Ionian Historians.* Oxford 1939.

Pickard-Cambridge, Sir Arthur Wallace. *The Dramatic Festivals of Athens.* 2d ed., revised by John Gould and D. M. Lewis. Oxford 1968.

Prakken, D. W. *Studies in Greek Genealogical Chronology.* Lancaster, Pa. 1943.

———. "The Boeotian Migration." *American Journal of Philology* 64 (1943) 417–23.

———. "Herodotus and the Spartan Kinglists." *Transactions of the American Philological Association* 71 (1940) 460–72.

Rohde, Erwin. "Γέγονε in den Biographica des Suidas." *Rheinisches Museum für Philologie* 33 (1878) 161–220, 620–22, 638. Reprinted *Kleine Schriften* I. Leipzig 1901. Pp. 114–84.

———. "Studien zur Chronologie der griechisches Litteraturgeschichte." *Rheinisches Museum für Philologie* 36 (1881) 380–434, 524–75. Reprinted *Kleine Schriften* I. Leipzig 1901. Pp. 1–113.

———. "Der Zeit des Pittacus." *Rheinisches Museum für Philologie* 42 (1887) 475–78. Reprinted *Kleine Schriften* I. Leipzig 1901. Pp. 185–88.

Samuel, A. E. *Greek and Roman Chronology.* Munich 1972.

Sandys, J. E. *A History of Classical Scholarship.* 3 vols. Cambridge, 1908. Reprint ed., New York: Hafner, 1958.

Scaliger, Joseph J. *Thesaurus Temporum.* Leiden 1606. 2d ed. (posthumous) Amsterdam 1658.

Schoene, Alfred, ed. *Eusebi Chronicorum Libri Duo.* Vol. I: *Eusebi Chronicorum Liber Prior. Armeniam uersionem latine ad libros manuscriptos recensuit* H. Petermann, *Graeca fragmenta collegit et recognouit, appendices chronographias sex adiecit* A. Schoene. Berlin 1875. Vol. II: *Eusebi Chronicorum Canonum Quae Supersunt. Armeniam uersionem latine factam e libris manuscriptis recensuit* H. Petermann, *Hieronymi uersionem e libris manuscriptis recensuit* Alfred Schoene, *Syriam epitomen latine factam e libro Londinensi* E. Roediger. Berlin 1866. Reprint ed., Dublin and Zurich: Weidmann Verlag, 1967.

———. *Die Weltchronik des Eusebius in ihrer Bearbeitung durch Hieronymus.* Berlin 1900.

Schwartz, Eduard. "Berossos." *Real-Encyclopädie der klassischen Altertumswissenschaft* 5 (1897) 309–16. Reprinted *Griechische Geschichtschreiber.* Leipzig 1959. Pp. 189–99.

———. "Eusebios." *Real-Encyclopädie der klassischen Altertumswissen-*

schaft VI (1907) 1370–1439. Reprinted *Griechische Geschicht-schreiber.* Leipzig 1959. Pp. 495–598.

———. "Die Königslisten des Eratosthenes und Kastor." Abhandlungen von der Gesellschaft der Wissenschaften zu Göttingen, phil.-hist. Klasse 40, no. 2 (1894–95) 1–96.

Seel, Otto. "Panodorus." *Real-Encyclopädie der klassischen Altertumswissenschaft* 36.2 (1958) 631–35.

Servais, J. "Hérodote et la Chronologie des Cypsélides." *L'Antiquité classique* 38 (1969) 28–81.

Siegfried, C., and Gelzer, H. *Eusebii Canonum Epitome ex Dionysii Telmaharensis Chronico petita.* Leipzig 1884.

Sirinelli, Jean. *Les Vues historiques d'Eusèbe de Césarée.* Paris 1961.

Smith, S. *Babylonian Historical Texts.* London 1924.

Spittler, L. T. "Historia Critica Chronici Eusebiani." *Commentationes societatis regiae scientiarum Gottingensis.* Phil.-Hist. Class 8 (1785–6) 39–67.

Starr, Chester G. "The Credibility of Early Spartan History." *Historia* 14 (1965) 257–72.

Strasburger, Hermann. "Herodots Zeitrechnung." *Historia* 5 (1956) 129–61.

Tarditi, Giovanni. "In margine alla cronologia di Archiloco." *Rivista di Filologia e d'Istruzione Classica* 87 (1959) 113–18.

Traube, Ludwig. *Hieronymi Chronicorum codicis Floriacensis fragmenta.* Codices Graeci et Latini photographice depicti. Supplement 1. Leyden 1902.

Treu, M. "Archilochos." *Real-Encyclopädie der klassischen Altertumswissenschaft.* Supplement 11 (1968) 136–49.

von Compernolle, R. *Étude de Chronologie et d'Historiographie Siciliotes.* Brussels 1959.

von Fritz, Kurt. *Die Griechische Geschichtsschreibung* I. 2 vols. Berlin 1967.

———. "Herodotus and the Growth of Greek Historiography." *Transactions of the American Philological Association* 67 (1936) 315–40.

———. "Pythagoras." *Real-Encyclopädie der klassischen Altertumswissenschaft* 47 (1963) 179–87.

von Gutschmid, Alfred. "De Temporum notis quibus Eusebius utitur in Chronicis Canonibus." *Schriften Kiel* 15 (1868) 3–28. Reprinted *Kleine Schriften* I. Leipzig 1889. Pp. 448–82.

———. "Über Schoenes Ausgabe der Chronik des Eusebius." *Kleine Schriften* I. Leipzig 1889. Pp. 417–47.

———. "Unterschuchungen über die syrische Epitome der Eusebischen Canones." *Kleine Schriften* I. Leipzig 1889. Pp. 483–529.

Wachsmuth, Curt. *Einleitung in der Studium der alten Geschichte.* Leipzig 1895.

Wade-Gery, Henry T. "A Note on the Origin of the Spartan Gymno-paidiai." *Classical Quarterly* 43 (1949) 79–81.

Wallace-Hadrill, D. S. *Eusebius of Caesarea.* London 1960.

————. "The Eusebian Chronicle: the Extent and Date of Composition of its Early Editions." *Journal of Theological Studies*, n.s. 6 (1955) 248–53.

Wehrli, Fritz R. *Die Schule des Aristoteles.* 2 vols. Basel 1944–59.

Westermann, A., ed. *Biographi Graeci Minores.* Braunschweig 1845. Reprinted Amsterdam 1964.

White, Mary E. "The Duration of the Samian Tyranny." *Journal of Hellenic Studies* 74 (1954) 36–43.

Index

G